Jon E. Lewis is a writer  s books include the best-selling *ze*, *The Mammoth Book of How* *mmoth Book of Wild Journeys*.

The Mammoth Book of

THE DEEP

True Stories of Danger
and Adventure Under the Sea

Edited by JON E. LEWIS

CARROLL & GRAF PUBLISHERS
NEW YORK

Carroll & Graf Publishers
An Imprint of Avalon Publishing Group, Inc.
245 W. 17th Street, 11th Floor
New York, NY 10011–5300
www.carrollandgraf.com

AVALON
publishing group incorporated

First published in the UK by Robinson,
an imprint of Constable & Robinson Ltd, 2007

First Carroll & Graf edition, 2007

ISBN-13: 978-0-78671-975-4
ISBN-10: 0-7867-1975-3

Printed and bound in the EU

Contents

Foreword   xi

Into the Abyss: A Chronology of
    Underwater Adventure and Exploration   xiii

PRELUDE: THE UNDERSEA ADVENTURE
    Philippe Diolé   1

THE KINGDOM OF THE HELMET
    William Beebe   10

GOGGLE FISHING
    Guy Gilpatric   16

MENFISH
    Jacques-Yves Cousteau   29

BENEATH THE ICE
    Andrew Todhunter   34

SHARKS! (AND OTHER BEHEMOTHS)
    Peter Benchley et al   38

FEAR IS THE LOCK
    Tim Ecott   67

ONE THOUSAND AND FOUR HUNDRED
      AND TWENTY SIX FEET UNDER THE SEA
    William Beebe   75

SAVED
    David Masters   101

DIVING TO ADVENTURE
    Hans Hass   107

THE SEA DEVILS
   Junio Valerio Borghese   123
FATAL DEPTH
   Joe Haberstroh   154
WOLF PACK
   Heinz Schaeffer   165
SOLE SURVIVOR
   John H. Capes   173
THE DISCOVERY OF THE *TITANIC*
   Robert D. Ballard   179
X-MEN
   T. J. Waldron and James Gleason   186
NIGHT DIVE
   Robert E. Schroeder   198
HIDDEN DEPTHS
   Philippe Tailliez   202
THE PIPE LINE
   Tom Shelnick   219
RAPTURE
   Jacques-Yves Cousteau   236
THE TRIALS OF A BATHYSCAPHE
   Pierre Willm   248
THE LOSS OF *TEMPEST*
   Charles Anscomb   275
KURSK: A Time to Die
   Robert Moore   281
DOWNTIME
   Keith Jessop   293
SPYING ON A RUSSIAN'S BOTTOM
   Don Camsell   299
THE GHOST OF SHIPWRECKS FUTURE
   Patrick Symmes   307
FISH DAYDREAMS
   Michael G. Zinsley   317
FREEDIVE
   Colin Beavan   321

BENEATH TROPIC SEAS
William Beebe 331
MORTAL BLOW
Edward Young 349
FROGMAN
Sydney Woollcott 363
THE BULL OF SCAPA FLOW
Wolfgang Frank 380
TRUK LAGOON
Sylvia A. Earle 391
THE HUNT FOR *MARY ROSE*
Alexander McKee 406
THREE MILES DOWN
James Hamilton-Paterson 425
ENVOI: A LESSON FROM THE SEA
Jacques-Yves Cousteau 439

Appendix: The History of Diving 444
Bibliography 489
Acknowledgements 491

Foreword

Space, it turned out, wasn't the final frontier: *Sea Hunt* proved to be a better pointer to the future of exploration than *Star Trek*. At the beginning of the 21st century, more people have flown to the Moon than have descended into the oceanic abyss; indeed, we know more about our lunar neighbour than we do about the sea around us. There may or may not be alien life forms on Mars, but strange new creatuers are discovered almost daily in the salt waters which cover three quarters of our world. By the estimate of oceanographers, humankind has explored less than 0.5 per cent of the undersea of the blue planet.

Welcome to the Deep, a watery world of endless beauty and sometimes, just sometimes, of danger and killer beasts.

The Deep has lured us all our existence. Descriptions of naked divers who could hold their breath are to be found in Ancient Mesopotamian and Egyptian texts, and there are early allusions to breathing tubes of hollow reeds. These first divers went down to the seas in the hunt for nature's bounty – fish, shellfish, but especially lucrative sponges and pearls – but it was not long before another reason suggested itself. War.

Alexander the Great is said to have supervised the siege of the port of Tyre in 322 BC from a glass barrel on the sea bed – the first recorded instance of a mechanical device to supply air to those under the sea. Warfare became a major stimulant on diving technology thereafter; in the 4th century AD the Roman military strategist Flavius Vegetius Renatus proposed that men should be issued with leather suits, with air hoses leading up to the surface, to enable sea-bed combat; in the 15th century, Leonardo da Vinci described underwater soldiers who were issued with "wine skins" to contain air; by the end of the 16th century Renaissance Europe was awash with real and proposed "diving bells", all of which might be put to martial use; the history of the greatest "diving bell" of them all, the submarine is inseparable from its development as a means of covertly attacking enemy shipping.

There were other reasons for going beneath the waves. To be found on the seabed were not only Nature's riches, but human ones too, for wherever people travelled their ships sank or their belongings fell overboard. Salavage, like war, prodded along diving technology. In 1691 Edmund Halley lodged a patent for an improved diving bell, which he tested himself in Pagham Harbour in Sussex, England. In his notes of the dive he recorded the sensation of pressure change: ". . . a pressure begins to be felt on each ear, which by degrees grows painful, like as if a quill were forcibly thrust into the hole of each ear; till at length, the force overcoming the obstacle, that which constrains these pores yields to the pressure, and letting some condensed air slip in, present ease ensues." Halley's dives in the bell, though recorded in pioneering scientific detail, had mercenary reasons – the recovery of the cargo from a sunken ship nearby. The men who backed Halley's patented bell were money-men who wished to become richer money-men.

The diving bell, while it allowed air to those within it, was limited in manoeuvrability. The free diver was manoeuvrable but unable to defy biology; his time underwater was short and absolute. A marriage of convenience between free diver and diving bell came with the invention of the diving helmet, the copper-and-glass bowl which enabled its wearer to see around him while he walked the seabed in a canvas suit with leaden feet, with air supplied via a tube to a boat on the ocean surface. Again salvage was the spur. As early as 1774, a diving helmet that allowed a man to walk around underwater was demonstrated to the King of Sweden, but the first truly practicable helmet was designed by Charles and John Deane from Deptford, England, who adapted the fireman's leather helmet (with the know-how of gunsmith Augustus Siebe) for salvage diving in the 1820s. Almost simultaneously, the processes of waterproofing developed by Charles Mackintosh enabled the waterproofing of canvas and later the making of vulcanized rubber diving suits. Equipped in his state-of-the-art kit, the deep-sea diver became the hero of the age, the Victorian equivalent of the 1960s astronaut. In penny dreadfuls and stage shows, the deep-sea diver was cast as the intrepid explorer of an alien world, where perils galore awaited, from giant squid to baddies who slashed the air line with gleaming blades and sneering lips.

One danger was seldom depicted on stage, for it was too horrible to contemplate let alone view. Now that the diver could go deeper and stay under longer he began to contract a mysterious disease with agonizing contortions that led to paralysis, pressure sores and oftentimes death: "the bends". Not until the French physiologist Paul Bert issued *La Pression Barometrique* in 1878 was the cause of "the bends" fully understood: that under pressure nirogen would dissolve into the bloodstream. Sudden decompression caused the nitrogen to bubble back to its free state at a rate which was disastrous for the human body. If the pressure was released slowly, Bert established, then the nitrogen could be released from the body in the normal respiratory process. Using Bert's discovery, tghe English physiologist J. S. Haldane was able to work out precise decompression times for dives down to thirty-four fathoms. Issued in 1907, Haldane's decompression tables removed the dread from diving.

The man who put the joy into diving was Jacques-Yves Cousteau, inventor in 1943 of the aqualung, a demand-valve regulator which fitted into the mouth and drew in compressed air from tanks on the diver's back. Cousteau set the diver free; he could now swim with the fishes: "From this day forward we would swim across miles of country no man had known, free and level, with our skin feeling what the fish sacles know . . ." Cousteau wrote of the aqualung in his memoir *Silent World*.

Cousteau did more than enable the creation of the "Manfish", he democratized diving. Henceforth anybody with an aqualung, a pair of goggles and flippers could neter the undersea world, and a circle had been closed, for the origins of humankind lay in that self same sea. To enter the undersea is not so much a return to the womb but, as the great aquatic explorer William Beebe found, a kind of home-coming.

The Mammoth Book of the Deep is a century-long literary journey beneath the sea in the company of Cousteau and Beebe and thirty other "aquanauts". They dive to explore, to dig gold, to kill, to lay pipes, to experience the sheer thrill of it all. They go in diving suits, they go in submersibles, they go near naked. What they all bring back are true and wondrous adventures from another place: the liquid world.

Jon E. Lewis

A Chronology
of Underwater Adventure and Exploration

332 BC   Alexander the Great reputed to have descended to seabed in glass barrel during siege of Tyre

1535 AD   Development of "true" diving bell by Guglielmo de Lorena

1536   Illustrated edition of Vegetius' *De Re Militari* depicts hood-and-tube diving equipment

1629   Francis Bacon's *Novum Organum* records use of "apparatus which has sometimes been used to work on submerged vessels, and which enables the diver, by returning to it from time to time to breathe, to remain for a very long time under water"

1623   Dutchman Cornelius Drebbel demonstrates first submarine, Thames, London, the vessel made out of wood and waterproofed leather

1690   Edmund Halley invents a diving bell with replenishable air supplies, enough for five divers to remain on bottom at ten fathoms for 90 minutes

1715   "Diving engine" built by John Lethbridge, supplied by compressed air from surface

1716   Edmund Halley publishes *The Art of Living Underwater*

1774   King of Sweden watches demonstation of diver walking underwater wearing helmet

1776   US *Turtle* engages British ship in NY harbour, the first recorded military attack by a submarine

1797   German scientist Klingert trials diving suit with bellows in Oder; later adds airtank

1818   British naval officer John Ross lowers a line more than mile in North Atlantic and hauls up large sea star

1819   Auguste Siebe makes his first diving suit; later (1837) refines this with addition of the Deane brothers' helmet

1839   Siebe diving suit used in salvage of HMS *Royal George*

1843   Royal Navy establishes first diving school

1858   First transatlantic telegraph cable operational

1865   Auguste Denayrouse and Benoit Rouquayrol patent underwater breathing apparatus consisting of steel tank of compressed air for use on diver's back, attached to mouth piece

1870   Publication of Jules Verne's *Twenty Thousand Leagues Under the Sea*

1878   "La Pression Barometrique", study of physiologic studies of pressure changes, published by Paul Bert

1913   Greek sponge-hunter Spitti free dives to 72 metres to free anchor of cruiser

1934   William Beebe and Otis Barton descend in a tethered "bathysphere" to a depth of mile

1933   Louis de Corlieu patents fins

1934   South African fisherman trawl up a coelacanth, a "fossil fish"; circa 1934 Guy Gilpatric promotes use of rubber goggles with glass lenses, French Riviera

1941   Italian "human torpedoes" sink two British battleships in Alexandria, Egypt

1943   Jacques-Yves Cousteau invents "aqualung"

1948   Launch of Auguste Piccard's "bathyscaphe", first independent deepsea submersible

1951   British ship *Challenger II* bounces sound off seabed near Guam, and discovers seven-mile deep chasm, the "Challenger Deep"

1953   *Trieste* "bathyscaphe" of Professor Auguste Piccard touches 1,750 fathoms down off Ponza, Italy; *Silent World* published by Jacques-Yves Cousteau

1954   French "bathyscaphe" FRNS3 descends to 2,250 fathoms (13,287 feet) off Dakar

1960   Jacques Piccard (son of Auguste) and Don Walsh dive in *Trieste* bathyscaphe to bottom of Challenger Deep

1963   American submarine *Thresher* sinks with loss of 129 men; wreckage later found by *Trieste*

1964   Launch of US Navy's piloted submersible, *Alvin*

1966   *Alvin* retrieves American hydrogen bomb from bottom of Mediterranean

1974   Peter Benchley publishes *Jaws*

1977   Tjeerd van Andel in *Alvin* becomes first person to see hydrothermal vents on ocean floors, together with hitherto unknown eco-system dependent on obtaining energy from oxidation of sulphur compounds ("chemosynthesis")

1984   US oceanographer Robert Ballard videos *Thresher* wreckage with towed submarine sledge Argo

1985   Ballard discovers wreck of *Titanic*, mid-Atlantic

1989   Ballard, using Argo, discovers *Bismarck*, three miles down on Atlantic floor

2000   Russian nuclear submarine *Kursk* sinks in accident, Barents Sea

2003   Tanya Streeter breaks freedive record, descending to 400 feet (122 meters)

"The greatest, most exciting adventure is the mere act of being alive where, amongst men, only the drowned visit you"

–Philippe Diolé

PRELUDE: THE UNDERSEA ADVENTURE

Philippe Diolé

Diolé, a colleague of the famous Captain Jacques-Yves Cousteau, has been called the "first contemplative diver" and his 1951 The Undersea Adventure *remains the classic book on the pleasures, principles and philosophy of diving. He died in 1977. From* The Undersea Adventure:

I have no "stories" to tell.

Breaking the surface of the sea, roaming about in the deep waters of the ocean, going down slowly, eyes open, watching the flicker of mullet and the dance of sea-bream, the butterflies of these liquid skies: this does not make up a "story".

But if I do not know any stories, I have perhaps lived a miracle, one which I want to talk about: I have travelled to another world in which "action is sister to the dream". I have swept away in the heart of the sea, at a depth of several fathoms, all my anxieties as a man. Worries of the moment, scientific curiosity, metaphysical doubts, have all been hurled into the sea and I do not regret any of them.

Like many others I do not feel in perfect harmony with our age and the solitude of diving lulls and stays a deep-rooted dissatisfaction. Down below, where dream and action move silently forward through the dense waters, side by side, man feels for a moment in tune with life.

Whether that is telling a story or not, I don't know. It is

always possible to write an account of journeys on land. I have been from one end of Europe to the other and made almost a complete tour of Africa. Every country I have visited can be described: it is simply a question of landscape, people, distances. But for three years my life has been entangled in the life of the sea. The only period of my existence worth anything in all this time has been spent far from other men, beyond a curtain of crystal, with fish or underwater animals more foreign in appearance and habits than anything one might come across if one travelled to the ends of the earth. It has been an adventure without incident, and it is not yet over. Probably it will only end with my death. For those who have once listened to the siren-songs of the ocean-bed never return to land.

Norbert Casteret, in his Pyreneean caves, my friend Guy de Lavaur, exploring Padirac, have both had adventures with quite definite beginning, middle, and end. You enter these subterranean grottoes, you go all over them, and finally you leave them. The explorer may find a river, rooms, stalactites, narrow passages filled with clay, obstacles to surmount . . . But once out in the open again he has only to relive his underground journey to make a tale of it.

But what am I to say, a sea-explorer whose objective is never reached, and who has never seen the end of those marine vaults, one minute black with shadows, the next hacked with swords of light? Here and there I have managed to snatch fragments of knowledge, I have tried to use my eyes and understand the meaning of what was before me, and to fit together where I could the pieces of a vague jig-saw of the sea.

But there is no need to organise expeditions to explore the sea. Anyone can go down where they want and come up when they want. All you need is a flask of compressed air, some goggles, a piece of lead round your waist . . . Excuses are not so easy to justify, for we are each judge of our own daring, alone witness of our fears and hesitations. There are often humble and unimportant victories over ourselves. I have known bitter March mornings when the flesh refused to advance into a sea that cut like ice. I have shivered, alone on a rock, while the rising sun climbed behind the tip of the Islettes, simply because I was determined to observe the underwater world through all its seasons and because it seemed especially important to me at that green and yellow moment of the Mediterranean dawn . . . But is that a "story"? It's not even an anecdote.

Dramatic incidents? Certainly, I know a few; but I am not sure they can be described. Mostly they were trifling dramas that were over in a few seconds. A pipe getting hooked on to a piece of jagged rock; air-cylinders refusing to work in an underwater grotto; moments of animal panic when I couldn't wait to surface, desperate to see another human being. None of that is worth talking about and even Fargue, who perished at a depth of 60 fathoms, would probably have had nothing to tell if he had survived.

But divers do certainly have "adventures". Only they are not what landsmen usually understand by that word. The greatest, most exciting adventure is the mere act of being alive where, amongst men, only the drowned visit you. And of making yourself at home there, living a comfortable, peaceful existence.

Frederick II, one of the outstanding figures of the Middle Ages, Emperor of Germany, King of the Romans, King of Sicily and Jerusalem, and a great lover of the Mediterranean, one day indulged in a whim. He threw his golden goblet into the sea in order to encourage a diver to go down and look for it. Frederick hoped, by questioning the diver, to learn some new facts about the sea-bed. But it was a vain hope. The diver's account was bound to be useless: the sea's secrets cannot be picked up like golden goblets. The two or three minutes during which a man can hold his breath are not long enough to reveal a world. The undertaking is of an altogether different nature. It is by no means certain that our generation and the next one will even complete it. We can only make a beginning.

I have often thought about this king's curiosity. He was a man in advance of his time and in more than one way. I think I can guess what he was looking for and what the diver could not tell him. Frederick wanted to know whether this sea, in which simple fishermen let down their nets, was worth the interest of a prince such as himself: a philosopher, a man of liberal and daring intellect. The King of Jerusalem and Sicily was that day on the way to a great discovery. If his diver had not been blinded by the idea of the golden goblet, he would at least have been able to reveal one of the basic mysteries of the deep: that there is a visible frontier between the two worlds of earth and water.

"Sire," this man would have been able to say, "at the depth which I was able to reach I only grazed the surface of whatever lay far beneath me; but at any rate I went through a screen, a veil of some kind, and that must mean something, for there was life of a sort going on there, too . . ."

In fact one does not go straight into the sea. Between the air and the water a steel wave quivers. What people call the surface is also a ceiling: a looking-glass above, watered silk below. Nothing is torn on the way through. Only a few bubbles mark the diver's channel and behind him the frontier soon closes. But once the threshold is crossed, you can turn back slowly and look up: that dazzling screen is the border between two worlds, as clear to one as to the other. Behind the looking-glass the sky is made of water.

Is this light spilling out in all directions, this pure and deep substance, really water? So much brilliance and clarity does not seem to belong to the green, frothing surface, the glaucous and resilient element through which the swimmer has to strike his path. Once he has broken the surface, the diver who is properly ballasted has no more weight, no more resistance: an aerial softness transports him where he wills. Here the world is sweetness. There is not a place in his body, from head to foot, which is not relaxed. It is a pleasure to stretch out, to lie on one's back and feel the perfect fluency of one's muscles. Dreams float very slowly up from the sea. Walled in silence and completely alone, the diver begins an interior monologue in the cell of his undreamed-of content.

At a depth of two or three fathoms all swell subsides. Not a weed moves. A carpet of sand gleams faintly in the cleft of a rock some yards farther down. A mysterious continent traces itself below me. I swim between the huge pages of an illuminated manuscript. Now I am dazzled by the purity of the light, the luminous beauty of the deep. A crystal quality in the atmosphere gives everything the cleanliness of a glass case. The opened pages end in a maze of rocks, beyond which a flow of blue water narrows out of sight and then widens. Over them is stretched a thick sky on which I glide until I reach shapes that turn under water into peaks of the sea-bed, or cathedrals rising out of plains on summer mornings. Inspecting these summits, feeling the hard rock under their soft exterior of weed, gives one a respite before the final slide towards an invisible bottom. I swim round a sapphire steeple. Everything in front of me is blue, but if I look down a whole purple universe seems to swing out of the depths. Shall I go down to the foot of this tower or give it up on the way? At 20 fathoms, everything is forbidding, congealed, and cold, and the sudden iciness stabs me. I don't know whether it freezes or paralyses me: I feel it in me like a living thing, a disease . . . What have I come here for? To explore the sea? I already know all that can be seen in it. I have come down in pursuit of a mirage. I have yielded to the dizzy madness of tearing open this blue canvas and making for the very heart of the dream. The Groupers, motionless in the shadow of their holes, gaze at the passer-by without stirring. Gorgonians spread their huge fans, quite still in the breathless water. Who has spoken of jungles? Not a single evasive flurry, not a moving shadow, brings this palace without walls to life. Were blood to flow, for example, it would not stain the crystal purity, for it would look blue. What is this vague terror from a Chamber of Horrors? The slightest rustle makes me tremble. I have even forgotten what the sky looks like, the real sky in which men can breathe without equipment.

Such is the aspect that submarine life presents, for the most part, today. Twenty fathoms is a good limit, needing care but within reasonable bounds. Even ten years ago we were less daring.

If Jacques Bainville did not care greatly for history when he was a boy, I did not have much interest in sea-bathing. Swimming without any particular purpose has always seemed to me pleasant enough when it is hot, but it soon becomes boring.

Like many others I have done some underwater hunting. It was during the period of cross-bows with rubber stretchers and harpoons two yards long. But it was also the time when goggles first made their appearance. The submarine depths appeared in a new and staggering light. A few yards from the shore, their unsuspected lustre, their virginal beauty, were awaiting man's attention. So the most treasured memories of these early days are not of more or less successful attempts at harpooning. But, closing my eyes, I can fetch images out of a sea forever opening to my gaze; seaweed of all kinds, grottoes, dishevelled rocks, sun-dazzle twining its trellising along the sea-bed, and fishes that were strange or friendly and familiar. It was a world so rich and so inconsequentially revealed that I felt I was on the way to an important personal discovery. It seemed to me that the sudden annexation of such huge territories could not be without influence on my life.

Having succeeded in reaching the threshold I began to stumble. Goggles and tube enabled me, while remaining on the surface, to study the sea near the coast: idly pursuing fish that could scarcely escape, picking weeds at random, I indulged in indiscriminating wonder. But it seemed to me that there should be more to it than this, and I began to grow impatient. I was the guest at a party where I knew no one. It was irritating to see without understanding, to visit a country in which everything, animals, plants, even the way of breathing, was strange. I was like a Martian on earth.

It was then that I met Commander Philippe Tailliez. He was at that time in charge of the Undersea Research Group, the scientific section of the Naval General Staff. And one day, in a little cover near Toulon, he sent me down with some bottles of compressed air on my back and made me bite the rubber tube: I breathed my first draughts of air . . . The sea opened. I crossed through the looking-glass, no longer the ghastly, pallid body with the jerky gestures that fish and divers observe with some disgust splashing on the edge.

This underwater baptism, in the freshness of the spring sea, not only crowned me with riches that nobody could ever take away, but provided me with keys to unlock certain parts of myself. Drunk with the discovery of a new continent, I began at first to learn more about myself than about it.

Valéry has written a line in *Charmes*, in which, with the foresight of true genius, he expresses the very essence of what I felt:

Heureuse vos corps fondus, eaux planes et profondes!

I was this "*corps fondu*", the idealized but lively image of myself, and I moved in a landscape of dazzling reflections. The reverse side of the looking-glass was inhabited: fish, sea-weed, now at eye-level, offered me the extension of a reality for which I was not prepared. I felt one by one, like a kind of arthritis, my land origins. The mind was less at home than the body. Freed of all anxieties about breathing, I moved around in the forbidden world. I was at least as much of a man in the water as I was on land: a man who could observe with discretion and no longer a wretch tortured by asphyxiation, blinded by splashes, going down a fathom or two only at the expense of great physical effort. The air was obedient to the call of my lungs. Everything became as simple as in a dream and this air which I breathed out climbed to the surface in great expanding bubbles, the supreme proofs of the miracle.

Lest anyone should misunderstand this story, let me repeat: I was a novice, a complete beginner. I have revisited the place of my first exploits: the depth of the cove is childish, but no act of daring today could ever give me so great a feeling of discovery, and of joy at wandering alone through a virginal forest and fashioning the sun into my own golden goblet.

On the rocks that day a family from Toulon was having lunch. It was a Sunday. I remember their loud voices, their amusement on the water's edge that anyone should bother to explore its depths. Were they aware, these Sunday revellers, that I was taking up all my promises to the sea and thanks to this second baptism renewing between man and the sea a contract broken 200,000,000 years ago? Did I even know myself?

Philippe Tailliez smiled at my enthusiasm. He didn't tell me that I had seen nothing and that I still had everything to learn. I discovered it for myself at my next dive. Then began a slow apprenticeship. To lose one's head over diving is only the beginning: the next step is knowing how to get the most benefit, once the sea has closed over you, out of this state of being a live, drowned man. One has to learn to be worthy of one's position as a "melted body". So a new life begins, with sterner pleasures.

The weight of our heredity, our whole past, dissuades us from accepting this sumptuous gift that the twentieth century offers us. Our ancestors, who lived in forests, have bequeathed us eyes that deceive us under water. Hunters have left us ears which are bad for diving and a sense of hearing which is useless in the sea. Accustomed for thousands of years to being warned, and to being able to avoid danger, by trusting to our eyes, our smell, our hearing, we are suddenly disarmed in an element where our horizon is limited to a few yards and where silence reigns. A fear born of ignorance keeps us company for a long time in this country, where we do not know how to distinguish dangerous from friendly creatures, plants from animals. We need this proof to be reminded of our ancient heritage, like those royal palaces one sees transformed into museums and which set the architect appalling problems. How many walls to knock down before we see the daylight, how many habits to renounce that we had taken to be the very marks of human intelligence: our idea of space, the hierarchy of our senses and the way to interpret their signals . . . Our disturbed brain asks to be reassured by a gradual and careful approach to these new truths of the sea. And these new marine truths are in the process of becoming new human truths, for in future this apprenticeship to the deep will interest the masses. A large public, more numerous each year, tries to learn about the sea, about conditions that scholars scarcely understand. Biology, the study of marine plants, hydrography, all still the preserve of specialists, are becoming subjects of holiday discussion. Civil servants and housewives, as soon as summer comes, put on goggles to gaze into the waters and to sample an enchantment which ten years ago was reserved for initiates. For children the magic of the sea is as commonplace as television and radar. I am not one of those who deplore it. So immediate an intimacy suggests that the underwater world is less impenetrable than it seems. New discoveries are worked out, future activities planned: the last has not been said about the evolution of human life.

But the underwater world escapes the hands that clutch at it. The fish are not the only ones to disappear. A fathom down, in full daylight, everything is deceptive: the plant the diver was going to grasp is not where he saw it. He looks for his own hand and it is no longer where it was. Thus, even his body deceives and takes advantage of him below the surface. He has to start all over again, like a child in the cradle that fumbles awkwardly for its rattle and has not learnt to co-ordinate its movements with its instincts. That all comes. Soon enough.

*"When I first put on a diving helmet . . . I knew that I had
added thousands upon thousands of wonderful miles to
my possible joy of earthly life"*

THE KINGDOM OF THE HELMET

William Beebe

*A director of the New York Zoological Society, Beebe always felt
at home under the sea, "a returning native rather than an intruding
stranger". Here he describes some early impressions seen "from the
kingdom of the helmet"; later, working with Otis Barton, he
descended to greater depths in the bathysphere (see pp 75–100).*

When first I put on a diving helmet and climbed down the
submerged ladder, then I knew that I had added thousands
upon thousands of wonderful miles to my possible joy of earthly
life: let me escape from dry-land etymology and say instead – the
joys of planetary life; for personal exploration under the ocean is
really unearthly – we are penetrating into a new world.

After we have dived hundreds of times we learn to discount
the fears upon which we have been nurtured since childhood.
And when the needless terrors of being water-enclosed, of the
imputed malignity of octopuses, sharks, and barracudas have
ceased to trouble our supreme delight in the strangeness and
unbelievable beauties of this newly conquered realm; then we
begin to appreciate the real significance of our achievement.

To enter into and to enjoy this new phase of life requires no
practice or rehearsal, no special skill or elaborate preparation. If
one dives and returns to the surface inarticulate with amazement
and with a deep realization of the marvel of what he has seen and
where he has been, then he deserves to go again and again. If he

is unmoved or disappointed, then there remains for him on earth only a longer or shorter period of waiting for death; there can be little worthwhile left for him.

Ten years of diving on New York Zoological Society expeditions have taught me all the primal necessities. The only requirements are a bathing-suit and a pair of rubber-soled shoes, a copper helmet with glass set in front, an ordinary rubber hose, and a small hand pump. A folding metal ladder is excellent, but a rope is quite sufficient. Now you go into two, four, six, eight fathoms, swallowing as you descend to offset the increase of pressure. If your ears hurt severely a few feet below the surface ascend at once and go to the nearest aurist, for something is wrong and should be attended to, whether you ever dive again or not.

Forty feet is a good limit to set, and indeed the most brilliant and exciting forms of shore and reef life will be found in shallower depths. There is no danger of falling. If you stumble over the edge of a submerged cliff or lofty terrace, you simply half drift, half float, gently to the bottom. But when you stand on the edge of a deep chasm, and are already eight or ten fathoms down, don't let any alluring shell or coral lure you much deeper. Ears cannot withstand too great pressure.

After you have made a dozen descents you will wish to do something more than stand amazed, or vainly try to catch fish which swim close to the glass and look in at you.

As we have done, you can begin to devise all sorts of new apparatus. You wish to make notes, so get sheet zinc or pads of waterproof paper, find a comfortable block of coral and write as easily as if you were sitting in the boat. Be sure to tie your pencil tightly around, for otherwise the wood will separate and float to the surface, while the core of lead sinks to the bottom, to be nibbled at excitedly by small fry.

Motion pictures can be taken, down to twenty or twenty-five feet, by placing the camera in a tight brass box with a bit of glass in front. If you wish to paint, weight your easel with lead, waterproof your canvas or skin, and sit down with your palette of oils. You will have to brush away small fish from time to time, for some of the paints give forth an alluring odour and your palette will sometimes be covered with a hungry school of inchlings.

If you take your seat in the midst of a coral reef you may be attacked – not by giant octopuses or barracudas, or sharks – don't give them a thought – but you may feel a faint nip or a push at your elbow and there is a little fish – a demoiselle shorter than your thumb, all azure and gold, furiously butting at you. Her home is nearby and in its defence she fears nothing which swims, crawls or dives. Soon she will accept you as a harmless new kind of sea creature, and off she goes to drive away an approaching snapper or surgeonfish.

If your tastes incline to sport, invent submarine sling-shots and crossbows and shoot what particular fish you wish with barbed arrows of brass wire. I now use dynamite caps on the end of a weighted fishpole, but sling-shots and stabbing grains are safer for the beginner.

If you wish to make a garden, choose some beautiful slope or reef grotto and with a hatchet chop and pry off coral boulders with waving purple sea-plumes and golden sea-fans and great parti-coloured anemones. Wedge these into crevices, and in a few days you will have a sunken garden in a new and miraculous sense. As birds collect about the luxuriant growths of a garden in the upper air, so hosts of fish will follow your labours, great crabs and starfish will creep thither, and now and then fairy jellyfish will throb past, superior in beauty to anything in the upper world, more delicate and graceful than any butterfly.

Our grandmothers lined their garden paths with conch shells, but undersea it is more difficult to do this, for the giant snails will insist on walking away as soon as you have planted them. But other exquisite shells can be scattered about, and the easiest and quickest way to discover these is to search until you have found the hiding-place of an octopus, and here you will be certain to find a collection of empty shells of all kinds. The octopus is an adept at searching out toothsome molluscs, and he then carries them to his lair and devours the inmates at his leisure. The shells, quite perfect, are then thrown outside into his kitchen-midden.

Finally, as a border to your marine plantation, collect a score of small, rounded brain corals all thickly covered with tube worms. When you lay them in place, they will be a drab, dirty white. It is their momentary winter, but wait patiently and in five minutes you can see spring approach, and a host of pastel buds appear; and in another five minutes full summer arrives and your ivory mounds are ablaze with scarlet, mauve, blue, yellow, and green animal blossoms. All are in motion, though there is no current, and we feel there would be nothing remarkable in their suddenly saying, like Alice's tiger-lily: "We *can* talk, when there's anybody worth talking to."

The wise diver will refrain from written descriptions of his experiences. What I have published of under-sea-scapes has aroused commendation on the part of the fireside and dry land readers. The moment, however, one of them puts on a helmet and goes to see for himself, thereafter all words and phrases, similes, and superlatives will become for him hopelessly inadequate. Just as the colours under-sea are nameless in the gamut of terrestrial hues, so our language becomes thin and vague when we try to fashion from it adequate submarine imagery. Even the commonest fishes and other organisms of our shallows are like different creatures when viewed from their element and their own level, instead of from man's vertical height above water: our human friends as we see them from a second-storey window are strangely unlike them face to face!

The Kingdom of the Helmet is not only a new experience for us, but the place in past aeons of time of fiercest competition and most spectacular evolution. It is a ribbon of a kingdom, of negligible depth – from six to sixty feet, and narrow in width – from a few inches to two miles. Its length is amazing – perhaps one hundred and fifty thousand miles of winding, submarine paths, rimming the rocks and cliffs of temperate fiords and bays; all along the palm-lined shores of southern continents, and the innumerable circles and rings of tropic isles and atolls. Perhaps the most interesting and exciting places are the reefs and shallows far from shore, like those of Bermuda which I have named Almost Island, where one can go overboard and to the bottom surrounded on all sides by depths forbidden to present ambulatory exploration.

When the summer's sun has warmed our northern waters, let us climb down the ladder off some rocky coast, say off Maine or Massachusetts. At once we begin to realize our new-found superiority: yesterday we crept painfully over legions of barnacles and peered ineffectually into outer depths. Now we pass quickly beyond the barnacle zone below lowest tide-mark, where things have been wet since creation. A little further down and the last of the steel-blue mussels passes from view, and then we perceive the great clinging roots of the giant seaweeds, with their leathery fronds stretching up and up to the surface. Green urchins give place to other larger species, and two or three fathoms down we enter the home of the beautiful basket starfish, hinting of the crinoids which have now almost vanished from earth.

We take our seat upon a mat of seaweed and watch the life of mid-water. Shrimps come in great numbers, drifting past like ghosts of living beings; the first squid, seen head on, will never be forgotten, nor will a galaxy of ctenophora jelly fish when the sunlight sets their cilia ablaze. Whelks and small curious crabs clamber upon our canvas shoes, and suddenly a thousand comets dash past – a school of herrings in search of spawning grounds. Only an impatient jerk on the hose will remind us that we have long overstayed our allotted time.

At the first dive in the tropics, say in the West Indies, we are impressed by the great increase in the amount of life and the unbelievable brilliancy of colour. Off New York we perhaps picked up a tiny crumb-of-bread sponge and on a clam shell found a bubble of coral the size of a marble. Here, in the midst of a tropical reef, corals form boulders six and eight feet across, or branched arborescent growths into which we climb. Anemones and fish are rainbow-tinted – harlequin angelfish and large-eyed scarlet squirrels. Horny corals send up unearthly purple branches like nothing conceivable above water, and the joy of it all is that everything that moves has little or no fear of us. We are made to feel at home – returning natives, not intruding strangers.

When many dives have been made at one place, so that the seascape has become familiar, and individual fish are known on sight and can be claimed as friends, then is the time to come out late some starlit evening, and go down in the dark. Choose a night when there is strong phosphorescence, and climb down the ladder very slowly. When your eyes pass just below the level of the water the illumination of the ripples is beyond any mere man-made fire. At first, as we stand on the bottom we seem to be in utter darkness, with only a glow coming down from above. A glance upward shows the keel of the boat turned to molten silver, and now our eyes have become re-adapted and our individual cosmos begins to be filled with galaxies and constellations, meteors and comets of blue and white light. These in turn are resolved by our intelligence into definite organisms. Some of them, such as jelly-fish and sea-worms, have lights of their own, but most of these shallow-water forms are illuminated by proxy. Every move they make evokes brilliance from the minute Noctiluca and other microscopic creatures. Now and then the passage of some great fish lights up all the surrounding reef with its caves and waving fronds, and memory, from our diurnal dives, supplies a host of details. Again, language fails us utterly; we can only stand and look and feel and later remember enough of the marvel of it all to wish to experience it again as soon as possible.

*"... I waved my companions away and prepared
to settle the thing, man to Merou"*

GOGGLE FISHING

Guy Gilpatric

*Gilpatric, sometime aviator and sometime vice president of a NY
advertising agency, moved to the French Riviera in the 1930s,
where he pioneered "goggle fishing" – hunting with a watertight
mask and harpoon. He also achieved a wider celebrity as the author
of the* Inchcliffe Castle *stories featuring the mariner "Mr Glen-
cannon".*

> *As inward love breeds outward talk,*
> *The hound some praise, and some the hawk;*
> *Some, better pleased with private sport,*
> *Use tennis; some a mistress court:*
> *But these delights I neither wish,*
> *Nor envy, while I freely fish.*
> *– The Compleat Angler*

For nearly three hundred years after Izaak Walton wrote his
masterly treatise on angling, the world was content to accept
him as final authority on the art, science, and mystery of
catching fish. From time to time false prophets arose with
patent hooks and chemical and electrical contrivances for
knocking fish cold in wholesale quantities, while during the
War the French infantry perfected an ingenious technique of
chucking hand grenades into the Moselle River, thereby blasting many a gasping and disillusioned mud-gubbin out into the

adjacent vineyards, and at the same time altering the course of the historic stream considerably. But all such devices of science, though effective, were flagrantly unsportsmanlike and therefore anathema to true amateurs of the rod and reel. However inefficient the old painstaking method, it was better, because fairer, than the new. Olde Izaak Walton, it seemed, had said the last word.

Then, suddenly, there came strange rumors. Somebody, somewhere, had evolved a radical and super-sportsmanlike manner of fishing – or, at least, so he claimed. His name (it was whispered by Seminole guides, Canuck gaffers, Highland gillies, and Negro boatmen) was olde Guyzaak Gilpatric. His method, they said, was called goggle fishing. Here is the dope on it.

First, because so many fish go through life handicapped by names like scrod, chub, guppy, and squid, I must explain that goggle fishing doesn't mean fishing for goggles, because goggles aren't fish. Goggle fishing is fishing with watertight eye-glasses and a spear – going down like McGinty to the bottom of the sea and scragging the wary denizens of the deep on their own home grounds. It is a sport so full of special tricks and dodges that I was minded to entitle this volume *The Sport of Kinks* until better judgment prevailed.

The first thing you need, to be a successful goggle fisher, is a body of good clear water. Personally I use the Mediterranean Sea and there is still plenty of room in it, but parts of the Atlantic, the Pacific, the Mexican Gulf, and the Caribbean will do just as well, and I know of many lakes and streams which would provide grand goggling. Next you need a pair of watertight goggles. I made my first pair myself from an old pair of flying goggles, plugging up the ventilating holes with putty and painting over it. The ones I now use were built for sponge and pearl diving.

In goggle fishing, the spear is thrust like a sword and is never thrown, for you cannot throw a spear much farther under water than you can throw a motorbus on land. The spear being of necessity fairly short, you will be wondering how it is possible to

approach within striking range of a fish. The answer is partly
skill but mostly the fact that a fish is less suspicious of a man
swimming under water, right in its own element, than of men or
boats floating on the surface. I discovered this characteristic
quite by accident, shortly after I began swimming with goggles
and before I had any thought of spearing fish. My idea,
originally, was merely to study the submarine scenery and
vegetation, which in the clear warm water of this Riviera region
I believed would be worth seeing. Accordingly, one day, I
shoved off from shore on an innocent sight-seeing trip. I had
ridden in the glass-bottomed boats of Catalina and Bermuda
and used waterscape boxes in the Gulf of Mexico, but I was
unprepared for the breathtaking sensation of free flight which
swimming with goggles gave me. It wasn't at all like flying in a
plane, where you are conscious of being borne by something
tangible; there was a nightmare quality to this sensation as in a
dream of falling, and in that instant I knew how Icarus felt when
his wings melted off. I jerked my head out of water and looked
around to reassure myself. The bottom was fifteen feet below
me, now, but every pebble and blade of grass was distinct as
though there were only air between. The light was a soft bluish-
green – even, restful, and somehow wholly appropriate to the
aching silence which lay upon those gently waving meadows and
fields of flowers. On the pinnacle of a rock like a little mountain
I saw a dwarf palm tree. I swam down to study it. I touched its
trunk and – zip! – the feathery foliage vanished as quickly as the
flame of a blown candle. I came up for air, a portion of which I
used in vowing to get the explanation of this flummery. I swam
along on the surface until I found another palm tree. This one I
sneaked up on (or rather, down to) stealthily. I reached forward,
touched the leaves and – they weren't! But this time it hadn't
fooled me. The trunk had simply sucked the leaves inside itself.
If my finger had been an anchovy or other small fish, it might
have been sucked in with them, there to be consumed for the
nourishment of the confounded plant. I have since learned that
this was the *Spirographis Spallanzanii*, not a plant at all, but an
animal; but I decided right then and there that it is as foolhardy

to go picking flowers on the sea bottom as it is in front of the cop in a public park.

Soaring on my way above hills and valleys upon which grew blossoms snowy white and flaming red, I came to a great submerged rock from one side of which projected a wide shelf. I could see small fish flashing in and out along its edges, and went down to have a look at them. The underside of the shelf, though only ten or twelve feet below the surface, was fifty feet above the bottom. It was heavily grown with weeds. Anchovies and sardines – thousands of them – were swimming around eating this foliage. But – I rubbed my goggles – they were swimming on their backs! Had I discovered a new species? At first I couldn't believe what I saw; then a larger fish happened along and he, too, was swimming on his back. I dove right under the ledge, where it was dark and cold, and shooed the whole crowd out. As soon as they left the shadow and saw the sunlight above them, they turned right side up and went their ways like any self-respecting fish. Now those fish did not have to turn on their backs in order to eat weeds on the ceiling, for fish can eat in any reasonable position as well as in several which I might call scandalous. No, those fish were not aware that they were on their backs. They thought that the ceiling was the floor; they didn't know up from down, being in practically the same fix as the oldtime aviators who, lacking instruments for flying in clouds and fog, used to lose all sense of direction and turn upside down without realizing it until loose objects, such as bottles, commenced falling upwards out of the cockpit. My discovery that sardines and anchovies can swim on their backs is fraught with significance and I have no doubt that after the publication of this book I will be the recipient of appropriate decorations and degrees from scientific organizations the world over.

Feeling pretty pleased with myself, I swam around to the other side of the rock. This face of it went down sheer until its base was lost in deep blue gloom. I had the sensation of flying in the chasm of a New York street. Below me I saw vague forms moving – fish, they were, and whoppers. I watched them for a long time as they lazed about in stately grace or poised in rumination, fearing that my slightest move would startle them. But presently a couple came up to within fifteen feet of me and seemed to be giving me the once-over. I thought I'd return the compliment. Swimming down as close to them as I dared, I hovered in suspense which they didn't seem to share. They were big fat dorades; I was so close that I could see the gold bands on their blue foreheads but I didn't hope that they'd let me come closer. I needed air and started upward. Suddenly, I found myself staring into the eyes of what looked like a German U-boat – a three-foot loup in a fine state of indignation, his dorsal fin jutting up like the bristles of a bulldog. Without stopping to think, I cut loose my right and pasted him square on the jaw. I heard a whirring sound like that of wings as Mr Loup departed under forced draught.

I came to the surface, gulped some air, and pondered on the sorry state to which I had fallen in being unable to knock out a three-foot fish. No use kidding myself, that blow wouldn't have bruised a stewed oyster. My knuckles were bleeding but this merely meant I'd scratched them on the little needles along the edge of his gill. I filled my lungs, swam down a way and indulged in some expert mental shadow boxing. I soon found the trouble. Being full of air and therefore lighter than water, my punches simply pushed me backward, and the harder I walloped, the faster I shoved myself away from what I was aiming to hit. Also, I was using a lot of energy in resisting my tendency to float up to the surface. I blew out my air, sank down further, and uncorked a couple of rights and lefts. Now, I felt that my blows really had a little steam behind them. My body being heavier than water, my punches had something to react against.

I was feeling pretty tired, and I noticed that the skin on my fingers was shrivelled from being in the water too long. As I swam toward the beach, I thought of what I'd learned – namely, that some fish are not afraid of swimmers, and that to exert power under water you have to empty your lungs. It occurred to me that in these discoveries might lie the basis of a new sport.

★   ★   ★

It was along toward the end of October and the days were pulling in pretty short. Sometimes the storm clouds would stack up on the mountains to the west of us and swallow the sun by four in the afternoon. Our front yard, the Mediterranean Sea, was as full of fish as ever and so clear that you could see bottom in sixty feet, but with the diminishing sunlight, its greens and blues and purples had taken on a grayish tinge and it was turning colder every day. All summer long we'd had priceless sport. For month after month, with water temperatures of between seventy degrees and eighty degrees, we goggled for six hours a day; and more than once, in August, we had worked the beach and harbor of Sainte Maxime for eight hours straight. We had learned things about fish and their habits which certainly no fisherman and perhaps no scientist had ever known; we had observed submarine phenomena which we couldn't explain ourselves and which were so strange that we hesitated to mention them to outsiders lest they stroke their chins and murmur "Oh, yair?"

Around the ends of the rocky capes of Antibes, Ferrat, and Roux, on the reefs beyond the Lerin Islands and at the foot of the red rock cliffs where the Esterel Mountains go into the sea, we had looked down upon scenes of grandeur beyond the dry land's grandest and had seen no billboards. But now, if we goggled for only half-an-hour, diving down fifteen or twenty feet or following the fish into the rock grottoes which the sun never penetrates, the cold knotted us up until we couldn't have speared a crate of dried codfish with a mile of picket fence. All along the Riviera, from Le Lavandou to Menton, people were complaining about the unmuffled speedboat motors when what they really heard was the chattering of goggle fishers' teeth.

1 November dawned a rotten day, with a high layer of clouds moving eastward and another scudding oppositely just above the sea. Ducks, geese, and herons were going over in bunches headed for Egypt, proving that ducks, geese, and herons do not believe all they read about the Riviera's winter climate. But at ten o'clock, faithful to our daily tryst, the Antibes Local of the Gogglers' Guild convened with spears on the wave-pounded

beach, and a solemn lot we were. Our number included a
Russian, two Frenchmen, an Irishman, and myself, so that
all we needed to make a comic dialect story was somebody
named Levinstein. But we didn't feel like comic stories, for any
of us could see with half a goggle that our sport was finished for
the season.

There was a long silence while we viewed the desolate
scene.

"Well, what shall we do?" asked somebody.

"What is there left to do?" snarled somebody else.

"I know!" I said, brightly. "Let's go fishing!"

For a moment they stood as men stunned; then—

"Fishing?" inquired an incredulous voice. "– Fishing? You
mean – fishing?"

"Yes, fishing. With hooks and lines and bait and boat.
Regular old-fashioned fishing."

Well, the sheer novelty of the stunt swept them off their feet,
and so an hour later we were bobbing at anchor just west of the
tip of Cap d'Antibes. We dropped our lines over the side and
waited for something to happen. For a long time nothing did
happen. It was a frightful bore. Even when we started pulling in
a few fair-sized ones our tackle kept getting tangled in our
yawns. Once a man has goggled – once he has hunted his fish,
stalked it, pursued it in its own element and finally speared it or
lost it as he or the fish was the smarter – the conventional
flummery of hooks and lines and rods and reels is merely so
much near beer.

By noon I'd had enough – and at noon, precisely, the sun
came out. "Madam Chairman and beloved lodge sisters," I said,
"I'm going overboard for a final hack at it." I peeled off, put on
goggles and knife belt, took my five-pronged spear and slid over
the gunwale into the (br-r-rh!) water. I swam toward the Cape,
which at that point goes down from the surface in sheer walls
like the facades of Florentine palaces. At some places the depth
was thirty or forty feet; at others I could not see bottom at all
and everything below was the dark velvety blue of February
evening sky. A school of black mullets like a flock of crows

passed under me. I saw a rock as big as a church swinging back and forth, back and forth; I lifted my face out of water to keep from feeling dizzy and to remind myself that I and not the rock was see-sawing in the swell. And when I put my face under again I saw Merou the Bonehead.

I didn't recognize him, at first. I only knew that the biggest fish I'd encountered to date was lying on a rock ledge twenty feet below me. I blew out my air and sank toward him. Before I was halfway down I realized that even if I speared him I'd have a tough time bringing him up. I stayed where I was, watching him. He returned the scrutiny with an eye the size of a horse's. His pectoral fins barely stirring, he moved majestically along the ledge and as a beam of sunlight struck him I saw that he was a merou. I swam up to the surface and back to the boat with the news.

Now the merou is a fish rarely landed in this part of the Mediterranean. They have a pair of them in the Oceanographical Museum of Monaco – their largest living specimens – who have been ogling the tourists through the plate glass side of a tank for over twenty-five years. Dr Oxner, the aquarium director, does not know how old this piscatorial Darby and Joan were when caught, nor can he say with any certainty which is Joan and which Darby. This is due to the merous' confusing habit of changing sex from time to time, so that, in meeting one socially, a person doesn't know whether to take off his hat and hand her an orchid or to slap him on the back and ask about the missus.

Well, we sat in the boat and discussed the merou problem while the wind from the snow-capped Alpes blew the clouds across the sun again and I developed a fine case of three-way shivers. All we knew about the merou was that he was a very athletic and very nasty fish and that, having speared him, you should not grab him by the throat lest he crush your fingers in his edged and armored gills. Or maybe hers. At length we decided to row to within fifty yards of the rocks, put a rope around me and my spear and try our luck. When I yanked on the line the people in the boat would yank me and (we hoped) the merou up to the surface; meanwhile I would be giving him appropriate treatment with my knife.

I went over the side again – and have you ever noticed how much colder cold water is the second time? It was awkward, swimming with the line around me; my feet kept getting tangled in it. The merou was still on his ledge but he had moved a little way along it to a spot where he could watch the proceedings better. He wasn't in the least afraid of me as I started down but as soon as he spotted the rope curling and snaking in the water, he ducked back into a crevice out of sight. Evidently, some time in his career, he'd had an unfortunate experience with a line with a hook at the end of it and he wasn't intending to fall for that gag again.

No, the rope wouldn't do. I went up for air, cast it off and called to the boat to stand by. I now planned to dive, plant the spear in him and then let go of it, hoping that once wounded he wouldn't be able to swim far. When he had tired himself by thrashing around I could go down again, do a little knife work on him and eventually bring him to the surface. Soon I saw the great brown snout come out of the crack – cautiously. I was about to dive when it bobbed in again. I lay on the surface and watched and shivered and cursed and shivered and watched for fifteen minutes. Yes, and shivered. Suddenly, further along the crack, I saw his whole head. I beckoned the boat to come closer; then, blowing out all my air to enable me to sink fast, deep and with minimum effort and water disturbance, I went for him. Just as I came within range – say four feet – he started back into the crevice. I couldn't see his body, only his head, and I knew I would have to hit him quickly and hard. "Alright, Sir or Madam, as the case may be!" I said. "How's – THIS?"

I let him have it smack on the dome. There was a frightful ruction, a brown flash and – Merou was gone!

All five spear teeth had struck him at once. The shock of the blow through the spear handle made my elbow tingle as though I'd hit a rock. Each of those teeth was needle-pointed and razor edged. But as far as I had seen or felt, not a single one of them had gone more than skin deep into Merou. Merou the Bone-head!

Well, the season was over, but though some of us had brought in well over a hundred fish, it ended on a sour note for me. It was easy enough to blame the loss of Merou on the cold water; perhaps, in August, I could have pasted him harder than I had done in November; and surely, if I hadn't had to strike him on the head. I would at least have put a dent in him. But still, I felt that something was wrong. I suspected my spear.

That spear, hand forged and highly tempered, had brought in some pretty big fish. With it I had landed an octopus measuring six feet seven inches across the tentacles, which is somewhat larger than the *octopus vulgaris* is supposed to grow. But it should have gone into that merou – and it hadn't. Why not? The answer came from India.

A Britisher just back from Benares was telling us how simple the *fakirs'* tricks are when you stop to figure them out. The famous couch of nails, for instance, is simply so chuckfull of nails that the holy man's weight, distributed over the points of all of them, does not bear down hard enough on any one point to puncture the skin. "But," said our friend, "I offered any number of the filthy brutes seventy-five rupees to sit on a single nail and there wasn't a sportsman in the lot." Right then and there we saw the trouble with our five-toothed spears. The force of the blow was divided among all the teeth and distributed over too great an area of the fish. What we needed was a spear with a single point in which the full force could concentrate.

For weeks, then, as the word went forth and good gogglers got together, the marble tops of cafe tables throughout the Alpes Maritimes were covered with pencilled designs for single-toothed harpoons. We went over to Monaco and studied the late Prince Albert's collection of native spears, as well as the various harpoons which he used on his expeditions. We whittled wooden models of harpoon heads and jabbed oranges and loaves of bread with them to study the nature of the wounds. At last we figured out a design which looked good to all of us. This was a steel shaft three-eighths of an inch square and forty inches long with a forged triangular head and a hinged barb. The barb would close tight against the shaft while entering the fish but would swing out at right angles at the slightest opposite pull, thus preventing the fish's escape. This entire gadget screwed into a tubular socket which accommodated the wooden handle, the handle varying in length to suit the individual owner. My own harpoon, when finished, was six feet long and weighed about two pounds. It was a mean weapon. The only trouble was, we didn't know whether we could hit anything with it. Our five-toothed spears had given us a margin of error of almost six inches, but with our new harpoons every shot had to be a bull's-eye.

By the middle of summer we began to realize that certain individual fish spend their time in fixed neighborhoods and that others, like some migratory birds, come back to the same spot at the same time year after year. We had known all along that many rock fish, such as the sargue and the serre, are confirmed stay-at-homes and we had come to know a number of them by their first names, but it surprised us to meet a giant linte for the third successive August in a little cove where no other linte is ever seen. At least three of us saw and recognized him and we believed that he recognized us. Then there was a big old loup who lived in a hole in the base of the jetty of the Port Mallet; as a rule loups are nomads, but this fellow didn't move twenty yards in seven months.

Thinking of this and talking it over with the others made me wonder if Merou – Merou the Bonehead, the only merou any of us had seen thus far – was not one of these confirmed home bodies. Certainly he'd known all the ins and outs of that crevice as though he'd lived there a long time. The rock ledge outside it was a comfortable front porch for him to loll around on, there were plenty of octopus for him to snag and all in all, if I had been a merou, I couldn't have asked for a nicer set-up myself.

The more we discussed it the more likely it seemed that we'd find him still in business – a year older, a little bigger but, we hoped, with arteries and skull no harder.

On 28 September, in calm, warm water and bright sunshine, four of us went out to look for him. Because I remembered the bottom from the year before (somehow a goggle fisher acquires the knack of finding his way by the bottom, unerringly, and rarely uses landmarks) I had no difficulty in leading the caravan to the proper territory. And there on his ledge, looking up at us with his horsy eye, lay Merou the Bonehead, exactly as I'd first seen him eleven months before!

I suppose I should have gone down and mingled with him at once. I could see his whole body and I believe I could have scragged him then and there. But a merou is not to be taken lightly, and at least two of our number had legitimate scientific reasons for wanting to see such a grand specimen at large. The grand specimen, however, had legitimate scientific reasons for getting to hell out of there, and he did so with a single caudal flip which took him into the crevice and out of sight. It was apparent that he didn't care for crowds.

Now by all rules of goggling, this merou was my own personal fish; and so, with the gesture of a matador ordering his *peons* from the ring and hoping to God that they won't take it seriously, I waved my companions away and prepared myself to settle the thing, man to Merou. They swam away twenty yards or so and lay with their faces under water to witness the drama of life and death which all of us felt would shortly unfold.

As for myself I floated with spear couched and knife loosened in its sheath, ready to sink down and deal the lethal blow. He didn't come out. I lay there for a long, long time – so long that I studied his old homestead in detail, even noting that the seaweed on his ledge – a species of white flower very like the gardenia of dry land – had a foot-wide path worn through it by the friction of his belly.

He stuck his head out exactly where I knew he would. I went down, just as I had planned and hoped and dreamed and known I'd go down. I drew back my arm, sighted along the spear, uncorked my soul and – SMACK!

There was a frightful ruction, a brown flash and – Merou the Bonehead was gone! When I came to the surface I found that the steel shaft of my harpoon was bent two inches out of line.

Excalibur had failed us!

Thus ended the goggling for another season.

*"No children ever opened a Christmas present with more excitement
than we did when we unpacked the first 'aqualung'"*

MENFISH

Jacques-Yves Cousteau

*Inventor of the aqualung and prolific maker of undersea documen-
tary films, the Frenchman Jacques-Yves Cousteau did more than
anyone else to bring the ocean to the notice of 20th-century man and
woman. He won Academy Awards for* The Silent World *(1956),*
The Golden Fish *(1960) and* World Without Sun *(1964); other
laurels accorded Cousteau, who was an early and passionate
environmentalist, included the* Legion d'Honneur *and the US
Presidential Medal of Freedom. Cousteau died in 1997, aged 87.*

One morning in June 1943, I went to the railway station at
Bandol on the French Riviera to collect a wooden case expressed
from Paris. In it was a new and promising device, the result of
years of struggle and dreams: an automatic compressed-air
diving lung conceived by Émile Gagnan and myself. I rushed
it to Villa Barry where my diving comrades, Philippe Tailliez
and Frédéric Dumas, were waiting. No children ever opened a
Christmas present with more excitement than we did when we
unpacked the first "aqualung". If it worked, diving could be
revolutionized.

We found an assembly of three moderate-sized cylinders of
compressed air, linked to an air regulator the size of an alarm
clock. The bottles contained air condensed to one hundred and
fifty times atmospheric pressure. From the regulator there
extended two tubes, joining on to a mouthpiece. With this

equipment harnessed to the back, a watertight glass mask over
the eyes and nose, and rubber foot fins, we intended to make
unencumbered flights in the depths of the sea.

We hurried to a sheltered cove which would conceal our
activity from curious bathers and Italian occupation troops. I
checked the air pressure. It was difficult to contain my excitement and discuss calmly the plan of the first dive. Dumas, the
best goggle diver in France, would stay on shore keeping warm
and rested, ready, if necessary, to dive to my aid. My wife,
Simone, would swim out on the surface with a schnorkel
breathing-tube and watch me through her submerged mask.
If she signalled anything had gone wrong, Dumas could dive to
me in seconds. "Didi", as he was known on the Riviera, could
"skin dive" to sixty feet.

My friends harnessed the three-cylinder block on my back
with the regulator riding at the nape of my neck and the hoses
looped over my head. I spat on the inside of my shatterproof
glass mask and rinsed it in the surf, so that mist would not form
inside. I moulded the soft rubber flanges of the mask tightly
over forehead and cheekbones and then I fitted the mouthpiece
under my lips and gripped the nodules between my teeth. A
vent the size of a paper clip was to pass my inhalations and
exhalations beneath the sea. Staggering under the fifty-pound
apparatus I walked with a Charlie Chaplin waddle into the sea.

The diving lung was designed to be slightly buoyant. I
reclined in the chilly water to estimate my compliance with
Archimedes' principle that a solid body immersed in liquid is
buoyed up by a force equal to the weight of the liquid displaced.
Dumas justified me with Archimedes by attaching seven
pounds of lead to my belt. I sank gently to the sand. I breathed
sweet effortless air. There was a faint whistle when I inhaled
and a light rippling sound of bubbles when I breathed out. The
regulator was adjusting pressure precisely to my needs.

I looked into the sea with the same sense of trespass that I
have felt on every dive. A modest canyon opened below, full of
dark green weeds, black sea urchins, and small flowerlike white
algae. Fingerlings browsed in the scene. The sand sloped down

into a clear blue infinity. The sun struck so brightly I had to squint. My arms hanging at my sides, I kicked the fins languidly and travelled down, gaining speed, watching the beach reeling past. I stopped kicking and the momentum carried me on a fabulous glide. When I stopped, I slowly emptied my lungs and held my breath. The diminished volume of my body decreased the lifting force of water, and I sank dreamily down. I inhaled a great chestful and retained it. I rose towards the surface.

My human lungs had a new role to play, that of a sensitive ballasting system. I took normal breaths in a slow rhythm, bowed my head, and swam smoothly down to thirty feet. I felt no increasing water pressure, which at that depth is twice that of the surface. The aqualung automatically fed me increased compressed air to meet the new pressure layer. Through the fragile human-lung linings this counter-pressure was being transmitted to the blood-stream and instantly spread throughout the incompressible body. My brain received no subjective news of the pressure and I was at ease, except for a pain in the middle ear and sinus cavities. I swallowed, as one does when landing in an aeroplane, to open my Eustachian tubes and stopped the pain. (I did not wear ear plugs, a dangerous practice when under water. Ear plugs would have trapped a pocket of air between them and the eardrums. Pressure building up in the Eustachian tubes would have forced my eardrums outward, eventually to the bursting point.)

I reached the bottom in a state of excitement. A school of silvery sars (goat bream), round and flat as saucers, swam in a rocky chaos. I looked up and saw the surface shining like a defective mirror. In the centre of the looking-glass was the trim silhouette of Simone, reduced to a doll. I waved. The doll waved at me.

I became fascinated with my exhalations. The bubbles swelled on the way up through lighter pressure layers, but were peculiarly flattened like mushroom caps by their eager push against the medium. I realized the importance bubbles were to have for us in the dives to come: as long as air bubbled on the surface all was well below. If the bubbles disappeared, there would be anxiety and emergency measures. They roared out of the regulator and kept me company. I felt less alone.

I swam across the rocks and compared myself favourably with the sars. To swim fishlike, horizontally, was the logical method in a medium eight hundred times denser than air. To halt and hang attached to nothing, no lines or air pipe to the surface, was a dream. At night I had often had visions of flying by extending my arms as wings. Now I flew without wings. (Since that first aqualung flight, I have never had a dream of flying.)

I thought of the helmet diver arriving on his ponderous boots at such a depth as this and struggling to walk a few yards, obsessed with his umbilici and his head imprisoned in copper. On "skin dives" I had seen him leaning dangerously forward to make a step, clamped in heavier pressure at the ankles than the head, a cripple in an alien land. From this day forward we would swim across miles of country no man had known, free and level, with our flesh feeling what the fish scales know.

I experimented with all possible manoeuvres of the aqualung-loops, somersaults, and barrel rolls. I stood upside down on one finger and burst out laughing – a shrill distorted laugh. Whatever I did, nothing altered the automatic rhythm of air. Delivered from gravity and buoyancy, I flew around in space.

I could attain a speed of almost two knots without using my arms; I soared vertically and passed my own bubbles; I went down to sixty feet. We had been there many times without breathing aids, but we did not know what happened below that boundary. How far could we go with this strange device?

Fifteen minutes had passed since I left the little cove. The regulator lisped in a steady cadence in the ten-fathom layer and I could spend an hour there on my air supply. I determined to stay as long as I could stand the chill. Here were tantalizing crevices we had been obliged to pass fleetingly before. I swam inch by inch into a dark narrow tunnel, scraping my chest on the floor and banging the air tanks on the ceiling. In such situations a man is of two minds. One urges him on towards mystery and the other reminds him that, if he will use it, he is a creature with good sense that can keep him alive. I bounced against the ceiling. I had used one-third of my air and was getting lighter. My brain complained that this foolishness might sever my air hoses. I turned over and hung on my back.

The roof of the cave was thronged with lobsters. They stood there like great flies on a ceiling. Their heads and antennae were pointed towards the cave entrance. I breathed lesser lungsful to keep my chest from touching them. Above water was occupied, ill-fed France. I thought of the hundreds of calories a diver loses in cold water. I selected a pair of one-pound lobsters and carefully plucked them from the roof without touching their stinging spines. I carried them towards the surface.

Simone had been floating, watching my bubbles wherever I went. She swam down towards me. I handed her the lobsters and went down again as she returned to the surface. She came up under a rock which bore a torpid Provençal citizen with a fishing rod. He saw a blonde girl emerge from the combers with lobsters wriggling in her hands. She said, "Could you please watch these for me?" and put them on the rock. The fisherman dropped his rod.

Simone made five more surface dives to take lobsters from me and carry them to the rock. I surfaced in the cove, out of the fisherman's sight. Simone claimed her lobster swarm. She said, "Keep one for yourself, monsieur. They are very easy to catch if you do as I did."

BENEATH THE ICE

Andrew Todhunter

The extreme sportsman Andrew Todhunter is the author of **Dangerous Games**, *2001.*

It takes a saw with an eighteen-inch bar to get through the ice in the middle of the lake. When the chain reaches the water, it throws back a clear, arcing fount as thick as my thumb.

I cut a triangle six feet on each side. When I'm finished, I press down on a corner with my boot: nothing. I sink the saw back into the notch and take another inch, rocking the bar. Another shove with the heel. Now the slab rocks, water pushing up through the cracks and pooling along the perimeter. Two of us sink the floe with our weight and slip it to one side beneath the ice. On the black surface of the water, drops of oil twist into paisleys of electric green and plum. Beside them, upside down, float the reflected summits of the High Sierra.

Over the expedition-weight Capilene underwear, a rag sweater, two pairs of wool socks, and a pile-jumpsuit known as a woolybear comes the dry suit. Of coated nylon, airtight, it seals with rubber gaskets at the neck and wrists. Then comes the brass-tinged body harness, followed by the weight belt: some twenty-five pounds of lead shot. Over this is an inflatable vest, called a buoyancy compensator, and then the tank, the regulator, neoprene mittens and hood, the fins, and the mask.

We clip lines to the rings on our harnesses. Flashlights,

secured by lanyards, are tucked into pockets in our vests. Inflator hoses are coupled with valves on the vest and the dry suit, and the air is turned on. We look at our gauges: 2,250 pounds of air; depth, 0; dive time, 0; residual nitrogen, 0. The compass swivels freely in its chamber of oil.

We are about to go ice-diving, which as a recreational sport is relatively new but is beginning to develop a following. Ice-diving is done professionally by ice salvage divers, who make a fair sum winching trucks and snowmobiles out of lakes. Search-and-rescue divers with the same skills save several lives nation-wide every year. To their ranks one can now add hundreds of Americans who go diving under the ice not because they have to but because they want to. Two of the nation's largest diving organizations, the Professional Association of Diving Instructors (800–729–7234) and the National Association of Underwater Instructors (800–553–6284), now offer instruction and certification in ice-diving, the prerequisites for which generally include certifications in open-water and advanced open-water diving.

Ice-diving as a recreational sport is practiced wherever conditions allow, from frozen lakes and quarries in divers' home states to the serpentine ice caverns that can be found beneath the polar ice caps.

But whether done at the North Pole or beneath the surface of a more accessible location, ice-diving offers displays and physical sensations that one can experience in no other way.

There are two of us who will make this dive, and a support team of four. Bobbing in the water, we go over the signals with our line-tenders. The slow bleed of adrenaline has sharpened the landscape. Low clouds tear their bellies on the peaks. We turn to the sun, gathering heat. Then we let the air out of our dry suits and descend.

In the first seconds the unprotected skin around the face protests and then goes numb. We sink, watching for the bottom. At fifty feet the mud plain looms out of the darkness. We pump a blast of air into the dry suits and arrest our descent, hovering with our fin tips five feet from the bottom. Had we landed in the silt, or even brushed it with our fins, we would have sent a cloud of decaying organic matter in all directions. As it is, the pulses of current from our fin blades strike the membranous surface of the silt. It quivers without tearing, like the coating on milk that has been boiled in a pan.

Far above, the triangle is aglow in the dimly translucent field of ice. Our lines stretch upward, vanishing. I give a firm tug: "Okay." A tug comes back from my tender: "Acknowledged." The trail of air bubbles works its way to the surface without hurry, rumbling faintly. I take a deep breath and expel it with one quick contraction of my diaphragm. The bolus of air breaks into three spheres that flatten into mushrooms the diameter of dinner plates, expanding as they climb.

We send two tugs up the lines: "Going out, give us slack." Keeping our distance from the silt, we move across the bottom. We follow a bearing due north. If we are separated from our lines, a 180-degree turn should bring us within sight of the hole.

A school of fingerling trout hangs motionless above a meadow of freshwater grass. We could pick them like apples if we cared to, collect them in a bag. They're sleeping out the winter, drunk with cold. I touch one with a mitten tip. A tremor in the gills, the tail flickers once, then nothing.

Farther on is a dinghy, perfectly intact. Right side up, it sits becalmed on the surface of the silt. As if abandoned on a winter beach, gathering snow, the benches and deck are blanketed with pale sediment. We sweep our lights beneath the benches, looking for a tackle box, an unopened bottle of beer. This wreck surrenders nothing – a sign of other divers here before us, or else a thorough abandonment of ship.

When we have used a third of our air, we ascend to the ice, still 500 lateral feet from the hole. We come up gradually, hands raised to cushion the landing. Our breaths lie pinned against the ice in shimmering pools. Expanding as we add to them with each exhalation, they elongate, break apart. Following ravines and valleys too subtle for the eye, they seek the highest place.

The ice seems to glow from its core. Palpable as mist, it is a pale light in which no shadows fall. The ice is smoked through with minute bubbles. Cracks lost deep within glitter like bayonets.

I inflate the dry suit until I am buoyant enough to "fall" upward and lie flat on my stomach against the ice. I crawl a few feet upside down on my hands and knees. With the heels of my fists I pound the ice. Whump. Whump. When struck, the ponds of air leap and scatter into quicksilver, spiraling in the current of the blow.

Pushing off the ice, I stand upside down and join my partner. Our exhalations tumble along our chests and break down our fins. There is a moment of vertigo before the inner ear accommodates the artificial gravity of this inverted world. Then we accept the illusion that we're standing upright on the ice.

The atmosphere above our heads – the deepening lake – is green darkening to black. The luminescent plain at our feet is as perfect and featureless as a glacier in the half light of a gathering storm. The horizon is uniform, impenetrable. My hands are getting colder.

We check our air. It's time to head back to the hole. Turning south, we take the lines in hand and send a fast series of tugs. We brace, leaning back.

On the other side of the ice our tenders set off like sled dogs at a run. The lines go taut and we begin to move, gaining speed. Howling through our regulators, we ski upside down across the ice.

The wedge of blue sky suddenly appears, hurtling toward us. As I dive head first through the triangle, I'm blinded. I look straight down into the sun.

SHARKS! (AND OTHER BEHEMOTHS)

Peter Benchley

More than 375 species of shark have been identified worldwide, of which a dozen or so are implicated in attacks on humans. Despite media frenzies such attacks are relatively scarce: there are on average 70, with 5–15 fatalities, each year across the globe. Of course, such figures do nothing to negate the primeval fear sharks inspire.

For the record, the list of so-called "man-eating" sharks is headed by the Great White, Tiger, Bull, and Oceanic Whitetip. And also for the record, for every human eaten by a shark some ten million sharks are eaten by humans. The real danger with sharks, which their negative press coverage does nothing help, is that they will be wiped out by humans, either from fear or for food.

Benchley, the author of, among other novels, Jaws, The Deep *and* The Beast, *died in 2006, aged 66. He had some awkward encounters with sharks in real life, as well as between the covers of his fiction:*

Then there's the oceanic whitetip, whose Latin name so aptly describes the creature that I'll burden you with it: *C. longimanus*, or "long-hands". This shark's pectoral fins are extraordinarily long and graceful, resembling the wings of a modern fighter jet. *Longimanus* tends to stay in the deep ocean, and nobody on earth has the vaguest notion about total numbers of long-hand attacks because the people they do attack are either adrift, alone, or survivors of shipwrecks, who don't much care *what* species of shark it is that's harassing them. I'd bet that many of the crewmen of the *Indianapolis*, in 1945, were killed by long-hands, but no one will ever know.

I do know, however, that *longimanus* is unpredictable, scary, and demonstrably capable of killing a human. There's a story about one that attacked two US Navy divers in the deep waters of the Tongue of the Ocean in the Bahamas. The shark took a big bite out of one of the divers and then, as the diver's mate fought it for possession of his friend, dragged the diver into the abyss. Finally, at a depth of about 300 feet – far beyond safe scuba depth – the mate had to choose between letting go of his friend and dying himself, and he watched as shark and body disappeared into the gloom.

Long-hands are my personal bêtes noires – one of the few species of shark of which I am genuinely and viscerally afraid. A couple of decades ago one made an honest effort to eat me. I don't blame the shark for trying, because my situation fell well within the bounds of Stupid Things You Should Avoid at All Costs, but the near-miss scared me – and scarred me permanently – nevertheless.

I was with an ABC-TV crew, also in the Tongue of the Ocean, in open water more than a mile deep. We had tied our boat to a Navy buoy that had become a popular spot to film because it had been in the water for so long that the sea had claimed it, transforming it into an artificial reef. Microscopic animals had taken shelter in the buoy and the chain and had been followed by tiny crustacea and other small critters. Then the larger ones had come to feed, and those larger still, until – in the magical way the sea has of generating life on all levels – the entire food chain had come to use buoy and chain as a feeding ground.

A school of yellowfin tuna was swarming around the buoy, attracted by something, and in the brilliant sunlight of the summer day the colors were so gorgeous that we decided to take some footage for the film segment about the Bahamas that we were working on for *The American Sportsman*.

I, as the so-called talent, was dispatched into the water. Stan Waterman followed to film whatever happened – presumably nothing more than the contrasting colours of the beautiful fish against the cobalt sea, interrupted now and then by a black-rubber-suited human wearing a yellow "horse-collar" buoy-ancy-compensator vest around his neck.

Back then I was still a pretty green blue-water diver. Blue-water diving is diving in water with no bottom visible or reachable; it can spark fears and phobias, for to look down into the darkling blue nothingness is to harken back to childhood nightmares about monsters and infinity. I wasn't accustomed to diving in water I knew to be more than five thousand feet deep, and once in a while I was haunted by a vision of my body drifting down, down, down, from light blue to darker blue, to purple and violet and the unknown black.

So, naturally, whenever I had to dive in blue water, I carried a security blanket: a sawed-off broomstick about three feet long, attached to my wrist by a rawhide thong. Exactly what it was supposed to protect me from I never determined, but my logic was unassailable: if cameramen could carry cameras with which to ward off attackers, and assistants could carry cameras and lights, why shouldn't I be allowed to carry a broomstick?

Thus armed, I jumped overboard and swam among the yellowfin tuna – or, rather, they swam around me. I held on to the barnacle-covered buoy chain to keep from being swept away by the current, and the school of tuna, which had scattered when I splashed into the water, re-formed and circled me. The shafts of sunlight piercing the surface glittered on their silver scales and yellow fins, and it seemed to me that Stan must be gathering an entire library of beauty shots.

The water was very clear, visibility more than a hundred feet, I was sure, though it's hard to tell in blue water, for there's nothing visible against which to gauge distances.

At the very edge of my vision I saw a shark swimming by. I couldn't discern what kind it was, and I didn't much care, for it was ambling, really, and showing no interest in me or the tuna.

Meanwhile, far up on the bow of the 55-foot boat, one of the crew – bored and tantalized by the sight of so many delicious meals swimming so close to the boat – rigged a fishing rod, dropped a baited hook into the water, and let it drift back into the school of tuna. He had not asked permission, nor had he told anyone what he was doing, for – hey, who cares? – he was staying out of the way and minding his own business. When he hooked a fish, he would simply drag it up to the bow and haul it aboard, and no one need be the wiser.

Stan gestured for me to move away from the buoy, so that he could frame me and the fish cleanly against the blue background. I let go of the chain and kicked my way out into open water. Obligingly, the tuna followed.

Suddenly I was gone, jerked downward by an irresistible force, with a searing pain in my lower leg, arms flung over my head, broomstick aiming at the surface. I could see Stan and the tuna receding above me. I looked around, panicked and confused, to see what had grabbed me. The shark? Had I been taken by the shark? I saw nothing.

I looked down. I was already in the dark blue; all that lay below were the violet and the black and . . . *wait . . . there, against the darkness . . . what could it possibly –*

A tuna, fleeing for the bottom, struggling, fighting . . . *fighting? Against WHAT?*

Then I saw the line, and the silvery leader. The fish was *hooked*, for God's sake. Somehow it had gotten . . . *no, impossible, no way it could have –*

A cloud billowed around my face, black as ink, thick as . . . blood. *My blood.*

I leaned backward and kicked forward, wanting to see my feet.

The steel leader was wrapped around my ankle. The wire had bitten deep, and a plume of black was rising from the wound, a sign that I was already down very, very deep, for blood doesn't become black till the twilight depths. (The sea consumes the visible spectrum of light, one colour at a time, beginning a few feet under water. Red disappears first, then orange, yellow, green, and so on, until, when you reach 150 or 200 feet, blood looks black.)

All I could guess was that, in some implausible fluke, as the fish had fled the surface it must have passed between my legs, or circled around my feet, or *somehow* wrapped the leader around my leg. And all I knew was that, somehow, I'd better find a way to free my leg before I was taken to depths from which no traveller returns.

I reached for my knife, to cut the line, but – encumbered by gear and disoriented by fear – first I couldn't find the knife, and then I couldn't release it.

The tuna stopped diving and turned, and the change in pressure against its mouth, the release of resistance, must have convinced it that it was free, for it swam upward, toward me.

The line slackened, the leader eased and spread, and I slid my foot and fin out through the widening coil.

Giddy with relief, I checked my air and depth gauges: 185 feet deep, 500 pounds of air, more than enough for a controlled ascent but nowhere near enough for a decompression stop, if one was necessary, a contingency about which I knew nothing. Diving computers were still years in the future (as were any computers for the common man). Because I hadn't intended to leave the surface, certainly not to venture deeper than, say, ten feet, I hadn't consulted the standard of the day: the US Navy's decompression tables, a reliable guide – though calibrated for a 25-year-old male in peak physical condition – to safe diving at various depths.

How long have I been at this depth? At any depth? How long have I been in the water? No idea.

I started up, slowly, and now the black blood no longer billowed around me but trailed behind. The pain in my leg had waned, and my foot seemed to be working, which meant that no major tendon had been cut.

I passed a hundred feet, then ninety, eighty . . . things were lighter now, visibility had returned, and I could see the rays of the sun angling down from the shimmering surface. Everything would be okay, after all. There was noth –

The shark came straight for me, emerging quickly from the blue haze, its fins forming a triangle of lopsided symmetry because of the slight downward curve of the extraordinary pectorals.

Ten, maybe fifteen feet from me it veered away, banked downward, and passed through the trail of blood leaking from my ankle. Convinced now of the source of the savoury scent it had picked up from far away, it rose again, levelled off before me, and began the final, almost ritual, stage of the hunt.

Because seawater acts as a refractive lens, sizes are difficult to ascertain under water. The generally accepted rule is that animals appear to be roughly a third again as large as they actually are. This shark looked ten or twelve feet long, which meant that, in fact, it was probably seven to nine feet long. But "in fact" didn't matter to me; all I cared about was that the closer this shark came, the bigger it looked, and near to me or far, it was very big.

It circled me twice, perhaps twenty feet away, establishing for itself a pattern and perimeter of comfort, and then began gradually to close the distance between us. With each circle, it shrank the perimeter by six inches, then by twelve, then fifteen.

I raised my broomstick and held it out like a sword, waving its blunt tip back and forth to impress upon the shark that I was a living being armed with the weapons and determination to defend myself.

Longimanus was not impressed. It circled closer, staying just beyond the reach of the broomstick. I could count the tiny black dots on its snout, the celebrated ampullae of Lorenzini, which carry untold megabytes of information, chemical and electro-magnetic, to the shark's control centre.

The mouth hung open about an inch, enough to give me a glimpse of the teeth in the lower jaw.

As I turned with the shark, trying to maintain some upward movement, I watched the eye – always the eye – for movement of the nictitating membrane, the signal that the threat display was ending and the attack itself beginning.

It quickened its pace, circling me faster than I could turn, so I began to kick backward as well as upward, to increase the distance between us.

I jabbed randomly with the broomstick, never touching flesh, never causing *longimanus* even to flinch.

I glanced upward and saw the bottom of the boat, a squat, grey black shape perhaps fifty feet away, forty-five, forty . . .

The shark appeared from behind me, a pectoral fin nearly touching my shoulder. The mouth opened, the membrane flickered upward, covering most of the eye, the upper jaw dropped down and forward, and the head turned toward me.

I remember seeing the tail sweep once, propelling *longimanus* forward.

I remember bending backward to avoid the gaping mouth.

I remember the ghostly, yellowish white eyeball, and I remember stabbing at it with the broomstick.

I *don't* remember hitting, instead, the roof of the shark's mouth, but that's what must have happened, for the next thing I knew, the shark bit down on the broomstick, shook its head back and forth to tear it loose, and, when that failed, lunged with its powerful tail, intent on fleeing with its prize.

The broomstick, of course, was attached to my wrist, and I was suddenly dragged through the water like a rag doll, flopping helplessly behind the (by now) frightened shark, which had taken a test bite from a strange, bleeding prey and now found itself dragging a great rubber *thing* through the water.

Breathing became difficult; I was running out of air.

I tried to peel the rawhide thong off my wrist, but the tension on it was too great and I couldn't budge it.

I was on my back now, upside down, my right arm over my head as *longimanus* towed me away from the safety of the boat. I could once again see blood trailing from my leg; at this depth it was dark blue, and it streamed behind me like a wake.

Everything stopped. At once. My arm was free, and I was floating, neutrally buoyant, about thirty feet beneath the surface. I looked at the broomstick – or at what remained of it:

longimanus had bitten through it, and the strands of mashed wood fiber looked splayed, like a flowering weed.

Far away, at the outer limits of my sight, I saw the black scythe of a tail fin vanish into the blue.

I sucked one final breath from my tank, opened my mouth, tipped my head back, and propelled by a couple of kicks, ascended to the kingdom of light and air.

Not until I reached the swim step at the stern of the boat did the weakness of fear overcome me, and the shock.

I spat out my mouthpiece, took off my mask, and gurgled something like, "Goddamn . . . son of a *bitch*! . . . mother –"

"No!" said the director. "No, no, no. You can't use that language on network television. Go back down and surface again and tell us what you saw."

San Francisco Chronicle, 16 September 1990

On a quiet day at the Farallon Islands a great white shark tried to eat scuba diver LeRoy French of Concord. "I could feel his mouth around my body and then he chomped me," French said. "When his teeth bit into my metal air tank, he let me go."

Last fall, also at the Farallons, a giant shark grabbed diver Mark Tiserand of San Francisco by the leg and dragged him off, as if looking for a quiet spot for a meal. "He was swimming off with me so fast I could feel the water rushing past," Tiserand recalled.

Last week, twenty-five yards off the beach near Jenner, Rodney Orr of Santa Rosa was knocked off his paddle board, then got a close look at some pearly whites. "My head was in its mouth, I could see the teeth."

Episodes like these are making the Bay Area coast the shark attack centre of the world. A search through this paper's files reveals there have been more than fifty shark incidents recorded off the Bay Area alone, though most receive little attention in the media. French, Tiserand and Orr all survived by fighting off their attacker. French and Tiserand had their lives saved when they were airlifted by helicopters to hospitals for emergency surgery. French ended up with a scar that runs four feet down his side, Tiserand with shark teeth souvenirs that doctors removed from his leg. Orr just about had his head bitten off, but escaped with big gashes around his left eye and neck. The shark lost interest when Orr clubbed him with his spear gun.

Waters off the Bay Area coast have sharks of mind-boggling size. In one fifty-minute period at the Farallon Islands, scientist Peter Klimely of Scripps Institute chummed up and tagged three different great whites that were all seventeen feet long. A few years back, at Ano Nuevo State Reserve in San Mateo County, a shark measuring nineteen feet and weighing an estimated 5,000 lbs washed up on the beach. That is as big as the one in the movie *Jaws*.

After a career of studying sharks, scientist John McCosker of the Steinhart Aquarium in San Francisco has identified the zone where the attacks are most common. "I call it the Red Triangle," said McCosker, who has travelled throughout the world to study maneaters. The Triangle is bordered by Ano Nuevo to the south, the Farallon Islands twenty-five miles out to sea to the west and Tomales Bay to the north.

Both Ano Nuevo and the Farallons are breeding grounds for elephant seals, and the young 200-pound pups make perfect meals for the big sharks. The mouth of Tomales Bay, meanwhile, is believed to be a breeding ground for great whites.

Anywhere near the Triangle, it may be foolish to spearfish, dive for abalone, surf, swim or kayak. Yet these sports remain popular because months can go by without an incident – and also because the history of danger is unpublicized. Yet the attacks just keep happening. In January a shark knocked surfer Sean Sullivan of Pacifica off his surfboard, leaving bite marks in the board. Sullivan reportedly escaped by getting back on his board and surfing into the beach with the shark chasing him.

I never gave the idea of a shark eating me any thought until a fall day about ten years ago. I had arrived at Pigeon Point lighthouse, where there are a few secluded coves nearby that are ideal for body surfing, but this time there was a crowd at the beach. It turned out that an abalone diver had just been bitten in half and killed at the exact spot I was planning to swim that day.

Since then there have been many other episodes. While fishing at the Farallon Islands with Abe Cuanang, the boat anchored, our depth finder was reading the bottom as ninety feet deep. Suddenly it was reading sixty-five feet, then fifty feet. It made no sense.

Then, all at once, it did make sense. "It's the Big Guy," Cuanang shouted. The Big Guy in this case was a great white so large under the boat that it was registering as the bottom of the ocean on the depth finder.

The same week Ski Ratto of Pacifica was fishing in his seventeen-foot Boston Whaler when he sensed "something was looking at me". Ratto looked behind him and a great white four feet across at the head, possibly longer than the boat, was on the surface, and it was indeed looking at him. "I started the engine and got the hell out of there."

Ever since these episodes I have not been one to dangle my legs over the side of the boat or body surf, abalone dive or anything else that means being in the water with the Big Guy. As long as other people do, it is inevitable that every once in a while someone will be attacked by a shark.

Adelaide Advertiser, 9 September 1991

An experienced diver told yesterday how he heard a "thunderous roar" when his diving partner was taken by a shark off Aldinga Beach. Off-duty police officer Mr Dave Roberts watched in horror underwater as the shark he estimated was four metres in length careered past him thrashing its head about.

"I could not see him, but I knew the shark had my buddy," Mr Roberts said. "The thunderous noise was so loud I couldn't hear anything else."

A police spokesman said the dead man "had no warning. He was literally taken in one big grab."

The dead man, 19, of One Tree Hill, was a student at the University of Adelaide and was the ninth person to die in a shark attack in South Australian waters. Police have not released his name.

The shark, which Mr Roberts believes was a white pointer [great white], took the young diver about 350 metres off Snapper Point, the main look-out at Aldinga Beach, at about 3 p.m. yesterday. The man was diving with a group of other students and members of the Adelaide University Skindiving Club in eighteen metres of water at a popular skindiving spot called the Drop Off. Three other people, including Mr Roberts, were in the water in the vicinity of the tragedy, but no one else was attacked. Four others who had been part of the diving group had climbed aboard their boat minutes earlier.

By nightfall yesterday police had recovered the dead man's air tank, his diving fins and a small part of his body. The search was called off at dark, but will resume at first light today. The tank's rubber hose, which led to the mouthpiece, was severed.

Mr Roberts, a senior constable in the police prosecuting branch, said the group was on its second dive of the day and he and his "buddy" (a diving term for partner) were returning to their boat when the shark struck.

"We were heading back to the boat, which was not far ahead of us, when I looked back at him and everything was all right," Mr Roberts recalled. "I turned back and went down to have a look at this colourful rock, and then suddenly heard this thunderous noise. I turned again and saw the shark. It was close to me and it was thrashing its head around. The noise was very loud. It was like a boat crashing over waves on top of you. The whole bottom was dusted up. The shark kept thrashing from side to side. I couldn't make him out clearly, but I knew he was there. I hung around and took a defensive position behind the rock and it moved away. It came within one and a half feet of me as it went past. It didn't look at me. It just took my buddy first – just dragged him past me as I was behind the rock. It was totally unexpected – you just never see them out there. I don't know if I'll dive again – this scared the life out of me."

Yesterday's dive had lasted about twenty minutes before the attack and had followed fourteen other dives by about thirty club members who were spending the day at Aldinga Beach. Ben Petersen, 18, of Aldgate, was first back to the boat and had helped three others into it when he suddenly heard screaming. "It was Dave Roberts screaming out 'Shark', so I pulled the anchor up and we drove the boat over to him," Mr Petersen said. "A tank, fins and other diving equipment floated by. We got Dave into the boat and he was saying a four-metre shark had come up and grabbed his mate."

Veteran Mr Rodney Fox recalled last night how he was attacked in the same place in 1963: "It's an interesting place to dive – lots of fish gather there near a big drop off the reef." Mr Fox had been defending his title as S.A. spear fishing champion when a white pointer hurled him through the water. He escaped after gouging its eyes and snout. Once he reached the surface he realized his chest was badly mutilated. Although he needed eighty-seven stitches, Mr Fox became fascinated with white pointers and continues to research them. Mr Fox continued with his sport and became involved in the making of several shark-attack movies, including *Jaws*, the Emmy-award-winning *Mysteries of the Sea*, and the South Australian Film Corporation's *Caged in Fear* television special. He is also a consultant to the Cousteau Society.

Los Angeles Times, 10 December 1994

A shark, apparently a great white, killed a commercial diver in the water off San Miguel Island on Friday – the state's first confirmed death from a shark attack in nearly six years.

Santa Barbara resident James Robinson, 42, was treading water near his boat when the shark swooped in for a swift, brutal attack. He had just finished a routine dive to scout for sea urchins and had deposited his equipment aboard his boat. His two crew members were putting away the equipment when they heard Robinson scream – and whirled around to see him drifting unconscious in a gush of blood.

"His right leg was nearly severed and his left leg had puncture wounds on it," said Francis Oliver, a diver who came to Robinson's aid after hearing his crewmates' distress call. "It was pretty gruesome."

A veteran diver, Robinson was attacked at about 9.45 a.m., half a mile off the coast of San Miguel Island, which lies about forty miles west of Santa Barbara. Crew members on Robinson's boat, the *Florentia Marie*, tried to revive him, but could not find a pulse. A Coast Guard helicopter rushed Robinson to Goleta Valley Community Hospital, where he was pronounced dead of massive trauma at 11.15 a.m.

Neither of the crew members saw the attack, but Coast Guard officials said they believe Robinson was targeted by a great white shark, a keen-eyed predator that can grow up to twenty feet in length and can sink its serrated teeth through a surfer and surfboard with one swift bite. "They say it's like a bullet – you never see the one that bit you," urchin diver Jeffery Gunning said. "I just hope it went quick for Jimmy."

Before entering the sea urchin business, Robinson had worked for years as a deep-sea diver for an offshore oil rig in the North Sea, near the English Channel. After settling in Santa Barbara, he quickly absorbed the California lifestyle. Deeply tanned with blond curly hair and an athletic build, Robinson loved surfing and diving – any activities which would keep him in the sun or in the water. Gracious and vivacious, Robinson was popular both in the harbour and in the neighbourhood. "You always hear about the good dying young and, golly, this guy was just one of the best," long-time diver Steve Rebuck said. "He will really be missed."

Most professional divers realize that gerat white sharks haunt the waters around San Miguel Island, where they feast on seals and sea lions, but their lurking presence has not deterred divers from prowling the ocean floor for valuable sea urchins, abalone and lobsters. It is a threat most divers take in their stride. "If you're frighted by it, you have no business being in the business," Rebuck said. "More people are killed by lightning and bee stings than by shark attacks."

Although great white sharks bump, bite and scare several people a year in California, fatalities are rare. No deadly attacks have been confirmed since UCLA graduate student Tamara McCallister was killed by a great white off Malibu in February 1989 . . . In a more recent incident, a woman's shark-bitten body was found off San Diego coast last April, but the county coroner said the victim may already have been dead when the great white gnawed at her body.

To protect themselves from attack, veteran divers usually descend to the ocean flor as quickly as possible. Once on the bottom, they can hide among rocks and shadows. Eventually, however, they must rise to the surface, where their wet-suited bodies are vulnerable. "It's one of the risks of diving," Gunning said. "We become part of the food chain when we enter the water." As a precaution, several divers in northern California have begun to tuck plastic pistols in their wet suits before jumping into shark-infested waters, Rebuck said. But most locals rely on more low-tech survival techniques – when face to face with a great white, they "say three Hail Marys and four Our Fathers," diver Matt Barnes said.

In the waters around San Miguel Island divers have learned to check for sharks by studying the behaviour of the sea lions and seals which carpet the beaches. If the animals look spooked or if any appear mauled, the divers know to stay away. Even the best precautions, however, are not fail safe. Sharks sometimes attack humans out of pure curiosity, marine biologist Gary Davis said, and they sometimes confuse divers in wet suits for sleek seals.

"They spend a lot of time bumping things on the surface and seeing if anything falls off," Davis said. "If it does, they taste it to see if it's something good to eat."

Divers are willing to face such risks in part because the sea urchin business can be quite lucrative. Sea urchin roe is a delicacy in Japan, prized for its rarity, freshness and delicate taste.

Los Angeles Times, 20 November 1996

It happened twenty-five years ago, but the image of sharks savagely attacking his diving partner and dragging him to the hazy depths of the Caribbean is as vivid in Bret Gilliam's mind today, in 1996, as it was in the days after the attack in 1971.

Gilliam wishes he *could* forget. Telling the story in its entirety for the first time, in a chilling article written for *Scuba Times* magazine, he describes that fateful day in the Virgin Islands.

Gilliam, now [in 1996] editor of the *Advanced Diving Journal* and president of Technical Diving International, was with Rod Temple and Robbie McIlvaine on a scientific expedition to recover samples for a research project being conducted at Cane Bay on the island of St Croix's north shore.

The plan was to inspect and to photograph the deepest project, at 210 feet, located on the wall of a steep drop-off. Temple was the dive leader and timekeeper, in charge of the paperwork and running the decompression schedule during the ascent.

But for him there would be no ascent.

"I watched his lifeless body drift into the abyss with the sharks still hitting him," Gilliam writes. And many believe that the hurried ascent made by Gilliam – from 400 feet with practically no air in his tanks – should have killed him.

Veterans of hundreds of deep dives, Gilliam, Temple and McIlvaine made their way down the wall at Cane Bay. They eventually reached the collection project – set during a previous dive – at 210 feet. As Gilliam and McIlvaine worked, Temple looked around. He spotted two white-tip sharks, one about twelve feet long and the other a bit bigger, swimming in the distance.

"This was nothing new to us, as we dove with sharks routinely," Gilliam says. "But it was rare to see these open-ocean species so close to shore."

After finishing their work, McIlvaine started up first. He spotted the sharks again, swimming over the coral and down a sandy chute. But the sharks didn't seem to be paying attention to the divers, which in itself Gilliam thought odd because he had had "nasty encounters" with white-tips before while diving farther offshore.

"Our plan called for Rod to be the last guy up," Gilliam writes. "I rendezvoused with Robbie at about 175 feet just over a ledge, and we both rested on the coral to wait for him to join us. He was late, and Robbie fidgeted, pointing to his pressure gauge, not wanting to run low on air.

"I shrugged and gave him a 'What am I supposed to do?' look, and we continued to wait. Suddenly Robbie dropped his extra gear and catapulted himself toward the wall, pointing at a mass of bubble exhaust coming from the deeper water.

"We both figured that Rod had had some sort of air failure . . . Since my air consumption was lower, I decided to send Robbie up, and I would go see if Rod needed help. As I descended into the bubble cloud, Robbie gave me an anxious OK sign and started up.

"But when I reached Rod, things were about as bad as they could get."

A twelve-foot white-tip shark had bitten into Temple's left thigh and was tearing violently at his flesh. Clouds of blood mixed in with the bubbles. The second shark appeared and made a blinding strike, ripping into Temple's calf.

Gilliam grabbed Temple by his shoulder harness and tried to pull him free. Both divers beat at the sharks with their fists, and the sharks finally let go, but only briefly.

They returned, bypassing Gilliam and striking Temple's bleeding legs. Temple had lost lots of blood and Gilliam felt Temple's body go limp in his arms. But he held on, and the divers and the sharks tumbled downward until the sharks finally ripped Temple from Gilliam's grasp, leaving Gilliam 400 feet beneath the surface, in shock and practically out of air.

"My depth gauge was pegged at 325 feet, but I knew we were far deeper than that," he recalls. "The grimness of my own situation forced itself on me through a fog of narcosis and exertion.

"That's when I ran out of air. I think that subconsciously I almost decided to stay there and die. It seemed so totally hopeless, and my strength was completely sapped. But I put my head back and put all my muscles into a wide, steady power kick for the surface.

"I forced all thoughts to maintaining that kick cycle and willed myself upward. After what seemed like an eternity, I sneaked a look at my depth gauge and it was still pegged at 325 feet. I sucked hard on the regulator and got a bit of a breath – not much, but it fueled my oxygen-starved brain a bit longer, and I prayed my legs would get me up shallow enough to get another breath before hypoxia (an abnormal condition caused by a decrease in oxygen to body tissue) shut down my systems for ever.

"There's really no way to describe what it's like to slowly starve the brain of oxygen in combination with adrenaline-induced survival instincts. But I remember thinking, if I could just concentrate on kicking, I could make it. After a while the sense of urgency faded, and I remember looking for the surface through a red haze that gradually closed down into a tunnel before I passed out. The panic was gone and I went to sleep, thinking, 'Damn, I almost made it.'"

Remarkably, Gilliam did make it. The small amount of air in his safety vest floated him to the surface.

"I woke up retching and expelling huge burps of air," he recalls. "But I still had to deal with an unknown amount of omitted decompression and the certainty that I was severely bent. Swimming to shore as fast as I could, I felt my legs going numb. By the time I reached the beach I could barely stand. A couple on their honeymoon waded out and dragged me up on the sand."

(McIlvaine, presuming both of his partners were dead, had already reached the beach and had gone to notify the authorities.)

"I gasped out instructions to get the oxygen unit from our van, and then I collapsed. In an incredible burst of good fortune, it turned out the wife was a [emergency room] nurse from Florida and understood the pathology of decompression sickness."

Gilliam, airlifted to a hospital in Puerto Rico, recovered and was released two days later, still numb in the legs and arms, and nearly blind in one eye. That blindness persists to this day, but in his mind he can still see – all too vividly – the sharks ripping his partner.

www.divernet.com, 2002

If the red-back spiders under loo seats don't get you, the blue-ringed octopus will. People delight in spreading shock-horror stories about Aussie wildlife, and often it works. Marie Davies has been instructing prospective divers Down Under and finds that many are terrified of being eaten by sharks – or worse. In this article she put matters in perspective:

Vast, diverse, exotic and home to the largest tropical reef system in the world, Australia is a diver's dream. Each year, lured by cheap air fares and strong currencies, Brits and other tourists flock Down Under to don their scuba gear and explore its underwater technicolour paradise.

Scuba diving in Australia is still a growing sport, if PADI qualification figures are any guide, and each year more and more reports surface of the potential dangers Down Under, with horrific headlines grabbing the imaginations of the public.

It's true – by dipping your fins into the Pacific Ocean, you could conceivably become a shark snack or fall victim to a potentially lethal bite or sting. But are these fears justified?

Sharks have killed more people in Australian waters than anywhere else in the world, averaging about one fatal attack per year – until 2000, when no fewer than five people died. Three of these attacks were by great whites. Previously, there had been only nine Australian fatalities in ten years, although the deaths of three other people are also believed to have resulted from shark attacks.

Worldwide attacks peaked at seventy-nine last year, the highest for forty years, according to the University of Florida's International Shark Attack File. But it is attacks on people at the surface, surfers and swimmers, which are the most common, accounting for almost four-fifths of all attacks.

Until 1994, not a single scuba diver had been killed by a shark Down Under. So can divers diverse easy? Not quite. Australia now has the second highest percentage of attacks on divers in the world after the USA. In 1999, eleven percent of Australian shark attacks were on divers and snorkellers, and this rose to 18.4 percent in 2000.

There are about 400 different species of shark, but only a handful have ever been known to attack humans, and most of these attacks were not fatal.

Over the past 200 years it is the grey nurse shark (known elsewhere as the sand tiger or raggedtooth) that has accounted for forty-three per cent of attacks worldwide. But the great white shark (*Carcharodon carcharia*) is the stuff of Hollywood legends, and is regarded as the most deadly shark found off Australia's coastline.

Last year, two surfers were killed off the coast of South Australia in attacks on two consecutive days, and two months later, a great white fatally bit off a swimmer's leg in waist-deep water in Perth, Western Australia. Why are such attacks on the increase? Chris McDonald, Shark Supervisor at Sydney Aquarium, says that one of the main reasons is the huge reduction in fish populations.

The amount of food available in the ocean is decreasing and sharks are now travelling further afield to feed. They are attracted to movement and sound in the water, but many experts believe that mistaken identity is the major reason for attacks on humans, especially in poor visibility such as in breaking surf. In such conditions swimmers, surfers or non-submerged divers can resemble seals at the surface, and seals are the great white's favourite snack.

"Global warming might also be a factor," says McDonald. "Changing temperatures in the water means changing patterns in shark migration." This means sharks are coming closer to shore and, with more holidaymakers taking up water pursuits such as diving and surfing, the odds of being attacked, whether mistakenly or not, increase accordingly.

Shark fans cite cage-diving as another reason for the incidence of attacks. By encouraging human interaction with sharks, they argue, we are associating ourselves with food. McDonald, however, does not believe that instigating a jaw-to-jaw encounter is one of the factors. "Contrary to what people believe, the great white isn't much of a threat to humans," he says. "The most common shark attacks are from tigers, dusky whalers and bull sharks.

Bull shark attacks are especially common, he says, as the species is attracted to people swimming in very shallow waters.

British backpacker Rob Collins was training as a PADI Dive Master in Airlee Beach, Queensland, when he had his first encounter with a potentially lethal shark. During a morning dive, a three-metre tiger shark circled the dive group while they were hanging on the descent line.

"The dive was awesome, but, just as we were coming up, I saw a large shadow out of the corner of my eye," he says. "We'd been diving with blacktips and whitetips, so I knew it was a shark. But this one scared me because it was three times as big.

"Then the sunlight just glinted off its body for a second and I realized it was a tiger. I'd heard loads of stories about them attacking divers and I felt a bit like bait just hanging there. Then I lost sight of it, which was even more scary."

Fortunately, the shark did not reappear and all the divers surfaced safely. Rob's buddy, Lisa McQuillin, was the only other diver to see the tiger. "I was really scared," she said, "and, when I told the other divers, they were a bit shocked. Some of them didn't want to go back in the water, even though we were moving to a different site."

However, like many divers, Lisa is quite nonchalant about the unexpected visitors. "You couldn't really blame the shark if it did attack. I mean, we were in its backyard, after all."

The dive began in the twilight hours of early morning, when sharks are at their most active and most hungry. Recently a man's head and limbs were found inside a tiger shark, caught off Lord Howe Island in New South Wales, which just goes to show how unpredictable these guys can be. But the fact is, only rarely do they attack divers.

If you want to dive in a statistically safe spot, choose Sydney. There are frequent sightings of sharks around the bay, but there hasn't been a fatal attack in the harbour since 1963. If you want the facts, top of the league for attacks is Queensland (37.5 percent), with New South Wales and Western Australia coming in joint second with less than half this number. Surprisingly, there has been only one recorded attack on a diver in Victona, and attacks are rare in Northern Australia too.

However, the North has other dangers for divers – if a crocodile doesn't get you, you could be prey to an extremely toxic tentacle. Australia is host to the most venomous marine creatures in the world, but the sting from a box jellyfish, or sea wasp, is definitely one to avoid.

Box jellyfish have between ten and sixty stinging tentacles, each armed with up to 5,000 stinging cells or nematocysts. Chemicals on human skin activate the cells and contact could be fatal for an adult. Last year there were about seventy reported deaths in Northern Australia between November and April.

These creatures are more likely than sharks to come into accidental contact with humans, which earns them the "Most Dangerous" title. Ricky Chan, a marine biologist from the University of New South Wales, says this is due mainly to their transparency, which makes them difficult to see in the water.

They are not aggressive creatures, but when swimmers fail to see them and bump into the tentacles, the jellyfish release their toxic cells in defence. "They probably can't penetrate through wetsuits, but in tropical waters divers normally wear a shorty, so there will inevitably be exposed bits," says Chan. Interestingly, turtles are not affected by their sting and even eat these invisible creatures! But, because of the risk box jellyfish pose to humans, for six months of the year (October–April), as they drift close to the shore, the beaches of Northern Australia are closed.

If you should get stung by a box jellyfish, you won't get off lightly. Victims have reported excruciating pain, which can last for weeks. Experts recommend that you don't try to remove the tentacles while they are still active, as it worsens the injury and leaves scars. On all beaches in Northern Australia you'll find tubs of vinegar, which deactivates the tentacles. Ice-packs can ease the pain; basic first aid, artificial ventilation and CPP may also be needed.

Another non-aggressive creature is the tiny blue-ringed octopus, which prefers to hide away from prying dive masks in rock pools and shallow coral. The chances of a diver being bitten by one are small, and the reason it is considered one of the most deadly organisms in the world, says Ricky Chan is because it attracts attention.

"When the blue-ringed octopus feels threatened, rings on its body change from dark brown to bright neon blue and it looks very pretty," he says. "But this is just its way of advertising its toxicity and is a warning for you to stay away."

When the octopus is not angry, it displays a yellowy-brownish colour, enobling it to blend with the sand and rock. This makes it hard to see, but any divers who accidentally put a hand on one could be in for a nasty surprise.

If you mistakenly touch a blue-ringed octopus, it will inject you with lethal enzymes that cause paralysis. The bite is painless, but the toxin travels through the saliva into your bloodstream. Death can occur within thirty minutes, usually from respiratory failure brought on by the venom, rather than drowning due to the paralysis. There is no anti-venom available in Australia, so, if you do get bitten, artificial ventilation is recommended until the effects of the venom disappear.

There have been very few diver fatalities from either box jellyfish or blue-ringed octopus, mainly because both creatures favour shallow near-shore waters and divers tend to dive a little deeper and usually off boats. They also tend to be more aware of the potential dangers of marine creatures than swimmers or surfers.

In the depths of Australian waters another venomous creature lurks – the sea snake. There are approximately fifty species worldwide, and about thirty-two live in Northern Australian waters. They like warm tropical water, though sightings have been reported as far south as Sydney.

Even though nine of the 10 deadliest snakes in the world live Down Under, there are no documented fatalities from sea snakes. They are usually pretty inoffensive and over the past ten years, only three incidences of bites have been recorded.

However, these slippery critters are predators and, even though they have small mouths, they can bite. Their venom is two to ten times as toxic as a cobra's but, luckily for divers, they usually transfer only a small amount to their victims. Only a quarter of those bitten show signs of poisoning. Distinct teeth marks are left, but there isn't much pain or swelling. The bad news is that "envenomation" can paralyse the nervous system, making breathing difficult. Eventually, the victim can suffocate to death. Kidney damage and heart failure may also occur, due to muscle destruction.

Anti-venom is available, though this has some nasty side effects, including rashes, fever and joint aches and pains. To treat a bite, remove the surface venom, apply a pressure bandage, remain calm and go immediately to a hospital.

Finally, sea snakes are incredibly curious. Fascinated with my hoses and fins, I fell victim to their inquisitiveness only recently whilst diving on Ningaloo Reef in Western Australia. It's amazing how fast you can fin when a yellow-belly sea snake is chasing your tail!

*   *   *

The best way to eliminate the chance of being picked on by a shark or bitten or stung by a venomous marine creature is to stay clear of the water, but as that advice is worse than useless to divers, just avoid touching anything and try to look as little like a seal as possible.

Attracting considerable attention in Australia these days is the shark repellent rod or SharkPOD (Protective Oceanic Device). It emits a type of electrowave that's supposed to annoy sharks and can keep them at bay for up to ten metres. Its effectiveness varies according to species, though tests show that it's pretty convincing around great whites.

As the power has to be turned low enough to prevent the diver getting shocks, the repellent is less effective than it might be. But there is now talk of the technology being miniaturized and put into BCs and lifejackets. The Australians seem to believe in it, and used such devices during the triathlon event at the Sydney 2000 Olympic Games. It wouldn't have done for any of the swimmers to have been chomped in front of millions of people worldwide!

If you don't have the luxury of a SharkPod and find yourself in the water with the most feared of sharks, you might not know it anyway. Great whites creep up on their prey, usually attacking from underneath. If you do see one, Ricky Chan suggests you drop to the bottom, if possible, and wait for it to disappear. "Make sure you know where the shark is and don't forget to look underneath you as well," he says. Studies have shown that aggressive behaviour also deters them. "They are very defensive creatures and they don't want to hurt themselves if they can help it."

from *Man-eaters*, Michael Bright

That orcas have little or no culinary interest in people was illustrated by an incident on 9 September 1972 at Point Sur, near Monterey, California. It is an area where many attacks on people by great white sharks have been recorded, but the

creature that came up behind Hans Kretscher that day was
something else altogether. Wearing a wet suit, Kretscher was
lying on his surfboard about 100ft (31m) offshore when he felt
something shove him from behind. He turned to see a glossy
black shape, and thought it was a shark. The creature grabbed
him and Kretscher banged it on the head with his fist. It let go
and he was able to body-surf to the beach. The Pacific Grove
Marine Rescue Patrol whisked him off to hospital where a
hundred or so stitches were needed to close three deep gashes
in his thigh. The surgeon, who had sewn up many shark-attack
wounds, said that Kretscher's wounds were definitely consistent with the kind of slashes he would expect from an orca's
teeth. Several witnesses at the beach consistently described an
animal with a tall dorsal fin, white undermarkings and a black
back.

Significantly, seals had been seen in the area before the attack,
and transient pods specialise in taking seals. Had the orca which
attacked Kretscher mistaken him for a seal and having realised
its mistake, moved on in search of more juicy prey?

There is no doubt that orcas are curious about humans, and
will often come towards people and boats just to check them out.
A predator must always explore any opportunity to feed, and in
the wild, this is usually all they do – investigate but not attack.
This was the case when Terry Anderson spent the night lashed
to his wrecked trimaran off Baja California in March 1972.
Orcas brushed close to the drifting boat but none attacked.

Scuba divers off New Zealand have had many encounters in
the water with orcas. Wade Doak gathered several stories for an
article in *Diver* magazine. One underwater photographer heard
the high-pitched whining sound of his twin strobe lights re-
charging and then heard something mimicking the sound.
Turning round, he came face to face with four large orcas,
and he just stared back at them in awe. The orcas looked at first,
then swam away.

Another diver was returning to his boat after looking for
lobsters when he felt his foot hit something solid. It was an orca,
and it took hold of one of his flippers. As he looked down, it let

go and swam away. A few seconds later it was back, and then began to inspect him, swimming in from all angles until his boat arrived and pulled him from the water. Several other divers have had similar experiences, the orcas appearing to be more inquisitive than dangerous. On one occasion, a marine biologist from the Leigh Marine Laboratory was in the water when a 16ft (5m) long orca approached him. To be on the safe side, the man dived towards the sea-bed, but the orca followed. It then opened its mouth and put its jaws around the diver's right ankle, foot and flipper, but did not bite. The man extricated his leg and tried to swim away, but the orca took his left foot into its mouth. Still it did not bite. He then kicked the orca with his free foot, but each time the whale came back and continued his game. After the sixth mouthing, the diver thought enough was enough and dived quickly to the bottom. The orca simply disappeared.

In the late 1990s, a shift in the ocean currents of the Pacific – the phenomenon known as El Nino – caused warm waters to flush the California coast; and with it came the jumbo-sized squid. Wednesday was designated by one fisherman out of Bodega Bay as squid-fishing day. On his fish finder he could see the squid hovering in mid-waters during the day, rather than in deep water, as was once thought. As soon as one is hooked and hauled to the surface, however, it changes colour immediately and the rest of the school is whipped up into a frenzy.

Underwater wildlife film-makers, Howard Hall, Bob Cranston, Mark Conlin and Alex Kerstitch were once in the middle of such a frenzy. They were diving at night in the Sea of Cortez near La Paz. Their boat drifted over an area where the bottom was over 1,000ft (305m) deep. They had bait over the side and lit up the water with enormous 1,200 watt lights. The squid arrived in ones and twos at first, and Kerstitch went in to look at them and take some still photographs. Below him were groups of large squid flashing colours at each other in an extraordinary luminescent body language. In the water, he was immediately "mugged" by three squid – each about 5ft (1.5m) long. At first he felt a tug, as a large squid wrapped its tentacles around his swim fin. It began to pull him down but as he kicked himself free another swam in and grabbed him by the back of the neck – the only part of his body not covered by his diving suit. "I felt the cold embrace of tentacles with their sharp-toothed suction cups digging into my bare skin," Kerstitch told reporters. "It was like somebody was throwing a cactus on to my neck."

Kerstitch was able to hit the squid with his diving light and it began to release its grip, but not before it grabbed the light and a gold chain around his neck. He made for the surface, but another squid wrapped its tentacles around his face and chest and dragged him under. Kerstitch dug his fingers into its body and it slid down to his waist, but it was also pulling him below. As he grabbed for the diving ladder, the squid made off with his decompression gauge, and Kerstitch was able to clamber aboard. He had a line of round, red scars circling his neck. This species of squid has serrated suckers which help capture and tear prey before it is sliced by the beak at the centre of the arms. Kerstitch had a lucky escape, although the sortie could have ended in tragedy. The three squid had pulled him down very deep before they let him go.

Some consider the squid among the most dangerous animals in the sea. This was evident during the Second World War. On 25 March 1941, the British troopship *Britannia* was sunk by the German raider *Santa Cruz* in mid-Atlantic. She was about 1,200 miles (1,931km) west of Freetown. Some men survived and clung to floating spars and life-rafts. Lieutenant R. E. G. Cox and eleven other men were supported by a very small raft; only their head and shoulders were above water. Sharks were the number one fear, but one night something far more sinister came up from the depths. A giant squid surfaced and wrapped a tentacle around one sailor and pulled him under. A little later Lieutenant Cox was seized by the leg, but the beast let go. Cox recalls incredible pain as the suckers were pulled off. The next day he noticed large ulcers had appeared where the suckers had gripped, and when he was rescued the medical orderlies were constantly treating the wounds. He wrote to Frank Lane, author of *Kingdom of the Octopus*, in 1956, telling him that the red marks were still there, and Professor John Cloudesly-Thompson at Birkbeck College of the University of London was allowed to examine them. He was able to confirm that they were sucker scars likely to have been from an attack by a giant squid.

The giant octopus is large and powerful, and will grip tenaciously with its suckers, but it tires quickly. This is because it has a copper-based blood pigment – haemocyanin – which is less efficient at binding with oxygen, as is the iron-based pigment haemoglobin in our own blood. Nevertheless, there are a few stories of it attacking and attempting to devour people. In October 1877, the *Weekly Oregonian* reported a North American woman going to the sea to bathe and being caught by an octopus and held under until she drowned. Her body was discovered, still in the monster's embrace, and some members of her tribe had to dive down and sever its arms before the corpse could be recovered.

In April 1935, a large Pacific octopus attacked a fisherman wading in waist-deep water near the entrance to San Francisco Bay. It wrapped its tentacles around the man's body, legs and left arm. He was being dragged to deeper water and cried out for help. Another fisherman ran to the rescue, and after a formidable struggle during which the rescuer hacked off some of the creature's arms, it was finally dispatched with a knife-blade between the eyes. It had a radial span of 15ft (4.5m) and weighed about 43lb (19.5kg).

Some years later Hollywood cameraman John Craig learned to have a healthy respect for the Pacific giant octopus. He wrote in his book *Danger Is My Business* about a time when he was lowered to the sea-bed, at San Benito Islands off Baja California, in an old-fashioned suit with brass helmet and lead boots. He spotted a large hole in the rocks, and entered a vertical shaft. At the bottom he found two large octopuses. Instead of rapidly back-tracking, he remembered the advice given to him by Japanese divers. They had said that you should not make any rapid movement that might attract the octopus's attention.

Rather, they suggested, you should remain quite still. The octopus might examine you with its arm but will ignore you if you are motionless. Craig stayed absolutely still and, sure enough, the octopuses behaved as the Japanese had said. One raised its arm, examined the outside of the diving suit, and then seemed to lose interest. Then Craig made his move. He slipped off his lead boots, inflated his diving suit, and began to float to the surface. But the move was premature. The larger of the two octopuses stretched out an arm and grabbed his leg. Fortunately it was sitting on gravel and had no hold on the rocks; it was jerked out of the hole and hauled to the surface still attached to Craig. On reaching the surface, the diving attendants hoisted Craig out of the water and saw that the octopus had smothered him completely. They tried to tear it off and went about attacking it with axes. They kept one of the severed arms. It was 8ft (2.4m) long. This meant that the octopus was about 18ft (5.5m) across. If it had been on rock rather than shingle, it would have killed the diver. Whether it would have eaten him too is unclear. The octopus, like the squid, has a formidable beak well capable of slicing through a diving suit and human flesh but more usually used for breaking into the carapace (shells) of crabs.

"I was aware that she was experiencing her very worst fears come to life: abandonment underwater"

FEAR IS THE LOCK

Tim Ecott

Tim Ecott, a BBC correspondent and producer, is the author of Neutral Buoyancy: Adventures in a Liquid World, *2001.*

Returning to London from a posting abroad, I decided to sign up for a dive in British waters. After the pleasure of clear, calm seas under the equatorial sun, I wanted to experience the underwater scenery of my own country. According to the diving magazines I had read, there was a wealth of marine life to be found off the south coast of England, and innumerable ship-wrecks waiting to be explored. Having found a diving club in London that made regular weekend excursions to the coast, I registered for an advanced diving course, imagining that diving with an instructor in attendance in these new conditions might be a good idea.

One Saturday in early spring found me standing on the quayside at Poole Harbour, where about a dozen people with large kit bags of diving paraphernalia were waiting for a fishing boat to take us offshore. On board, I was introduced to a slightly built middle-aged woman named Susan. She too was enrolled for an "advanced" course and I was to dive with Susan and the instructor, with whom she had recently completed her basic diving certification. The instructor was a diminutive female in her early twenties. As I made conversation with Susan, it became clear that she had reservations about the day's diving.

She smoked four cigarettes during the half-hour journey to the first dive site, and told me that she had never dived in the sea before. In common with many British divers, her training certificate had been issued after a series of dives in inland quarries, where an instructor can easily monitor and assist students without the hazards of coastal currents and excessive depth. Susan told me that she had an abiding fear that she would surface from a dive and find herself alone in the expansive Channel with no boat to retrieve her from the water. Her training in a quarry, an artificial body of water, had seemed safer, a self-contained environment no more alarming than a giant swimming pool. The open sea frightened her with its vastness, and like many divers she felt dwarfed by its scope. I assured her that in my experience the scenario of being left behind by the boat was a most unlikely prospect.

A short distance west from the entrance to Poole Harbour we prepared to make our first dive. The instructor had chosen a shallow area of seabed, no more than thirty-five feet deep, where we could practise a drift-dive, an exercise in letting the prevailing current take you along underwater to rendezvous with the diving boat after a pre-arranged time. To allow the diving boat to locate the divers easily, one of the group would hold a nylon rope-line attached to an inflatable marker buoy which would float on the surface throughout the dive.

As we put on our equipment, I struggled with the thick wetsuit which would cover all of my body. It restricted my limbs and felt tight around my chest. When I pulled on the rubber hood I found that I had difficulty rotating my neck or tilting my head downwards to look at the equipment clipped to my chest. The prospect of jumping from the fishing boat into the grey waters around us thus handicapped made me slightly apprehensive. With gloves on my hands, would I be able to operate my equipment easily? Surely this could not be fun.

Once overboard, I discovered that the wetsuit and its accoutrements worked exactly as promised. There was little sensation of cold, and the water around me liberated me from the stiffness I had felt on deck. And I could see underwater, albeit no further than twenty feet or so in any direction. As I had expected, the underwater colours were dull, yes, but there was seaweed and fish and interesting underwater rocks covered in anemones to discover. The problem was Susan. She seemed to have no control of her position in the water. One minute she would be head down, feet up; the next floating upwards towards the surface headfirst. The instructor and I would grasp her by the fins, or by her buoyancy jacket and pull her back down, and then she would roll over on to her back like a stranded tortoise. The entire forty-minute dive was spent guiding Susan through the water like a wayward torpedo. Except that a torpedo would have been hydrodynamic; she was more like a badly behaved dog on a lead.

After completing the drift-dive I decided to talk to the instructor and ask if it might be possible to join one of the other diving groups on board, so that she could give Susan some personal attention underwater. To my mind, Susan was too nervous to enjoy her dives and would be better off diving alone with her instructor at her own pace. The instructor told me that the difficulties on the morning dive had just been a case of "teething problems", and having certified Susan as a diver in inland waters she was confident that she would handle the afternoon dive more competently. After lunch, she told me, we would attempt the next stage of our course, a so-called deep dive where we would demonstrate our ability to dive below twenty metres, a depth I had already exceeded in warm waters on several occasions. Yet again, I wondered what the underwater visibility would be like in this part of the world, but I was now at least confident that I would not be cold.

As we approached the dive site, Susan and I were told that the skipper of the fishing boat had forecast rough conditions for the area. A strong current was running, perhaps as high as four knots, and we would have to take care to stay together once we entered the water. The instructor emphasized that the current would be likely to be much stronger at the surface, and so as to avoid being separated we should be ready to jump into the sea in unison and swim straight down without lingering on the surface.

Soon afterwards, our boat drew near to a large oil barrel, a fishing buoy tethered to the seabed by a heavy metal chain. In the surging current the large barrel was being tugged below the waves, straining at the chain like a dog on a leash. Watching the barrel, I overheard the boat's skipper asking the leader of the dive club if he was sure he wanted anyone diving in the prevailing conditions. The leader seemed to think the current was only a problem at the surface, and so after a short conversation we were given the go-ahead to dive. We kitted up and stood shoulder to shoulder at the side of the boat. Other divers held on to our air cylinders from behind, steadying us against the dangerous pitching of the deck. We were poised like paratroopers waiting for the green light to hurl ourselves through the aircraft's open door. With a final OK signal from the instructor we were ready, and I took a giant stride into the dark water. To my surprise, Susan, the instructor and I all hit the water at the same time and quickly signalled that we were OK to descend. We sank beneath the violent swell and were alone in the dim water, a trio of rubber-clad shapes communicating only with our eyes and a wave of the hand. Once underwater it was clear that the current was too strong to do anything other than drift along with it. We made our gradual descent through the half-lit world of water shadows, peering below for a sign that we were reaching the seabed.

A minute later we hit bottom at around twenty-three metres and found ourselves in a submarine landscape of granite shelves. Large slabs of flattened rock like king-sized double beds lay on the seafloor. The water around us seemed to have a greenish tint, a cool illumination which dampened the emotions. Visibility was poor, and in order to collect ourselves we knelt on the bottom in the lee of the rocks, ducking down behind them to stay out of the current. As I held on to the edge of a rock next to the instructor, it was clear that Susan had a problem. Like us she was pinned against one side of a large slab by the current, not moving, but there was something unnerving about the way she looked. Susan showed no emotion or reaction to the instructor's hand signals. Behind her mask she stared straight ahead, as if in a trance. She was frozen with fear, destabilized by the knowledge that once she left her anchorage in the rocks she would be at the mercy of the current. After her performance in the morning it was clear that she felt unable to orientate herself properly in the swift flow. I imagined her rolling like a tumbleweed along the rocky ledges, propelled by the drifting water but unable to right herself and steer herself beside us in the gloom. Confronted with the deep, dark water and the impelling current, her mind refused to think about anything practical. She clung to the edge of the slab as though it was the edge of a precipice, gripped by a condition known as passive panic.

The light on the seabed was dim. Desperately, we tried to pull ourselves hand over hand across the rock slab to reach her. The current was too much for the instructor. I had almost reached Susan, fighting to keep myself out of the flow, hugging the face of the slab to minimize the amount of my body exposed to the ripping force of the tide. Just as I was within arm's length, and ready to pull Susan forcibly from where she was rooted against the rock, I felt something grasp me around the neck. Somehow, in our attempt to scramble across the rock, the instructor had allowed the rope line attached to the marker buoy to become entangled about my throat.

I could feel the tug of the nylon cord threatening to pull the regulator from my mouth. I turned to see the instructor struggling to maintain her position on the rock. Seeing my predicament, she signalled for me to release my hold on the slab. In the strong current we flew off the rock, tied together by the nylon line which was clipped to her buoyancy jacket. As I looked back, Susan was still pinned to the rock, unmoving, and seemingly unaware of what was happening. As we drifted away she was gone, a ghostly image hidden by the grey-green waters. Then the instructor and I were alone, bound together by the fouled line.

I pulled at the cord around my throat, trying to keep it away from my regulator hose, feeling the nylon biting into my fingers.

I can clearly remember thinking to myself, "This is not good", and then wondering why I was thinking in speech bubbles, like a character in a cartoon. Then I wondered why I was being so calm, and I fleetingly considered the imminent danger of drowning. It all seemed strangely academic. I was enveloped in this world of green dream water, more concerned about what might be happening to Susan than my own predicament. I was aware that she was experiencing her very worst fears come to life: abandonment underwater. She was an insignificant speck on the seabed surrounded by the infinite space of the ocean.

After a time I felt the noose around my throat go slack. I did not know it, but the marker buoy on the surface above had separated from the nylon line with the force of my weight pulling against it underwater. I held on to the instructor as we kicked slowly for the surface, still drifting, revolving like ornaments on a fairground merry-go-round in the current. Her eyes, as round as saucers, stared back at me from behind her mask. Slowly we kicked upwards towards the light and air. I felt a warm glow at the idea that I was leaving the green dreamworld behind.

Breaking the surface, the instructor and I maintained a hold on one another, and realized that we were drifting in the swell with nothing to signal our position. Released from its tether, the marker buoy had flown across the wave tops. Waves hit our faces at unpredictable intervals and we breathed air from our cylinders so as to avoid being swamped for as long as possible. When they ran dry we used our snorkels, kicking as best we could to maintain our breathing tubes away from the prevailing wind. We dropped our weight belts so as to lighten the load on our buoyancy jackets. Neither of us could speak except in occasional snatches of shouted instructions, but we were undoubtedly thinking the same thing. What had become of Susan? The image of her stricken face receding from my sight as we were torn from the rocks kept flashing through my head.

In dull-coloured wetsuits we were mere dots on the surface of the Channel. The swell lifted us high enough to see a panoramic view of the coastline in the distance, with several diving and fishing boats in the vicinity but all too far away to hear us call out for help. We waved at several boats and were not seen, and all the time we wondered what had happened to Susan. We barely spoke, breathing through our snorkels so as to avoid the buffeting waves which threatened to make us swallow seawater. I recalled stories I had heard about divers left adrift in cold water for hours. For about forty minutes we floated with the tide, until a charter fishing boat spotted us. The men on board were divers who had abandoned their own diving plans that afternoon due to the rough seas and strong currents. Although there were six divers and a skipper on the fishing boat, only one man had seen us waving. After we were pulled from the water we made radio contact with our own boat, which until then had no idea of our fate.

An alert was issued on the ship's VHF radio and all boats in the area began searching for Susan. The instructor and I did not speak to each other; it was clear she was responsible for the accident, and there was no point in stating the obvious. We sipped hot tea provided by our rescuers and stood apart at the ship's rail scanning the sea for signs of Susan. Forty-five minutes later we received the radio call that she had been found by another diving boat. They had to drag her from the water like a hooked fish. She sobbed uncontrollably with fear and relief.

Later that day, I spoke to Susan about what had happened. She was still shaken by her experience and brought to tears as she recounted her story. She would have to consider carefully whether she would ever dive in England again. Finding herself alone underwater after we became separated, she said she waited for us to return, somehow imagining that we would be able to find her. She felt powerless to help herself, and terrified of letting go of her niche in the rocks. After several minutes alone in the dark, she said the reality of her predicament struck her. On only her second sea dive, she had been abandoned in a strong current and in relatively deep water. She had a choice: swim to the surface alone, or die. Conquering her panic, she pulled herself from her rocky nook, mustering all her inner courage to force herself to ascend slowly to avoid decompression injury.

Once on the surface safely, her nightmare was only half over. Now she was alone, and drifting in the open water, a tiny piece of flotsam in a rolling sea.

Officially, my instructor left the diving club by "mutual agreement" the following week. As diving accidents go, our incident was quite minor, but at sea, and underwater, there is a narrow line between mishap and disaster. People die every year with great regularity diving in British waters, and now I understood why. I carried on diving with the club and soon found a regular buddy whom I trusted, but my introduction to the Channel had been a valuable lesson.

Susan did not dive again.

"We stepped out of the bathysphere at 11.52 . . . with the memory
of living scenes in a world as strange as that of Mars"

ONE THOUSAND AND FOUR HUNDRED AND TWENTY SIX FEET BELOW THE SEA

William Beebe

William Beebe (see pp 10–15) made a number of pioneering
descents into the ocean in a "bathysphere". From Beebe's Half
Mile Down, *1934:*

A certain day and hour and second are approaching rapidly
when a human face will peer out through a tiny window and
signals will be passed back to companions, or to breathlessly
waiting hosts on earth, with such sentences as:

"We are above the level of Everest."

"Can now see the whole Atlantic coastline."

"Clouds blot out the earth."

"Temperature and air pressure have dropped to minus
minus."

"Can see the whole circumference of Earth."

"The moon appears ten times its usual size."

"We now . . ." etc.

Both by daylight and by moonlight I have looked from a plane
down on the earth from a height of over four miles, so I know
the first kindergarten sensations of such a trip. But until I
actually am enclosed within some futuristic rocket and start on a
voyage into interstellar space, I shall never experience such a
feeling of complete isolation from the surface of the planet Earth
as when I first dangled in a hollow pea on a swaying cobweb a
quarter of a mile below the deck of a ship rolling in mid-ocean.

We were able to adumbrate the above imaginary news items from a rocket mounting into interplanetary space, by the following actual messages sent from the bathysphere up our telephone wire:

"We have just splashed below the surface."
"We are at our deepest helmet dive."   60 feet
"The *Lusitania* is resting at this level."   285 feet
"This is the greatest depth reached in a regulation
suit by Navy divers."   306 feet
"We are passing the deepest submarine record."   383 feet
"The *Egypt* was found at this level by divers in
rigid shells."   400 feet
"A diver in an armored suit descended this far into
a Bavarian lake – the deepest point which a live
human has ever reached."   525 feet
"Only dead men have sunk below this."   600 feet
"We are still alive and one-quarter of a mile down." 1,426 feet

A young gale blew itself out, and on 3 June 1930, the sun rose on a calm, slowly heaving sea. On Nonsuch Island we ran up the prearranged flag signal and the working crew saw it from St Georges and put out. On this day we only made a trial submergence with the bathysphere empty, to test the working of the crew and the whole apparatus.

It was let down 2,000 feet, averaging two minutes for each 100 feet. Two clamps were attached, fastening the rubber hose to the cable every 200 feet. When the cable began to come in we found there were several turns of the hose about the cable. It was beyond our power to revolve the cable so we were compelled to remove the clamps and let the hose drop down, still twisted. As more and more clamps were removed, the ascent became increasingly difficult, the rubber hose becoming a regular snarl. By great good luck we were able to push the tangle down and down until at last the bathysphere itself appeared and we got it aboard. Draped and looped about and below it were forty-five twists of the half-mile of rubber hose.

We imagined the contained light and telephone wires bent and broken, and our entire venture seemed to be at an end. It looked as if we were to pay penalty at the very start for daring to attempt to delve into forbidden depths.

The crew went to work and within twenty-four hours the half-mile of hose was again neatly arranged in its great loops on the deck and when we tested the four wires we found the electric circuit was unbroken, light and sound passing through as perfectly as before the catastrophe.

When we wound the great steel cable onto the winch on deck, from the wooden spool on which it came from the factory, without our knowing it, there must have been a slow twisting. This was not apparent until we let down the bathysphere, and began attaching the rubber hose. Little by little the cable unwound, carrying around with it the pliable hose, until, when the cable was hanging straight and quiet, it had revolved forty-five times. On subsequent dives the cable never made a single turn, and the two elements came up as they went down.

6 June was another day of almost perfect calm with only a long, heaving swell in mid-ocean. We were on board the barge early, and, as soon as the tug *Gladisfen* came alongside, took her tow-rope, described a circle around the reefs, and headed out to sea through Castle Roads. The great jagged cliffs towered high on both sides, and on their summits the ruined battlements of the old forts frowned down upon us. I wondered what old Governor Richard Moore would have said, three hundred odd years ago, leaning his elbows on the parapet, if he could have watched our strange procession steaming past. In all likelihood, the steaming part would have mystified and interested him far more than our chief object.

As we cleared the outer head of Brangman's, we felt the first gentle heave and settling of the swell of the ocean, and in a few minutes the foam-ringed mass of Gurnet Rock passed astern, and we steered south straight into the open sea. An hour later the angle of the two lighthouses showed that we were about eight miles off shore, with a generous mile of water beneath us. Choosing a favorable spot under such conditions is like looking around and trying to decide on the exact location of the North Pole. I think it was Dooley who said that finding the North Pole was like sitting down on the ice anywhere. And so I felt when they all awaited my signal to stop. I looked about, could detect no unusually favorable swell or especially satisfying wave, so I resorted to a temporal decision, and exactly at nine o'clock ordered the *Gladisfen* to stop. We headed up wind and up swell, and lowered the bathysphere again with only a motion picture camera inside. At a depth of 1500 feet this was exposed by electricity and the sphere pulled up after an hour and a half of submersion. There was nothing visible on the film, and, what was of far greater interest to us, we found not a single twist of the hose, the windows were intact, and only a quart of water was collected in the bottom.

We dried and cleaned it thoroughly, then put in the oxygen tanks, and the chemicals. There were two wire racks for holding the latter, one, as I have said, for calcium chloride for absorbing moisture, the other of soda lime for removing the excess of carbon dioxide from the air. Finally we were all ready and I looked around at the sea and sky, the boats and my friends, and not being able to think of any pithy saying which might echo down the ages, I said nothing, crawled painfully over the steel bolts, fell inside and curled up on the cold, hard bottom of the sphere. This aroused me to speech and I called for a cushion only to find that we had none on hand. Otis Barton climbed in after me, and we disentangled our legs and got set. I had no idea that there was so much room in the inside of a sphere only four and a half feet in diameter, and although the longer we were in it the smaller it seemed to get, yet, thanks to our adequate physique, we had room and to spare. At Barton's suggestion I took up my position at the windows, while he hitched himself over to the side of the door, where he could keep watch on the various instruments. He also put on the ear-phones.

Miss Hollister on deck took charge of the other end of the telephone and arranged the duplicate control electric light so that she could watch it. Mr Tee-Van assumed control of the deck crew.

At our signal, the four-hundred-pound door was hoisted and clanged into place, sliding snugly over the ten great steel bolts. Then the huge nuts were screwed on. If either of us had had time to be nervous, this would have been an excellent opportunity – carrying out Poe's idea of being sealed up, not all at once, but little by little. For after the door was securely fastened, there remained a four-inch round opening in the center, through which we could see and talk and just slip a hand. Then this mighty bolt was screwed in place, and there began the most infernal racket I have ever heard. It was necessary, not only to screw the nuts down hard, but to pound the wrenches with hammers to take up all possible slack. I was sure the windows would be cracked, but having forcibly expressed our feelings through the telephone we gradually got used to the ear-shattering reverberations. Then utter silence settled down.

I turned my attention to the windows, cleaned them thoroughly and tested the visual angles which I could attain by pressing my face close to the surface. I could see a narrow sector of the deck with much scurrying about, and as we rolled I caught sight of the ultramarine sea and the *Gladisfen* dipping at the end of the slack tow rope. Faint scuffling sounds reached us now and then, and an occasional hollow beating. Then it seemed as if the steel walls fell away, and we were again free among our fellows, for a voice came down the half mile of hose coiled on the deck, and such is the human mind, that slender vocal connection seemed to restore physical as well as mental contact. While waiting for the take-off, Barton readjusted the phone, tested the searchlight, and opened the delicate oxygen valve. He turned it until we both verified the flow as two litres a minute – that being the amount suggested to us for two people. I remembered what I had read of Houdini's method of remaining in a closed coffin for a long time, and we both began conscientiously regulating our breathing, and conversing in low tones.

Another glance through my porthole showed Tee-Van looking for a signal from old Captain Millet. I knew that now it was actually a propitious wave or rather a propitious lack of one for which they waited. Soon Millet waved his hand, and exactly at one o'clock the winch grumbled, the wire on the deck tightened, and we felt our circular home tremble, lean over, and lift clear. Up we went to the yard-arm, then a half-score of the crew pulled with all their might and swung us out over the side. This all between two, big, heaving swells. We were dangling in mid-air and slowly we revolved until I was facing in toward the side of the *Ready*. And now our quartz windows played a trick on us. Twice already, in an experimental test submergence, we had not gauged correctly the roll of the ship or the distance outboard and the sphere had crashed into the half-rotten bulwarks. Now as I watched, I saw us begin to swing and my eyes told me that we were much too close, and that a slightly heavier roll would crash us, windows first, into the side of the vessel. Barton could not see the imminent danger, and the next message I got was, "Gloria wants to know why the Director is swearing so." By this time we had swung far out, and I realized that every word which we spoke to each other in our tiny hollow chamber was clearly audible at the other end of the wire. I sent up word that any language was justifiable at such gross neglect as to allow our window to swing back and forth only a yard from the boat. And very decisively the word came back that fifteen feet was the nearest it had ever been, and we were now twenty-five feet away. Barton looked out with me and we could not believe our eyes. Fused quartz, as I have said, is the clearest, the most transparent material in the world, and the side of the *Ready* seemed only a yard away. My apologies must have cost us several litres of good oxygen.

To avoid any further comment on our part, profane or otherwise, we were lowered 20 feet. I sensed the weight and sturdy resistance of the bathysphere more at this moment than at any other time. We were lowered gently but we struck the surface with a splash which would have crushed a rowboat like an eggshell. Yet within we hardly noticed the impact, until a froth of foam and bubbles surged up over the glass and our chamber was dimmed to a pleasant green. We swung quietly while the first hose clamp was put on the cable. At the end of the first revolution the great hull of the barge came into view. This was a familiar landscape, which I had often seen from the diving helmet – a transitory, swaying reef with waving banners of seaweed, long tubular sponges, jet black blobs of ascidians and tissue-thin plates of rough-spined pearl shells. Then the keel passed slowly upward, becoming one with the green water overhead.

With this passed our last visible link with the upper world; from now on we had to depend on distant spoken words for knowledge of our depth, or speed, or the weather, or the sunlight, or anything having to do with the world of air on the surface of the Earth.

A few seconds after we lost sight of the hull of the *Ready*, word came down the hose that we were at 50 feet, and I looked out at the brilliant bluish-green haze and could not realize that this was almost my limit in the diving helmet. Then "100 feet" was called out, and still the only change was a slight twilighting and chilling of the green. As we sank slowly I knew that we must be passing the 132-foot level, the depth where Commander Ellsberg labored so gallantly to free the men in the Submarine S-57. "200 feet" came and we stopped with the slightest possible jerk and hung suspended while a clamp was attached – a double gripping bit of brass which bound the cable and hose together to prevent the latter from breaking by its own weight. Then the call came that all was clear and again I knew that we were sinking, although only by the upward passing of small motes of life in the water.

We were now very far from any touch of Mother Earth; ten miles south of the shore of Bermuda, and one and a half miles from the sea bottom far beneath us. At 300 feet, Barton gave a sudden exclamation and I turned the flash on the door and saw a slow trickle of water beneath it. About a pint had already collected in the bottom of the sphere. I wiped away the meandering stream and still it came. There flashed across my mind the memory of gentle rain falling on a window pane, and the first drops finding their way with difficulty over the dry surface of the glass. Then I looked out through the crystal clear quartz at the pale blue, and the contrast closed in on my mind like the ever deepening twilight.

We watched the trickle. I knew the door was solid enough – a mass of 400 pounds of steel – and I knew the inward pressure would increase with every foot of depth. So I gave the signal to descend quickly. After that, the flashlight was turned on the door-sill a dozen times during our descent, but the stream did not increase.

Two minutes more and "400 feet" was called out; 500 and 600 feet came and passed overhead, then 700 feet where we remained for a while.

Ever since the beginnings of human history, when first the Phoenicians dared to sail the open sea, thousands upon thousands of human beings had reached the depth at which we were now suspended, and had passed on to lower levels. But all of these were dead, drowned victims of war, tempest, or other Acts of God. We were the first living men to look out at the strange illumination: And it was stranger than any imagination could have conceived. It was of an indefinable translucent blue quite unlike anything I have ever seen in the upper world, and it excited our optic nerves in a most confusing manner. We kept thinking and calling it brilliant, and again and again I picked up a book to read the type, only to find that I could not tell the difference between a blank page and a colored plate. I brought all my logic to bear, I put out of mind the excitement of our position in watery space and tried to think sanely of comparative color, and I failed utterly. I flashed on the searchlight, which seemed the yellowest thing I have ever seen, and let it soak into my eyes, yet the moment it was switched off, it was like the long vanished sunlight – it was as though it never had been – and the blueness of the blue, both outside and inside our sphere, seemed to pass materially through the eye into our very beings. This is all very unscientific; quite worthy of being jeered at by optician or physicist, but there it was. I was excited by the fishes that I was seeing perhaps more than I have ever been by other organisms, but it was only an intensification of my surface and laboratory interest: I have seen strange fluorescence and ultra-violet illumination in the laboratories of physicists: I recall the weird effects of color shifting through distant snow crystals on the high Himalayas, and I have been impressed by the eerie illumination, or lack of it, during a full eclipse of the sun. But this was beyond and outside all or any of these. I think we both experienced a wholly new kind of mental reception of color impression. I felt I was dealing with something too different to be classified in usual terms.

All our remarks were recorded by Miss Hollister and when I read them later, the repetition of our insistence upon the brilliance, which yet was not brilliance, was almost absurd. Yet I find that I must continue to write about it, if only to prove how utterly inadequate language is to translate vividly, feeling and sensations under a condition as unique as submersion at this depth.

The electric searchlight now became visible. Heretofore we could see no change whatever in the outside water when it was turned on, but now a pale shaft of yellow – intensely yellow – light shot out through the blue, very faint but serving to illuminate anything which crossed it. Most of the time I chose to have it cut off, for I wanted more than anything else to see all that I could of the luminescence of the living creatures.

After a few minutes I sent up an order, and I knew that we were again sinking. The twilight (the word had become absurd, but I could coin no other) deepened, but we still spoke of its brilliance. It seemed to me that it must be like the last terrific upflare of a flame before it is quenched. I found we were both expecting at any moment to have it blown out, and to enter a zone of absolute darkness. But only by shutting my eyes and opening them again could I realize the terrible *slowness* of the change from dark blue to blacker blue. On the earth at night in moonlight I can always imagine the yellow of sunshine, the scarlet of invisible blossoms, but here, when the searchlight was off, yellow and orange and red were unthinkable. The blue which filled all space admitted no thought of other colors.

We spoke very seldom now. Barton examined the dripping floor, took the temperatures, watched and adjusted the oxygen tank, and now and then asked, "What depth now?" "Yes, we're all right." "No, the leak's not increasing." "It's as brilliant as ever."

And we both knew it was not as brilliant as ever, but our eyes kept telling us to say so. It actually seemed to me to have a brilliance and intensity which the sunshine lacked; sunshine, that is, as I remembered it in what seemed ages ago.

"800 feet" now came down the wire and I called a halt. There seemed no reason why we should not go on to a thousand; the leak was no worse, our palm-leaf fan kept the oxygen circulating so that we had no sense of stuffiness and yet some hunch – some mental warning which I have had at half a dozen critical times in my life – spelled *bottom* for this trip. This settled, I concentrated on the window for five minutes.

The three exciting internal events which marked this first trip were, first, the discovery of the slight leak through the door at 300 feet, which lessened as we went down; next, the sudden short-circuiting of the electric light switch, with attendant splutterings and sparks, which was soon remedied. The third was absurd, for it was only Barton pulling out his palm-leaf fan from between the wall of the sphere and the wire lining of the chemical rack. I was wholly absorbed at the time in watching some small fish, when the sudden shrieking rasp in the confines of our tiny cell gave me all the reactions which we might imagine from the simultaneous caving in of both windows and door! After that, out of regard for each other's nerves, we squirmed about and carried on our various duties silently.

Coming up to the surface and through it was like hitting a hard ceiling – I unconsciously ducked, ready for the impact, but there followed only a slather of foam and bubbles, and the rest was sky.

We reached the deck again just one hour after our start, and sat quietly while the middle bolt was slowly unscrewed. We could hear our compressed air hissing outward through the threads until finally the bolt popped off, and our ear-drums vibrated very slightly. After a piece of boiler-factory pounding the big door finally swung off. I started to follow and suddenly realized how the human body could be completely subordinated to the mind. For a full hour I had sat in almost the same position with no thought either of comfort or discomfort, and now I had severally to untwist my feet and legs and bring them to life. The sweater which was to have served as cushion, I found reposing on one of the chemical racks, while I had sat on the hard cold steel in a good-sized puddle of greasy water. I also bore the distinct imprint of a monkey wrench for several days. I followed Barton out on deck into the glaring sunshine, whose yellowness can never hereafter be as wonderful as blue can be.

While still upside down, creeping painfully, sea-lionwise, over the protruding circle of bolts, I fancied that I heard a strange, inexplicable ringing in my ears. When I stood up, I found it was the screeching whistles on the boilers and the deeper toned siren of the *Gladisfen* giving us, all to ourselves, a little celebration in mid-ocean. The wind was right and my staff on Nonsuch ten miles away saw the escaping steam through the telescope binoculars, later heard the sound faintly, and knew that we had made our dive and ascent in safety.

Four days later we were able to put to sea again, and sent the bathysphere down empty to 2000 feet. By the judicious use of white lead we had effectively stopped the leak in the door, and there was no tangle or twist of hose. A tiny flaw which we had watched with suspicion on the outer rim of one of the quartz windows had not increased. The only novelty in the way of unexpected happenings after this two hours' submergence, was that about three feet of the hose had been forced inside the sphere. When this was rectified, Barton and I climbed inside and started enthusiastically for a deeper plunge. Everything went well until at 150 feet we began to experience bad static on the phone. A sentence would come through clearly and then only a mixture of spluttered words. It improved for a while, but at 250 feet Barton said, "My God! The phone is broken." It was a tragic exclamation, and I felt exactly as he did. The leak on our other trip, the short circuiting, the static today – these were all annoying but not terrifying, and as I have already mentioned, the sound of the human voice had, all unconsciously to us, seemed a much surer bond than the steel cable or the sturdiness of the sphere. We had neither of us felt before quite the same realization of our position in space as we did now. It seemed as if hose, cable, and all had gone. We had become veritable plankton. I visualized us as hanging in midwater for as long as the Flying Dutchman roamed the surface above. The silence was oppressive and ominous, and our whispers to each other did nothing to alleviate it. The greenish blue outside became cold and inimical. We did our best to signal with the searchlight, knowing that answering flickering must be reflected in the checking bulb on deck. We felt a sudden weight beneath us and knew that we were being reeled swiftly to the surface.

This was Dive Number Seven for the bathysphere, and we climbed in at 9:50 a.m. We had made a number of improvements since the first dive. The inside had been painted black so as not to interfere with observations. Barton had come to look upon his very greasy leather skull-cap as a mascot, so when he could not find it, the central bolt was unscrewed, and the *Ready* searched thoroughly for five minutes, after which he found he was sitting on it. We now had a special place for fans and monkey wrenches and I arranged a shelf for my notebook and pencil, specimens of scarlet crustaceans, and a book with type and plates to test the pseudo-brilliance of the light. The cushion was in its right place, and we had built a shield to shut out the lateral glare from the searchlight. We had also learned to cover the *chevaux-de-frise* of bolts at the entrance with sacking, and so to soften the effects of our frantic wrigglings in and out. The shackle of the cable had been shifted from the central to the posterior hole so that the sphere tipped slightly forward and downward when swinging free. This gave me a better outlook in a slightly oblique, downward direction. The hose fastening on the sphere had been tightened so that there was less chance of our being smothered in its entering, entwining coils, which would have been an undramatic, *Laocoön* ending.

This time we took a chance on everything being in good order, and did not make an experimental submergence. We fastened the Tropical Research house flag of the New York Zoölogical Society and that of the Explorers' Club to the bathysphere, and tied a very ancient squid wrapped in cheese-cloth just beneath the observation windows. Dangling in front and just to one side was a cluster of luminous hooks attractively baited. With the searchlight ready to turn on, I felt that I had contrived all the enticements possible for luring deep-sea fish within my observational zone.

Barton and I were screwed down and bolted in at ten o'clock, and four minutes later touched water. The surface was crossed with small wavelets, and three times before we were completely submerged the distant *Gladisfen* and the level horizon were etched clearly on the glass, and as instantly erased by a green and white smother. We sank slowly and I peered upward and watched the under side of the surface rise above me. When the rush of silvery bubble-smoke imprisoned beneath the sphere had passed, the surface showed clear. From the point of view of a submarine creature, I should by rights call it the floor of the air, and not the ceiling of the water. Even when diving in the helmet I am always conscious of the falsity of calling the water wet when I am once immersed in it. Spray blows in one's face and leaves it wet, but down below, the imprisoned air sailing upward, slips through one's fingers like balloon pearls, dry, mobile beauty, leaving only a pleasant sensation.

And now I looked up at our vertical wake of thousands of iridescent swimming bits of air, and, for a moment, forgot whither we were bound.

The boundary of air and water above me appeared perfectly solid, and like a slowly waving, pale green canopy, quilted everywhere with deep, pale puckers – the sharp apexes of the wavelets above showing as smooth, rounded indentations below. The sunlight sifted down in long, oblique rays as if through some unearthly beautiful cathedral window. The host of motes of dust had their exact counterpart in mid-water, only the general feeling of color was cool green, not yellow. The water was so clear that I could see dimly the distant keel of the *Gladisfen*, rolling gently. And here and there, like bunches of mistletoe hanging from a chandelier, were clusters of golden sargassum weed, with only their upper tips hidden, breaking through into the air. A stray berry went past my window and I saw an amusing likeness between its diminutive air-filled sphere and that which was at present my home.

The last thing in focus, of the upper world, was a long, undulating sea serpent of a rope dangling down from the side of the *Ready*.

We had asked to be lowered slowly. When less than 50 feet beneath the surface I happened to glance at a large, deep-sea prawn which I had taken for color experiment. To my astonishment it was no longer scarlet, but a deep velvety black. I opened my copy of *Depths of the Ocean* and the plate of bright red shrimps was dark as night: No wonder I thought of the light as cool.

On this and other dives I carefully studied the changing colors, both by direct observation and by means of the spectroscope. Just beneath the surface the red diminished to one-half its normal width. At 20 feet there was only a thread of red and at 50 the orange was dominant. This in turn vanished at 150 feet. 300 feet found the whole spectrum dimmed, the yellow almost gone and the blue appreciably narrowed. At 350 I should give as a rough summary of the spectrum fifty per cent blue violet, twenty-five per cent green, and an equal amount of colorless pale light. At 450 feet no blue remained, only violet, and green too faint for naming. At 800 feet there was nothing visible but a narrow line of pale grayish-white in the green-blue area, due of course to the small amount of light reaching my eye. Yet when I looked outside I saw only the deepest, blackest-blue imaginable. On every dive this unearthly color brought excitement to our eyes and minds.

A few familiar aurelia jellyfish drifted past while we were sinking to 50 feet, and at 100 feet a cloud of brown thimble jellies vibrated by the window. These were identical with those which we had observed in vast swarms in Haiti.* They are

* *Beneath Tropic Seas*, William Beebe, 1928.

supposed to be surface forms, but here they were pushing against my window 20 fathoms down. They were the first organisms which showed that the fused quartz did away with all distortion. Full 20 feet away I could see them coming, and the knowledge of their actual size – that of a thimble – gave me a gauge of comparison which helped in estimating distance, size, and speed of unknown organisms.

I found that little things could change my whole mental outlook in the bathysphere. Up to this moment I had been watching the surface or seeing surface organisms, and I had focused so intensely upward that what was beneath had not yet become vivid. As the last thimble jelly passed, an air bubble broke loose from some hidden corner of the sphere, and writhing from the impetus of its wrenching free, rose swiftly, breaking into three just overhead, and the trio vanished. Now I felt the isolation and the awe which increased with the dimming of the light; the bubble seemed the last link with my upper world, and I wondered whether any of the watchers saw it coming, silver at first, then clothing itself in orange and red iridescence as it reached the surface – to break and merge and be lost forever.

At 200 feet there occurred my first real deep-sea experience on this dive, something which could never be duplicated on the surface of the water. A six-inch fish suddenly appeared, nosed the bag of ancient squid and then took up its position close to the glass of my window, less than a foot away from my face. Something about it seemed familiar, yet it was strange. In size, shape, and general pattern it was very like a pilot-fish, *Naucrates ductor*. Twice it swam back to the delectable bait and three times returned to where it almost diametered my circular outlook. Then I knew what the trouble was – it was the ghost of a pilot-fish – pure white with eight wide, black, upright bands. At 200 feet a pilot-fish could not be the color he is at the surface, and, like Einstein's halfsized world, here was a case where only the faulty, transient memory of man sealed up in a steel sphere had any right to assert that under different conditions the fish would show any colors other than the dark upright bands. I am certain that the fish itself aided this pale appearance, for it has considerable power of color change, but this was very different from the mere expansion and contraction of dermal chromatophores. At 250 feet I saw the pilot-fish going *upward*.

There was a similarity between 200- and 300-foot levels in that most of the fish seen were carangids, such as pilot-fish and *Psenes* (this has no human or Christian name, but its technical one is so interesting to pronounce that this can be excused!). Long strings of siphonophores drifted past, lovely as the finest lace, and schools of jellyfish throbbed on their directionless but energetic road through life. Small vibrating motes passed in clouds, wholly mysterious until I could focus exactly and knew them for pteropods, or flying snails, each of which lived within a delicate, tissue shell, and flew through life with a pair of flapping, fleshy wings.

At 400 feet there came into view the first real deep-sea fish – *Cyclothones* or round-mouths, lanternfish, and bronze eels. The former meant nothing at first; I took them for dark-colored worms or shrimps. Only when I saw them at greater depths in the searchlight did I recognize them. Of all the many thousands of these fish which I have netted, I never saw one alive until now. The lanternfish (Myctophids) came close to the glass and were easy to call by name. Instead of having only a half dozen scales left, like those caught in the nets, these fish were ablaze with their full armor of iridescence. Twice I caught the flash of their light organs, but only for an instant. An absurdly small and rotund puffer appeared quite out of place at this depth, but with much more reason he probably thought the same of me.

Big silvery bronze eels came nosing about the bait, although what they expected to accomplish with their exceedingly slender and delicate jaws is hard to imagine. Their transparent larva also appeared, swimming by itself, a waving sheet of watery tissue. Pale shrimps drifted by, their transparency almost removing them from vision. Now and then came a flash as from an opal, probably the strange, flat crustacean, well-named *Sapphirina*. Ghosts of pilot-fish swam into view again at this level.

Here, at 400 feet, we found that we could just read ordinary print with an effort, and yet to the unfocused eye the illumination seemed very brilliant. I found that the two hours' difference between 10 a.m. and noon, marking the two dives, Numbers Four and Seven, although both were made in full sunlight, resulted in fifty percent less illumination at 10 A.M. than at noon.

At 500 feet I had fleeting glimpses of fish nearly two feet long, perhaps surface forms, and here for the first time I saw strange, ghostly, dark forms hovering in the distance, – forms which never came nearer, but reappeared at deeper, darker depths. Flying snails passed in companies of fifty or more, looking like brown bubbles. I had seen them alive in the net hauls, but here they were at home in thousands. As they perished from old age or accident or what-not, their shells drifted slowly to the bottom, a mile and a half down, and several times when my net had accidentally touched bottom it had brought up quarts of the empty, tinkling shells.

Small, ordinary-looking squids balanced in mid-water. I hoped to see some of the larger ones, those with orange, bull's-eye lights at the tips of their arms, or the ones which glow with blue, yellow, and red light organs. None came close enough, however, or it may be I must wait until I can descend a mile and still live, before I can come to their haunts.

A four-inch fish came into view and nosed the baited hook. It was almost transparent, the vertebræ and body organs being plainly visible, the eyes and the food-filled stomach the only opaque parts. Since making the dive I have twice captured this fish, the pinkish, semi-transparent young of the scarlet, big-eyed snapper.

At 550 feet I found the temperature inside the bell was seventy-six degrees, twelve degrees lower than on deck. Near here a big leptocephalus undulated past, a pale ribbon of transparent gelatine with only the two iridescent eyes to indicate its arrival. As it moved I could see the outline faintly – ten inches long at least, and as it passed close, even the parted jaws were visible. This was the larva of some great sea eel.

As 600 feet came and passed I saw flashes of light in the

distance and at once turned on the searchlight, but although the blue outside seemed dark, yet the electric glare had no visible effect, and we turned it off. The sparks of light and the distant flashes kept on from time to time showing the power of these animal illuminations.

A pale blue fish appeared, yet the blue of the pilot-fish does not exist at this depth. Several seriola-like forms nosed toward me. They must have drifted down from the surface waters into these great pressures without injury. Dark jellyfish twice came to my eyes, and the silvery eels again. The flying snails looked dull gold and I saw my first shrimps with minute but very distinct port-holes where the lights must be. Again a great cloud of a body moved in the distance – this time pale, much lighter than the water. How I longed for a single near view, or telescopic eyes which could pierce the murk. I felt as if some astonishing discovery lay just beyond the power of my eyes.

At another hundred feet a dozen fish passed the sphere swimming almost straight upright, yet they were not unduly elongate like the trumpetfish which occasionally assume this position in shallow waters near shore. I had a flash only of the biggest fish yet – dark, with long, tapering tail and quite a foot in length. Shrimps and snails drifted past like flakes of unheard-of storms. Also a large transparent jellyfish bumped against the glass, its stomach filled with a glowing mass of luminous food.

Here and at 800 feet a human being was permitted for the first time the sight of living, silver hatchet-fish, heliographing their silver sides. I made Barton look quickly out so he could verify the unexpected sight.

Here is an excerpt, of a very full seventeen minutes, direct from the transcription which Miss Hollister took of my notes telephoned up from 800 feet on Dive Number Eleven:

19 June 1930. 1:24 p.m. Depth 800 feet: 2 black fish, 8 inches long going by, rat-tailed, probably *Idiacanthus*. 2 long, silver, eel-like fish, probably *Serrivomer*, Fish and invertebrates go up and down the shaft of light like insects. 3 Myctophids with headlights; *Diaphus*. (Work with a mirror next time.) 2 more

different Myctophids. The same 3 Myctophids with headlights. 20 Pteropods and 6 or 8 *Argyropelecus* together. 3 more
Pteropods. Little twinkling lights in the distance all the time,
pale greenish in color. Eels, 1 dark and 1 light. Big *Argyropelecus* coming; looks like a worm head on. *Eustomias*-like fish 5
inches long. 30 *Cyclothones*, greyish white.

We had left the deck at ten o'clock, and it was twenty-five
minutes later that we had again reached our record floor – 800
feet. This time I had no hunch – reasonable or unreasonable –
and three minutes later we were passing through a mist of
crustaceans and flapping snails at 900 feet. We both agreed
that the light was quite bright enough to read by and then we
tried Pica type and found that our eyes showed nothing definite
whatever. With the utmost straining I could just distinguish a
plate of figures from a page of type. Again the word "brilliant"
slipped wholly free of its usual meaning, and we looked up from
our effort to see a real deep-sea eel undulating close to the glass –
a slender-jawed *Serrivomer*, bronzy-red as I knew in the dimly-
remembered upper world, but here black and white.

At 1,000 feet we had a moment's excitement when a loop of
black, sea-serpenty hose swung around before us, a jet-black
line against blackish-blue.

Almost at once the sparks we had seen higher up became more
abundant and larger. At 1050 feet I saw a series of luminous,
colored dots moving along slowly, or jerking unsteadily past,
similar and yet independent. I turned on the searchlight and
found it effective at last. At 600 feet it could not be distinguished; here it cut a swathe almost material, across my field of
vision, and for the first time, as far as I know, in the history of
scientific inquiry, the life of these depths was visible. The
searing beams revealed my colored lights to be a school of
silver hatchet-fish, *Argyropelecus*, from a half to two inches
in length and gleaming like tinsel. The marvel of the searchlight
was that up to its sharp-cut border the blue-blackness revealed
nothing but the lights of the fish. In this species these burned
steadily, and each showed a colorful swath directed downward –

the little iridescent channels of glowing reflections beneath the source of the actual light. These jerked and jogged along until they reached the sharp-edged border-line of the searchlight's beam, and as they entered it, every light was quenched, at least to my vision, and they showed as spots of shining silver, revealing every detail of fin and eye and utterly absurd outline. When I switched off the electricity or the fish moved out of its path, their pyrotechnics again rushed into visibility. The only effect of the yellow rays was to deflect the path of each fish slightly away from their course. Like active little rays of light entering a new medium, the Argyros passed into the searchlight at right angles to my eye and left it headed slightly away. With them was a mist of jerking pteropods with their delicate shields, frisking in and out among the hatchet-fish like a pack of dogs around the mounts.

My hand turned the switch and I looked out into a world of inky blueness where constellations formed and reformed and passed without ceasing. At this moment I heard Miss Hollister's voice faintly seeping through Barton's head-phone, and it seemed as if the sun-drenched deck of the *Ready* must surely be hundreds of miles away.

I used the searchlight intermittently, and by waiting until I saw some striking illumination I could suddenly turn it on and catch sight of the author before it dashed away.

At 1,100 feet we surveyed our sphere carefully. There was no evidence of the hose coming inside, the door was dry as a bone, the oxygen tanks were working well and by occasional use of our palm-leaf fans, the air was kept sweet. The walls of the bathysphere were dripping with moisture, probably sweating from the heat of our bodies condensing on the cold steel. The chemicals were working well, and we had a grand shifting of legs and feet, and settled down for what was ahead of us.

In the darkness of these levels I had not been able to see the actual forms of the hatchet-fish, yet a glance out of the window now showed distinctly several rat-tailed macrourid-like fish twisting around the bend of the hose. They were distinct, and were wholly new to me. Their profiles were of no macrourid

I had ever seen. As I watched, from the sides of at least two, there flashed six or more dull greenish lights, and the effect on my eyes was such that the fish vanished as if dissolved into water, and the searchlight showed not a trace. I have no idea of what they were.

At 1,200 feet there dashed into the searchlight, without any previous hint of illumination, what I identified as *Idiacanthus*; or golden-tailed serpent dragon, a long, slender, eel-like form, which twisted and turned about in the glare, excited by some form of emotion. Twice it touched the edge and turned back as if in a hollow cylinder of light. I saw it when at last it left, and I could see no hint of its own light, although it possesses at least three hundred light organs. The great advantage of the electric light was that even transparent fins – as in the present case – reflected a sheen and were momentarily visible.

From this point on I tied a handkerchief about my face just below the eyes, thus shunting my breath downward and keeping the glass clear, for I was watching with every available rod and cone of both eyes, at what was going on outside the six-inch circle of the quartz.

At 1,250 feet several more of the silver hatchets passed, going upward, and shrimps became abundant. Between this depth and 1,300 feet not a light or an organism was seen: it was 50 feet of terrible emptiness, with the blue mostly of some wholly new color term – a term quite absent from any human language. It was probably sheer imagination but the characteristic most vivid was its transparency. As I looked out I never thought of feet or yards of visibility, but of the hundreds of miles of this color stretching over so much of the world. And with this I will try to leave color alone for a space.

Life again became evident around 1,300 feet and mostly luminous. After watching a dozen or more firefly-like flashes I turned on the searchlight and saw nothing whatever. These sparks, brilliant though they were, were kindled into conflagration and quenched in the same instant upon invisible bodies. Whatever made them was too small to reach my eyes, as was almost the host of copepods or tiny crustaceans through which we passed now and then. At one time I kept the electric light going for a full minute while we were descending, and I distinctly observed two zones of abundance and a wide interval of very scanty, mote-like life. When they were very close to the glass I could clearly make out the jerking movements of cope-pods, but they were too small to show anything more. The milky sagitta, or arrow worms, were more easily detected, the eye catching their swift dart and then focusing on their quiet forms. While still near 1300 feet a group of eight large shrimps passed, showing an indeterminate coloration. We never took large shrimps at these comparatively shallow levels in the trawling nets.

Barton had just read the thermometer as seventy-two degrees when I dragged him over to the window to see two more hatchet-fish and what I had at last recognized as round-mouths. These are the most abundant of deep-sea fish and we take them in our nets by the thousand. Flickering forms had been bother-ing me for some time, giving out no light that I could detect, and twisting and wriggling more than any shrimp should be able to do. Just as my eyes had at first refused to recognize pteropods by their right names, I now knew that several times in the last few hundred feet I had seen *Cyclothones*, or roundmouths. In the searchlight they invariably headed uplight, so that only their thin-lipped mouths and tiny eyes were turned toward me.

Before Barton went back to his instruments, three squids shot into the light, out and in again, changing from black to barred to white as they moved. They showed no luminescence.

At 10:44 we were sitting in absolute silence, our faces reflect-ing a faint bluish sheen. I became conscious of the pulse-throb in my temples and remember that I kept time to it with my fingers on the cold, damp steel of the window ledge. I shifted the handkerchief on my face and carefully wiped the glass, and at this moment we felt the sphere check in its course – we felt ourselves press slightly more heavily on the floor and the telephone said "1,400 feet." I had the feeling of a few more meters' descent and then we swung quietly at our lowest floor, over a quarter of a mile beneath the surface.

I pressed my face against the glass and looked upward and in the slight segment which I could manage I saw a faint paling of the blue. I peered down and again I felt the old longing to go further, although it looked like the black pit-mouth of hell itself – yet still showed blue. I thought I saw a new fish flapping close to the sphere, but it proved to be the waving edge of the Explorers' Club flag – black as jet at this depth.

My window was clear as crystal, in fact clearer, for, as I have said before and want to emphasize, fused quartz is one of the most transparent of all substances and transmits all wavelengths of sunlight. The outside world I now saw through it was, however, a solid, blue-black world, one which seemed born of a single vibration – blue, blue, forever and forever blue.

Once, in a tropical jungle, I had a mighty tree felled. Indians and convicts worked for many days before its downfall was accomplished, and after the cloud of branches, leaves, and dust had settled, a small, white moth fluttered up from the very heart of the wreckage. As I looked out of my window now I saw a tiny, semi-transparent jellyfish throbbing slowly past. I had seen numerous jellyfish during my descent and this one aroused only a mental note that this particular species was found at a greater depth than I expected. Barton's voice was droning out something, and when it was repeated I found that he had casually informed me that on every square inch of glass on my window there was a pressure of slightly more than six hundred and fifty pounds. The little moth flying unharmed from the terrific tangle, and the jellyfish drifting gently past seemed to have something in common. After this I breathed rather more gently in front of my window and wiped the glass with a softer touch, having in mind the nine tons of pressure on its outer surface!

However, it was not until I had ascended that the further information was vouchsafed me that the pressure of the water at our greatest depth, upon the bathysphere from all directions, was more than six and a half million pounds, or more concisely, 3366.2 tons. So far from bringing about an anticlimax of worry, this meant hardly more than the statement that the spiral nebula in Andromeda is 900,000 light years away. Nevertheless I am rather glad that this bit of information was withheld until I had returned to the surface. If I had known it at the time I think the two-tenths of a ton might have distracted my attention – that 400 pounds being fraught with rather a last-straw-on-the-camel's-back significance!

Like making oneself speak of earthrise instead of sunset, there was nothing but continued mental reassertion which made the pressure believable. A six-inch dragonfish, or Stomias, passed – lights first visible, then three seconds of *searchlight* for identification, then lights alone – and there seemed no reason why we should not swing the door open and swim out. The baited hooks waved to and fro, and the edge of one of the flags flapped idly and I had to call upon all my imagination to realize that instant, unthinkably instant death would result from the least fracture of glass or collapse of metal. There was no possible chance of being drowned, for the first drops would have shot through flesh and bone like steel bullets.

The duration of all this rather maudlin comment and unnecessary philosophizing occupied possibly ten seconds of the time we spent at 1,426 feet.

When, at any time in our earthly life, we come to a moment or place of tremendous interest it often happens that we realize the full significance only after it is all over. In the present instance the opposite was true and this very fact makes any vivid record of feelings and emotions a very difficult thing. At the very deepest point we reached I deliberately took stock of the interior of the bathysphere; I was curled up in a ball on the cold, damp steel, Barton's voice relayed my observations and assurances of our safety, a fan swished back and forth through the air and the ticking of my wrist-watch came as a strange sound of another world.

Soon after this there came a moment which stands out clearly, unpunctuated by any word of ours, with no fish or other creature visible outside. I sat crouched with mouth and nose wrapped in a handkerchief, and my forehead pressed close to the cold glass – that transparent bit of old earth which so sturdily held back nine tons of water from my face. There came to me at that instant a tremendous wave of emotion, a real appreciation of what was momentarily almost superhuman, cosmic, of the whole situation; our barge slowly rolling high overhead in the blazing sunlight, like the merest chip in the midst of ocean, the long cobweb of cable leading down through the spectrum to our lonely sphere, where, sealed tight, two conscious human beings sat and peered into the abyssal darkness as we dangled in mid-water, isolated as a lost planet in outermost space. Here, under a pressure which, if loosened, in a fraction of a second would make amorphous tissue of our bodies, breathing our own home-made atmosphere, sending a few comforting words chasing up and down a string of hose – here I was privileged to peer out and actually see the creatures which had evolved in the blackness of a blue midnight which, since the ocean was born, had known no following day; here I was privileged to sit and try to crystallize what I observed through inadequate eyes and interpret with a mind wholly unequal to the task. To the ever-recurring question, "How did it feel?", etc., I can only quote the words of Herbert Spencer, I felt like "an infinitesimal atom floating in illimitable space." No wonder my sole written contribution to science and literature at the time was, "Am writing at a depth of a quarter of a mile. A luminous fish is outside the window."

The return trip was made in forty-three minutes, an average of one foot every two seconds. Twice during the ascent I was aware of one or more indefinite, large bodies moving about at a distance. On the way down I had accredited them to an over-excited imagination, but after having the experience repeated on several deep dives I am sure that I did see shadowy shapes of large and very real living creatures. What they were I can only guess, and live in hopes of seeing them closer on some future descent.

We had ascended to 1,000 feet when Miss Hollister sent down word that a gull was flying about the *Ready*, and a moment later said that it was a young herring gull. I relayed the information that I had made a note of it – qualifying thus as the first ornithologist who had ever made a submarine bird note, and then contradicted it by remembering that when diving in a helmet off Marlborough in the Galàpagos I had recorded on my zinc tablet a passing visit from two penguins.

Immediately after, to a question as to what was happening, I retorted that two *Ipnops* had taken our hooks – this fish being one that we much desired but had not yet seen or caught. Down came the statement that one of the men had just scooped up a big deep-sea fish with his hands on the surface. I jeered – and then, seeing a luminous fish, snapped into an excited account of what began to come into view. When we returned to the surface I was astonished to discover that the capture of the deep-sea fish was not a rather pointless joke but a fact. In some way a giant specimen of the lanternfish, *Myctophum affine*, had got mixed up with the sphere or hose, and had come to the surface somewhat damaged. Once disabled it had *fallen up*, as is the horrible fate of deep-sea fish in trouble. It was the world's record for size.

We stepped out of the bathysphere at 11:52 after a submergence of almost two hours, with good air to breathe, perfect telephonic communication, and the memory of living scenes in a world as strange as that of Mars.

"Never will men be nearer death than those saved from the K13"

SAVED

David Masters

On 29 January 1917, K13, a steam-driven British submarine, sank when her engine-room ventilators were left open. Not only did she carry her normal complement of crew but observers from her makers, the shipbuilders Fairfields, making seventy-three men in all. Thirty-one men perished immediately but, as Masters recounts below, there then began a race against time and dying oxygen to save the remainder:

Although we live in an enlightened age, superstition is still rife, and not many people would care to dive for the first time in a submarine bearing the unlucky number thirteen. Yet in spite of the fact that sailors are generally credited with being more superstitious than most people, no thought of danger crossed the minds of the seventy-three men who during the First World War stepped aboard the British submarine K13 in order to carry out her trials. She was a wonderful craft, 334 feet long, just under 27 feet wide amidships, and as she lay at her moorings she displaced 1,880 tons.

Like her sister ships of the same type, she was one of the fastest submarines afloat, capable on the surface of overtaking most battleships in order to send them to their doom, able to take her place with the Grand Fleet and steam along with them at top speed without being left behind. This wonderful speed was attained by fitting her with steam turbines in addition to the usual oil engines and electric motors. Her stumpy funnels folded down when she was diving, and the introduction of steam made it essential to get fairly big ventilators. In order to dive she could take into her ballast tanks 800 tons of water in four minutes, but with a big submarine over 100 yards long, all divided into many compartments, diving was a delicate operation that depended for its safety upon all men carrying out their duties instantly. It was necessary that the crew should be quite conversant with their craft and that there should be perfect team work. But an absolutely new craft is bound to present some strange features to her first crew. In this case she was a new development in submarine practice, and it was probably the fact that the K13 was unfamiliar that brought about the ensuing disaster.

Built on the Clyde, she was taken along to the Gareloch to be put through her paces. The Gareloch was quiet, away from spying eyes, free of the attentions of the unwelcome enemy submarine, and here the K13 carried out her surface trials satisfactorily. The conning tower was closed, the funnels were dropped back flush with the deck, and orders were given to trim the boat for diving. The watertight doors were shut and the sea began to flow into the tanks. Then, as the craft submerged, came disaster. A mighty rush of water swept into the after part of the ship, drowning instantly the 31 men on duty there, and carrying the K13 stern downwards to the bottom. It was afterwards discovered that in diving some of the ventilating scuttles had been left open and these had flooded the stern of the ship. It was a tragic oversight that in a moment swept thirty-one men into eternity.

In the forward part of the K13 42 men were imprisoned, held fast on the sea-bed by the weight of water in the ship. There was no trace of panic. Nobody turned a hair. As quietly as though they still floated serenely on the surface, they stood by and carried out their commander's orders.

For hours they strove to get the ship to move to lighten the tanks sufficiently to bring her to the surface again. The ship remained fast. No trace of movement was to be detected. The watertight bulkhead across the centre of the vessel held death at bay for the moment, but no one knew how long it could withstand the terrific pressure. At the other side of the bulkhead lay their dead companions, and the hungry sea was waiting to engulf the living. Death threatened them from all quarters, death from drowning, death from asphyxiation owing to the exhaustion of their air supply, death from starvation even if the air held out. Hour by hour death came nearer. They realized it only too well, but still they remained cheerful.

When it was seen that all their efforts were useless, Commander Godfrey Herbert, D.S.O., who was in command, and Commander F.H.M. Goodhart, D.S.O., who was aboard to watch the behaviour of the vessel before taking over the command of the K14, conferred and agreed to try to get to the surface, 90 feet above their heads, in order to obtain help. They knew perfectly well that they were probably going to their deaths, that the odds were so tremendously against them that they were not worth considering. They did not think of themselves; they thought only of the 40 men caught in that death-trap.

The one way of getting to the surface was through the conning tower. But the terrific weight of the water above closed the lid so tightly that the strongest giant in the world would never lift it. To raise it was beyond the mere strength of human beings. The only way of accomplishing the feat was to let into the conning tower compressed air until the pressure of the air equalled the pressure of the sea, and as the air burst away upwards the gallant officers hoped to be carried to the surface with it.

Quietly they entered the conning tower, and partially flooded it. The compressed air was turned on. Minute by minute the pressure increased, minute by minute the officers waited, wondering if death or life was to be theirs, whether their attempt was to succeed or fail.

So great grew the pressure that the air could no longer be kept within bounds. With incredible strength it burst upwards and Commander Goodhart was dashed violently against the steel sides of the conning tower and killed instantly.

By the greatest good fortune Commander Herbert missed the full force of that deadly upthrust of air. Still, he too, was hurled upwards, and, as the water rushed in and the air gushed out, was carried clean through the conning tower to the surface.

Already the disappearance of K13 was arousing anxiety up above, and a salvage craft had been called to the spot. A couple of men in a boat, noticing the figure of Commander Herbert as he came up in the Gareloch, pulled quickly towards him and dragged him over the side. He was almost dead with exhaustion, and the wonder is that he survived that terrible ordeal.

As soon as he was sufficiently recovered, he gave an account of what had happened and told how the men were trapped in the submarine. The urgency of the case was obvious. It needed no stressing.

Then began a most thrilling salvage fight. It was a fight, not for treasure, but for human life. It was a race against time, a long tussle with death.

Divers dropped down the shot-ropes to the bed of the Gareloch and began to search for the sunken submarine. The light was none too good, owing to the water being fogged with mud, but they were searching only for a short time when the dark hull of the submarine loomed in front of them. They hurried up to it. One drew an axe from his belt, and hammered hard at the side.

Answering knocks came from within, and those waiting anxiously on the surface heaved a sigh of relief as the divers telephoned up: "We've found her. They're still alive!"

Surveying the wreck, the divers discovered that the bow of the submarine was about 20 feet higher than the stern, which was already covered by a dozen feet of mud. Wading in slime sometimes up to the armpits, the divers worked their way round her, then quickly sped to the surface and reported her position.

At once the experts summed up the situation. The K13 with her stern full of water, covered up aft by a dozen feet of mud, was too heavy to raise bodily. She was well over 3,000 tons, and up to that time nothing like this weight had ever been lifted from the seabed. The only thing to be done, the sole hope of saving the imprisoned men, was to strive to lift the nose of the craft to the surface, while leaving the stern resting on the bottom. Nothing else was possible.

"The first thing to do is to get through supplies of food and air to them," the salvage officer remarked.

The divers slid down to the bottom and, disregarding all thought of their own safety, laboured hard and long to connect up with the entombed men. They must have broken the endurance record, for one worked for over twelve hours continuously on the sea-bed without taking food, without resting. Time was too precious for them to waste a second. They realized the risk, but they accepted it as gladly as Commander Goodhart ran the risk which led to his death. They worked until they were ill and dizzy, floundering in the mud, wrestling with giant steel cables.

Forty men were depending on them for their lives. The thought nerved the divers to do prodigious things. It was essential to communicate with the imprisoned men, to let them know that everything possible was being done for them, to strive to sustain their spirits. Commander Kay of the Salvage Section found the way. Sending down a submarine flash-lamp, he instructed the divers to rig it up in front of the periscope. By peering into this instrument the prisoners were thus able to read the messages that were flashed to them in Morse Code, and were made to understand that they were not entirely cut off from the world after all. With many a struggle, the divers managed to open a valve in the hull and to attach a pipe through which food such as Bovril, bottles of hot soup and chocolate, as well as life-giving air, were passed from the surface. All this entailed long hours of endeavour.

The coolness of the men in the submarine was almost unbelievable.

"Send us down a pack of cards to while away the time," one shouted up the pipe.

The cards were procured and sent down, and these British seamen played cards while Death peeped over their shoulders.

Up until then the men had been carefully conserving their supplies of compressed air, not knowing how long they would need them to keep alive. Now that air was being pumped from the surface, they were able to use what was left of their own supplies to blow all the oil out of the forward tanks. This lightened their craft considerably.

After a terrific struggle, the divers managed to fix mighty steel cables under the nose of the submarine. Salvage craft and lifting vessels strained away. For a time they made no impression. Then slowly the grip of the mud began to relax and the bow of the submarine, lightened by the blowing out of the oil tanks, began to rise nearer and nearer the surface until, about midnight, it broke clear into view.

It was a weird sight. Great arc lamps lit the scene, and under their glare the salvage men attacked the steel hull of the K13 with oxy-acetylene blow-pipes. Everyone was desperately anxious, afraid that the submarine might slip. Under the intense heat of the blow-pipes, the steel grew soft and melted. Gradually, laboriously, the salvors burned their way through the stout outer plates.

They now made an onslaught on the inner hull, directing the flame on the steel shell. The metal glowed and flowed. A rush of air leaped upwards from the interior of the vessel and blew out the roaring flame of the blow-pipe.

"Get us some matches!" the divers called to those above.

Under their very noses a hand from inside the ship suddenly slid through the hole in the metal, the fingers holding up a box of matches.

"Here you are," said a cheery voice, and the divers knew that all was well.

Another period of strenuous endeavour and the hole in the metal was big enough for a man to squeeze through. Then, as the forty prisoners were helped and carried to freedom, the cheers of the salvage men echoed to the shore.

Never will men be nearer death than those saved from the K13. For fifty-seven hours they were imprisoned in the sunken submarine at the bottom of the sea, for two and a half days they lived with death at their elbows, not knowing when the end would come.

"The moray was almost as tall as I am"

DIVING TO ADVENTURE

Hans Hass

Second only to Cousteau, the Austrian diver Hass was the man responsible for bringing the ocean into the modern home; his books and TV films were staple viewing in the 1950s and 1960s. The extracts below are from Hass' first book, Diving to Adventure, *and tell of a long sojourn in Curaçao, a Dutch island in the Caribbean, on the very eve of World War II.*

At the mouth of the *boca* we pulled up the boat on a little bright, sandy beach. We were now directly on the sea, which was comparatively calm. Only beyond the opening of the channel the waves broke in white spray. This was the starting point of a coral reef, which went out in a broad curve along the coast. On our side of the mouth there seemed to be no coral reefs, so we had first to cross the channel, whose water looked fairly turbid and muddy. Over at the reefs, however, it was clear; we could see that plainly by the blue colour. Another companion, who was following our hunting preparations attentively, mentioned that sharks very seldom came as far as the mouth of the *boca*. So much the better!

I slid into the water, and Alfred followed. Within a very few strokes of our fins the steeply shelving sand bottom vanished from our sight, and all was impenetrably grey around us, just as in Puerto Cabello. We kept close together, constantly peering in every direction. The disagreeable part was that in this water we could not judge how far we really saw. Nowhere was there a fish or any other indication of what distance a creature would appear at if it were coming towards us; very possibly it might suddenly take shape directly beside us! We hurried along, and could see plainly by the surface how far we still were from clear water. The dividing line must be very abrupt. The closer it came, the more excited we grew. And then the grey clouds did indeed flow away, and the dirty wall of fog remained behind us.

We paused.

There are pictures you never forget all your life; this was one. Before us, or rather diagonally below us, lay a most remarkable reddish forest, some of whose trees grew nearly up to the surface. These trees did not in the least recall seaweed or such growing things as you see on land. They were perfectly rigid, and their gnawed, shovel-like branches thrust out in all direc-tions like antlers. They were trees of stone – corals.

Stiff, motionless, and like a lunar landscape as this forest on the ocean floor seemed, the surface sunlight dancing upon it and the variegated life among the branches were all the gayer and livelier. Fish large and small whisked hither and thither every-where, some of them so dainty and colourful that they reminded you more of butterflies than of water creatures. As if in some blissful waltz they swung through the enchanted grove. Some of them appeared for only a moment, then vanished again in the uncertain shade of the branches; of others I never saw anything but the eyes, dancing like will-o'-the-wisps in the darkness of the wood.

And it was perfectly still in this forest. Over the whole bright bustle there spread a mysterious, unearthly, Sleeping Beauty silence.

I caught my breath, and carefully glanced at the shore. There stood a few dry bushes, and beyond them dirty-grey cacti. A piebald bird was walking up and down along the beach, uttering loud, cawing cries. I slipped under again, and dived back into this other world.

I came close now to one of the coral trees, and touched a branch with my finger-tip. It was at once rough and slippery. So this was a coral branch! At that moment a monstrous head appeared below the branch. I clutched my harpoon tighter, but the head had already vanished, and in its stead there was a fat, radiantly blue fish, nibbling with yellowish teeth at one of the rust-red branches. This activity seemed to occupy his whole attention. Now and then he would swim backwards a little, as if to observe the spot he was gnawing at from a slightly greater distance; then he would suddenly rush forward again, and his teeth would rasp over the rough surface. I was about to aim my harpoon when I saw just above him a winged crab. Or could that be a fish too? Or perhaps two, embracing each other?

An involuntary motion on my part, and the mysterious creature was gone. Where to? It had suddenly dissolved into nothingness, like the reflections of the sun that danced about in the coral forest like many-coloured kobolds, appearing unexpectedly and as suddenly vanishing again. But wait! Over there was a gigantic fish. I could plainly see its tail fin jutting out behind a tree; it waved steadily to and fro, recalling a big, soft fan. With pounding heart and harpoon at the ready I sneaked around the tree. But instead of a fish I saw nothing but more fins of the same kind – they were some sort of fan-like coral growing up from the bottom like great leaves, not stiff, but swinging elastically to and fro in the swell.

I came up, and waited until Alfred, too, appeared on the surface again. But he did not even notice me. I only saw him gasp hastily for breath, then he was gone below the waves again, like a walrus or a dolphin, only surfacing briefly in all haste to catch another breath.

So I dived again, too, and swam on, peering attentively into the darkness of the forest. Then I swam in among the trees, pursuing this and that fish, but I could never spear any, because before I got round to the thrust I was always distracted by some other creature. You would have had to wear blinkers to shut out the bewildering multiplicity. I came to an open spot covered over with the most remarkable corals. Some of them looked like flowers, others were a sort of hedge, others again recalled shed antlers. Among them, arranged in tufts, were yellow plates, along with blubbery, finger-like growths and big balls, some of which displayed the meandering pattern of a human brain.

I felt everything, and burned my fingers on the yellow plates. Strange, unknown creatures appeared, luring me on. I saw corals that I had never dreamed of, and wonderful, powerful fish passing by out yonder in the deeper water. Only sharks were not to be seen.

We swam across a flat, tiresome bottom, with merely some spherical coral shapes sprinkled among green and grey plants, and then reached a sharp edge thirty or thirty-five feet down, along which the bottom fell away abruptly. As it was already fairly late, the scene under water was sombre and uncanny. We looked around frequently; I had a vague feeling that a shark was bound to turn up suddenly somewhere. It was strange enough that we had not met a single one as yet.

Suddenly Joerg pointed downwards. A broad, dark shape had appeared in the distance and came swimming along the pitch just above the bottom – a big ray, beating the water with its winglike sides. Like a ghost in the night it fluttered along the bottom, its long, whiplike tail behind it. On this tail the creature has a poisonous spine, provided with such a dreadful barb that it can be removed only in the direction it was driven in. If you are struck in the leg – says Brehm's famous book on animals – you have to pierce a hole from the opposite side of the leg, and pull the spine out straight through. What you are to do if you get a spine in the stomach the author does not say.

I did not dawdle, but dived to meet the ray. He took no notice of me, going calmly on his way. Even when I drove the harpoon with great force into his body, he paid no attention. It was several seconds before he noticed what had happened. Then, indeed, he quickened his pace, and headed directly for deep water. As so often before, I clutched the harpoon shaft, and tried to check the creature's speed. But the ray was considerably the stronger, and easily pulled me after him. What had become of Joerg? We kept going down and down, and I was quite out of breath.

I looked round, but Joerg was nowhere to be seen. Then, all at once, I noticed he was beside me. He reached for the rope, I let go, and he was pulled away below me. I caught a flash of him bracing himself with desperate strokes of his fins against the water, then I shot to the surface as fast as I could go.

When, after a few deep breaths, I stared downwards again, I saw a trail of mud leading across the bottom far below me. Joerg and the ray were almost out of sight. I raced frantically after, and when I finally overtook draft animal and driver, Joerg was already at the end of his strength. I took over the rope, and he shot upwards. Then he came back, and I shot upwards. We went up and down several times; we passed the rope to each other like the baton in a relay race. And slowly it turned out that the ray was tiring. His movements grew heavier, the pull weaker, he flapped around in circles, lashing his tail, and after half an hour we had the great creature in shallow water, and pulled it ashore fairly exhausted. As the ray was still lashing around, we threw the harpoon across its tail, pressed it to the ground, and Joerg cut it off. Not until then could we kill the brute.

As Joerg was slightly put out that he had not harpooned the ray, we swam out again immediately, although by now it was very dark and uncanny indeed. Sure enough, we met a second ray, even bigger, even darker, fiercer-looking. Joerg harpooned it with a delight that made it plainly evident how eagerly he had longed for this moment, and for safety's sake I drove my harpoon into the creature's back as well. Thus we were able to hold on by two ropes. But this ray was too strong for us. It pulled us with irresistible force down the slope into the depths, and there was nothing for it but to cut the lines, so that we lost two heads at once.

When native fishermen came past in their boats, and saw us swimming around among the reefs, they usually rowed over to warn us against the "tribon", the shark. But day after day passed without our seeing a single one. We ventured farther and farther out into deep water, and our excitement kept growing, until finally the great moment really came.

There were three of us, just turning a reef, when a big body materialized out of the distance and came towards us with calm, steady movements. By the blue colour we could see that it was a blue shark – a man-eater. How often I had studied its picture in Brehm's *Animal Life*.

This was it.

I don't know what got into me. From everything I knew about sharks I should really have been afraid. But this creature was so handsome, so graceful, looked so unlike a bloodthirsty man-killer, that for the moment I could think only how fine a photograph of it would be. I forgot I had not even a knife on me, and I swam towards the shark, armed only with the camera. I had not the slightest misgivings; the voice of reason was completely silenced.

Every detail I saw in those seconds stamped itself indelibly upon me. To this moment I can see the plump body fairly exuding power, the sharp pectoral fins, thrusting forward on both sides like the fins of a bomb. I see the big, crescent tail fin, almost imperceptibly beating the water, and the dorsal fin, curved backwards – the dreaded "black triangle above the waves". The shark's body was perfectly streamlined in shape; as the creature was swimming between me and deep water, it stood out in the round against the background; its outlines were bathed in sunlight.

Abominable beast? No! Without doubt it was the most beautiful of all living animals!

The shark came closer; strangely enough, I did not see its eyes. They must have been too small, hidden somewhere between the pointed nose and the five sharply marked gill openings in the shadow. I could make out the maw below. Twenty feet . . . Fifteen feet . . . Closer and closer the shark came!

When the thirteen-foot creature was within what my companions judged to be eight feet of me, its massive body gave a sudden jerk. With a cat-like suppleness quite incompatible with the calm majesty of its previous movements, the shark spun around almost on the spot. A few quick fin strokes vibrated audibly through the water, then it was out of sight.

Not until we got to the surface did we really take in what had just happened. The shark, the king of the sea, had fled before a small, unarmed human being. How could that be?

Actually the explanation was obvious enough. The shark is accustomed to having all creatures flee before him; it has always been so since time immemorial. And now, suddenly, it had met a strange creature that had shown no fear, but actually swam at it as if to attack. This must have been most unusual to the shark. Was the simple-minded creature not bound to think that this strange being was stronger than it?

After this we often met sharks, and always with the same result: no matter whether they were large or small, blue, grey, or the light-grey ones especially feared on some coasts, they all fled when we swam towards them, just as if we, not they, were the dreaded tigers of the sea. This reached such a point that I had real difficulty in getting good shark photographs. I soon discovered that one seldom comes as close as had been the case in our first encounter; usually the creatures turned away at a distance of fifty or sixty feet. Once, when, as usual, I was vainly trying to photograph a shark, Joerg summoned me to him for some reason or other. I left the creature behind, hurried towards Joerg, and found that the shark, so timid but a moment ago, now came after me in a most interested fashion. The faster I tried to get away, the faster it followed. This discovery led me to a method that may be classed with applied animal psychology. Henceforth if I wanted to photograph a shark I pretended to flee as conspicuously as possible, thus awakening the instinct in every beast of prey to chase what tries to escape. And I actually succeeded thus in luring sharks after me. When I saw that they were close enough, I would suddenly spin and swim towards them with camera at the ready. And before the creatures had recovered from their surprise and turned away in disgust I already had their image on film.

I must admit that some months later, when we were hunting on the stormy north coast of Curaçao, it turned out that sharks are not always so good-natured. Once, after a successful stalking hunt, we were swimming back to the coast, and since I had a lot of fish with me, I lagged behind my companions. Suddenly I noticed that two sharks had appeared behind me. They followed, looking like twin brothers. Both were equally big, equally grey, both approached simultaneously, both turned away simultaneously when I hit out in their direction with my fins. Obviously the blood of the dead fish was what attracted them. They kept coming back, and since I felt perfectly safe, I even let them get close to the fish several times, and then snatched them away from in front of the sharks' noses. I never dreamed for a moment that the situation might grow dangerous. And yet it did. As a strong surf was running, the water was turbid for some distance from shore; besides, it was just ebb tide, and muddy water was coming out of the neighbouring cove, whence the current carried it along the coast. In short, about a hundred and fifty feet from shore I got into muddy water that lay like a wall of cloud between me and the coast. I had to get through this dark zone. I strove to scare away the sharks, but now they seemed more interested in my company than ever. Giving up the fish was obviously out of the question. There was nothing for it but to swim into the foggy water despite the sharks, relying on the creatures' cowardice. But at the moment when I could see nothing, and thus lost my own assurance, the timidity of the twins vanished. The two of them now appeared unexpectedly behind me, beside me, below me, and finally even in front of me, always close together, with wily, wicked eyes. I pulled my fish close to me, swivelled my head frantically in all directions, and swam as fast as my fins would carry me. But I grew so nervous that I finally thought I saw the sharks even where they were not. I hit about me with the fins like a madman. The more scared I got, the saucier grew the twins.

It was a hundred and fifty feet to the coast, and then another hundred to the place where one got out of the water – a short, and yet, I can assure you, extraordinarily long, distance!

*   *   *

While we were still camping at Jan Thiel, Curaçao, I once harpooned a fish that fled into the nearest cleft in the coral and literally stuck there. Only its tail projected from the hole. I tugged at it, and also at the line, but I could not get the fish out. I looked to see whether it had wedged itself in after the fashion of the grouper, but this was not the answer either.

So I braced my feet right and left against the coral, and this time tugged quite violently at the tail. Sure enough, the creature emerged inch by inch. But when I relaxed for a second it promptly snapped back to its former position. Yet the fish was stiff and lifeless – a complete mystery. The brute seemed to have a rubber band fastened to its head, keeping it in the hole.

I tugged again, and again the fish snapped back. But this time I saw why it was: a great snake, hidden in the cleft, was holding my fish by the nose and pulling it back each time. This snake-like creature – a fish, actually – had the most malignant eyes I had ever seen.

It was a moray.

The first time I ever saw a moray was in the pictures, when I was a small boy. It was for Adults Only, and I had sneaked in with an old hat of my father's. The film was a rather sexy affair laid in ancient Rome, in which we saw a banquet with lavish courses and exceedingly voluptuous dancing girls. During the dinner the morays were also fed. Hundreds of serpentine shapes boiled on the surface of a pond; sharp, poisonous teeth sparkled in avidly gaping maws, and then some slaves were tossed into the pond. Human flesh to fatten the morays! The corpulent Romans hooted, the slaves struggled, and the voluptuous girls danced. The scene was very gruesome; the director had done himself proud. And yet he forgot the most effective bit of all. He should have shown the morays' eyes, incomparably cold and malignant, the way I once saw them . . .

It was the day after Mynheer Gezaghebber's visit. I was fishing alone on the north shore of our islet, fairly late in the afternoon. The reefs rose dark and silhouette-like from the ocean floor. I was swimming twenty-five feet under, intending just to go as far as the corner of this particular reef and then return to shore with the two fish I already had, when I saw something I shall never forget.

A big snapper, weighing easily thirty pounds, which had swum rather slowly up from the depths, suddenly whipped the water with a frightened blow of its fins and raced off with every sign of terror. At the spot where it had just been there gaped the yawning jaws of a giant moray whose body rose erect from a cleft in the reef, a ghostly silhouette with the light behind it.

Before I realized what I was doing I had driven my harpoon through the monster's fat green throat. That very instant the harpoon was snatched from my hand to go dancing off among the coral masses. Then all was still again, and I saw the harpoon cord now leading into a hole from which a thin thread of blood curled up.

I struggled to get the creature out of its hiding place, but an hour passed without bringing me the slightest success. My nose was beginning to bleed from constant diving, and the sun sank ever closer to the horizon. Finally I gave one last yank, with redoubled fury, at the harpoon line, and suddenly the whole coral mass exploded as if by dynamite, and the moray, which had produced this blast with its own frenzied power, shot out of the ruins straight at me.

Not until now did I realize what a monster I had tangled with. The moray was as tall as I am.

It rushed me at once; I parried with the harpoon shaft. And so began a regular duel. Again and again the brute tried to get at me by every imaginable feint. For instance, several times the moray shot perpendicularly down, dragging me after it, then turned like a flash and shot straight up again, at me. It came from every quarter, squirming through the water like a snake, with venomous eyes and wide-open jaws. I defended myself with the harpoon shaft, and toiled to drag the raging creature towards shore.

Twice the moray got quite close to me, and then, finally, I had it up to the reef, and flung it over into the shallow water of the lagoon. Unfortunately I now discovered that the lagoon bottom, like that at Jan Thiel, was paved with thousands of sea urchins. How was I to get across with the savage moray?

Since the sun was already approaching the horizon, I had little time for reflection. I was determined not to give up the moray; Joerg and Alfred simply must see it. I looked across the lagoon again, hunting some possible way over the grisly black fields, and resolved to try it in spite of all. I wound the harpoon line as often as I could around the shaft, to give the moray less play, and off I started on my arduous journey.

For a while I managed, then I reached a spot where there seemed to be no clear space at all among the sea urchins. Just one little round ball of coal arose from the bed of spines. I stepped cautiously upon it, shifted my weight, and then my foot skidded off the slippery surface, and I lost my balance. To break my fall and shield face and body from the spines, I flung my arms forward; they were impaled in twenty places. At the same time I involuntarily pulled back the harpoon, and this gave the moray a chance to get at me.

As I opened my eyes wide with pain in the water, I saw slavering jaws and wicked, venomous eyes just in front of my face.

Somehow I managed to stretch my arm away, and so to pull the creature back by the harpoon shaft at the last moment. I still wonder how I did it. The eyes of that moray I shall never forget. Their expression was so evil, so hateful, that it would be hard to imagine anything more fiendish. I believe there are only two other living things capable of such a look – the fabled sea serpent and man.

On the one hundred and tenth and one hundred and thirteenth day of our expedition we had two unusual experiences.

The first began with me swearing most blasphemously. For one thing because the dorado-like fish I was labouring over could not be made to see that picture-taking is a perfectly innocent pastime; and for another, because each time I did manage, with great difficulty, to get within snapping distance of the fish, a cloud would invariably pass over the sun. That day turned me into a meteorologist. Shivering and squinting up-wards, I marked the formation and movement of the clouds in detail, longingly following the passage of the little blue holes among them. Whenever I saw one of these holes moving towards the fiery ball of sun that shone behind the clouds, I would take a deep breath, dive, and creep up, in order to snap the shutter if the seascape turned bright and sunny for a moment. Mostly, however, these holes missed the sun, or the fish would just be vanishing in a coral crack, showing me nothing but their hastily disappearing tail fins. An easy job it was not.

Suddenly I noticed out in the deep sea a peculiar three-pointed dorsal fin, almost motionless above the waves. Little as I know of zoology, I did know that there is no creature with a three-pointed dorsal fin. So what could it be? The jagged comb of a gigantic lizard? Possibly the sea serpent?

Joerg and Alfred were nowhere to be seen, so I ventured out alone. It was a long trip across bottomless water, which seemed doubly far to me because my heart was pounding twice as fast as usual. Once the three-pointed hat upon the waves disappeared, and I was afraid my curiosity was not going to be satisfied, but then, luckily, it bobbed up again. Finally came the eagerly awaited moment when the first delicate outlines stood out under water in the distance. I stared ahead. Why, there was not one three-pointed creature swimming there, but two others as well, completely under water. Each, in addition to its three-pointed dorsal fin, had also a three-pointed fin on its tail!

After a moment's blank amazement I realized what was what. It was not individual creatures I saw, but groups of three dolphins each, snuggling so close together that a group looked like a single creature. And these dolphins moved so evenly that they seemed to be glued side to side. Not until the click of my camera cut the silence did the groups suddenly break up and the creatures shoot perpendicularly into the depths, where the blue-black abyss swallowed them within a matter of seconds. Some time later they reappeared, enormously swift and supple, and came straight up towards me. At the same time I heard a definite squeaking in the water, rather like the cries of young pigs.

The second experience began at midnight with a curse from Joerg. Someone had burst into our cabin, turned on the light, and waked us out of a sound sleep. He was a member of the ship's crew. Could we keep quiet? he asked us. When Joerg, instead of keeping quiet, began to bellow, he asked whether we wanted to make ten guilders.

That was another matter. To us ten guilders was the same as catching, lugging, and selling thirty-five pounds of fish. Joerg fell silent.

Fifteen minutes later, in beach robes, and carrying spears, we left the ship, which was then lashed alongside the pier to discharge cargo. The customs official who was standing guard at the gangway blankly looked at us and then after us, but as we were considered crazy anyway, he thought it quite possible that we might be going fishing at midnight. So he only shook his head, relaxed, and went back to sleep.

It was a matter of smuggling. Our nocturnal visitor had tried to smuggle paint ashore from the ship, and his little skiff had tipped over, sinking to the bottom of the harbour along with the heavy paint cans. But it happened that he had collected an advance payment of half the price for his goods and had already turned the advance into alchohol. First he had gone to a native diver, who, however, demanded sixty guilders. So the man reflected that the Viennese students would undoubtedly do it cheaper. And, as you see, he was right as rain.

It was perfectly dark, without a star; only a few lanterns burned on the far side of the pier. We groped for a while through the darkness, then the man stopped on the edge of the pier. This was the place, he whispered. The paint cans, he said, were about thirty-five feet out; the water was about thirty feet deep. The fact that a half-inch scum of oil lay on top of the water the man chose not to mention; I soon discovered it, with little or no satisfaction, when I started swimming, as I usually do, with my mouth open. I had volunteered for the first attempt, and regretted it even before I dived. The water below me was perfectly black. What might not be lying or prowling on the bottom of the harbour? What would be the first thing I touched when I got below?

The fellow called from the shore in an undertone that I was exactly over the spot. I waved my arms irresolutely in the water, causing it to gleam brightly around me, because the sea was phosphorescent that night.

Getting a grip on myself, I dived with a quick turn. The farther I went into that black soup, where only a tiny dot of light flashed here and there, the slower grew my movements. Suppose something were to touch my face? I groped cautiously ahead with my hands. And suddenly I was startled as one almost never is. All grew suddenly bright around me! I had expected anything, but not that. Whence came this glow? Here, in the pitch-black night, twenty-five feet down in the black harbour water?

I could see plainly all about me for twenty-five or thirty feet. Just below lay the flat, sandy bottom, and close ahead of me three paint cans. I quickly grabbed two in my right hand and the third in my left hand, and pushed off from the bottom with all my might. The brightness fell away below me, and I rose again into the murk. But the very next moment I was in brightness again. I had expected too much of myself; all three cans at once were too heavy. They pulled me straight down again. So I dropped one of them, and pushed off again.

This time the darkness held me. I swam upwards, swam as hard as I could, swam, swam – and suddenly realized that I could not tell whether I was moving up at all. Above and below and round about me lay uniform pitch blackness. Everywhere the water had the same disgusting smell, and everywhere the same tiny creatures gleamed. But only so briefly that I could form no idea of my motion. I could not even tell by the pressure in my ears whether I was moving up, because my ears were already roaring and whistling from want of breath. Now there was an uncanny ringing about me, and I wondered briefly why I did not drop the paint cans. Then the ringing grew louder.

When I regained consciousness, I was lying on the pier, and

Joerg was working over me. I had a revolting oily taste in my throat – obviously I had swallowed water. Joerg told me that after an absolutely endless absence I had come to the surface for just a moment, and had then sunk away again, gurgling. He had jumped in after me and pulled me out. Along with the two paint cans, which I still clutched rigidly. They weighed nearly sixty pounds.

Then Joerg went down for the third paint can, and saw the same strange brightness. Where might it come from? We do not really know. Presumably the light of the innumerable little luminous animals in the water, reflected in all directions by the sandy bottom, creates a faintly lit zone. But perhaps it was the ghost lanterns of drowned pirates, wanting to give me a good view of the paint cans and then drown me in the attempt.

On this our farewell day the north coast is perfectly calm for a change, and the visibility under water is gloriously clear. Even close to the cliffs, where the breakers usually befog everything. And everywhere among the cleft rocks and shattered stone fragments the water gleams with fish large and small, some of them shimmering in the colours of the rainbow. Joerg and Alfred have each shot a tarpon, so that I hardly know which one to photograph. A funny situation: each of them is drawn hither and thither through the water by his tarpon, with each fish in turn leaping into the air like a silver streak. There are sharks, too, including the smallest I have ever seen, a baby eighteen inches long.

Unfortunately my camera is not at its best. It, too, seems weary of long service. I hastily rush ashore, open the box, and give the spring another little poke.

Then I am back in the water, arriving just in time for a spectacle such as we will never see again. In a little cove, below a cliff, rests a medium-sized grouper. Alfred hands me his tarpon, and sneaks up on the creature. All eyes are upon him: our eyes, those of the grouper, still undecided as yet, the eyes of the many bright-coloured fish around – and also one hidden pair of eyes. Quite unexpectedly a massive blue body fades in out of a cleft in the cliff, swoops forward, and the grouper vanishes like greased lightning, and just as Alfred is about to thrust, he has before his harpoon not the grouper but a thirteen-foot blue shark! For a moment Alfred shoots upwards with a sudden motion.

I just have time to hear him say something about "of all the nerve", then I am under water myself, pursuing the big blue shark, who propels his fat body into deep water. I snap twice, then hurry back.

"We're better men than the sharks, all the same!" Joerg grins at me, having meanwhile caught Alfred's grouper.

"Quick, look, look!" Alfred interrupts, waving his arms excitedly.

Close behind us a creature has suddenly appeared that reminds one more of a steam roller than of any fish. It is a hammerhead! And bigger than the one we saw with Meyringh! Its body is almost as thick as we are tall – like the trunk of an ancient oak. And of course the camera balks again. I pound furiously on the case with my fist, and the steam roller slowly swims off.

Here indeed is a situation worthy of an anniversary and a farewell hunt. Round about us the crystal water, ahead and to one side the little cove with the great rock mass and the many bright, shimmering fish. On Joerg's harpoon the medium-sized grouper, on Alfred's face even now the traces of his utter amazement, at my belt the bunch of fish with the big tarpon. And then the tiny, the big blue, and the even bigger steam roller hammerhead shark. And now this illustrious company is joined by a three-foot hawkbill turtle. Slowly, overgrown with barnacles, it paddles through the water, and Joerg and Alfred are off after it, trying to take it alive.

How happy I am that this expedition came true! How fully every effort has been repaid! Everything we had hoped for has happened.

". . . the air bubbles attracted the attention of the watch aft:
He switched on a searchlight and we surfaced right into its rays"

THE SEA DEVILS

Junio Valerio Borghese

Count Borghese was the head of the Italian Navy's underwater
division during World War II. Below Borghese recounts the raid
by Italian "human torpedoes" – frogmen riding electric underwater
chariots – on the British Mediterranean Fleet at Alexandria,
Egypt, on 18–19 December 1941:

The operation against Alexandria was most carefully thought
out. The most important requirement was the maintenance of
absolute secrecy, that indispensable co-efficient of success in
any action, and particularly in those where the vulnerability of a
handful of half-naked men, plunged underwater in the dark
depths of an enemy harbour, had to overcome armour-plates,
barriers and a hundred methods of watching for and spotting
them, and also thousands of people on dry land, operating from
cover and behind defences on mole and ships, whose business it
was to discover and destroy the assailant.

Wide use was made of air reconnaissance for the obtaining of
information and photographs with a view to keeping us informed about the usual moorings of vessels and the nature of the
protective measures employed (net obstructions, etc.). Great
care was also taken in preparing materials: the human torpedoes, which were now in good shape, as had been verified
during the last mission to Gibraltar, were brought to the highest
level of efficiency.

The *Scirè* was again appointed to carry out the approach. Her gallant crew, now thoroughly accustomed to such experiences, remained unchanged. All its members, after their usual period of rest in the Alto Adige, were in excellent physical trim.

The senior group of pilots had been given a long training by myself in carrying out exercises similar to the performances they would have to accomplish at Alexandria (they were, however, not told the final object of the courses and defence negotiating they were ordered to do). In other words, practice took place at night in the actual conditions prevalent in the enemy harbour, their difficulties being, wherever possible, increased. Thus, while the operators were being trained to economize their strength in view of the prolonged and difficult nature of the assigned task, we ourselves were obtaining the data necessary for the study of the plan of operations and had the opportunity of verifying, as if we had made a survey on the spot, the methods to be adopted for the job, the periods required to complete the various stages and the precautions needed to circumvent difficulties and elude enemy detection, as well as, lastly, to check the degrees of skill acquired by individual operators.

One day we called them all together; Forza made the following very brief speech to them: "Now, boys, we want three crews for an operation in the very near future; all I can tell you about it is that it differs from the Gibraltar operations in the fact that return from it is extremely problematical. Is there anyone who would like to take part in it?" Without an instant's hesitation they all volunteered. Accordingly, we of the Command had the delicate task of making a selection. Finally, the crews were as follows: Lieutenant Luigi Durand de la Penne and P.O./diver Emilio Vianchi; Engineer Captain Antonio Marceglia and P.O./diver Spartaco Schergat; Gunner Captain Vincenzo Martellotta and P.O./diver Mario Marino.

These men were chosen because they were the pick of the bunch. De la Penne, leader of the group, was a veteran of the previous missions to Gibraltar and the rest were all equally vigorous, steady and resolute fellows, in mind as in body. It was pure chance that the three officers represented three different services of the Navy: deck, engines and guns.

The reserve crew consisted of Surgeon Sub-Lieutenant Spaccarelli and Engineer Lieutenant Feltrinelli, both belonging to a lower age group than the others but equally keen.

The usual instructions were given: absolute secrecy was to be maintained without exception for anyone, whether comrades, superior officers or, naturally, relatives; training, now openly designed for this particular operation, was to be intensified; each man's private affairs were to be settled in view of his imminent departure for a length of time which could not be foreseen; at worst, it might be for ever, at best there would be some years of imprisonment.

Meanwhile, all the wheels of the machine began to go round. This kind of operation, if it were to have any decent chance of success, had to be thought out to the last detail; the whole of an extensive organization had to be got ready; there were a thousand details to be studied and put into practice: from the collection of hydrographic and meteorological data to intelligence as to enemy vigilance; from the taking of aerial photographs of the harbour to the arrangement of safe and extremely rapid channels of radio liaison with the submarine, so that the latter could be informed, immediately before the operators were dropped, as to the number and disposition of units on the night of the operation; from the determination of suitable ciphers to getting materials ready for action; from composition of the series of operational orders to the training of operators so as to bring them to the maximum of physical efficiency by the pre-arranged day; from the study of navigation and the best routes of approach for the submarine and those for the forcing of the harbour by the pilots, to research on new devices for causing the enemy maximum damage should the occasion arise; in a word, the proceedings were exactly the opposite of what the phrase "assault craft" might be supposed to mean; there was to be nothing in the nature of making a dash, nothing was to be left to chance, all impulsiveness was to be held in check; on the contrary, everything was to be coolly calculated and every technical and ingenious resource was to be exploited to the fullest extent possible.

During this preparatory phase, we were afflicted by the grievous loss of a valued collaborator; this was Lieutenant Sogos, belonging to the Command of the Tenth. While he was in transit to Athens for consultation with the military authorities there, his young and promising life was cut short by a wretched traffic accident.

At last the time came to start. On 3 December the *Scirè* left La Spezia, ostensibly on an ordinary cruise, so as not to arouse curiosity among the crews of the other submarines at the base.

My gallant, steady and reliable crew neither knew nor wished to know where we were going, so as not to be burdened with a secret which, like all secrets, would be difficult to keep; they only knew that we were on another dangerous operation, perhaps as dangerous as the former ones, perhaps more so; they had confidence in their commander and in their vessel, to which each of them had devoted every care during the period of preparation, knowing well that it was on the proper functioning of the elements of which it was composed that the outcome of the venture, its success and the very lives of all aboard depended.

We had scarcely left harbour, at twilight, so as to elude any indiscreet watchers, when a lighter approached us; it was carrying the human torpedoes 221, 222 and 223, which had just left the works at San Bartolomeo in the pink of condition, as well as the operators' clothing and breathing sets; such was the slight equipment necessary to transform three pairs of men into three engines of destruction.

The operators checked over their craft with a sort of tender solicitude. Each possessed his own; he had done his training with it and knew its good points, its shortcomings and its caprices; he placed it in the appropriate cylinder (de la Penne's was forward, those of Marceglia and Martellotta astern), settling it in such a way as to avoid risking shocks and injury to it. Finally, late at night, everything was fixed to rights; we took leave of the lads, who would rejoin us at the last moment by 'plane, and set out, hugging Tino Island, along the safety route through the minefields. It was 2300 hours on 3 December 1941. "Operation EA 3", the third attempt of the Tenth Light Flotilla against Alexandria and the ships of the British Eastern Mediterranean Fleet, had begun.

We proceeded normally along the courses set until we made the Sicilian coast; here a curious episode occurred which is worth relating. The Cape Pelorias signal station sent out a Donath (nocturnal signalling lamp) message in clear: "Submarine *Scirè*." A piece of madness! Did they want everyone to know that the *Scirè*, the only submarine in the Italian Navy equipped to carry assault craft, was at sea? Not much of a secret, apparently, though such trouble had been taken to keep it! Off the San Ranieri (Messina) light-house a launch belonging to the Naval Command approached us. I was handed an envelope; we immediately resumed navigation. The note was from the Supreme Naval Command informing me of the position of the allied vessels then at sea in case I met them. And the Messina Naval Command told me that an enemy submarine had been seen a few hours before close to Cape dell'Armi, firing torpedoes at one of our convoys.

I had, in fact, to pass near Cape dell'Armi; I decided to give it a wide berth and cruised along the coast of Sicily as far as Taormina. There I sighted a submarine which appeared to be motionless. I kept my bows turned towards it (one can never take too many precautions) and signalled it. I couldn't make head or tail of the answer: the vessel was clearly one of the enemy's. The situation being what it was, both of us being surfaced and visible to each other (it was a bright moonlight night), and considering my orders and my special task, as well, finally, as the fact that my adversary had two guns and I had none, I sent a signal to the Messina Naval Command that I had seen an enemy vessel and continued straight on my course towards the Eastern Mediterranean. And the enemy submarine? Well, she started off on a course parallel to my own! We proceeded in this way, side by side, with about 3,000 metres between us, like the best of friends, for about an hour; after this, the other submarine, as unexpectedly as it had joined me, left me to myself and turned back towards Taormina. Strange things happen at sea in time of war! The next day we encountered a melancholy spectacle. We were passing through waters strewn with wreckage and flotsam of every description, including many life-belts; one of our convoys had been surprised during the past few days. On the 9th we reached Leros and entered Port Lago, which I knew well, having made a long stay there, years before, while in charge of the *Iride*. It is a magnificent natural inlet, protected on three sides by high, rocky mountains, while on the other lies a pleasant little village, built entirely during the last few years, with its inn, church and town hall; it looked like a corner of Italy transferred to this Aegean island. I moored at the pier outside the submarine barracks; and was at once visited by Spigai, a career colleague of mine, in command of the 5th Submarine Flotilla at Leros. He put himself at my disposal with the affection of a good comrade. The first thing I did was to cover the *Scirè*'s cylinders with enormous tarpaulins; we were ostensibly a submarine belonging to another base which had put in here on account of serious damage sustained while fighting and was in need of prolonged repairs. Leros was full of Greeks and no precaution could be excessive. Six technicians flown from Italy for the purpose proceeded, meanwhile, to give the "pigs" a final check-over.

On the 12th, the 10 operators arrived, also by air. To keep them out of sight, they were given quarters in the transport *Asmara*, which was moored in the deserted bay of Parteni, at the opposite end of the island; the same anchorage had been used by Faggioni's detachment and the Suda *E*-boats. The lads spent the last few hours before their operation in the peace and quiet of that isolated roadstead, with nothing to distract them and no dangers to be encountered; on the 13th, I paid them a visit and we studied the operational plan in detail, also examining the latest aerial photographs of the harbour and the data I had been receiving (only very few messages up to now); we also gossiped a little, possibly to distract our minds for a while from the subject on which we had been concentrating our whole attention for the last month.

Admiral Biancheri, Commander-in-Chief of the Aegean naval sector, arrived at Leros from Rhodes. He wanted us to carry out exercises and tests in his presence, there and then, at Port Lago! I took advantage of my orders giving me full authority during the operation to decline the invitation. The admiral expressed his disappointment and his convinced opinion that "we shan't do any good if we cut training short".

I could not lose time. The favourable lunar phase had begun, the nights being absolutely dark; weather reports were good. I resolved to start on 14 December. I kept in continuous touch with Forza, who had gone to Athens on the 9th to take charge of and co-ordinate air reconnaissance services, intelligence reports, the issue of weather bulletins and radio liaison with the *Scirè*.

The plan of operations provided for the arrival of the *Scirè* on a certain evening, a few thousand metres from the entrance to Alexandria harbour; as it was assumed that everything would be in darkness (owing to the black-out), it had been arranged that, in order to facilitate the submarine's landfall, the coast being low-lying and without conspicuous features, and to allow her to identify the harbour (for the success of the operators' raid would depend largely on the precision with which the point of their release was determined), on the evening before, and also on the one of the action, our aircraft would bomb the harbour. The submarine would then release the operators. The latter, proceeding on courses laid down beforehand, as soon as they arrived in front of the harbour, would have to overcome the obstructions and attack the targets previously assigned to them by the commander of the *Scirè*, who would base his orders on the latest data transmitted to him by radio. After attaching the charges to the hulls of the targets, the operators were to lay a certain number of floating incendiary bombs with which they had been supplied. These bombs would go off about an hour after the warheads had exploded and were intended to set alight the oil which would by then have spread from the ships which had been attacked; it was expected that this would cause fire to break out in the harbour, affecting all the vessels therein, together with the floating docks, the harbour installations and the warehouses, thus putting the chief enemy naval base in the Eastern Mediterranean utterly out of action.

The *Scirè*, directly the operators had been dropped, was to start back. The pilots had been told which zones of the interior of the harbour were considered the least vigilantly watched, where they were to land on conclusion of the operation and what routes they were to take to get clear of the harbour area in the shortest possible time. Plans had also been laid for their rescue: on the days following the action the submarine *Zaffiro* (commanded by Giovanni Lombardi) would shuttle for two consecutive nights 10 miles off Rosetta in the Nile delta; such operators as eluded immediate capture would be able to reach her by any boat they could find on the coast.

The *Scirè*, with the pilots aboard, left Leros on the morning of the 14th. She proceeded without incident and, so to speak, in secret; by day we submerged, surfacing only at night, to charge the batteries and freshen up the atmosphere aboard. The task of the *Scirè* was, as usual, to find a method of getting as close as possible to the enemy harbour, without arousing prohibitive alarm or allowing her presence to be suspected. Discovery would mean arousing anti-submarine measures; a remorseless pursuit would begin, which would prevent us from carrying out the operation. We therefore took the strictest precautions. And as we might be detected by hydrophones as a result of normal sounds aboard the submarine, we had to proceed noiselessly, muffling the machinery. The intelligence we had received on setting out was to the effect that Alexandria harbour was surrounded, like all other harbours in time of war, by mine-fields. To quote the report: "*Fixed and mobile defences ascertained*: (a) minefield 20 miles NW of harbour; (b) line of 'lobster-pots' arranged at a depth of 30 fathoms in a circle with a radius of about six miles; (c) line of detector cables closer in; (d) groups of 'lobster-pots' in known positions; (e) net barriers relatively easy to force; (f) advanced observation line beyond minefield."

How could all these dangers be circumvented? How could the minefields be evaded if we did not know the security routes? Or the "lobster-pots"? Or the detector cables?

In order to reach the target we were obliged, after a certain stage, to trust to luck; there was nothing else to do. But luck can be "assisted", especially when the matter in hand is a complex one. I had therefore decided that, as soon as we reached a depth of 400 metres (which would probably be where the minefields started), we would proceed at a depth of not less than 60 metres, since I assumed that the mines, even if they were anti-submarine, would be located at a higher level; if the submarine should then collide with one of the mooring cables, I felt sure that the latter would slide along her sides, which were accurately streamlined and carefully cleared of all adherent matter, without getting caught up anywhere, till it fell harmlessly astern. There was nothing else I could do to elude the peril of the mines, except, naturally, to trust to luck.

The other difficulty was that of taking the submarine to the *precise* point prearranged; in other words, to navigate with the exactitude of a draughtsman working with compass and ruler, despite the drifting caused by underwater currents, which are always difficult to deal with, and despite, above all, the impossibility of ascertaining one's position from the moment when, at dawn of the day appointed for the operation, the submarine would be obliged to submerge (so as not to be detected from the enemy base) and proceed at a great depth (to avoid mines), until the time came to release the operators.

The solution of this problem of underwater navigation cannot be reached without perfect control of the speed of the vessel; the course has to be laid and kept to with great precision (so as to eliminate errors due to faulty steering) and finally position has to be determined from variations in depth quota, the only hydrographic factor which can be ascertained in a submerged submarine; here we are in a sphere closer to that of art than to the science of navigation.

Everyone aboard gave me effective help, officers, petty officers and seamen. Each man, in his own special department, took care that his services should be regularly maintained and that his machinery should function in such a way as to prevent any unforeseen accident which might compromise the success of the operation.

Ursano, my second-in-command, had the general supervision of routine aboard; Benini and Olcese, the two efficient navigation officers, helped me in following the course and with the tricky business of dealing with codes and communication; while Tajer, the chief engineer, regulated the performance of the machinery (engines, electric batteries, air supply, etc.) and kept the respective services in order. The petty officers were first-rate: Ravera was chief mechanic, Farina chief torpedo-gunner, and Rapetti chief electrician; the wireless operators kept us in continuous touch with Rome and Athens; all were praiseworthy in the discharge of their various duties. Last but not least there was the cook (a seaman to whom this task had been allotted; he was a mason in civil life) who became the martyr aboard; he was on his feet 24 hours out of 24 at the tiny, red-hot electric stoves, whatever the sea was like, concocting from dry rations dishes to satisfy the tastes and digestions of 60 people, as well as hot drinks for those on night watch and solid meals to keep up the spirits of the operators.

The latter, meanwhile, in perfect serenity (for the die was now cast) stored up their energy by resting. De la Penne, with his big fair head of rumpled hair, was generally to be found lying in his bunk asleep. Even as he slumbered he would every now and then stretch out an arm, put his hand into a drawer and extract a large fruit cake, which he ate up at a great rate. Then he would blissfully turn over and go back to his dreams.

Martellotta, permanently in good spirits, occupied another bunk. "Peace and good will!" was his invariable greeting; a heartening phrase. Marceglia, a giant of a man, with a tranquil temperament and something stately about him, was absorbed in study: his *basso profondo* tones were rarely heard and, when they were, it was to make some technical request or utter some comment on the operation. Feltrinelli, Bianchi, Marino, Schergat, Favale and Memoli all managed to find acceptable accommodation among the ship's equipment and spent their days in unbroken repose, only interrupted for the necessary more than substantial meals.

Public health was in the hands of Spaccarelli, surgeon, diver and reserve crew leader; every day he put the pilots through a thorough medical examination; it was essential to have them in the pink of condition on the day of the operation, which was now at hand.

The pilots remained very calm: the difficulties and dangers of which they were naturally well aware did not make them uneasy but merely increased their determination; anxiety and strain were inevitable, but did not find expression; talk went on at the ordinary level of cheerful tranquillity characteristic of life aboard; there were periods of gay hilarity, when facetious repartees were exchanged.

They were really extraordinary fellows, those lads; they were about to undertake action which would require the exploitation of their whole physical and moral energy and put their lives in peril at every moment, hour after hour; it would be a mission from which, *at best*, they could only hope to emerge as prisoners of war, and yet they preserved the attitude of a team of sportsmen off to play their customary Sunday game.

Meanwhile the *Scirè* encountered, on 16 December, a heavy storm.

In order to avoid exposing materials, and above all our operators, to excessive strain, I remained submerged even at night, the moment our supplies of air and electricity had been taken in.

The same day I wrote:

In consequence of the bad weather and the lack of exact information as to the number and size of the enemy units in harbour, I decided to postpone the operation for 24 hours from the night of the 17th/18th to that of the 18th/19th. (From my official report.)

On 17 December I added:

> In view of the ship's position and the favourable weather
> conditions I decided that the operation should take place on
> the evening of the 18th, hoping that I should meanwhile
> receive precise intelligence regarding the presence of vessels
> in harbour.

This was a hope that was soon realized. The same evening we
obtained at last, to our great delight, confirmation from Athens
that both the two battleships were at Alexandria.

The word was now: forward! Throughout the day, on the
18th, the *Scirè* proceeded through a zone which we presumed to be mined, at a depth of 60 metres, over bottoms
which rose rapidly as we approached the coast, till we
slipped over them like a silent and invisible tank, "continually regulating our movements in accordance with the
rise of the sea-bed, till at 1840 hours we found ourselves at
the prearranged point, 1.3 miles by 356° from the lighthouse
at the west mole of the commercial harbour of Alexandria,
at a depth of 15 metres".

Preparations were made for release of the operators. As soon
as I had discovered, by a survey taken through the periscope,
that the darkness was complete, I surfaced just sufficiently to
enable the trapdoor to be opened ("outcrop level", as it is
technically known) and came out on the conning tower. The
weather was perfect: it was pitch-dark; the sea very smooth and
the sky unclouded. Alexandria was right ahead of me, very
close. I identified some of its characteristic buildings and
determined my position; to my great satisfaction I found that
we were within a metre of the pre-arranged point. This was an
exceptional result after 16 hours of blind navigation! Immediately afterwards, with the pilots wrapped in their rubber suits
and wearing their breathing sets, the ceremony of leave-taking
began; we neither spoke nor embraced one another: "Commander," was all they said, "give us the good-luck kick, will you?"
And with this strange rite, into which I put all I knew, so that

my good wishes might be evident, the farewell ceremony terminated.

The first to go up were the two leaders of the reserve crews, Feltrinelli and Spaccarelli. Their job was to open the cylinder doors, to save the operators the fatigue of doing so.

One by one, de la Penne and Bianchi, Marceglia and Schergat, Martellotta and Marino, covered from head to foot in their black suits, their movements encumbered by their breathing gear, went up the ladder and disappeared into the darkness of the night and the sea. I submerged to the bottom.

A few minutes later the hydrophones told us that the three crews were on their way. "God be with them," I prayed, "and speed them well!"

Inside the submarine we waited for the sounds of blows struck against the deck, the agreed signal to be made when the doors of the cylinders, now empty, had been closed and the reserves were ready to be taken aboard again. When at last we heard them, I surfaced. Feltrinelli told me, in a voice broken by emotion, that as he could see no sign of Spaccarelli, he had gone astern to look for him: by pure chance he had stumbled against something soft on deck; he had discovered by groping (for we must not forget that the scene took place underwater at night) that it was the missing Spaccarelli, who seemed lifeless. I instantly sent up two other divers, who had been kept ready for any emergency; Spaccarelli was lifted up and lowered down the ladder into the interior of the submarine. I descended to the bottom again and began to head for home, following precisely the same course which had proved to be safe during my approach.

The unfortunate Spaccarelli was forthwith relieved of his mask, breathing set and diver's suit and put to bed; he was quite blue in the face, his pulse was imperceptible and he was not breathing; he showed every normal symptom of having been drowned.

What was to be done? The mission's surgeon was not much use to us in this extremity, for he himself was the victim. I arranged for two men to give him continuous artificial respiration; I rummaged in the medicine chest and had him injected with the contents of all the phials that, judging from the description of the ingredients, seemed capable of exercising a stimulating action on the heart and circulation; others gave him oxygen (the air aboard was emphatically unsuitable in this case); all the resources of our extremely slender store of medicaments and of our still slenderer knowledge of medicine were brought into play in the attempt to achieve what appeared to be an utter impossibility, the resuscitation of a dead man.

Meanwhile the *Scirè*, with this dramatic episode taking place aboard her, slipped along the sea-bed, further and further away from Alexandria. We took care not to reveal our presence in any way; discovery would have been fatal to the six adventurous lads who were at that very moment engaged in the crucial phase of the operation. But the submarine was not responding very well to my directions: the cylinder doors astern had been left open, a circumstance which made it difficult for me to keep my depth and maintain trim. As soon as we were some miles from the coast I surfaced to close them. I noticed that the Ras el Tin Lighthouse was functioning; a number of lights which I had not seen before showed at the entrance to the harbour; units were evidently going in or out; I hoped the operators would be able to take advantage of the fact. As for the cylinders, I found that they could not be closed on account of damage to one of the doors.

I continued on my course of withdrawal, remaining submerged, for the zone we were now crossing had been notified as constituting the minefield. After three and a half hours' continuous artificial respiration, a number of injections and some applications of oxygen, our surgeon, who had till then shown not the smallest sign of life, drew his first wheezing breath; it was a deep, hoarse sound, resembling a death-rattle. But it meant he was alive and we could save him! A few hours later, in fact, though his condition was still serious, he got back the use of his voice and was able to tell us that while he was making a terrific effort to close the starboard cylinder door, which stubbornly resisted every attempt he made, the effects of the oxygen he was breathing and those of water pressure at the depth involved had caused him to faint; luckily he fell on deck and did not slip overboard, as might very easily have happened, for there were no rails or bulwarks to the vessel (they had been removed to prevent the mine-cables from catching on them).

At last, on the evening of the 19th, since we were now presumably clear of the minefields, the *Scirè* surfaced, after 39 hours of submersion, and set course for Leros. On the evening of the 20th we received the following wireless communication from the Naval Supreme Command: "Photographic reconnaissance indicates two battleships hit." There was great enthusiasm aboard; no one had doubted it would be a success, but to have our expectations confirmed so soon gave us great satisfaction.

On the evening of the 21st, as soon as we had docked at Port Lago, we took Spaccarelli ashore to the local naval hospital. He was now out of danger but still required a good deal of attention in consequence of the severe shock he had experienced.

The return of the *Scirè* from Leros to La Spezia proceeded without any notable incidents, except that on Christmas Day, while the submarine was off Bengazi and the crew were listening to the Pope's speech on the loudspeaker, an aircraft of unidentified nationality came a little too close to the vessel and got within range of our four 13.2 machine-guns; the natural retaliation was the dropping of five bombs about 80 metres astern of us, which did no damage. Our Christmas pies!

On 29 December the *Scirè* arrived at La Spezia. Admiral Bacci, now chief of the North Tyrrhenean Sector, was waiting for us, on the pier; he brought us greetings and congratulations from Admiral Riccardi, Under Secretary of State for the Navy.

I was glad of this tribute to my gallant crew, who had worked so hard, with such efficiency and courage, in bringing our submarine back to harbour after 27 days of operational service, 22 of them at sea, and had covered without mishap 3,500 miles, thus contributing to a great victory for Italy.

How had it fared with the operators, whom we had left in the open sea, outside Alexandria harbour, astride their fragile torpedoes, plunged beneath the waves in the darkness of night, surrounded by enemies in ambush? The three crews had left the submarine in company and commenced approach along the pre-arranged routes.

The sea was very calm, the night dark. Lights in the harbour permitted the pilots to determine their position, which they found to be precisely as planned. They went ahead so coolly that at one point, as de la Penne relates in his report, "as we were ahead of schedule, we opened our ration tins and had a meal. We were then 500 metres from the Ras el Tin Lighthouse."

At last they reached the net defences at the harbour's entrance.

> We saw some people at the end of the pier and heard them talking; one of them was walking about with a lighted oil-lamp. We also saw a large motorboat cruising in silence off the pier and dropping depth-charges. These charges were rather a nuisance to us.

While the six heads, only just above water, were looking, with all the concentrated attention of which they were capable, for a gap in the net, three British destroyers suddenly appeared at the entrance to the harbour, waiting to go in: guide lights were switched on to show them the way and the net gates were thrown wide open. Without a second's hesitation our three assault craft slipped into the harbour with the British destroyers: they were in! They had lost sight of one another during this manœuvre, but they were now close to their targets. The latter had been distributed as follows: de la Penne was to take the battleship *Valiant*, Marceglia the battleship *Queen Elizabeth* and Martellotta was to look for the aircraft-carrier; if she were not in harbour, he was to attack a loaded tanker in the hope that the oil or petrol which would issue from it would spread over the water and thus furnish excellent fuel for the floating incendiary bombs the operators were to scatter before abandoning their "pigs".

We will now take up the stories of the individual crews.

De La Penne – Bianchi

Inside the harbour, after passing the interned French warships, the presence of which was well known, de la Penne sighted, at the presumed anchorage, the huge dark mass of the target assigned to him, the 32,000 ton battleship *Valiant*. As he approached her, he encountered the anti-torpedo net barrier: he got through it *surfaced* "in order to lose as little time as possible, for I found that my physical condition, owing to the cold, would be unlikely to let me hold out much longer". (His diver's suit had been leaking ever since he had left the submarine.) He had no difficulty with negotiation of the net: he was now 30 metres from the *Valiant*; it was 19 minutes past two. He touched the hull, giving it a slight bump; in performing the evolution necessary to get beneath the hull, his "pig" seemed to take on extra weight and went to the bottom in 17 metres of water; de la Penne dived after it and discovered to his amazement that there was no sign of his second pilot. He rose to the surface to look for him, but could not see him; everything was quiet aboard the battleship; no alarm had been given. De la Penne left Bianchi to his fate, returned to the bottom and tried to start the engine of his craft to get it underneath the hull, as it had meanwhile moved some distance away. But the engine would not start; a rapid check-over soon showed what the trouble was: a steel wire had got entangled in the propeller.

What was to be done? All alone, with his craft immobilized on the sea-bed a few metres from the target, de la Penne resolved to try the only possible expedient: this was to drag the "pig" by main force, finding his direction from the compass, beneath the battleship. Speed was essential, for he feared that at any moment the British might pick up his second pilot, who had probably fainted and would be floating about close by . . .; the alarm would be given, depth-charges would be dropped, his operation and those of his companions would be doomed to certain failure, for they would be at work only a few hundred metres away. With all his strength, panting and sweating, he dragged at the craft; his goggles became obscured and the mud he was stirring up prevented his reading the compass, his breath began to come in great gasps and it became difficult to breathe at all through the mask, but he stuck to it and made progress; he could hear, close above him, the noises made aboard the ship, especially the sound of an alternating pump, which he used to find his direction. After 40 minutes of superhuman effort, making a few inches at every pull, he at last bumped his head against the hull. He made a cursory survey of the position: he seemed to be at about the middle of the ship, an excellent spot for causing maximum damage. He was now almost exhausted; but he used the last vestiges of his strength to set the time fuses; in accordance with the orders he had received he regulated them so as to cause the explosion at five o'clock precisely (Italian time, corresponding with six o'clock local time). He did not release his incendiary bombs, for when they rose to the surface they would reveal the presence and the position of the threat now established under the hull with the fuses in action. He left his craft on the sea-bed under the vessel and swam to the surface. The moment he got his head above water he removed his mask and sank it; the fresh, pure air revived him; he began to swim slowly away from the ship. But someone called out to him, a searchlight picked him out, a burst of machine-gun fire brought him to a halt. He swam back towards the vessel and climbed out of the water on to the mooring-buoy at the bows of the *Valiant*. He found there his second pilot Bianchi, who, after fainting, had risen to the surface like a balloon and on regaining consciousness had hidden himself on the buoy so as not risk causing an alarm which would have disturbed the work of his leader. "Aboard they were making facetious remarks, believing that our operation had failed; they were talking contemptuously about Italians. I called Bianchi's attention to the probability that in a few hours they would have changed their minds about the Italians." It was then about 3.30. At last a motorboat turned up and the two "shipwrecked" men were picked up by it and taken aboard the battleship. A British officer asked who they were, where they had come from and expressed ironical sympathy with their lack of success. The two operators, who were now prisoners of war, made clear who they were, by handing over their military identity cards. They refused to answer any other questions. They were taken in the motorboat, separated from each other, to a hut ashore, near the Ras el Tin Lighthouse. Bianchi was the first to be cross-examined: on leaving the hut he made a sign to de la Penne indicating that he had said nothing. It was then the latter's turn: naturally, he held his tongue; the Britisher, who had a revolver in his hand, seemed to be an excitable sort of fellow, "I'll soon find a way to make you talk," he said, in excellent Italian. The men were taken back aboard the *Valiant*: it was then four o'clock.

They were received by the commanding officer, Captain Morgan, who asked them where the charge was located. On their refusing to answer, the two men, accompanied by the officer of the watch and escorted by an armed picket, were placed in one of the holds forward, between the two gun-turrets, not very far from the point at which the charge would explode.

We will now let de la Penne take up the tale.

Our escort were rather white about the gills and behaved very nicely to us; they gave me rum to drink and offered me cigarettes; they also tried to make us talk. Bianchi sat down and went to sleep. I perceived from the ribbons on the sailors' caps that we were aboard the battleship *Valiant*. When there were about 10 minutes left before the explosion, I asked if I could speak to the commanding officer. I was taken aft, into his presence. I told him that in a few minutes his ship would blow up, that there was nothing he could do about it and that, if he wished, he could still get his crew into a place of safety. He again asked me where I had placed the charge and as I did not reply had me escorted back to the hold. As we went along I heard the loudspeakers giving orders to abandon ship, as the vessel had been attacked by Italians, and saw people running aft. When I was again in the hold I said to Bianchi, as I came down the ladder, that things had turned out badly and that it was all up with us, but that we could be content, since we had succeeded, in spite of everything, in bringing the operation to

a successful conclusion. Bianchi, however, did not answer me.
I looked for him and could not find him. I supposed that the
British, believing that I had confessed, had removed him. A
few minutes passed (they were infernal ones for me: would
the explosion take place?) and then it came. The vessel reared,
with extreme violence. All the lights went out and the hold
became filled with smoke. I was surrounded by shackles
which had been hanging from the ceiling and had now fallen.
I was unhurt, except for pain in a knee, which had been
grazed by one of the shackles in its fall. The vessel was listing
to port. I opened one of the port-holes very near sea level,
hoping to be able to get through it and escape. This proved to
be impossible, as the port-hole was too small, and I gave up
the idea: but I left the port open, hoping that through it more
water would enter. I waited for a few moments. The hold was
now illuminated by the light which entered through the port.
I concluded that it would be rash to stay there any longer,
noticing that the vessel was now lying on the bottom and
continuing slowly to list to port. I climbed up the ladder and,
finding the hatchway open, began to walk aft; there was no
one about. But there were still many of the crew at the stern.
They got up as I passed them; I went on till I reached the
Captain. At that moment he was engaged in giving orders for
salvaging his ship. I asked him what he had done with my
diver. He did not reply and the officer of the watch told me to
be silent. The ship had now listed through 4–5 degrees and
come to a standstill. I saw from a clock that it was a quarter
past six. I went further aft, where a number of officers were
standing, and began to watch the battleship *Queen Elizabeth*,
which lay about 500 metres astern of us.

The crew of that battleship were standing in her bows. A few
seconds passed and then the *Queen Elizabeth*, too, blew up. She
rose a few inches out of the water and fragments of iron and
other objects flew out of her funnel, mixed with oil which even
reached the deck of the *Valiant*, splashing everyone of us
standing on her stern. An officer came up and asked me to tell

him on my word of honour if there were any other charges under the ship. I made no reply and was then again taken back to the hold. After about a quarter of an hour I was escorted up to the officers' mess, where at last I could sit down, and where I found Bianchi. Shortly afterwards I was put aboard a motor-boat, which took me back to Ras el Tin. I noticed that the anchor, which had been hanging at the bows, was now underwater. During transit an officer asked me whether we had got in through the gaps in the mole. At Ras el Tin we were locked in two cells and kept there until towards evening. I asked whether I could be given a little sunlight, as I was again very cold. A soldier came, felt my pulse and told me that I was perfectly all right.

Towards evening we were put into a small lorry and transported therein to a prisoner-of-war camp in Alexandria. I found some Italians in the camp who had heard the explosions that morning. We lay down on the ground, without having had any food, and, though we were soaked through, we slept till the following morning. I was taken to the infirmary for treatment of my knee injury and some Italian orderlies gave me an excellent dish of macaroni. The next morning I was removed to Cairo. (From the report handed in by Lieutenant Luigi de la Penne on his return from prison.)

In 1944, after de la Penne and Bianchi had come back to Italy from prison, they were awarded the gold medal for gallantry in war. And he who pinned the medal on the chest of de la Penne was none other than Admiral Morgan, formerly commanding officer of the *Valiant* and at that time chief of the allied naval mission in Italy.

Marceglia – Schergat

Approach commenced in company with de la Penne on the pre-arranged course. About midnight they saw the guide lights at the entrance to the harbour switched on; it was clear that units were either going in or coming out. Violent shocks were felt against the casing of the "pig", as though it had crashed against some metallic obstacle, accompanied by strong contraction of the leg muscles of the pilots: these were the effects of depth-charges dropped by the enemy at the entrance to the harbour to prevent "unwelcome visits". As they slipped into the entrance channel they noticed, much to their surprise and satisfaction, that the net gates had been opened. Shortly afterwards, towards one o'clock, they had to take rapid evasive action to avoid being run down by three destroyers which were just coming in. Marceglia resumed the pre-arranged course: "in no time at all found myself face to face with the whole massive bulk of my target." He came upon the anti-torpedo net, got through it and, now that the way was clear, submerged beneath the hull, in line with the funnel. With the aid of his second pilot, Marceglia precisely carried out manoeuvre: he clamped a loop-line connecting the two bilge keels and attached the warhead of his torpedo to the central point of the line, so that it hung about a metre and a half below the hull; then he set the fuse in motion. It was then 3.15 a.m. (Italian time).

I tried to analyse my sensations at that moment. I found that I did not feel particularly thrilled, but only rather tired and just starting to get cold. We got astride our craft again: my diver made me urgent signs to surface, as he was just about all in. I pumped in air to surface; the craft only detached itself from the bottom with difficulty, then at last it started to rise, at first slowly, later more rapidly. So as not to burst out of the water too suddenly, I had to exhaust; the air bubbles attracted the attention of the watch aft. He switched on a searchlight and we surfaced right into its rays. We ducked down on the craft to make the target as small as possible and prevent our goggles from reflecting the light. Shortly afterwards the searchlight was switched off; we started on our return, which took us past the bows of the ship; a man was walking up and down the fo'c'sle deck, I could see his cigarette glowing; everything was quiet aboard. We got out of the obstructed zone and, at last, took off our masks; it was very cold; I couldn't prevent my teeth chattering. We stopped again and began distributing our incendiaries after setting the fuses. (From a report by Engineer Captain Antonio Marceglia.)

They then set off for the spot on which they were to land: it was the area which, according to our maps and intelligence reports, was the least strictly guarded and furnished the most convenient access to the city.

While still some distance from land they set going the fuse of the craft's self-destructor and sank her; they swam ashore, removed their breathing sets and rubber suits, cut everything to pieces and buried the strips under the rocks. Then they waded ashore: it was 4.30 a.m.; they had been in the water exactly eight hours.

Marceglia and Schergat succeeded in leaving the harbour area unobserved. Posing as French sailors, they entered the city of Alexandria; after wandering about for some time, they made their way to the station to take the train for Rosetta and try to rejoin the submarine which would be lying about 10 miles out to sea at certain pre-arranged times, a night or two later. But at this point their troubles began: the sterling with which they were supplied did not circulate in Egypt; they wasted a lot of time trying to get it changed and were not able to leave until the evening. At Rosetta they spent the night in a squalid little inn, hiding from frequent visits by the police; next day, in the evening, they made for the seashore, but were stopped by the Egyptian police, recognized as Italians and turned over to the British naval authorities.

Their attempt to evade capture was thus frustrated.

Marceglia's operation may be characterized as a "perfect" one, meaning by this phrase that it was performed without a hitch at every stage and nothing unforeseen happened. In a letter he wrote me some years later he observed: "As you can see, Sir, our performance had nothing heroic about it; its success was due solely to the preparations made, the specially favourable conditions under which it took place and above all the determination to succeed at all costs."

Preparations, determination and luck were rewarded with the gold medal for gallantry in war, which both Marceglia and Schergat obtained on their release from prison.

Martellotta – Marino

Martellotta writes in his report:

> Aboard the submarine *Scirè* at 1630 on 18 December 1941, I received from Lieutenant-Commander Borghese the following operational orders: "Attack to be made on a large loaded tanker and six incendiaries to be distributed in its immediate neighbourhood."

The presence which had been notified of 12 loaded tankers in harbour at Alexandria, with a total tonnage of 120,000, was sufficient indication of the importance of the order received: the fire which might be started would be capable of reaching such proportions as to bring about the entire destruction of the harbour itself, with all the units present and all the shore installations.

Nevertheless, I felt obliged to reply: "Sir, I shall obey your orders; but I should like you to know that my diver and I would rather have attacked a warship."

The Captain smiled at this remark of mine and, to please me, since he was aware that there was a possibility of an aircraft-carrier having returned to the harbour, he modified the original operational orders to read: "Search to be made for the aircraft-carrier at its two normal anchorages and attack to be made on it if found; otherwise, all other targets consisting of active war units to be ignored and a large loaded tanker to be attacked with distribution of the six incendiaries in its immediate neighbourhood."

Martellotta had a certain amount of trouble in opening the door of the cylinder and asked Spaccarelli to help him (this was the difficulty which involved Spaccarelli in the adventure related above); he finally joined the other two crews and continued approach in their company as far as the entrance net gate.

> I felt shocks from depth-charges and violent pressure against my legs, as though they were being crushed against the craft by some heavy object. I put on my mask and, so as to avoid injury from the frequent shocks being inflicted at vulnerable parts of my body, I ducked in such a way as to lie low in the water, but with heart, lungs and head above the surface. I told Marino, my diver, to put on his mask also and to take up a similar position, but facing aft, since I was unable myself to keep an eye open in that direction, engaged as I was in looking ahead and having only the limited area of visibility which the mask allowed.

We arrived in these positions at the entrance to the harbour . . . We did not find obstructions, as we had expected, at the pier-heads: the channel was clear.

We went ahead very slowly. Suddenly, my diver, Marino, thumped me on the shoulder and said: "Hard a-starboard." I instantly swerved in the direction indicated, putting on speed, but the craft struck the buoys of the fixed interior barrier, being driven against them by the waves from the bow of a ship which had caught me up as it entered the harbour. It was a destroyer, showing no lights and going at about 10 knots; I distinctly heard chains clashing at her bows and saw members of the crew on deck getting ready to moor. It was then 0030 hours on 19 December. I got going again and, taking advantage of the waves made by a second destroyer as it entered the harbour, I slipped in with it, still surfaced and passing within about 20 metres of the guardship.

Martellotta, therefore, was now inside the harbour; he started looking for the aircraft-carrier at its two habitual anchorages; he could not find her (as a matter of fact she was not in harbour that night).

But he did sight a large warship; believing her to be a battleship, he initiated attack; he had already got under her

hull when he discovered that she was, on the contrary, a
cruiser and with great reluctance, in obedience to orders
received, abandoned the attack; just as he was clearing her
after-davits he was caught in the rays of a pocket-torch aboard
her: some seconds of utter immobility ensued, during which
he felt as if even his heart had stopped beating; then the torch
went out. He made for the zone of the tankers. Martellotta was
now beginning to notice signs of strain: his head ached and he
had to vomit; he could no longer keep the mouthpiece of the
mask between his lips; he took it off and went ahead surfaced.
There were the tankers. "I sighted a large one, heavily loaded,
which I guessed to be about 16,000 tons." Not being able to
submerge, he decided to carry out the attack from the surface:
while Martellotta kept the "pig" under the stern of the tanker,
the second pilot, Marino, fastened the charge beneath the hull.
By 2.55 the fuse had been set going. While this operation was
proceeding, a smaller tanker had come alongside the one under
attack.

> When Marino rose to the surface and saw her, he said: "Let's
> hope she stays here another three hours and then she'll have
> her hash settled too." Next, we started off again, for dis-
> tribution of the incendiaries: we moored them, after setting
> their fuses, about 100 metres from the tanker and 20 metres
> apart.

The operation having been carried out in detail so far, the final
stage began: this would be the attempt to escape so as not to fall
into the hands of the enemy. They got ashore at the agreed place
without incident, destroyed, by way of preventive action, their
breathing sets and divers' suits and sank the "pig" after setting
the self-destructor fuse. Then they went ashore.

> I set off with Marino to get clear of the harbour zone and
> enter the city: we were stopped at a control point and arrested
> by some Egyptian customs officials and police, who sum-
> moned a second lieutenant and six privates of the British

Marines. We were taken to an office occupied by two lieutenants of the Egyptian police, who started cross-examining
us; while I was answering the questions put to me in as
evasive and vague a manner as I could, a British naval
commander arrived and requested the senior of the two
Egyptian officers to hand us over to the British. The Egyptian
refused to do so in the absence of any authority from his
Government, pointing out that, as he had found us to be
Italians from the documents we carried and Egypt was not at
war with Italy, he would have to get special instructions.

The British Commander, after obtaining the necessary author-
ization from his Admiral, made a personal application to the
Egyptian Government for the instructions required and succeeded in getting us handed over.

My waterproof watch was on the table with the other articles
taken possession of and I never took my eyes off it. Shortly after
5.54 a.m. a violent explosion was heard, which shook the whole
building. A few minutes later, as we were getting into a car to
follow the British officer, a second explosion was heard, further
away, and after the car had started a third. At the Ras el Tin
naval headquarters we were briefly interrogated, courteously
enough, and then despatched to the concentration camp for
prisoners of war at Cairo. (From the report of Gunner Captain
Vincenzo Martellotta.)

Martellotta and Marino, on their release from captivity, were
also awarded the gold medal for gallantry in war.

The Italian War Bulletin N. 585 of 8 January 1942, gives the
following account of the success of the operation:

On the night of 18 December assault craft of the Italian
Royal Navy entered the harbour of Alexandria and attacked
two British battleships anchored there. It has only just been
confirmed that a battleship of the *Valiant* class was seriously damaged and put into dock for repairs, and is still
there.

The following Bulletin, N. 586 of 9 January rounds off the information as follows:

> In the operation conducted by assault craft of the Italian Royal Navy in the harbour of Alexandria and reported in yesterday's Bulletin we now have definite further intelligence that, in addition to the *Valiant*, a second battleship of the *Barham* class was also damaged.

Such was the modest announcement of a naval victory unparalleled throughout the war for precision of execution and importance of strategic results. At the cost of six men captured, there had been sunk, in addition to a large tanker, two 32,000 ton battleships, the last of those at the disposal of the British in the Mediterranean. Crippled by the charges applied to their hulls by the daring members of the Tenth Light Flotilla, the vessels were at a later date, after much expenditure of energy and materials, refloated, patched up for the time being and then transferred to quiet and distant yards for refit: but they made no further contribution to the war and immediately after the cessation of hostilities they were removed for demolition.

The losses of the *Valiant* and the *Queen Elizabeth*, following those of the *Ark Royal* and the *Barham* in the Mediterranean and almost contemporaneous with the destruction of the *Repulse* and the extremely recent *Prince of Wales* in Indonesia at the hands of Japanese aviators, brought about a most critical situation for the British Navy, which was only retrieved after a long lapse of time and then only by means of American assistance.

The strategic position in the Mediterranean was now reversed: for the first (and last) time in the course of the war the Italian Navy achieved crushing superiority and dominated the Mediterranean; it could therefore resume, with practical immunity, supplies to the armies overseas and carry out transport of the German *Afrika Corps* to Libya, thus causing the defeat, a few months later, of the British Army, which was driven out of Cyrenaica.

Even more could have been done: Italy's naval superiority at that time was such as to permit her armed forces to undertake a direct attack against the pivot of the war in the Mediterranean (and perhaps not only in that theatre of war), namely, Malta. An invasion force transported by a convoy protected by the entire Italian Fleet, when our battleships would be opposed by *no* such British vessels, would have eliminated that obstacle in the heart of the Mediterranean, which had done us so much harm already and was to do us even more later on. Such an operation would have disposed of the difficulties which the Italian Navy had to encounter, for months afterwards, in supplying our African army.

In view of the disproportion between naval forces, the operation would certainly have succeeded, though it might have been accompanied by serious losses. When the thorn in the flank of Italy's line of communication across the Mediterranean had thus been eliminated, the occupation of Egypt would only have been a question of time, bringing with it incalculable consequences for the outcome of the war.

The responsibility for losing this opportunity rests, in my opinion, on the Italian General Staff and, still more, upon the German High Command which, by refusing to supply the necessary fuel for our warships and aircraft, "again displayed its underestimation of sea power in the general conduct of the war and in particular of the importance of the Mediterranean in the general picture of the entire conflict". (From the report of Admiral Weichold, a German liaison officer attached to the Italian Supreme Naval Command, submitted to the Anglo-Americans after the war.)

The great victory at Alexandria was therefore only partially exploited: the British were given time to draw naval and air reinforcements to the Mediterranean to such an extent that a few months later the situation was again reversed, to our disadvantage; it continued to deteriorate until the final collapse, of which the withdrawal from North Africa in May 1943 was the obvious proof.

But how great the danger which threatened the enemy was, and how near we were, after the blow delivered at Alexandria, to achieving decisive victory, was indicated, more clearly than by anyone else, by the man who, being in charge of the conduct of the war on the other side, realized it most fully: Winston Churchill. In a speech before a secret session of the House of Commons on 23 April 1942, after announcing the loss of the *Ark Royal*, the *Barham*, the *Repulse* and the *Prince of Wales*, he continued as follows:

> A further sinister stroke was to come. On the early morning of December 19 half a dozen Italians in unusual diving suits were captured floundering about in the harbour of Alexandria. Extreme precautions have been taken for some time past against the varieties of human torpedo or one-man submarine entering our harbours. Not only are nets and other, obstructions used but underwater charges are exploded at frequent irregular intervals in the fairway. None the less these men had penetrated the harbour. Four hours later explosions occurred in the bottoms of the *Valiant* and the *Queen Elizabeth*, produced by limpet bombs fixed with extraordinary courage and ingenuity, the effect of which was to blow large holes in the bottoms of both ships and to flood several compartments, thus putting them both out of action for many months. One ship will soon be ready again, the other is still in the floating dock at Alexandria, a constant target for enemy air attack. Thus we no longer had any battle squadron in the Mediterranean. *Barham* had gone and now *Valiant* and *Queen Elizabeth* were completely out of action. Both these ships floated on an even keel, they looked all right from the air. The enemy were for some time unaware of the success of their attack,* and it is only now that I feel it possible to make this disclosure to the House even in the strictness of a Secret Session. The Italian fleet still contains four or five battleships, several times repaired, of the new *Littorio* or of the modernized class. The sea defence of the Nile valley had to be confided to our

---

* This assertion is disproved by the Italian War Bulletins quoted above. (Borghese's note.)

submarine and destroyer flotillas, with a few cruisers, and of course to shore based Air forces. For this reason it was necessary to transfer a part of our shore based torpedo-carrying aircraft from the south and east coasts of England, where they were soon to be needed, to the north African shore . . .

The decoration, that of the Military Order of Savoy, which was conferred upon me, on the King's own initiative, after the Alexandria operations, was accompanied by the following citation:

Commanding officer of a submarine detailed to the Tenth Light Flotilla for special assault craft operations, he had already successfully carried out three daring and difficult undertakings; he studied and prepared, with great technical competence and shrewdness, the plan of a fourth operation, for forcing a further enemy base. He took his submarine close in to the heavily fortified harbour, facing with cool determination the risks incurred from the defence measures and vigilance of the enemy, in order to put the assault craft in the best possible position for forcing the enemy base. He then launched the assault craft in an action which achieved a brilliant success, leading as it did to the infliction of serious damage upon two enemy battleships.

FATAL DEPTH

Joe Haberstroh

Trinkets from the sunken Italian liner the Andrea Doria, *which lies 250 feet down in the approaches to New York, are among scuba diving's most coveted trophies. In 1998 Craig Sicola joined the roll of those who died diving to the wreck:*

Eighteen people, including Dan Crowell and his crew of five, were aboard the *Seeker* that night by the time Dan steered the boat through the inlet and out to the dark ocean. It would take about eight hours to get to the waters above the *Andrea Doria.* Craig was aboard with a Long Beach Island contingent that included Ken Mason, Paul Whittaker, and Jim Schultz.

"We were all attracted to it for the artifacts, first of all," said Schultz. "Then, just the challenge of it. You could say, 'I'm a *Doria* diver.' You had the bragging rights. Craig liked that. You dive the *Doria*, it means a guy knows what he's doing."

The *Seeker* left by 10 that night and made it to the wreck by 6:30 a.m. Dan had long ago punched in the *Andrea Doria*'s coordinates on the navigation computer in the *Seeker*'s wheelhouse. People tried to sleep on the voyage, which was not easy with the boat's twin, 325-horsepower Detroit Diesels churning through the night. A little before 8, two members of Dan's crew, Tom Packer and Steve Gatto, made the first dives and secured the *Seeker*'s anchor line to the mooring attached to the *Andrea Doria* below. The mooring was in the same slot along the ship's bow through which the *Andrea Doria*'s crew had long ago winched the liner's anchor chain.

Gary Gentile had been the third diver that morning, after Packer and Gatto. As usual, Gentile had come up with a few pieces of china. Paul Whittaker and Craig decided they would use their afternoon dive to scout around for the china hole. They went in a few minutes after 2. It took them four minutes to descend to the wreck. Visibility was average: about forty feet. Beyond that, walls of blackness. It was Whittaker's second dive on the ship and he found himself in awe. The anemones and hydroids had taken over, so every surface of the tipped-over liner, where rusty plates of steel did not show through, had a sort of shaggy, meaty look to it, but it was undeniably still a magnificent passenger liner. Long railings and stacked window frames and the S-shaped lifeboat davits – even in the murky depths, the array of geometric shapes together made clear that this was not a pile of rubble, but still vividly a ship, albeit a stricken one. And it did look completely wrong somehow here, at the bottom.

From the anchor line, Whittaker and Craig swam about seventy-five feet toward the ship's stern and dropped into Gimbel's Hole. The two then swam some distance back from the hole. Whittaker began to appreciate the topsy-turvy nature of the wreck, where old decks and ceilings were walls, and old walls were floors and ceilings. None of the once exquisite paneling was left, of course, having long ago been ingested by worms. So the divers proceed deliberately through what effectively are massive steel chutes. It wasn't like any other wreck Whittaker had been on. "You're not worried about getting crammed into a spot that you're not going to get out of," he said. "It's more like getting lost. That's the worry."

The two had been swimming along, with Craig in the lead, when Whittaker realized they had passed the spot that might reveal the china hole. He had kept a wary eye on his depth gauge. The ship rested at 250 feet but the china hole, or at least what they thought was the china hole, was at 210 feet. Working in unfamiliar surroundings, the two men had drifted down to

220. Whittaker, who was diving on air (79 percent nitrogen, 21 percent oxygen), wasn't comfortable with the depth because oxygen can become toxic past 215 feet. He began waving his light back and forth to get Craig's attention. Craig eventually noticed, and Whittaker signaled he was turning around and getting out. Craig agreed, and they made their way out of the wreck. By the time they both pulled themselves back onto the *Seeker*, they had been in the water for almost exactly one hour. Whittaker had planned twenty minutes of bottom time. Craig, breathing Trimix (17 percent oxygen, 35 percent helium and 58 percent nitrogen), had a bit more bottom time – twenty-three minutes.

The two men perspired heavily as they struggled over to the shin-high table that took up about half the *Seeker*'s stern cockpit, where – as was the frequent practice – other divers lifted their tanks from their shoulders. Then Whittaker and Craig tugged off their thick gloves, peeled back their snug-fitting hoods, unzipped their dry suits, and began to step out of their fleece-lined jumpsuits underneath. Both men were also wide-eyed at the haul of china brought up that morning by Gary Gentile.

Gentile brought up another load when he surfaced from his second dive at 6 p.m. Gentile kept generally to himself on the *Seeker*, but no one questioned his skills, his experience, and his instincts. While his prose sometimes bordered on the wacky (the *Andrea Doria* is, Gentile has written, "a beckoning Siren to those whose ears are unwaxed"), it was clear that Gentile was also plainly courageous. If there is a pre-eminent *Andrea Doria* diver (other than Peter Gimbel, who did it first but who has been dead for several years), Gentile would unquestionably be a candidate for the honor. Maybe he overplays the adventurer-photojournalist role – an author's photo on the back of his self-published *The Technical Diving Handbook* shows him in full hunter's khaki "during a month-long wilderness canoe trip down the George River in Labrador" – but he has also achieved serious victories, such as when he won a permit from the US government in 1989 to dive on the *Monitor*.

On 23 June 1998, he had brought up the most china. It was in the best condition. It was the talk of the boat. His score was highest.

Craig tried to convince Gentile and Dan Crowell to tell him the location of the china trove. He peppered both with questions all evening, and he spoke to John Moyer as well. Moyer was another diving heavyweight, less self-consciously so than either Dan or Gentile, but he wasn't helpful to Craig. Certainly greed drove the senior divers, but they also had a genuine sense that it was safer not to try to explain to Craig how to get to the china hole. Craig had made four dives on the shipwreck. Gentile, Dan, Moyer, and other senior men aboard such as Bart Malone and Steve Gatto had each made more than a hundred dives on the *Andrea Doria*. If they didn't know how best to approach the ship safely, then who did?

At the same time, however, Bart Malone did not approve of Gentile's behavior that day. Malone well understood the craving for china; he had a twenty-by-twenty-four-foot building near his home in Bellmawr, New Jersey, stacked high with *Andrea Doria* loot. No, he didn't exactly sell it, he said. What he meant was, he did not actively, routinely solicit sales. But, he offered cheerily by way of clarification, if you traded him three hundred dollars for a crystal glass etched with ITALIA, well, of course he could do that. Malone was a digger. He found stuff in the muck of the *Andrea Doria* that eluded other people. He wasn't the first guy to find the china hole in any particular year. He was a gifted scavenger. He worked a second-class china cabinet for six straight years in the 1990s. During the 1991 diving season, he bagged more than five hundred pieces from the ship.

So, he acknowledged, he might not have been the right person to sniff at Gentile that day, but he did anyway. He wondered why Gentile did not stow the china to remove it from the gaze of agitated divers such as Craig. It was obvious to Malone that Craig had China Fever, even if he thought the term a stupid one. Craig did not impress Malone as a patient person.

"Hey, Gary, why don't you put this stuff away? It'll psych people out," Malone told Gentile.

Gentile was eating in the *Seeker*'s main cabin. "It's okay, it's okay," he said.

"Gary," Malone continued, "they're fucking beautiful. Gary, you can't leave this stuff here."

Gentile, said Malone, continued to eat.

That night, Craig tried again to get the senior divers to tell him the location of the china hole. He found Gentile and Dan's code for the china hole – "Secret Spot No. 26" – to be condescending. Malone offered to explain how to get to the second-class china cache, but Craig had done enough research to know that this required a three-hundred-foot swim from where the *Seeker*'s anchor line was tied in to the *Andrea Doria*. The long swim meant a lot less time looking for that second-class stuff, and anyway, it wasn't the first class he so fiercely wanted. Gatto tied to convince Craig that when Gary Gentile described the new china hole as a tricky spot, that really meant something. If Gentile deemed it tricky, then it certainly was tricky.

"You want china off the wreck? Be patient," Gatto told Craig. "If you're patient, the dishes will come. Take it easy." With that Gatto walked back inside the main cabin, and Craig studied the *Andrea Doria* deck plans that were posted outside. Someone had said something about the kitchen during the course of the day. Maybe that was the place to go.

The weather degraded the next day. A haze had settled. Surface visibility had cranked down to perhaps two miles. But it was sixty-five degrees and the current moved at less than a mile an hour. The divers at the *Andrea Doria* cared more about current speed than any other measurement of the conditions at the dive site. A fast current would force them to hang on tight to the anchor line during their decompression stops and it could also stir silt on the wreck itself, which could hamper visibility.

Craig was scheduled to dive with Paul Whittaker and Lyn Del Corio. But he wasn't ready to go, or at least it seemed he wasn't ready. So Whittaker and Del Corio went as a two-man team.

Whittaker entered the water at 10:26, according to the logs kept by Jenn Samulski. Del Corio followed at 10:27. Craig went in at 10:37, by himself, with his own ideas on the whereabouts of the china hole.

Craig's decision to dive alone did not concern most of those who were aboard the *Seeker*. Diving solo was contrary to a basic rule of recreational scuba diving, which held that people should pair up for safety. But *Andrea Doria* divers are what Himalayan climbers are to weekend hikers. The "rules", which aren't enforced by any law or regulation anyhow, don't apply to these divers. Dan estimates that about 40 percent of the divers enter the water by themselves. The bottom times are short at the *Andrea Doria* – fifteen to twenty minutes maximum – and the divers don't want to be concerned with another diver's safety. Bart Malone called it "big-boy diving", and the big boys did not buddy up. The less experienced divers, however, did work together, and Dan encouraged this even if he did not do it himself. Down on the wreck, Whittaker and Del Corio worked as a team inside the wreck, which they had entered through the big opening everyone called Gimbel's Hole. They found a cache of china. It was a picked-over spot but good enough for them, and they took a few pieces. They took turns holding the light for each other. At some point Whittaker moved a few large panels, and the area in which they were working started to cloud up with billowing silt. Time to go.

Craig saw the white flare of their diving lights as he approached Gimbel's Hole. It was about 10:45 a.m. They all drew together in the darkness there. Whittaker flashed Craig the OK sign with his thumb and index finger. He intended it as a question. Was Craig all right? Craig returned the gesture. He was good. Whittaker then lifted a thumbs-up sign. His dive had gone well. His eyes smiled through his mask. Craig nodded enthusiastically.

Whittaker and Del Corio watched Craig enter Gimbel's Hole. His disappearing form was replaced by a fizzy trail marking his exhalation, but the bubbles burst in moments, vanishing as quickly as chimney smoke wiped away by a hard breeze. Whittaker and Del Corio kicked their fins and headed to the *Seeker*'s anchor line.

Craig dropped into the oval-shaped room that gave the Foyer Deck its name. *Ponte Vestiboli*. He then made a turn toward the *Andrea Doria*'s stern, down a passageway that led to the dining room. The U-shaped dining room straddled the width of the ship, which meant that ninety feet separated the bulwark above Craig's head (this was the wall when the ship rested in its proper orientation) and the bottom of the room – that is, the other original wall. Table legs, long ago bolted to the floor, now jutted from the side like tree branches. Negotiating the dining room is a feat for divers because they must maintain a consistent depth (by monitoring their depth gauge) as they proceed through the sprawling chamber. If they drop down, they could find themselves stumbling upon hallways or companionways they have not memorized from the deck plans. Using time to reorient here eats the clock, as divers already have only fifteen to twenty minutes of bottom time. With five dives to the ship, two of which were surveys outside the hull, Craig had opted for a decidedly problematic penetration.

Somehow Craig made it beyond the dining room to the kitchen. Of course it was a logical place to find china, and he did find some. He dug out three pieces. One was so faded it looked bone white. Two others had rust-colored blotches but bore the unmistakable maroon-and-gold braid that indicated this was first-class china. At the top, capital letters spelled ITALIA and above that hovered the line's classic logo, a red crown.

He stashed the three pieces in the mesh goodie bag clipped to his harness. Then he began to puzzle his exit from the wreck.

Craig's depth gauge showed that in his strenuous effort to bag the china he slipped to a depth of 226 feet. This either happened as he worked his way back to the kitchen or on his return. He had sunk almost fifty feet from when he dropped in the ship through Gimbel's Hole. At some point he got out of the ship, but this had taken some amount of time, and he opted not to ascend the anchor line. If, as was likely, he came out of the ship back through Gimbel's Hole, he would have faced a seventy-foot swim against the current to the anchor line.

Instead, he reached back for his emergency ascent reel – his up line. He tied off the lightweight nylon line to something on the old ship. He then attached a lift bag to the other end and sent it slowly up to the surface. It would act as buoy to let the others know he was ascending on the emergency reel and not on the anchor line.

The lift bag hit the surface at 11:12 a.m. At first, for the *Seeker* crew members, no cause for concern was apparent. Divers sometimes sent their loot ahead of them on lift bags so they wouldn't have to hold on to it as they executed their decompression stops. At the time, thirteen *Seeker* divers were still in the water. The bag could have been anyone's. Steve Gatto had just climbed back on deck after his dive when he and Dan spotted the lift bag flopping in the gray swells. Both men climbed down into the *Seeker*'s Zodiac-style outboard boat and sped over to the lift bag. They pulled it out of the water, but found nothing attached – no bag of goodies. They knew it was Craig's, however, because two laminated tables with decompression stop information were attached. Gatto drew in the line that descended from the bag and found it chafed and almost parted about eighteen inches from the end that had been tied off below.

People did the math in their heads. It said right on the divers' log that Craig planned to be in the water for seventy minutes, including twenty-three minutes on the wreck. If he entered the water at 10:37, and you then added four minutes for the descent, that meant that Craig's bottom time should have run from about 10:41 to 11:01. But the lift bag's appearance on the surface at 11:12 suggested that at perhaps ten minutes after 11 he had been tying off the lift bag when he should have been a solid ten minutes into his series of decompression stops. He was way off schedule. Where was he?

Ten minutes later, at 11:22 a.m., Craig heaved to the surface, facedown. Dan, Gatto, and Moyer had been scanning the surface since the lift bag appeared, and they had no problem picking up Craig's red-and-black dry suit rolling in the water off the *Seeker*'s port bow. This time, Gene Peterson bounced over to Craig in the Zodiac with Dan and another diver, Joe Zeisweiss. Peterson climbed out and unclipped Craig's double air tanks, which plummeted more than two hundred feet to the bottom. He rolled Craig on his back. Craig's eyes were bloodshot and he was unresponsive. Blue blotches bloomed on his face. Peterson began mouth-to-mouth resuscitation. Dan and Zeisweiss lifted some of Craig's gear aboard the Zodiac, then hauled Craig aboard.

Craig was on his back on the *Seeker* in a few minutes. A red foam bubbled from the corner of his mouth. A succession of divers emerged from their time underwater unaware of what greeted them on the boat – Tom Packer, Terry Zeller, then Craig's friend Paul Whittaker.

Jim Schultz had not dived that day, and he and John Moyer cut Craig out of his dry suit. Both men joined in the CPR rounds, along with Peterson and Whittaker and Gatto. They placed an oxygen mask over Craig's mouth while doing chest compressions. The stunned men whispered quiet words of encouragement.

"C'mon, Craig," they said. "C'mon, Craig." But Craig never had vital signs from the moment they got to him in the Zodiac. Even as they attempted to revive him, they called the Coast Guard. Their signal at 11:34 a.m. was garbled, though, so they relayed the information through a passing fishing boat. The call went to the Coast Guard station at Woods Hole, Massachusetts, on Cape Cod. The radio channel finally cleared at 11:51 and Dan was able to relay the situation. The Coast Guard then called Dr Bruce Gelphia, the on-call physician at the Divers Alert Network, a leading diving-safety organization based at the Duke Medical School in Durham, North Carolina, and Gelphia suggested that Craig be evacuated to Massachusetts General Hospital in Boston. At 12:26, a Coast Guard helicopter was taking off from the air station on Cape Cod, and by 1:00 it had dropped a rescue swimmer near the *Seeker*. He helped secure Craig in the rescue basket.

While the crew and customers of the *Seeker* continued their effort to somehow revive Craig, not everyone could help. Unnoticed, Bart Malone had taken Craig's goodie bag and carried it inside to the *Seeker*'s main cabin. He didn't want Craig's prizes disturbed. He examined them. It was obvious where mud had fallen away as they ascended quickly – too quickly – with Craig. From his experience as a digger on the wreck, Malone decided that these pieces had also been concealed in muck when Craig found them. Craig had dug them out. He could also see that the pieces were the kind that more experienced divers had, on occasion, found in the kitchen. There was a dinner plate, an oval serving dish, and a first-class bowl. Malone placed them in the sink.

Later, after Craig had been whisked away by the Coast Guard helicopter, Dan, Gentile, and a few of the other men went inside to rest. Dan wanted everyone to write out statements as soon as they could for the Coast Guard. Best not to leave it for Montauk, because that was an eight-hour ride back. As if in one of their training courses, their discussion focused on re-creating the accident as they thought it might have unfolded. Who saw Craig last? Did anyone know his dive plan? Dan stood up and moved over to the sink. He looked down at Craig's dishes and to no one in particular said: "Where the fuck did he go?"

He took one of the pieces in his hand. "Well," he said, "I know where he got this one from." He looked over at Gentile.

"Yeah," Gentile said, "he got it from the kitchen."

A hush fell. The men eyed each other. Streams of emotion ran through Jim Schultz. He was happy for Craig that he had achieved his goal on the wreck, yet angry and pained that Craig's thinking process had been seized up with plain greed. Wasn't Craig smarter than that? They had dived together for several years, and they had a schtick they did when deciding whether to go ahead with a dangerous penetration on one of the wrecks close to Jersey.

"That's not worth it to me!" Schultz would say.

"It's worth it to me!" Craig would say.

The crew got the *Seeker* under way at ten minutes after one, just a few minutes after they watched the Coast Guard helicopter thunder north into the haze, to Boston. A doctor at the medical examiner's office there pronounced Craig dead at 2:09 p.m., moments after he was wheeled inside Massachusetts General. Dr Stanton Kessler concluded that the cause of death was "drowning and barotrauma due to rapid ascent in salt water."

Craig had rocketed to the surface so fast that his bloodstream had flooded with nitrogen bubbles. An autopsy had also shown that Craig had an enlarged heart; Kessler told the Coast Guard that the condition of the Craig's heart could not be ruled out as a contributing factor in his death.

As one of the Long Beach Island contingent aboard the *Seeker*, Schultz helped organize Craig's stuff to take home. Everyone talked about the fact that Craig had made it out of the wreck and managed to send up the lift bag. He had escaped from some trouble inside the wreck and had gotten out. Gene Peterson examined Craig's nylon up line. Its end was apparently worn through. The rope now measured about 150 feet. Some of the divers wondered if Craig had tied the line off, only to have it get caught somewhere on the wreck and sawed through. Craig had apparently been in a hurry. One of his knives was missing. What had he used the knife for? No one knew. Gary Gentile, who had almost twenty years on some of the divers, said some thoughtful words about the risky nature of deep diving. But as Jim Schultz packed his dead friend's things, his mind framed the situation in a less noble way. "Fuck! Why was it worth it? Why?"

"The hundredth depth-charge bursts.
Beads of sweat stand out on every forehead"

WOLF PACK

Heinz Schaeffer

Schaeffer was a U-boat midshipman (later commander) during
World War II. With Germany's defeat in May 1945 he and 30
crew sailed U-977 to freedom in Argentina.

Our destination this time was mid-Atlantic – we had already
crossed longitude 15° W., beyond which point the wireless was
generally silent. This meridian was, so to speak, a frontier, and we
generally referred to waters west of it as our "Western zone";
after we had crossed it we received an increase in pay. For days on
end there was the same monotonous routine; nothing different
ever happened, and we began to long for something to turn up. At
last there came an urgent signal, which the wireless operator laid
before our Commander – it was news of a convoy.

It was still far off but coming our way, if it didn't alter its
course, and we proceeded at half-speed towards our intercep-
tion point. We should have sighted it in two days, but still we
saw no smoke. However, it must have been a very important
convoy, for the High Command sent us out a reconnaissance
plane although we were 3,000 kilometres from the nearest
airfield. A U-boat is a small object to make out, however,
and we were doubtful if it would find us. The wireless operator
tried to make contact so as to give him our exact position and, if
possible, our bearing, but this wasn't an easy job, for aeroplane
transmitters are not powerful.

We kept on sending out signals at short intervals, and in the end it all worked out amazingly. The plane came into view, a B.V. 138 built by Blohm and Voss for special tasks, and we flashed the probable position of the convoy. The B.V. flew away. Two hours passed, and we went ahead without any more news. Our Commander personally had not much faith in radio. Although under favourable conditions European transmissions can be picked up in America, messages from ships can normally only be picked up 20 miles away.

In the end our B.V. 138 returned, and flashed this message: *Convoy. Square 10. About 50 ships escorted by 10 destroyers.* We went full speed ahead, with the whole watch standing by, the petty-officer torpedoman checking up on his torpedoes, and the plane still flying over us. At three in the afternoon we sighted the first column of smoke. Then another, and a third. We sped ahead. Next the first masts showed up, more and more of them.

"Why, it's a whole forest," said someone on the bridge. "We've certainly got a job."

"Stop chattering and get on with your work," the Commander snapped back, without lowering his binoculars. The B.V. 138 made off, wishing us luck, and vanished.

"Those airmen don't have such a bad time. Home to mother every night. I wouldn't mind being in their shoes."

We sent out a twenty-word signal – position of the convoy, course, speed, strength and escort – so as to put High Command in the picture. Every two hours we transmitted fuller details. We were the first U-boat to contact the convoy and our job now was to call in all other U-boats in the area, that being the whole point of our wolf-pack tactics. But I do not mean to imply by this that we were all acting under a unified command. United action in the Battle of the Atlantic merely meant calling up all available forces, for once in touch with the convoy every ship acted on its own, yet in this way we could annihilate convoys of fifty ships and more in actions that went on for days.

The night, which was pitch dark without a moon, was in our favour. But some U-boats were failing to show up. As far as we could judge from the reports we got we might be six in all by dawn. It was an important convoy – fifty ships with war materials bound for England.

"Make call-signs," the Commander ordered.

Rather a nerve, sending out wireless messages right in among the enemy ships. If our wavelength was known we were finished. But it couldn't be helped, we had to have more U-boats.

Wireless operator to Commander: "U X has contacted the convoy."

Next thing we learned was that another of our boats had done so too.

So we were now three in all, and our Commander decided to attack. Bearing indications to the other ships were no longer required, as you can see the flash of a torpedo miles away, and if one ship went up in flames it would light the way for the other U-boats. We wanted to torpedo four ships, so we picked out the big ones, preparing to attack the furthest first and the rest afterwards, allotting two torpedoes to the largest ship, and one each to the others. If possible all four must hit simultaneously, so as to leave no time for alterations of course. We were quite close to the nearest ship already – 650 metres perhaps.

"*Fire!*"

The ship throbbed five times – we were using our after tube along with the rest. In fifteen seconds the torpedoes should hit. We grew impatient; they seemed such very long seconds. Perhaps the tinfish hadn't run properly. Was anything wrong?

A spurt of flame and then two thuds. Sound travels through water faster than through the air. One more explosion aboard the same ship. She was breaking apart now, and in a moment she had gone down. There could be few survivors. Then came two more explosions – one torpedo had evidently missed. In a moment the convoy which had been peacefully pursuing its course sprang to action with much flashing of red and blue lights and signals to change course. The British knew their job. To handle blacked-out ships in convoy at night is no easy task, yet there was no collision. A pity for us, it would have saved us extra work.

The destroyers now pounced on their prey. Searchlights switched on, guns opened fire, depth-charges detonated. But we were not discovered, for we were still in among the convoy, which was probably the last place they expected to find us. Instead of making off or diving we went further in. Our Commander guessed they'd overlook us there, and he was right. With a small range of vision you can easily overlook a submarine from the high bridge of a merchant-ship. It's hard to make out that dark streak on the water, to distinguish it from the shadows cast by the higher waves.

The rear doors of the torpedo tubes swung open, one torpedo after another sliding in. The crew were bathed in sweat, working like mad. It was a matter of life and death, no time or place for reflection. If they found us now we were utterly lost, for without our torpedoes secured we couldn't dive. This was war – "Go in and sink".

It lasted thirty-five minutes. Already we were making ready for the next attack.

Torpedo control officer to Commander: "Tubes one to four ready!"

Heavy explosions. Ships were breaking up, others letting off steam and coming to a standstill, thick smoke mounting skywards. Searchlights played on the dark water and the starry blaze of oil. SOS calls never stopped going out on the 600-metre wavelength. More U-boats were coming up. Still more explosions.

"Hope we don't buy one of the 'overs'," said the second officer of the watch. "It would be the limit if our own people sent us all to hell."

And it might so easily happen, seeing that we were all mixed up with the escort ships.

At last the convoy was really breaking up, ships making off in all directions. That was bad for us for we could only take one target at a time now. Besides, they'd had their warning – some were zig-zagging, others steaming on a circular course.

Hard a-starboard. Our next victim, an 8,000-ton ship, was held in the crosswires. "*Fire!*" Almost simultaneously with this fresh command a flash went up from her. But we only scored one hit, though she was listing heavily aft.

"Object ahead!"

We tried to get away – but the object moved more quickly than we could. Gradually it loomed larger. "Watch out! They're after us!" As we rushed below we heard more explosions. We were just robots. Things were happening spontaneously, events taking charge of us.

Our High Command had warned us about fast launches shipped aboard the convoys and launched when U-boats attacked at night. Their strength lay in their small size, amazing speed and strong armament of quick-firing guns. You could only see these craft when they were right on top of you, if you saw them at all.

Down to 50 fathoms. With 40 degrees load and all our power we sank into the depths. . . . Was our engineer by any chance related to a fish? He dived the boat to the exact depth, put her on an even keel, closed the vents and finally reported "All clear".

"Well done," the Commander congratulated him.

Our friend the enemy had always got a new card up his sleeve. Well, the war would be very dull if he hadn't. Anyhow, we'd know better next time. The watch on the bridge were pretty alert in my opinion.

The first depth-charges were exploding now, but a long way off. We were still too close to the convoy and the destroyers couldn't pick us up because of all the other din – a happy state that could hardly last long. The Commander gave the order to proceed at silent speed. The electric engines were almost inaudible, and the auxiliaries shut off; words of command whispered, the ratings went around in felt shoes. Everybody not needed for immediate duty went off to lie down, as in that way we expended less oxygen. Nobody knew how long we would have to survive on what we had, and you consume less lying down than standing up and talking.

The convoy was steaming away now, its propellers barely audible. But three destroyers were after us, and before long the sound of their Asdic, like fingernails run over a comb, grew all too familiar. Another of their Asdic devices rattled like peas in a tin, a third screeched like an ancient tramcar taking a curve. We weren't likely to forget this experience. I thought of the man who went out to discover what fear meant. He should have been there.

The destroyers surrounded us, their explosions sounding closer and closer, usually in threes. My action-station was cramped up aft at the speaking-tube, and every time a charge exploded I had to report if there was any damage. The tube ran between the hull and the torpedo tube, and in this minute space I had to support myself leaning on one hand and aching in every limb. There was an almighty roar, and the boat sank like a stone for 20 metres: the light went out, and the emergency lighting came on automatically. It was no joke, when the enemy had us held like this on the dials of his instruments. Engine noises got louder – and the depth-charges ever nearer. The electricians were moving about the boat repairing damage: meanwhile the lights were switched over to the second of the two ring-main electrical circuits with which the boat was fitted. It went on for hours. Our wireless operators maintained contact with the destroyers, and kept the Commander posted; when they came closer he went to the wireless room himself to give orders. Every time a destroyer was on top of us we altered course – you have to react instinctively. Fortunately our Commander knew exactly what he was about. He betrayed no feeling, and indeed everyone gave an appearance of self-control, but we were all uneasy, myself not least. It had never been as bad as this – we couldn't see, we couldn't shoot, we just had to last it out, though it was almost more than we could stand. We counted sixty-eight depth-charges.

How long could this unreal combat, not man to man or even weapon against weapon, this inhuman strain go on, this mixture of luck, blind tactics and instinctively doing the right thing at the right time? We were caught up in a mechanism, everyone getting down to their work in a dead, automatic silence. There was something uncanny about the whole atmosphere aboard. The ratings looked like phantoms.

There is a frightful crack, just as if the boat has been struck by a gigantic hammer. Electric bulbs and glasses fly about, leaving fragments everywhere. The motors have stopped. Reports from all stations show, thank God, that there are no leaks – just the main fuses blown. The damage is made good. We are now using special breathing apparatus to guard against the deadly carbon-monoxide which may be in the boat. The rubber mouthpiece tastes horrible. This is war all right, real war, not a film-war of waving flags and blaring music.

Yet the instinct of self-preservation is active in every man of us, and if we had been asked if we really felt frightened I doubt if we could have given a plain yes or no in reply.

The hundredth depth-charge bursts. Beads of sweat stand out on every forehead. As our last hope we discharge the *Bold* – the Asdic decoy to which so many U-boats owe their survival, its chemical components creating a film which hangs like a curtain in the water and gives an echo like a submarine to the destroyer's Asdic.

Our tactics then are to turn, intentionally, broadside on to our hunters, so as to make sure they get our echo, then turn away sharply and show them our stern, sneaking away and leaving the *Bold* for the hunting pack to worry.

Our *Bold* evidently helped us, for fewer depth-charges were exploding now, and it did seem the enemy had been tricked. After counting one hundred and sixty-eight charges in eight hours, we at last began to breathe again. The destroyers were steaming away. They had to pick up their convoy, for it needed an escort for the coming night. If every U-boat had pinned down three destroyers, then only one of the ten could still be with the convoy, and things would be easier for other U-boats.

Our kind of warfare is not what the layman thinks it is, just slinking up under water, shooting and stealing away like a thief in the night. On the contrary, most ships are torpedoed in an escorted convoy by a surfaced submarine; and although the size of a destroyer doesn't allow for an unlimited number of depth-charges – I imagine that they must make do with about eighty –

what they have can make things hot enough while the action lasts.

We waited for an hour and then we surfaced.

Full speed ahead.

The batteries were then recharged, which was the chief thing, for without our batteries we could not dive and in effect would cease to be a submarine. We reloaded our tubes and once more we were ready for action, only a bit worn out. I remembered our training advice on Dänholm: "No sailor gets worn out – if you can't keep your eyes open jam matches into them." Instead of matches we took caffeine and pervitin tablets, which wasn't ideal for our health but we had to go without sleep for days and just could not do without them.

That night we failed to overtake the convoy, and reported our success to date to headquarters: four ships sunk, 24,000 tons in all.

The Admiral replied: *Not 24,000–36,000. The ships were . . .* and he listed them. *Well done. Go on in and sink the rest.* Our intelligence service was superb, and this time they had decoded the enemy wireless signals. Altogether 100,000 tons had been sunk, and we hoped that there was something left for the following night; we had already forgotten the counterattack with depth-charges, and counted on the destroyers having exhausted their supply. But in fact we found ourselves unable to keep up with the convoy, for our fuel was almost exhausted and we had to turn back to base. Later on we learnt that the convoy had been almost annihilated.

SOLE SURVIVOR

John H. Capes

On the night of 6 December 1941 the British submarine Perseus *struck a mine off Greece, sinking in 270 feet of water. All her crew of 56 were lost; the only survivor was chief stoker John H. Capes, who was taking passage to join his own submarine,* Thrasher.

Suddenly a devastating explosion rocked the boat from stem to stern. My makeshift bed reared up throwing me in a complete somersault on to the deck . . . or what I thought to be the deck. The lights went out but not before I realized that the real deck was standing up and that I had been tossed on the forward bulkhead, normally a vertical wall of steel. I knew that *Perseus* was plunging to the bottom in a nose dive.

The bows hit the bottom with a nerve shattering jolt, the boat hung poised for a moment, standing on her head. Then the stern, where I was, fell back settling on the sea bed, possibly for ever. Finally, the boat lay stretched on the uneven sea bed, listing almost 30 degrees on the starboard side, the stern was now lower than the bows.

I guessed we had hit a mine, but by some miracle the after compartments were not yet flooded, and by another miracle, I was still alive, although the thump of hitting the bulkhead on my backside was very painful. No time for pains now. How about the chaps in the engine room? I groped for the torch near the escape hatch, "Thank Heaven," I thought, it was in its position, and it worked! The powerful rays pierced the dank foggy air already beginning to stink of paint pouring from an upturned drum. The bulkhead on which I was tossed was more or less vertical again.

Through the watertight door, I went forrard, searching the stokers mess deck, then the bulkhead to the motor room. Electricians had apparently been killed by falling on live switches. As the rays fingered through the gloom of the engine room they revealed a ghastly sight, half of the cylinder heads at the front end of the engines had sheared off from the studs, with the operation gear hurled against the engine room forrard, thrown there by the sudden jerk of the last dive.

Beyond them was the bulkhead door, shut . . . but not by human hands. No clips had been secured. It must have been slammed by the first blast of the explosion, and was now held in place by water . . . crushing on the other side. It was creaking under the great pressure. Jets and trickles from the rubber joint seeped through. That door saved me and the three injured men I found alive in the debris. Our plight was one of vital horror. The water was rising in the engine room bilges and we were surrounded by the mangled bodies of a dozen dead. *Perseus* had become a cold steel tomb surrounded by the relentless sea.

With the cold already gnawing into me I thought of the rum in my blitz bottle. That would warm us up all right. I nipped back aft, had a stiff livener and handed the bottle round for a swift pick-me-up. I didn't dwell on the very doubtful chance of escape. So far so good. I was still alive in one piece. My immediate thought was to help the others. One by one I guided them to the stern compartment. No time to be fussy about wounds. There was only one thing to do . . . to get out. The next problem was somehow to flood up the after compartment and get the men through to the surface, if by luck nothing had fallen on the escape hatch to jam it.

Willing or not, in pain or no, I dragged them aft to the escape hatch. Had the explosion warped it? Would the heavy list of the boat prevent it opening? I didn't know, but would jolly soon find out. The depth gauge, if still functioning, showed a little over two seventy feet, that had to be overcome anyhow. No one as far as I knew, had ever attempted anything like it. I didn't give it further thought. If death was going to claim me it would not be without a fight.

It took half an hour to drag three wounded shipmates to the after escape compartment. By the light of my torch I gave them another noggin of rum each and had two myself. Liquor at least kept out the damp cold for the moment. The boat was leaking and would soon be flooded through-out. No time to waste. I shut the after water-tight door, isolating us in the stern compartment. I broke the seals of the four lockers and strapped the rubber escape sets on my companions. This device consists of a rubber lung, worn on the chest, a small bottle of high pressure oxygen across the stomach, a nose clip, goggles and a tightly fitting mouthpiece with adjustable rubber band around the neck, securing fairly comfortably. I soon had our sets in place. The atmosphere in this small space was becoming foul. I lowered the collapsible canvas trunk from a recess fitted around the escape hatch, and secured it by lashings to the deck. At the top of the trunk inside was the escape hatch, with four nuts holding four large clips securing the hatch firmly on the rubber seating joints all round the rim.

Reminding them of the drill, I found the valve in the most suitable position to flood the compartment from sea. I knew the water would rise around the escape trunk, leaving a small space of air considerably compressed. This would stop the water rising further. Then we would have to insert our mouthpieces, duck down under the water coming up into the trunk and then out into the open sea through the escape hatch. The first job was to open the hatch, then return to the compartment to see the lads out. I found the valve in starboard bilge, but the spindle was bent and immovable, we were trapped. If I could not move it, no one could. Was there an alternative?

If there was it had to be found quickly before we were all frozen to death. Torpedo tubes? Could I flood them into the compartment by opening the front and back doors? I pondered but decided that as the hydraulic tele-motor system had lost all pressure this would be impossible. What else then? The under water gun! That was it. Thank God we were in the compartment with the gun in position in the lowest part of the compartment. This was normally used to send smoke signals to the surface for instruction purposes. It had a four-inch bore for rapid flooding. I knew the drill book advised us to avoid rapid flooding so we would have time to get used to the pressure gradually, but I had to chance it, we were waist deep now and the water was rising steadily, the only chance was to flood quickly, release the hatch and leave without a minute's delay. I splashed down to the gun and opened the breech, I tried the sluice valve gently and could feel the thrust of water entering. It increased to a steady whirl as the sea gushed in and then steadied, the air space round the hatch diminished rapidly. Here it came . . . the sea that would save us, drown us or freeze us to death.

Almost three hundred feet above, a strong wind was passing over a short choppy sea. As the water swirled around us almost chest high, a thick oily scum of paint spread itself across the dark swell in the small confined space. We still breathed this putrid air, slightly warmer from its own compression. I swiftly fitted my mouthpiece, settled on the nose clip and manipulated the needle valve on the oxygen bottle, flat across my stomach. I opened the mouthpiece cock and oxygen flowed into my lungs. Oxygen, the life saver, and at the same time, a killer. To breathe this gas under a pressure of fifteen atmospheres was risking oxygen poisoning in a matter of a few minutes.

Breathing painfully, I ducked down through the paint scum, groped for the bottom rim of the escape trunk, braced myself against the slippery angle of the deck and dragged myself upwards. Suddenly I found my head above water in the little pocket of air in the air lock below the hatch itself. I stretched out a hand and unscrewed the small vent cock in the centre of the steel lid. The air whistled out to sea above, the slimy water rose above my face. My teeth were chattering, I realized the oxygen would not give me long . . . I had much to do still. Using all my weight, I put my remaining strength on the tommy bar in the tube spanner to undo the dog nuts. Fortunately they were not corroded with salt and came away without difficulty. The vital moment came as the last nut dropped below me as I gave a mighty heave. The hatch flew wide open, a giant bubble of air escaped. I clung to the top rungs and rim of the hatch. I was free to ascend. I lost my mouthpiece, but managed to recover it and stuffed it back. Breath came again, and a few bubbles from the lung streamed upward.

The battle was almost won. I pulled myself back down, bobbed out from under the bottom of the trunk and poked my head into the foul air still trapped in the roof of the compartment. . . . My torch showed the others to be still breathing. . . . Quick now – first one bobbed down and out, next one, and a third, all gone. All now on their way to the surface, rising slowly through the freezing black water. Not too quickly or lungs would burst. I rubbed my goggles and dipped into the trunk for the last time. On coming out of the hatch, I felt overhead for the jumping wire, it had apparently snapped and fallen away. I flashed the torch around but was unable to see further than a few feet of rear casing steel deck, this was my last glimpse of the valiant *Perseus*.

I let go, the buoyant oxygen lifted me quickly upward. Suddenly I was alone in the middle of the great ocean with only a torch . . . that faithful steel torch . . . to make a friendly glimmer on the scene. The pain became frantic, my lungs and whole body were fit to burst apart. Agony made me dizzy. I realised I was coming up too quickly, so I unrolled the small apron and held it out in front of me, designed to act like a parachute in reverse. Theoretically, it was supposed to trap the water and slow the ascent, in fact all it did was to unbalance me and tip me head over heels.

I let go and became upright again. The torch illuminated dirty looking wires, one brushed close, I passed a large cylindrical object. Wires hanging from it were caught in the light of my torch. I tried to hold my breath, but felt like a balloon about to burst. Dear God! How long can I last? A prayer was a natural

suffix. With the suddenness of certainty, I burst to the surface
and wallowed in a slight swell with whitecaps here and there.
Had I returned to the land of the living? But where was this
land?

"... the Golden Fleece of undersea exploration ..."

THE DISCOVERY OF THE *TITANIC*

Robert D. Ballard

Robert D. Ballard is Director of the Center for Maritime Exploration at the Woods Hole Oceanographic Institution in the USA. The events recounted below happened in early September 1985, 350 miles off the coast of Newfoundland, using a specially developed remote controlled submarine, Argo:

After a sandwich and a beer in the galley, the pent-up fatigue of the past week hit me. But I stayed awake until midnight to be sure the Watch of Quiet Excellence understood their instructions for line number ten. Leaning over the plotting table, I noticed that the end of line nine would take *Argo* past the northeastern limit of the earlier SAR coverage. In an hour or so, we would be sweeping a section of sea bottom that Jean-Louis had missed, a sliver of territory 1 mile wide and 5 miles long.

It didn't take Jean-Louis's watch long to settle in, and they were living up to their nickname: the only sounds in the van were the habitually chirping computers, the whirr of data printers, and the metronome ping of the sonars. Then someone slipped a cassette into the stereo machine.

"Golden oldies," he said, scanning the plastic tape box.

"I'm going to grab some sleep," I told Jean-Louis, the watch leader.

As I left the van, "I Heard It Through the Grapevine" was playing on the stereo.

Up in my cabin, I felt the chill of the approaching weather and pulled on a pair of thick flannel pajamas. In order to purge my mind of the foundering expedition, I picked up Chuck Yeager's autobiography, hoping the tales of adventure in the sky would make me forget about failure.

Down in the control van, video-tech Bill Lange turned to Stu Harris.

"What are we going to do to keep ourselves awake tonight?" he asked.

The video monitors scrolled the same monotonous image: soft gray mud, low rippling sand hills. It was 0048 hours, twelve minutes before one a.m.

Stu did not answer. His eyes were fixed on the screen. "There's something," he said quietly, pointing at the monitor.

Everyone in the van was suddenly alert.

Stu flipped switches, changing the monitor view from the forward-scanning camera to the down-looking zoom. A moment later, Stu burst with excitement: "It's coming in!"

Bill Lange leaned close to the screen, then shouted, "Wreckage!"

Stu Harris gazed at the flickering gray image. It was angular, probably steel, clearly debris from a ship, but there was no way of knowing if it was from *Titanic*. In 1912, the liner had sunk in the regular trans-Atlantic shipping lanes, but over the intervening years, so had scores of other ships, particularly during World War II when German U-boats had prowled these waters searching for helpless cargo ships. It was more likely that *Argo* had found the debris from one of the wartime wrecks than from *Titanic*.

As *Argo*'s floodlights cast their full power, the crew in the van could distinguish twisted rusty pipes and fittings. The debris appeared considerably older than the wreckage at the *Thresher* and *Scorpion* sites. But how old was the question.

There was no doubt, however, that this material was large.

Lieutenant George Rey, the sonar operator, called out distinctly, "I'm getting a hard contact."

"Bingo!" cried Stu.

Argo passed beyond the metallic objects. The screen revealed only a few small glacial boulders.

The people in the van stared quizzically at each other, as Stu was rewinding the video tape to the 0048 time hack. Had they all seen the same thing? Then, at 0058 hours, more metallic debris, including unmistakable sheets of riveted hull plate, slid across the TV monitors.

There could be no doubt. *Argo* was gliding 30 feet above *Titanic*'s debris field. Search line number nine had just entered the wedge of unsurveyed terrain that Jean-Louis Michel's SAR sweep had missed a month before.

Now all manner of metallic wreckage flowed across the video monitors.

"Someone should go get Bob," Bill Lange suggested.

But no one wanted to leave the van at this moment of triumph.

Then, at four minutes after one a.m., Stu Harris said, "Let's go get Bob." But still, there were no volunteers.

Finally, the ship's cook, John Bartolomei, who was visiting the van for the first time, volunteered to fetch me.

While the cook headed aft toward my cabin, the sketchy gray image of a circular object suddenly filled the screen. It was 0105 Hours. *Argo* flew at 14.6 meters above the bottom, at a depth of 12,230 feet. In the bright floodlights, three smaller circular shapes appeared on the larger metallic face.

"A boiler?" Jean-Louis mused.

Bill Lange was practically jumping up and down. "It's a boiler!" he yelled.

But Jean-Louis, ever the precise engineer, was cautious. He grabbed the book containing the 1911 *Shipbuilder* article on the construction of *Titanic* and her sister ship *Olympic*. After flipping to the pictures of the huge boilers in their Belfast foundry, then studying the image on the screen, Jean-Louis spoke with conviction.

"Yes. It *ees* a boiler."

John Bartolomei leaned into my cabin and spoke with a strange tone of suppressed excitement. "Uh, the guys think you should come down to the van."

There were only two things that would have caused them to interrupt my rest at this time: either we had a serious problem with the equipment, or we had found *Titanic*'s debris field.

I dragged on my jumpsuit over my flannel pajamas and scrambled down three decks, my boat shoes slipping on the damp stairs.

When I burst through the doorway of the van, Stu Harris rushed up to me, his face full of joy. The first word that registered was "boiler."

In the three minutes it had taken the cook to call for me, *Argo* had indeed passed over and videotaped one of *Titanic*'s twenty-nine gargantuan boilers, unmistakable from the three side-by-side circular vents on the top plate.

I was twanging with excitement, my eyes shooting around the van like a strobe, registering splintered images: the position of the plotline, the depth, the time, both here on the Atlantic and back in the States.

Stu was rewinding the videotape to replay the boiler image. Earle Young flew *Argo* steadily, his face neutral, determined to stay at his station, working well, while the others in the van exploded with our triumph.

Suddenly, the enormity of what had happened washed over me. The film crew was documenting this historic event, and I knew I should have some fitting words to say. But words failed me. All these years, dreaming of this moment. I turned to Jean-Louis and clapped him on the shoulder. His dark eyes were moist, brimming with pride. We had found *Titanic*.

"It was not luck," Jean-Louis said softly. "We earned it."

But I could only reply with stunned incredulity, "God damn . . . God damn."

Argo had found *Titanic*, the Golden Fleece of undersea exploration.

The voices in the control van rose to a loud babble, then subsided.

"Look at it," someone whispered. "Just look at all of it."

On *Argo*'s monitors we watched a procession of bronze portholes, twisted sections of railing, hull plating and small deck equipment stream by on the rolling gray mud of the bottom.

Most of us had forgotten how huge a ship *Titanic* had been, that she had been assembled from hundreds and thousands of these individual bits and pieces, now revealed to human eyes in the glare of *Argo*'s floodlights for the first time in seventy-three years.

Titanic had been an abstraction to us, a dream; we were not prepared for the mundane reality of the deck-lamp stanchion, bent like a shepherd's crook, the fragile old lightbulb still in place, or the clustered spouts of the ship's steam whistle, now forever mute.

Momentarily, we forgot the exhaustion and anxiety of the past weeks. This collection of light debris – stripped from the great liner by the violence of its long plunge to the bottom and winnowed by the currents to their final resting places on the soft deep-sea sediment – gripped us with absolute fascination.

But I snapped out of the near-hypnotic trance, realizing *Argo* might be in grave danger as we gazed like a herd of stunned deer at the images on the screen. *Titanic*'s massive hull could be looming in *Argo*'s path, only a few meters ahead. Worse, the ship's funnels, jutting cranes, and maybe even its mast-rigged radio antennae might still be intact but, made jagged by seventy-three years of rust, could act as scythes and sever the camera sled's umbilical cable like a stalk of dry grass.

"What's your altitude?" I asked Earl Young.

"Ten meters," he replied instantly.

"Take her up to fifty meters," I shot back, "fast."

Earl hit the winch lever, and we heard the cable whine above the roof of the van.

As we winched *Argo* to an altitude of 50 meters over the bottom, I tried to calculate if that would be adequate to clear the obstacles – provided the hull was intact and nearby – and still give us video coverage.

"Make it sixty," I said, just to be sure.

Even as *Argo* rose from its run across the debris field, we saw images of deck rails, the bronze frames of teak benches long ago consumed by worms, even tantalizing evidence of that final night at sea such as wine bottles and crockery.

Certainly the occasion called for champagne. If this had been *Le Suroit*, we'd be popping the corks on bottles of good Veuve Cliquot. But there was no champagne on board, just plenty of Budweiser and Wild Turkey. We toasted our victory with paper cups of warm sparkling Mateus we'd picked up in the Azores.

For some reason I glanced at the large electric clock on the bulkhead.

"Oh, my God," I exclaimed.

It was just after two a.m., local time. We had found *Titanic* almost at the hour of her death. She had sunk beneath the calm, cold surface of the Atlantic at 2:20 a.m. on 15 April 1912.

Suddenly, the debris strewn across the undulating gray sediment 2.5 miles below was no longer a fascinating Edwardian time capsule but the resting place of 1,522 fellow human beings.

I mumbled a few words to Steve Gegg and Cathy Offinger, and they spread the word through the van. Most of the members of the expedition and the available crew joined me on the fantail. At exactly 2:20 a.m., Lieutenant George Rey helped me raise the red-white-gold-and-black flag of *Titanic*'s builder, Harland & Wolff, with the taffrail halyard.

I spoke only a few words. "I really don't have much to say, but I thought we might just observe a few moments of silence."

We bared our heads for a long time in respect for the souls of those whose remains rested in the icy black embrace of the deep-sea bottom below. The forecast storm front had stalled to the west and the weather was serene, better than in midsummer. The cloudless sky was velvety with stars, reflecting brightly from the flat surface. Except for the quarter moon overhead, the scene was almost identical to the night *Titanic* sank.

". . . underwater work . . . calls for the very highest qualities
of courage, self-control, and self-sacrifice"

X-MEN

T. J. Waldron and James Gleason

The use of frogmen and mini-submarines was pioneered by the
Italian Navy (see pp 123–153), which used them to considerable
effect in attacks on the British fleet at Gibraltar and Alexandria in
1941. The British soon returned the compliment, not least with a
spectacular attack on the Tirpitz, *the battleship of Italy's axis*
partner, Germany.

It will be seen that underwater work is such that it calls for the
very highest qualities of courage, self-control, and self-sacrifice.
Courage alone is not enough, there are other physical and
mental qualities that can only be brought out by a rigorous
and indeed ruthless training. The men were unquestionably the
best we could produce for this particular form of activity. These
men – with all their personal qualities, must, in order to give of
their best, have supreme confidence in their equipment, and in
their leaders. Not only did the British catch up – but they
excelled in the use of this new and powerful weapon.

What of their equipment – that little word which covers the
production of a thousand and one pieces of design, of feats of
engineering, of the application of known scientific principles,
and of experimenting with the unknown. Well, from the perfect
little "X" craft midget submarine of the Royal Navy, to the
tiniest, and least detectable single-seater underwater craft in the
world – Britain had them. Improved two-man human torpe-

does, a different diving dress and oxygen set for each type of operation, silent motorised floats for swimmers, parachuting gear for dropping frogmen in the sea, high-explosive charges of every type and size, fuses, time delays, anti-removal switches, sympathetic detonation devices, they were all designed, made, and perfected. Britannia's discomfiture passed. She took the new weapon perhaps a trifle awkwardly at first, maybe a little self-consciously, and then blazed away with men and material second to none.

Things were beginning to take shape by now. A new offensive arm of the Royal Navy was being forged in the "X" craft, sturdy little midget submarines with a crew of four. They were forty-eight feet long, with a maximum diameter of five feet six inches, except under the periscopes, where it was just possible for an average-sized man to stand upright. They weighed thirty-nine tons fully stored and loaded. They were divided into four compartments – the for'ard one contained the battery that was always in use supplying power for pumps, auxiliary machinery, cooking and lights, and which, of course, drove the submarine when submerged. The store room was located here and the divers' suits and breathing apparatus also were kept here. When everything was in place there was just room for one man to lie down.

The second compartment was known as the W. and D., or wet and dry compartment. It was an escape chamber, built on the principle of the Davis escape chambers in big submarines. The purpose of the compartment was to allow the divers to leave and re-enter the submarine while submerged, without disturbing the trim and stability of the craft or allowing water to enter any other compartment. It was about three feet high, two feet six inches long and four feet wide.

The third compartment was the main one and contained a mass of complicated machinery. At the forward end the helmsman sat surrounded by various levers and wheels, which he had to operate in addition to his duties as helmsman. Next came the slightly raised dome, where there was a wide field bifocal periscope, which could be used when under targets or for looking for hostile aircraft. There, also, was the attacking periscope, which could be raised telescopically nine feet. This was as slender as a wireless antenna and beautifully clear. Two inches of this periscope above the water gave the Captain an excellent view of all that was going on above him, and it was nearly invisible, even to the keenest submarine look-out. Abaft the dome sat the First Lieutenant at the hydroplane controls surrounded, like the helmsman, by switches, levers and wheels. Other space in this compartment was taken up with a multitude of things – air purifiers, periscope raising gear, pumps and their motors, wheels, levers and gauges. In addition, there was the second bunk in which the occupant was forced to lie curved round various pipes and handles. Cooking was done on a double saucepan electrically heated. In this one made coffee, heated tinned foods, boiled potatoes and eggs, and washed up when finished with. The fourth compartment was almost inaccessible. It housed the gyro compass, a high-pressure air compressor, and a score of gauges and pipes and wheels and valves, not to mention the air-conditioning plant.

The "X" craft had an amazing steaming range on their diesel engines, and could dive for thirty-six hours on their batteries. They were safe, and frequently exercised, at very great depth, and apart from the acute discomfort common to all cigar-shaped ships of their size, they were remarkably seaworthy, and spent many long days and nights in the worst Atlantic and Arctic winter weather. The crew of four worked in two watches, four hours on and four off. One man dived, steered, and controlled the boat while the other carried out maintenance routine and mopped up the endless condensation that was a menace to the maze of electrical equipment. He also prepared the meals. At action stations all four were at their respective posts; the Captain working his attack instruments, doing the chart work and conning the ship by occasional glimpses through his periscope; the First Lieutenant at the main motor and hydroplanes control; the third hand, who was generally an officer but sometimes a rating, was dressed for shallow-water diving, with his oxygen breathing bag on and all ready, except for his facepiece.

He was also helmsman. The Engine Room Artificer was a Jack-of-all-trades – helping the Captain, the First Lieutenant and relieving the third hand when he left the craft to cut a way through nets or fix a mine to the target's bottom; and, of course, he was in general charge of all machinery.

Their operational role was to make their way into a protected enemy anchorage and either lay themselves alongside the target and drop large explosive charges underneath, fused to explode in about an hour's time, or to attack by means of attaching limpet charges to the bottom of the target. In this case it was necessary for one member of the crew, the diver, to make his exit through the escape hatch of the submarine while she lay submerged under the target. It was then his duty to place his limpet charges in position on the bottom of the target – rejoin the submarine and enter via the escape hatch once more.

The diver was an extremely important member of the crew of an "X" craft because, apart from his role of attaching limpet mines, he frequently had another task allotted to him. All these protected anchorages, apart from being mined, apart from watchful patrol boats, shore defences, asdic and radar appliances, had a defence system of steel mesh nets, both at the boom defence of the harbour, and in many cases around the more important vessels lying at anchor. In such cases as this a method of entry frequently used was for the "X" craft to nose her way underwater up to the net defence, whereupon the diver would make his exit through the escape hatch armed with mechanical cutters. He would then start to cut strand by strand from the forepart of the submarine, often indeed swarming on to the net itself like a spider on its web until the defences had been breached enough to let the craft through. Even then his job was not finished. He would regain the slippery hull of the "X" craft and as it went slowly ahead he would walk with the passing strands of the net to the after part of the craft to keep the net from becoming snarled in any part of the slow-moving "X" craft. After this operation he would regain the submarine by means of the escape hatch. This method of penetration was often practised at night when it was pitch dark on the surface, let alone thirty to forty feet down; from which it will be gathered that these divers had unusual qualities.

In an isolated fiord in northern Norway there still lurked that potential menace to our vital merchant convoys – the German battleship *Tirpitz*. *Tirpitz* lay a thousand miles from the nearest British base. Nevertheless, it was decided that the battleship would have to be attacked. The manner in which the situation was tackled is perhaps best expressed in the words of an official citation:

"The King has approved the award of the Victoria Cross for valour to Lieutenant Basil Charles Godfrey Place, D.S.C., R.N., and Lieutenant Donald Cameron, R.N.R., the Commanding Officers of two of His Majesty's Midget Submarines X 6 and X 7, which on 22 September 1943 carried out a most daring and successful attack on the German battleship *Tirpitz*, moored in the protected anchorage of Kaafjord, North Norway." The citation continued – "To reach the anchorage necessitated the penetration of an enemy minefield and a passage of fifty miles up the fiord, known to be vigilantly patrolled by the enemy, and to be guarded by nets, gun defences and listening posts, this, after a passage of at least a thousand miles from base.

"Having successfully eluded all these hazards and entered the fleet anchorage, Lieutenants Cameron and Place, with complete disregard for danger, worked their small craft past the close anti-submarine and torpedo nets surrounding the *Tirpitz* and from a position inside these nets, carried out a cool and determined attack.

"Whilst they were still inside the nets, a fierce enemy counter attack by guns and depth charges developed which made their withdrawal impossible. Lieutenants Place and Cameron, therefore, scuttled their craft to prevent them from falling into the hands of the enemy. Before doing so, they took every measure to ensure the safety of their crews, the majority of whom, together with themselves, were subsequently taken prisoner.

"In the course of this operation, these very small craft pressed home their attack to the full, in doing so accepting all the dangers inherent in such vessels, and facing every possible hazard which ingenuity could devise for the protection, in harbour, of vitally important fleet units. The courage, endurance, and utter contempt for danger in the immediate face of the enemy shown by Lieutenants Cameron and Place during this determined and successful attack were supreme.

"His Majesty has also approved the appointment to the Distinguished Service Order of Sub-Lt. Robert Aitken, R.N.V.R., Sub-Lt. Haddon Kendall, R.N.V.R., and Sub-Lt. John Thornton Lorimer, R.N.V.R., and the award of the Conspicuous Gallantry Medal to Engine Room Artificer, Fourth Class, Edmund Goddard for their gallantry, skill and daring during the successful attack on the *Tirpitz*."

Both Donald Cameron, now a Lieutenant-Commander, and Godfrey Place are still in the Navy. They are modest and quietly-spoken young men, but there is a directness in their manner of speech which loses nothing because of the quiet delivery. Cameron's voice still has enough of the Doric in it to confirm his Scottish ancestry. Place has the well-modulated tone of an educated young Englishman. When asked about the attack on *Tirpitz*, this is what Godfrey Place said:

"In this particular operation the chance of return was better than in many others, because the training had been long and thorough, and the design of the boats was such that we could come back under our own steam. But in this rather novel type of warfare it is impossible to plan for everything. One of the difficulties we encountered was minor mechanical failures, which had not been bowled out during the 'working-up.' In the passage to the operation we were submerged for twenty-three hours out of twenty-four for ten days on end.

"The actual attack took place in daylight, in the most heavily defended anchorage of the German North Norwegian Fiords. In the essentials, the attack was simple. A question of getting under the *Tirpitz* and laying heavy mines which exploded after a time lag. I myself encountered some difficulties in the form of net defences, which were rather more complex than we had thought, and my eventual form of attack was to pass underneath them, which took longer than I had anticipated. It was, in fact, these close net defences which made it impossible for me to get out after the completion of the attack."

Donald Cameron's story of his part in the attack is equally understated. This is what he said:

"How incongruous the affair was, was brought home to us on the night before the attack. There we were, in an enemy harbour, about to attack the big fellow himself – or herself – with earphones clamped to our ears, listening with one ear to a BBC programme, and to harbour craft circling about us with the other.

"My difficulties were mechanical. My periscope was flooded, and one of my explosive charges had flooded, which added to trimming difficulties and gave me a fifteen degree list. We managed to navigate the outer defences – more by luck than good judgment or skill, and found ourselves outside the steel nets which surrounded the ship herself – her last line of defence. Fortunately there was a gap in the close defences used for the passage of small craft. We learned subsequently that this gap had been opened about half an hour previously to admit normal boat traffic to and from the *Tirpitz* and the surrounding ships. We passed through, and on turning to attack, betrayed our presence by grounding on an uncharted sandbank. The alarm was raised on *Tirpitz* by an observant look-out who reported 'a large fish' to the officer of the watch. As large fish were apparently extremely uncommon in that particular area, he was told not to be a bloody fool. However, the buzz had got around of something unusual. Due to our navigating apparatus being put out of action when we grounded, we were totally blind and floundered around inside the nets. We were forced to carry out our attack on the surface against *Tirpitz*. We closed in on *Tirpitz* from fifty yards range under a constant barrage. Laying ourselves alongside, we dropped our charges with a time-setting of one hour. Having laid the charges, and considering the chances of escape with the craft to be negligible, I decided to scuttle the craft on top of the charges to prevent her falling into enemy hands. We did this, and were picked up by motor launch and taken on board *Tirpitz* for interrogation. I was in *Tirpitz* being interrogated when the charges exploded."

It is rather extraordinary that de La Penes' experience when attacking one of our great battleships in Alexandria should have been repeated so closely by Cameron on this attack on another great battleship. Like de La Pene, Cameron did not talk because the Captain could have saved his ship by just moving it and, like de La Pene, Cameron knows what it means to wait a few feet from his own explosive charge and wonder what will happen when it goes off.

Many other vessels were sought out as they lay at anchor in that maze of intricate sea inlets along the Norwegian coast. An Australian, Lt. "Maxie" Shean of the R.A.N.V.R., sank the *Barenfels*, and Lt. H. P. Westmacott, R.N., even sank a floating dock, for which he was awarded the D.S.O. After a long journey up the long fiord he described the last part of his attack like this:

"This stretch of the West Byfjord was mined and my route was a dog-leg, so I wanted to keep in the channel, if possible, but there was a lot of traffic and I was rather jostled up to the north side of my route. For various reasons I didn't want to go below periscope depth because I wanted to take a quick peep every few seconds. At last Puddefjord opened up in front of us, and we began to identify objects like the observatory – the cathedral – and other things. At 09.00 hrs. I sighted the floating dock. As we crept towards it the water became restricted, and the traffic denser. I was crawling around the deck – the periscope popping up and down like a piston. This, of course, was the moment ordained for Practical Jokes Co-ordination Ltd. – the periscope had to jam up and smoke started from its works. We managed to fix it with a screwdriver.

"We were pretty near the dock now – no nets in sight – and –

what a shame – nothing in the dock. However, there were two small ships alongside.

"We still had a hundred yards to go when I saw the mast of the *Barenfels*, which Maxie Shean had accounted for on the last trip. It had a notice on it saying 'Langsam Fahren' which means 'GO SLOW.' That was fine – I was only doing two and a half knots. About 09.30 hrs. we went astern under the dock and I let her settle on the bottom while we placed the first charge, then we manoeuvred two hundred feet under the other end, and dropped the other one off. The job was done by 10.15 hrs. and with the craft now lightened I let her go for a thousand yards clear – took one fix – tucked her head down, and went like a racehorse for the entrance of the West Byfjord."

So the Norwegian fiords were no longer a safe lurking place for enemy shipping. Targets were sought out and damaged or destroyed by individuals and units of up to four men working by themselves a thousand miles from the nearest base, not only in the Norwegian fiords, but wherever the enemy was to be found; men who achieved their objectives by their supremely high sense of duty, their fearlessness, and their disregard for danger. And they were all volunteers. Things were beginning to hum since that September morning when a dull boom was heard in Gibraltar harbour, the results of which set tongues wagging in Whitehall.

The Royal Navy has an ancient tradition of getting things done quietly and efficiently. This quietness and efficiency is perhaps epitomised in the action that takes place in the tiny interior of an "X" craft as she slips through the water, submerged on the last leg of an attack in an enemy harbour. The only sound is the quiet whine of the battery-driven motors, the crew are silent and intent at their stations. The craft is at forty feet.

The Engine Room Artificer is manipulating his Asdic Transmission Set. This acts like a powerful invisible searchlight underwater. It sends out a wireless signal in a straight line like the beam of a searchlight and when the beam hits a solid body

underwater it sends back an echo. The frequency and strength
of the echo tells the operator how far away the object is and gives
him a good clue also of what it is.

Now the E.R.A. reports an echo from straight ahead.

"Give me the earphones," says the C.O., "bring her up to
periscope depth, Number One," to the First Lieutenant.

"Periscope depth, sir," replies Number One, and as the craft
rises he slowly intones "fifteen feet – fourteen feet – thirteen feet
– twelve feet."

"Up periscope" orders the C.O., the periscope whines up, the
C.O. glues his eyes to it. "Nothing in sight," he says. "Down
periscope – bearing of those echoes again?"

"Right ahead, sir," replies the E.R.A.

"Seems like harbour defence asdic to me. I'll give you a fix to
check on that. Stand by bearings, up periscope – ship's head
now?"

"275, sir."

"Green 37 – now?"

"276, sir."

"Green 18 – now?"

"276, sir."

"Red 25 – now?"

"277, sir."

"Red 112. Down periscope. Time and log reading?"

"0609, sir."

The C.O. peruses the chart. "First bearing is that point,
second the left-hand edge, third is that, fourth is that beacon.
Up periscope – Ah! There's a coaster, green 7, and I can see two
ships now probably boom gate vessels. Steer 275."

"Steer 275, sir."

"Down periscope."

"Asdic echoes getting louder, sir," says the E.R.A.

"Where are they coming from?"

"Just off the starboard bow, sir."

"Very good – up periscope. That coaster's coming straight at
us. I should say she's about two miles away. Can't you hear any
hydrophone effect?"

"Might be something, sir – on the starboard bow."

"Down periscope. How's the trim, Number One?"

"Excellent, sir, no trouble at all. It's all right at this speed, of course."

"Yes, I don't want to go any slower while I'm at periscope depth," says the C.O.

"I can hear her hydrophone effect now, sir," says the E.R.A. "about a hundred revs. reciprocating, I should say."

"Up periscope. Bearing green 6. Range is fifteen minutes. Down periscope. How far away is she?"

"Three thousand three hundred yards, sir."

"Good. At ten knots she'll be up to us in nine minutes. Up periscope. I can see a motor-boat with her too. It's just crossing ahead of her. Down periscope."

"That coaster's doing a hundred and forty revs. now, sir."

"Up periscope. Bearing green 5, range forty-five minutes. Down periscope, that's one thousand one hundred yards, isn't it? Motor-boat's gone back towards the harbour. Up periscope, the coaster's coming up fast. She's only about four hundred yards off. Down periscope. Flood Q!" There is a sudden rush of water as the tanks are flooded for an emergency crash dive away from the oncoming coaster.

"Full ahead," cries the C.O. above the roar of water. "Take her down, Number One – forty-five feet."

The rush of water ceases and there is silence once more except for the faint beat of the coaster's propeller above them. Louder and louder it gets – the uneven beat thunders in their ears – it is like a monstrous elliptical wheel of steel rumbling across an iron bridge. Gradually it recedes.

"Bring her up to periscope depth, Number One," says the C.O.

"Aye, aye, sir."

"Where have those asdic echoes gone," the C.O. asks the E.R.A.

"They're pretty loud now, sir, on the starboard side."

"Do they seem to be in contact?"

"No, sir."

"Thirteen feet, sir," says Number One.

"Up periscope. Port ten, steer 250. Plot our position, Smith – we'll do a little coast-crawling now. Down periscope. Sixty feet. Jones – go and get into your diving dress."

And so – calmly, efficiently and relentlessly – they move in for the kill.

"Stream-lined blood-red worms,
attracted by the light, swam around us in circles"

NIGHT DIVE

Robert E. Schroeder

Into Salt Pond Bay, the US Virgin Islands, where Schroeder
worked as a member of the Fisheries Research Project in the 1970s:

The ocean was oily black, and the night moonless. The shore,
where the ripples softly washed the rocks, was blacker still, a
silhouette against the stars. Fumbling in the dark, I slipped into
the harness of my aqualung and fastened the weight-belt.

Jack (Dr John Randall), in charge of the research station,
lowered the long cord of our improvized diving light to the
bottom, forty feet down. I put on my mask and leaned over the
side. All I could see was a pale circle of sand and coral,
pathetically small and far away in the deep dark ocean.

I cast off the little dinghy that carried the battery. A sudden
splash told me that Jack was on his way, and a moment later his
ripple-distorted figure appeared under the skiff, barely visible
in the dim light. Gathering my courage I slid over the gunwale
and the warm, dark Caribbean closed over my head.

The light seemed miles away, and we swam toward it down a
long wavery tunnel of darkness, accompanied by excited finger-
length shadow-fishes that darted about in the eerie glow. Jack
grasped the light, and to my profound relief swung the beam
about to reassure himself that nothing was lurking in the dark.
No monsters! But the ruby-bright eyes of night-walking lobsters blazed from the corals, and pale fish swam over the sands.

An ivory-white mantis shrimp at my feet lifted huge refractile eyes to stare blindly from its burrow, and a sand-dwelling anemone stretched gracefully curving tentacles of crimson and gold.

I had been diving in tropical waters for pleasure and science for several years and had collected reef fishes in the Bahamas and the Florida Keys, but this was my first experience with night diving. Strange creatures I had never seen on the sunny daytime reefs indulged in mysterious pursuits. Familiar organisms had so changed their colours and their habits that they were almost unrecognizable. My initial anxiety was quickly forgotten in the wonder of a scene transmuted by darkness. I realized I had been unaware of half the problems in the sea; that night was as important as day, and almost entirely different.

We soon found what we were looking for near the bay's mouth on a stretch of sand and coral rubble. Baby conch do indeed burrow by day to come out at night to feed. Jack swam about excitedly grabbing every one he could find; but to me the conch were incidental to the wonders of the ocean at night.

Stream-lined blood-red worms, attracted by the light, swam around us in circles. Blotchy black and white goatfish, which school along reefs by day, had assumed coats of mottled scarlet and were sleeping on the sand. Scorpionfish, blinded by our light, allowed me to scoop them up in my palm. Cardinalfish, which by day are orange-red and hide deep in the coral, were translucent ghosts of themselves, swimming high above the reef. I dragged Jack away from his baby conch, appropriated the light, and went sightseeing.

A brick-red octopus the size of a grapefruit sat bolt upright and motionless on the coral rubble. Light-blinded, it did not move until Jack urged it into the mouth of his collecting bag. The creature crawled into the bag, revealing that it had been sitting on the overturned shell of a large queen conch, its tentacles and mantle completely enclosing the aperture.

The conch had withdrawn far into its shell, but did not appear the worse for its experience. Was the octopus waiting for it to emerge to be paralysed by a poisonous bite, or had a poison already been secreted into the enclosed shell cavity? The octopus is a flexible creature, and easily could have squeezed far enough into the shell to bite the occupant. Perhaps the siege had only begun.

The poisonous bite of the octopus may explain the presence of conch in the stomach of fish which have no means of removing the big snail from its shell. Jack once found both a conch and an octopus in a snapper's stomach. Had a snapper attacked the octopus after it paralysed the conch, it would have gotten both the octopus and its victim. Or the conch might have been left on the bottom to be scavenged by crabs or carnivorous snails, such as Murex, that are incapable of attacking a healthy conch.

We made several night dives at Salt Pond Bay. One night two small manta rays, perhaps ten feet in wing span, circled briefly above us in the glow of the light. I was afraid they would hit the extension cord, capsizing the battery boat and plunging us into darkness, but after two circuits they slipped out of the light and disappeared. Another night I was examining expanded coral polyps when Jack tapped me on the shoulder and pointed. Floating above us were four huge tarpon. I watched in awe as they hung mesmerized by the blinding glare before slowly drifting towards us, their expressionless eyes casting pale reflections.

Tarpon are among the more primitive bony fish. To me they always had an ancient and alien look, as if belonging to a bygone age. Their appearance this night in ghostly silver against the darkness did nothing to reduce this impression. It was as though we were diving on a fossil reef sixty million years ago, when mammals were still new.

I looked at Jack. He pointed at the nearest tarpon. I also pointed, questioningly, with my spear. We had collected no tarpon. Jack nodded. I assumed he meant we were to break our night-time rule against spearing except in self-defence.

Drawing a careful bead on the nearest five-footer, I fired. The spear rebounded, a great scale impaled on its tip. The tarpon disappeared straight up, and its companion zipped out of sight.

I waited a moment, but failed to see where the first one broke the surface.

Jack and I both went up after that. In the skiff, Jean (Mrs Robert Schroeder) was calling at the top of her lungs: "What was it? Bob, are you all right? What on earth . . .?" We swam to the skiff, where she was jumping up and down excitedly. "A great silvery thing! It soared out of the water like a rocket! I didn't see where it came down!" Handing her our equipment, we hauled ourselves aboard. "It was a tarpon, a big one. We didn't see where it came down either. It went through the surface and just disappeared." Jack looked at the sky speculatively and said wryly: "Maybe it went into orbit!"

"It proved impossible to revive him"

HIDDEN DEPTHS

Philippe Tailliez

Captain Tailliez was co-founder, with Jacques-Yves Cousteau and Frederic Dumas, of the famed Undersea Research Group of the French navy, and the unit's first commander.

But the sea, in the course of so many dives, had marked us for its own more profoundly than it had the majority of our naval colleagues, and in a different way. From the beginning man's ancient instinct for the chase had been at the bottom of our zealous pursuit of fish and pictures. Then the game, after having occupied so much of our thought, had grown into a passion so powerful that we could not have renounced it without destroying our very selves. We were of the opinion that it was possible for our technique to be applied to utilitarian purposes within the framework of the navy even better than outside it. Our ruined harbours strewn with wrecks, our coasts, channels and mine-infested quays required years of underwater labour to clear them. It was imperative to get on with the job, and in it the new tool – the independent diver – could and should find an accepted place. Within the framework of the navy itself, which we knew so well and which had been almost entirely destroyed, we should be contributing to its rebirth if, by deed and example, we could spread the realization of a simple but often overlooked truth: the sea, the highway of shipping, is also a world in itself, a huge three-dimensional world awaiting exploration by man.

As it turned out, we were re-established with our former ranks, and when Admiral Lemonnier, having returned to France, became Chief of Staff, Cousteau presented *Sunken Ships* to him.

Dumas had also been taken on by the navy in the capacity of scientific expert, and the three of us found ourselves at Toulon in April 1945 provided with a tolerably vague schedule of work concerned with diving equipment, mine-sweeping, the salvage of wrecks and the training of divers. We would see how it would all work out, though at the moment we had not the faintest idea to what it was going to lead.

The town, the arsenal and the harbour were one mass of ruins, from which rose the dull growling of excavators and concrete-mixers. As I walked past I cast a fraternal glance upon the workers with their picks and shovels: we, too, were going to rebuild. Admiral Lambert, the Préfet maritime, gave us the use of a first floor in a building which had belonged to the Port Authority. Though its roof and ceilings were in a state of collapse, we deposited our luggage there, viz., an aqualung outfit, a coil of tubing and underwater goggles and paddles, all much the worse for wear. Brick by brick, the three of us began to build the edifice which is now the G.E.R.S., the Groupe d'Études et de Recherches Sous-marines, the Undersea Study and Research Group.

If we had not toiled so joyously it would simply have been the most grinding hard labour, for each one of the bricks we assembled cost its full price. Everything was in disorder as liberation fever swept the country; and in the arsenal, where every single department had to rise from the ashes, no place for us had been contemplated. To obtain it was in itself a major operation.

Soon, however, our team became very well known in No. 3 région maritime, for it was ready to lend itself to any kind of underwater operation. We would hardly have emerged from the water before we would be leaping into offices, demanding a chair, a table, a lorry, a motor-bicycle, a compressor, abandoned diving equipment, a typewriter or a man from the depot.

Gradually, sailors were added to our team, for we had asked for volunteers. Some of those who turned up were often a little bantering and ironical, for they had heard talk of three madmen who spent their time drilling holes in fishes' bellies. They had sent in their names, just to see, for the fun of it. Well, we would put their noses in the water and teach them to dive. And, indeed, after a fortnight those who had not thrown in their hand were as keen as ourselves.

The first naval officer to volunteer was Chief Petty Officer Maurice Fargues, a splendid type and an old hand of the *Casablanca*, who before the war had been the best instructor at the École des Scaphandriers, where he had been the first to experiment at a depth of four hundred feet with rigid diving equipment. A trainer of men, and soon a really remarkable diver, he was placed in charge of a patrol launch, the VP8, which we had managed to obtain and equip for traditional heavy diving and aqualung diving, with a powerful compressed-air unit and a recompression chamber for the treatment of casualties.

After that we were joined by Petty Officer Morandière, a former aviator who had become a fanatical diver; and by Torpedo Petty Officer Pinard, also a former diving instructor, a man of extraordinary vitality, whose resourcefulness in replenishing our stores was unequalled.

Our numbers were finally made up by M. Chasseriaud, an experienced photographer from the former Toulon Study Centre; M. Agnès, a draughtsman from the submarine section of the arsenal, who was already a diver of the traditional kind and soon became an excellent aqualung diver; and Mlle Ferrero, our secretary, the shrewd, loyal, unique siren of the Undersea Group.

Our first underwater assignment consisted of removing two torpedoes from a scuttled German submarine which had been cast ashore off the Saint-Mandrier peninsula. These torpedoes, assumed to be acoustic, were of the greatest interest to our naval construction service. Dumas and I dived into the torpedo compartment to open its doors and unscrew the torpedoes. Then, from the outside, with great care, we unscrewed the fuses. A towline was slipped round the explosive cones, and the launch, moving gently forward, caused the steel tubes to slide out into the water.

Then came mines, and again mines. While Lieutenant Porcher with his team of helmeted divers was performing a wonderful clean-up of the harbours and seaboard of the Atlantic and the North Sea, we came to grips with the Mediterranean mines at the same time as Commandant Serre and his Toulon team were rapidly being initiated into the science of diving.

The removal of obstructions known as katymines along the beaches of Languedoc was entrusted to Captain Bourragué and Lieutenant Cousteau. It was a vast and intricate problem. In the harbours, where visibility is practically nil, one is reduced, in the search for mines which may have sunk away in the mud, to spreading a network of cables along the bottom and letting helmeted divers follow these with their hands. To follow such a procedure along mile upon mile of coastline would have needed an army of divers. Cousteau, however, thought out and elaborated a method of exploration which made it possible to carry out the vast operation efficiently and cheaply. (This method was again applied by the Group in 1953, with Lieutenant Alinat in the Bay of Quiberon.) Cousteau had equipped his craft with long tuna-fishing rods provided with tackles, the distance between which depended on the degree of underwater visibility. Weighted halyards served the purpose of tow-ropes, to which the divers clung, very near the sea bottom. The moment they came across a mine or any suspicious object they marked it without interrupting their search by releasing a weighted reel with a marker buoy, which rose to the surface.

In the course of our clean-up of the Toulon roads Cousteau, Dumas and I found ourselves during one dive in the hold of a lighter, where, side by side, were ranged twenty-seven ugly-looking cylinders. We took photographs, and the experts, upon investigation, declared them to be German magnetic and acoustic mines. Logically speaking, we ought to have been blown to smithereens. I then asked for the magnetic field of our diving apparatus to be measured, for at the time these were made of steel. It was found that it was dangerous to approach within ten feet of such mines with our equipment. Nobody henceforth would be venturing anywhere near the lighter *Sainte-Geneviève* by the Lazaret. For eight years, until they were removed by Messrs. Grandmange, a ring of buoys remained in place round those twenty tons of high explosive. Any shock, or the passage of some vessel, might have set off those mines and caused an explosion catastrophic in its effects on the harbour and the town.

Our work along the coast was carried on in co-operation with the chief of the mine-sweeping organization. He asked us, in order to guide the work of his vessels, to reconnoitre the channels in the Hyères roads which the Germans had amply provided with mines and barrage-nets. Our launch was peacefully following the course indicated to us as safe, when the brigadier signalled the presence of a mine near our bows. A mighty wrench at the wheel – and we missed it by inches. The next moment we saw another to starboard, ten feet below the surface, and yet another – we were right in the middle of a minefield. We dived in, and it was a most impressive experience, in this limpid water, to swim round those large spheres with their pointing horns, covered as they were in algae and barnacles, gently bobbing at the ends of their cables. While Cousteau, for the benefit of the experts, filmed the mines from every angle – but keeping his distance – Dumas and I prowled round, full of interest, oblivious of the strong current that was carrying us towards one of them. At one point we actually got pressed firmly against the mine, and it took us several seconds to free ourselves with the aid of our fins. They were long, crowded, disagreeable seconds, which reminded me of a similar experience in Syria, in 1942, with an Italian mine which had been washed ashore and the fuses of which I, as a qualified torpedo officer, had to remove.

Back on board, we prepared charges at the end of an electric cable and, this time without any diving equipment at all, plunged in to fix them to the lowest antenna of each mine. The launch then made herself scarce, unrolling some three hundred feet of cable, and before long enormous geysers of water could be seen rising, one after the other, into the sky.

Mine clearance, for all its risks, was by no means the hardest of our tasks. Sometimes aeroplanes would fall into the sea and bodies have to be recovered.

In September 1946 a naval flying-boat was making for the Palyvestre base. Presumably the pilot was misled by a mirage, and the aircraft hit the water in the Bay of Giens. Having received a radio call, we were on the spot within an hour. Fishermen had already collected the body of the pilot officer, one of our friends, who at the moment of impact had been flung from his seat and literally slashed to pieces. Air bubbles and oil were rising to the surface from some hundred and thirty-five feet below. Cousteau went down with Dumas, eager to take a film which would be of use to the experts in determining the cause of the accident.

I went down in turn with Morandière, at the end of a rope lowered from the launch. A large white cross began to stand out against the sea bottom. It was the wreckage. And above this cross a corpse was rising – Dumas had already fixed the body of a passenger to a rope which was being hauled in. As it rose – as rigid as a wax model, one arm pointing stiffly upward, one leg severed – it nearly touched us. Behind him, his parachute had opened, and the enormous white rosette was also floating gently to the surface.

We reached the fuselage. One of the engines had broken loose and lay some thirty feet away. There was still one body left in the cabin, and we succeeded in freeing it. A hundred and thirty feet below the surface of the sea, we handled it as if we were in a dream – it had no weight and was in no way repulsive but, on the contrary, inspired us with a kind of tender pity. Ophiurians, those disc-shaped stars with long, thin, supple arms like rat-tails which divers encounter at great depths, were already crawling on its face and eyes. We were just about to slip the rope under its shoulders and make a knot, when I felt myself being violently pulled upwards. In the boat they apparently thought I had given the signal to hoist. I was furious at this setback, but could do nothing but hang on to the rope so that I could go down again without a pause. I broke surface by the side of the launch and, clinging to the rail, opened my mouth to protest, when I saw all eyes fixed on me in unbelieving amazement. It wasn't me, a living diver, whom they had expected to see rising from the water.

The research departments from time to time used to approach us to ask for data – direct observation or film – on the underwater behaviour of their apparatus. Our first efforts in this field were made in collaboration with the submarine *Narval*. Our task was to check the shape of the cloud of anti-asdic bubbles emitted by a dived submarine to counteract the effect of enemy radar.

Accompanied by Dumas, I took up my position with my camera some sixty-five feet under a launch. Two-thirds of a mile away the *Narval* had dived to periscope depth and was heading towards us. The wait was depressing. We were revolving on our axis, having lost our sense of direction, vaguely giddy in the blue water. And the worst of it was that we could hear the dull rumble coming nearer and nearer and yet did not know in which direction to turn. At last her stem, fine and dark, with its saw-toothed net-cutting device, came straight at us. We had just enough time to turn the right way, and the huge shark slid past us at a speed of eight knots, its flag unfurled at the stern, without as much as an eddy. It was an extraordinary spectacle, and the performance had to be repeated several times to make sure we had properly filmed the bubbles.

After our tests with the *Narval* came life-saving tests with the personnel on board submerged submarines. Parallel tests were made at Brest and at Toulon by the submarine *Rubis*. Before the war Commander Seyeux and Lieutenants Lancelot and Jéhenne had already made good their escape from submarines with diving suits provided with an independent oxygen-fed helmet, but in the course of one of their tests Jéhenne had lost his life. It was now important to show that it was possible to leave the flooding chamber of a submarine with the aid of the "Cousteau-Gagnan" apparatus, and, moreover, that it had become a simple and safe operation not only for specialists but also for all properly trained naval personnel – at any rate in waters a hundred and thirty to a hundred and forty feet deep, at which level intoxication due to nitrogen breathed under pressure is not yet felt.

The *Rubis*, commanded by Lieutenant Ricoul, was a fine mine-laying submarine which had done brilliant work in the Allied cause. Perfect understanding between her crew and the divers prevailed throughout the experiments. The submarine had settled down on the sea-bed at a depth of a hundred and twenty feet. The divers, alone or in groups, entered or left the submarine through the flooding chamber, amidst the folds of the ensign flapping in the water: a perfectly simple thing to do. In another operation Cousteau, taking his position by a launching tube, filmed the firing of a torpedo. It sped past him at forty knots. We were everywhere, along the back, the sides and the keel of the submarine, clinging on to her as long as possible as she dived and gathered speed. Her captain, who at first had been a little anxious about the cluster of divers round his vessel, ended up by being as indifferent to our presence as a shark is to that of its pilot fish.

In the course of these tests a documentary film was made called *Une Plongée du "Rubis"*. Never before had the cinema shown a submarine in her element, releasing men from her flooding chamber, firing torpedoes, laying mines, and settling down on the sea bottom.

The sequence showing mine-laying was shot off Cap Brun and cost a vast amount of film. Cousteau, suspended from a buoy, waited, camera in hand, for the submarine to pass as she followed a set course, her periscope just at water level. To the stem of the *Rubis* there clung a pilot-diver – Dumas, as it happened – whose job it was to give the signal for the release of the mines. Clutching the net-cutter with one hand and a hammer in the other, he was hard put to it not to lose his underwater goggles at the five knots they were doing. When

Dumas, who had accurately calculated the inevitable delay, caught sight of Cousteau, he struck a loud blow on the hull just at the right moment. Inside the submarine a man was listening, his ear pressed against the hull. The moment he heard the signal he pressed a bell warning the men in the mine-laying compartment, and the string of mines was released immediately in front of the camera.

The mines had been dropped in their places and it was now my task to film an operation which few submarine men can possibly have seen: the way in which an underwater mine behaves. This type of mine is provided with an anchor-weight called a sinker, which, before the launching, has been bolted to the body of the mine by means of a cylinder of rock-salt. Upon launching, both sinker and mine go down to the bottom together. Then the cylinder of salt begins to dissolve; this done, the mine rises upwards, as it goes, unrolling its cable which locks again once the mine reaches its appointed distance from the surface.

I had stationed myself in front of one of them, seated on the bottom, my finger on the camera button. Time passed, and I had to switch over to my air reserves. A mine, with its devilish horns, has an expressive look, and I began to feel that my mine was laughing at me. So I turned my back on it and watched its neighbour. At that very moment a fearful clatter arose. My original mine had released itself and was leaping skyward, raising a thick cloud of mud.

Full of resentment, I had to surface after having handed the camera to Morandière, who was laughing behind his goggles. Five minutes later he also was surfacing, having run out of air, angrier even than I was. Warned by my experience, he had refrained from turning away from his own mine, which turned out to be the only one that refused to rise.

To complete the sequence, another string of mines had to be launched.

We were constantly having to train officers, petty officers and men, and not only naval personnel but also men belonging to organisations interested for various reasons in the training of aqualung divers: infantry, engineers, firemen, life-saving organisations, the Ministry of Works. And they, in turn, spread the art.

The General Staff would at times send us biologists, physiologists, geologists, or oceanographers on a course. We sailors and divers lacked their scientific training, but it seemed inconceivable to us that people should claim to embody the laws of the sea in learned tomes without once having been below its surface with open eyes. We thought that the step taken by the General Staff would do much to open the way to a more sure and human approach to underwater studies. We felt amply rewarded when, upon their return from a dive, we heard the experts expressing this feeling and read in their eyes the animation and excitement of their first real contact with the sea.

We ourselves felt enriched, having learned to look at the sea from another angle than the seaman's – to discover its place in the branches of science.

Deep diving continued to attract us.

It is not altogether certain that any kind of record-making or breaking should be rejected, whatever the field and the spirit in which it is made, for such records extend the limits within which man can operate and increase his powers. They establish the point to which research has progressed, the extreme frontiers of risk which are being continually pushed back through the daring of pioneers, under whose cover humanity takes stock with fresh confidence. They have their place among the evolutionary factors of our species, and translate its instinct of preservation into a long-term policy: not to perish because of changed conditions in its milieu as so many animal forms in the earth's various ages have perished – indeed maybe not to perish with the earth itself when its day comes, but to be prepared for prolonging our destiny at some other point in space.

In how many years could that be, in what span of millions or billions of years? Immaterial. Time passes like lightning.

But in our case, as divers, what drove us down below the

surface was not the vainglorious and abstract craving for records, nor the certainty that every foot gained added to the
impressive number of cubic feet of possible under-sea exploration. Rather, far more simply, and without our even giving it
much thought, it was the outcome of a double curiosity: to see
how the seven colours behaved below water, and to explore the
world of coral. We longed to see with our own eyes as we dived
deeper the progressive absorption of the solar spectrum below
the sea, the disappearance of red with its low vibrations, from
the first feet, and of the blues and greens last of all, until we
came to the region of the total extinction of light at about sixteen
hundred feet.

We had already observed the star-fish, brown or dull red on
the bottom, brighten in our hands as we rose towards the
surface, where they took on startling vermillion hues. At San-
ary, by the Embiez archipelago, Dumas and Cousteau had
drifted down one hundred and fifty feet to a sumptuous field
of dark-blue, almost black, gorgonians or sea-fans. With their
daggers they had cut off an armful of these living flowers which
are actually animal colonies, coelenterata like the corals, but
whose branches are supple, and which orient themselves along a
single plane in vast fans, on to which the porbeagles like to hook
their eggs, those translucent, horny capsules with tendrils at
each corner. When thrown into the launch, these sea-fans, too,
were red.

I do not know which of us discovered the ideal method of
pursuing these observations: we let ourselves sink along the tall
cliffs, under the narrow caves scooped out in the coastline
between Marseilles and Cassis, the sides of which go down
vertically before linking up with the sandy plain sometimes well
over three hundred feet below the surface. Like unroped Alpine
climbers we would plane in the silence, the slow beat of our fins
steering us effortlessly past the needles protruding from the
smooth rocky walls where flourished flora and fauna, whose
shapes and tints varied with the depth, but more rapidly so than
they do with the altitude on mountains. Here change was
sharply defined from fathom to fathom.

In this way a new sport was originated: inverted Alpine climbing, as revealed in the film *Paysages du Silence* (*Landscapes of Silence*), under the impact of which many ardent divers, at the suggestion of Henri Broussard, formed the Club Alpin Sous-Marin at Cannes.

It was the start, or rather the revival, of underwater photography with artificial light, for as early as 1893 Louis Boutan at the Arago Marine Laboratory at Banyuls had already made a number of experiments.

Never have I been so moved as I was while diving along the face of Les Empereurs off Marseilles. We were going down this mighty, steep reef – also called Les Impériaux – which proudly stands out south of Riou Island, a few hundred yards away from the Grand Congloué, the islet where Cousteau with his *Calypso* a few years later was to tackle the sunken wreck of a Roman galley with her formidable cargo of amphoras, jars and crockery.

The walls of Les Empereurs led us down to sands lying at a depth of about two hundred and fifty feet. To the habitual intoxication of the sea-floor was now added a different and more subtle rapture, that of colour, which man knows on dry land in the contemplation of flowers or objects such as a painting or a Disney cartoon.

Before our eyes passed variety upon variety of sponges, the round or Marseilles sponge, the Greek or matapan, the elephant's ear, the silicious sponges, the Neptune's cup, hollow like vases or cylinders; primitive sponges, those which form a sulphurous orange lepra on the rocks but whose name I do not know, and the homocoela, which come off the rock in violet patches when one's hand brushes them. Among the bryozoa is the *Cellulosa retepora*, Neptune's lace, tufts of rosettes with pale, fragile, perforated petals. These wonderful fungosities softly irradiated the gloom with a luminous glow which the eye perceived when one moved close enough to touch them with one's goggles.

Words, paltry words – not even those that poets create have the power to suggest the sight of a deep underwater rockface; in this vision, no doubt, the diver's intoxication plays its part. Yet among poets I would make an exception of Rimbaud, on account of a few lines like these in his *Bateau Ivre*:

> *I dreamed the green night of extravagant snow;*
> *Kiss of the ocean, unhurried, climbing the eyes,*
> *Stirred saps, ineffable humours whirled away;*
> *And phosphorus singers, a blue and gold alarm.**

Was this only coincidence, a coincidence noticed by me alone? But it is Rimbaud speaking, Rimbaud the damned, the technician of the disorder of the senses. "I accustomed myself," he said, "to pure hallucination. I clearly saw a mosque where had stood a factory, coaches on the roads of the sky . . . a drawing-room at the bottom of a lake."

I know of physiologists and neurologists, passionate divers themselves, who are beginning to show a loving interest in those unknown laws governing our senses, in the mysterious correspondences, the profound unity of their vibrations.

In any case at the foot of the wall of Les Impériaux I felt that day filled with euphoria and glory. Within three feet of me I spotted Cousteau, his nose almost flattened against the rock, also lost in contemplation. I had not noticed him before. It was then that an idea worthy of a deep-sea drunkard occurred to me. I got as near to him as I could and began to sing the *Marseillaise*, a doughty *Marseillaise*, making it ring in my mouthpiece, and jumping from one of his ears to the other to make sure he heard me. No one has ever played such a trick on me under water, and the effect, it seems, is terrifying. As, after a short pause, I began on the second stanza with renewed vigour and a fresh stream of air-bubbles, Cousteau seized me round the waist and hoisted me back to the surface.

Sometimes along a crack at the mouth of a cave grottoes would open up, deep and menacing. We explored them, preceded by

---

* Rimbaud, A., "The Drunken Boat", in *Four Poems by Rimbaud*, translated by Ben Belitt, Sylvan Press, 1948.

the beam of our electric torches. Cousteau discovered some marvellous ones in the Vayron plateau, in the vicinity of Planier Island. We named them Ali Baba's caves, a legendary appellation which they fully deserved. The far end, a hundred feet deep, was perforated by vertical chimneys, the larger of which would permit a diver to pass through. Having slid through these, one landed on a singularly pure white sand. Then began an inextricable maze of galleries, low-roofed halls held up by rocky columns splaying into Gothic arches. The sun, through the holes in the roofs, drew slanting pillars in the water with shafts of light. Eight divers together, our bubbly plumes above us, we wandered in this palace of shadows, circling pillars, scaring the morays, the mérous and the sars.

We still had to discover the coral, that noble growth, *coralium rubrum*, the sacred, living shrub round which history has woven so many legends and superstitions and which has chosen to live only in the divine sea. This, to us underwater climbers, was our edelweiss. We were well aware that we would, in our own eyes, be entitled to the name of diver only after we had plucked with our own hands from the floor of a dark grotto the precious flower of blood.

It was Catsulianis, the famous old-style diver, who lived in retirement at Cassis, who initiated us. He lived in a narrow alley leading down to the harbour. This son of the ocean, remarkably hale for all his seventy years, his gestures quick, his eyes bright with mischief, knew the sea better than we did. We could have listened to him for days on end.

At the age of eighteen he had started diving, mother naked. He told us how some fifty years ago certain shipowners, unscrupulous villains all of them, set about recruiting the needy and starving of the Athens taverns. When they were drunk they were thrown, at dead of night, into the hold of a felucca and there they would wake to find themselves on the high sea, bound for the Syrian coast. Thus would start the hell of sponge-fishing. Each diver had his guide who was at the same time his guardian and his executioner, for there were plenty of revolts and fights on board. The guide would hold in his hand the diver's cable and his life. A heavy stone tied on his back, the diver was provided with a short, sharp dagger, while the rope was passed under his armpits.

"At times," Catsulianis told us, "we had to go down as much as a hundred and fifty feet. The diver was stark naked, and even at that depth we could do more than a helmet diver. It would happen that a diver 'went to sleep' at the bottom. They would haul him up, beat him back into consciousness and send him down again."

After that Catsulianis became a helmet diver, sometimes a wreck-pirate and sometimes a sponge-diver. In the Red Sea his equipment had been painted black to keep away the sharks. He had seen most of his companions die in accidents, or become paralysed for the rest of their days. "At a great depth," he said, "one's clothing sticks and the blood begins to froth. As one comes up, it curdles." When a diver came up feeling ill they took his helmet off and threw buckets of water in his face. We wondered by what miracle our friend had survived, for he had no knowledge at all of the rules of diving.

Nevertheless he taught us a thousand wiles that are not to be found in books; for example, how to capture a crayfish which shows only its feelers beyond the edge of its hole. We were keenly interested, for it is considered doubly shameful to break these feelers: a disgrace for the diver to come up with a pair of pincers only, a disaster for the crustacean which is unjustly deprived of a fine and useful ornament.

Like all divers, Catsulianis talked with his hands, and mimed his captures: "First, you stroke the corselet gently, very gently, with your fingers. *Giligili*. It begins to move its legs and feelers and advances a little. Hop! You seize the pincers at the base, one in each hand, and you draw him out by bending them a little down towards the tummy. . . ."

He told us where in the vicinity of Cassis coral beds were to be found, and confirmed the story that round about 1910 all the coral along the coast had been gathered by Greek divers for the Naples jewellers. He showed us a twig, the thickness of a finger, which he had kept because one branch formed a cross at right angles with it, which is very rare. He also explained how the coral hides beneath its screen, the crest, invariably pointing towards the bottom in a single plane, its dark-blue skeleton speckled with minute six-petalled anemones, which contract at the slightest shock. And how one breaks them, with a light hammer, with small sharp taps – *tocatocato*.

In the course of our dives along the cliffs we had already analysed our physiological and psychological reactions at various depths. We had been able to gauge, while searching for torpedoes, aeroplanes and mines along the deep sea-floor, the difficulty of performing even a simple task, how dangerous any effort was and what an individual and subjective thing diving became under such conditions.

Eight of us had gone down in turn along a cable to three hundred feet, each recording in indelible pencil on boards attached to the cable at every thirty feet what our reactions were. Dumas had gone down to three hundred and ten feet to free the dredger of a patrol vessel engaged in the channel.

The intoxication of great depths is attributed to the progressive dissolving of nitrogen in the nervous tissues; but it is probable that this process is accelerated by the presence of exhaled carbon dioxide, which is all the more harmful as the depth becomes greater. In the diving helmet carbon dioxide cannot be altogether eliminated, but we thought that with a breathing apparatus in which all vitiated air is expelled after each exhalation to be replaced by pure air originating from a reservoir, it should be possible to go down deeper. An attempt at controlled diving, in a team, below three hundred feet was undertaken on 17 September 1947 off Toulon, from the despatch-boat *Elie-Monnier*.

The order in which the eight individual attempts were to be made had been determined by drawing lots. Chief Petty Officer Fargues, a ballast of pig-iron in his hand, was the first to slip down the long cable, with, as an extra precaution, a thin rope fixed round his belt for transmitting signals. A remarkable diver, of great coolness in action, and who had started as a helmet diver, he was the least likely of us all to suffer from nitrogen intoxication. He went down rapidly, leaving short phrases on the little planks which, from two hundred feet down, were attached to the cable. It took him three minutes to reach three hundred and eighty-five feet. At four hundred feet he merely wrote his initials, lost consciousness and let go his mouthpiece. As he was no longer answering, he was pulled up and Torpedo Petty Officer Pinard went down to two hundred feet to meet him. We saw Fargues brought to the surface, inanimate, his mouthpiece floating above his head and releasing a stream of bubbles.

It proved impossible to revive him.

"Water was cascading into his helmet . . ."

THE PIPE LINE

Tom Shelnick

Shelnick, born in Pittsburgh in 1936, served with the US Navy before becoming one of the best-known American deep-sea divers of the 50s and 60s, the first to be employed by Miami's Seaquarium and a regular TV presenter. At the behest of the police and FBI, he liberated some 200 bodies from watery graves, and at the behest of the US government retrieved test bombs at Cape Kennedy. Below Shelnick recounts a commercial pipe-laying operation in the early 60s that went awry.

The shortest distance between two Philippine islands is a pipe line – and it had to be straight. The two islands lay a mile apart in green water. The pipe line was to carry drinking water from a tank on the large island to the smaller one, which presently was supplied by tugboat and barrel. Although we had laid a quarter of the line without running into obstacles, now a rock formation blocked our way. We had to blast. I had just set the charge below.

My diving partner and I were sprawled on the deck of the tug, waiting for the engineer to press the plunger. We wanted to go back down and inspect the blast site before we quit for the day. But the engineer was having trouble clearing the water of fishing boats. With his hands on his belly, he squeezed out French like a wheezy accordion, and his three workmen shouted Filipino across the water. The *bancas* kept circling.

My partner was impatient. Sunday Tanner was from Kentucky, and he didn't have much patience with the rest of the world. But his complaining – like GI griping – wasn't really as sour as it sounded. It was just a way to pass the time, a habit he had never lost from his days in the Navy.

Now – tow-headed and lanky, his helmet on the deck beside him – he looked at me with a grin and I knew a gripe was coming on.

"Look at them damn sea buzzards," he said. He waved his arm over the scene. "You know what they're waiting for? They're waiting to see if any dead fish float up. They love to fish with dynamite, you know that?"

He cupped his hands and shouted at the boats – "*Sauve qui peut!*" Then he wiped his grin away and waited for me to ask the question.

"What's that mean?" I said.

"That's what Napoleon hollered to his troops at Waterloo. It means, 'Save your skins'."

He cupped his hands again and this time he shouted, "Now hear this! Skidaddle!"

We all laughed, except the French engineer. The engineer scowled, either because he didn't like Sunday or because he didn't like his French.

But the Filipinos did like Sunday, and they laughed at whatever he said – even though they seldom understood the words. From their scattered English they had grubbed up an affectionate title for him. They called him "Sea Monster".

Somehow, Sunday's meaning had carried across the water. The outriggers were heading slowly in toward Yankee Island – which is what Sunday called the big island. To him, anyone who didn't come from Kentucky or thereabouts was a Yankee, and that included, the French, the British, and the Americans on "that damn Yankee island."

Soon the area was clear. The sea glittered like an acre of glass. The wind lifted the spray and rubbed the tug against the barge alongside, which squatted under a stack of black pipe.

We all waited for the blast. The three Filipinos sat on the deck

and faced the spot where the dynamite was planted, 225 feet
down. The engineer leaned over the plunger.

"Bet he can't find it under that fat gut of his," Sunday said.
He chuckled and began to sing—

> *"Goin' up Cripple Creek,*
> *Goin' on the run,*
> *Goin' up Cripple Creek*
> *To have a little fun—"*

Then he stopped.

The plunger squeaked down into its black box. The engineer
grunted, slowly sat down, and rubbed a finger under his sweaty
chin. He looked out at the water.

There was a dull roar, far far away in some other county.
Then, fifty yards off the bow, a slug of black water humped out
of the sea and riffled on the surface.

One second, two seconds, three seconds – it was all over, I
thought.

Sunday stood up. "That's it," he said. "Let's get back to
work."

But suddenly another blast let loose. A shock wave hit the tug
and crunched it up against the barge. "Mother!" Sunday yelled,
and he rolled to the deck beside me.

A geyser of water shot into the sky, pumping up bubbles and
foam. It settled into a pool of froth about twenty-five yards off
the beam.

"Damn it all, mate" – Sunday said – "that was a mine!"

"You bet it was," I replied. And then, I don't know why, a
weak laugh started out of me. Lying helpless on my side, in a
heavy canvas suit and weighted shoes, I looked into Sunday's
indignant face. "Don't sell him short," I said.

"Who?"

"That's one hell of a plunger when he finds it."

"He's some kind of a nut!" Sunday said.

We pushed ourselves to our feet.

All around the boat the water flowed in black streams like

lava. A deadness hung over the spot, and everything but the silence seemed remote – the chatter of the three Filipinos, the sunlit sea, and the two green islands beyond. Suddenly I knew the feeling of the war as it must have been in these Pacific islands – the heat, the salt, the slice of steel through green water, and the surprise from below, the murderous surprise. How many ships had we lost in these waters?

The engineer came over to me. "How does this happen?" he asked.

"A mine," I said.

He shrugged helplessly and walked away.

Sunday looked after him with disgust. "If I kick a spike off one of those sisters," he said, and he clanked a shoe against his helmet, "I hope I shoot through this tub like a torpedo."

"You want to go down and take a look?" I asked.

This time it was he who shrugged helplessly. "*Magkano ang halaga?*" he asked. It was one of the few Filipino expressions he knew – "How much does it cost?"

A half hour later we were on the bottom. The water in the beam of our lamps was filled with white sand. The charge had wiped away the rock pile and lifted the sand, and now a shallow crater remained. We went over it with the lights foot by foot. It was solid.

"Solid, man, solid," Sunday kept saying on the phone.

"Shut up, Sunday," I said, but I knew it was useless. The only one who could shut him up was the engineer. When he pressed a switch to talk to the two of us, all we could do was listen. Maybe that's why Sunday didn't like him.

"Cheez, what a grouch," Sunday replied.

"How can I tell if you've got nitrogen narcosis," I said, "when you talk like a drunken sailor half the time as it is?"

"What d'ya do with a drunken sailor . . ." he sang.

Despite the kidding, nitrogen narcosis was a real worry at this depth. Below 200 feet, some "intoxication" was inevitable – which was one reason we shouldn't stay down too long at a time. Concentration was an effort. Reflexes were slow. Worst of all, a diver who was too tired to fight off the "rapture" might do any crazy thing. The temptation was always there to let go – and I knew, as well as anyone, that will power holds out only so long. Then, laughing bubbles into the water, you step into a dream from which you might never awake.

Sunday and I, moving slowly along together in our merging lights, inspected the last two sections of twenty-foot pipe to see if the joint had been loosened by the explosion. It looked tight. But I could see that the level of the line was higher than the crater dug out by the charge.

"Maybe I used too much powder," I said. "We'll have to sandbag."

"No sandbagging," Sunday said. "We've got work to do." He chuckled.

The engineer's voice cut in – "Sandbags?"

"Not today," I said. "Tomorrow morning."

"Why not?" Sunday asked. "Hell, it's still daylight out."

He flashed his light around the black pool of the ocean bottom, and then he turned it out. In the fog of my light, he looked like the "sea monster" the Filipinos called him – a huge grey figure with a metal head, breathing bubbles.

"Let's get the bags down here anyhow," he said, "and then tomorrow—"

"Mister Shelnick," the engineer cut in. "Have you need for the sandbags?"

"No. We're coming up."

This time Sunday's voice had an edge in it – "We'll be on this job for months at this rate. Why hurry home?"

"How much decompression time do you figure, Sunday?" I asked.

"You think I carry those tables around in my head?"

He knew I was baiting him.

"Let the engineer figure it," he said. "He's the tender. That's his job."

"Sure, let George do it. He figured it yesterday and I went home with one hell of a headache." I didn't mind that the man topside was listening. "I checked his figures last night and he had us seven minutes short. He's okay on a single dive, but he gets lost in the repetitive dive tables."

"So do I," Sunday said.

"That's great. That's just great. What the hell would you do if I got knocked out down here?"

There was silence on the phone.

"I don't know about you," I added, "but I don't want to end up with a bubble in my brain."

I had planned this dive on paper before descending. It was time to go up. I knew the decompression time that would compensate for nitrogen absorbed in the present dive, plus residual nitrogen in our bodies from the previous dive. But if we overstayed our time, my figures would be wrong.

"Topside!" I said. "Take us up to forty feet."

We began our ascent up the guideline. With my light, I checked off the twenty-five-foot markers as they passed.

"Look, Sunday," I said. "We've piled up a decompression time of 131 minutes. I don't like to be hanging by my hat longer than that. Not when we don't have to. If the tug gets hit by a storm topside – and, damn it, you know how quick they come up – that means we've got to come out fast and take a chance on the bends, or else be dragged through the channel ass-over-teacups. I don't care for either choice."

"Yes, suh, Captain," Sunday said. "I read you."

But by the time we reached the first decompression stage, he had brushed it off. Hanging motionless in the dark, he resorted to his usual way of passing the decompression time he hated—

> *"For it's dark as a dungeon,*
> *And damp as the dew,*
> *Where the dangers are double*
> *And the pleasures are few . . ."*

The dangers are double, all right, I thought. I was still irritated, and I was more worried about Sunday than I was about the danger of another stray mine. The most dangerous thing to contend with on the bottom is a reckless partner. You're committed to him. You've got a thousand-ton commitment pressing in on all sides, isolating the two of you in your own locked world, and if one of you gets into trouble – the other one's in trouble.

It wasn't that Sunday didn't know his business. He didn't forget things – he just skipped them. He skipped equipment checks before he went down. He laughed off the danger of nitrogen narcosis. He even seemed willing to take chances with the bends.

Was it just plain carelessness? If so, maybe I could jolt him out of that. But I wasn't sure. What really bothered me was that it might be something other than carelessness – something more deadly. I'd known a diver or two who had courted disaster, it seemed, almost deliberately. They'd found it, in time . . . because it's always there waiting for you at the bottom of the sea.

I would have to watch Sunday, I thought. And then I turned off my mind. But the voice in my helmet sang on—

> *"Where the rain never falls*
> *And the sun never shines,*
> *It's dark as a dungeon*
> *Way down in the mines."*

That night Sunday went into a talking spree that lasted all evening. It started over the kitchen table in the two-room apartment we had shared for three weeks – furnished by the French construction company bossing the job – and it continued later over beer glasses at the local *tindahan*. He talked and talked, and all of it was about the past.

I listened, of course, partly because it wasn't convenient not to, partly because I was looking for clues to his real nature, and partly because I was tired – too tired to do anything but sit and listen to his voice washing over me like the sound of waves on a distant beach. I didn't mind his talking, but I couldn't understand why this sunny boy from the hill country – with his blue eyes and butter-coloured hair – wasn't as tired as I was.

His first story began when he served me the eggs he had

scrambled for supper. He liked to cook, thank goodness, and he saved me that chore.

"If I waited for you to make something, I'd starve to death," he said. "I had this buddy once, in the US bloomin' Navy, and he was a natural-born cook. He was always heating up something. Half the time I didn't know what it was, but I do know he had a fishing line trailing from his porthole clean across the Pacific.

"We were buddies because we were both mountain boys – or maybe just because he liked to cook and I liked to eat. He was from West Virginia. He always used to say – from West by God Virginia.

"Well, somehow we found ourselves once in a land party – taking orders from an Army *sergeant*, if you can imagine that. It seems the Army needed some *real* men for some important matters, they said, and we were volunteered. Anyhow, we're living on C-rations. Now C-rations don't give a cook a hell'uva lot to work with – not even a good cook. Rocky had procured some petrol – or, as he said, 'I stole it' – to heat the rations. I claimed he was using it for seasoning. It was pretty damn awful.

"Anyhow, one evening Rocky and I were busy, and we crawled into this wrecked farmhouse. The elements were rough at the time. We made a search of the place, and darned if we didn't find something hard to believe. Back in a hole – safe from the weather and things – we found a real live Leghorn chicken. And it was plunked down on two whole eggs. Two eggs! An egg apiece and a chicken between us.

"We decided the eggs should go first, because they might break. I was in such a hurry I was going to swallow mine raw, but Rocky said they should be fried – it was no trouble. He set up this C-ration can with a handful of dirt in the bottom. Then he poured petrol over the dirt and lit it. Then he poured a little water into his mess gear, and a little into mine, and he fried us each an egg. I claimed they were poached, but he was the cook and he said they were fried. Either way, they didn't last long.

"Now we had the chicken to consider. It was a hard decision, I tell you. I wanted to eat it right away, but Rocky said we should save it. Since no other volunteer had found her, he said, we should let her keep producing eggs until we were ordered to move. *Then* we could eat her.

"I guess it was the taste of that egg still fresh in my mouth that made me go along with him. That very night – and I'll hold it against sergeants as long as I live – we had to go out on one of those important matters. We had to crawl over the hill in front of us and find out what was on the other side. The sergeant said 'Just go over there, count the Gooks, and come back and get some shut-eye. Tomorrow we move out.' What could we do?

"We didn't get back for three days. In the meantime, the C-B's had put a four-lane highway through our hen-house."

He looked so miserable as he finished the story that I snickered through the rest of the meal.

It had rained while we were eating, and, as we walked to the store in the late sunlight, the ground steamed and the air was cool. Children played around the stilts of their slatted huts or peeked out at us from the shade beneath. Filipino men, bringing home baskets of fish, nodded gravely as we passed them. And, once in a while, a woman glanced from a darkened doorway and stepped back out of sight.

Sunday was aware of the women.

"Doggone, Tom," he said, "did you notice something funny?"

"What's that?"

"Every time one of these gals pops out to take a look at me, she sees you and pops back in again. Now how do you explain that?"

"I thought it was the other way around."

"Aw, come on," he laughed, "I'm the fair-haired boy of the islands, didn't you know? Those li'l ol' Hawaiian gals – why they'd get so excited they used to shimmy their skirts right down to their ankles." He laughed again. "Ain't it the truth."

"Maybe so," I said, "But I don't see you stepping over any skirts around here."

"Yah, ain't *that* the truth." He suddenly grew sober. "Now how do you explain that?"

"Well," I said, "to these people, you're just half-baked."

"Come on – what kind of an answer is that?"

"No, I mean it. You see, they have a legend. When God made people, first he baked them too long, and they're the black people. Then he didn't bake them long enough, and they're the white people. And finally he baked them just right – and they're the Filipinos. You're just half-baked."

"That's an awful *mean* theory. Where the hell did you hear that?"

"I read it in an Armed Services guidebook."

"You sure?" he replied. "Sounds like Commie propaganda to me."

When we reached the *tindahan*, the community store, we sat at one of the tables outside, ordered some American beer, and leaned back in our rattan chairs.

There were two Englishmen at another table, in khaki shorts and shirts and white jungle hats, but the Filipinos didn't drink here. I had never seen a Filipino drink anything but his coconut brew on his own front porch.

We drank a couple of cans of beer apiece and then it was dark. One minute it was daylight, and then the next minute it was dark. Why? I wondered.

The beer had made me sleepy. I was thinking vaguely about the next day's work, but not really. I was in that strange sort of mood which is half pleasant, half irritable – or was I pleased at my own irritableness, or what? I was thinking I should go to bed, but the idea wasn't strong enough to make me move.

And I hadn't learned anything about Sunday. I had almost forgotten what it was I was supposed to learn.

"How come you hate Mr Froggie so much?" I asked.

"Cause he sits on top of the water and croaks, and every time he croaks in my ear like that, he makes me feel like a tadpole."

"What the hell does that mean?"

"I don't know," he replied.

We were both silent for a while, and then he began to ramble on about some island while we drank our third beer – an island in the bay of San Francisco.

"Yerba Buena," he said. "Goat Island. Hilly. I was in O.G.U. there for weeks, waiting for a berth, waiting, waiting, waiting. . . . Anyhow, the Bay Bridge passed overhead and was anchored right on the island. We used to lean against this big immense pillar . . . cement . . . about a hundred feet high – and talk."

"Talk, talk, talk," I said.

"And the trains would go right over our heads. Those yellow trains, you know? And they drowned us out, naturally. But we got so used to it, it didn't matter. It got so that you would stop right in the middle of a sentence, and wait, maybe wait like ten or fifteen seconds, and then go right on and finish the sentence. Nobody even noticed it."

"Then how come you don't like Mr Froggie?"

"That bridge meant a lot to me," he went on. "There's something about living under a bridge – boy, I've never figured it out. All I know is, without that bridge, I'd have been a real prisoner. I'd have died on that goddamn island. That bridge was my lifeline out of there, and I used to go ashore every night."

"All ashore that's goin' ashore."

"You're corked."

"I'm sleepy."

The girl came with two more cans of beer. She was Filipino, and her name was Esther, and I thought she was beautiful. I thought so even when I wasn't drinking, even when I just came in to buy a pack of cigarettes. She was part Chinese, and her skin, I swear, was pure gold, while her hair and eyebrows were coal black, and her eyes were so big and dark they always looked brimful . . .

Sunday pulled her into his lap.

I was surprised. So was Esther. She sat there timidly with her hands folded, waiting to be released, or to be kissed, or I don't know what.

"Do you know my name?" Sunday asked.

"Sonnee," she said. And she smiled.

"That's good," he said. "That's very, very good."

I stood up.

"Don't you want your beer, matey?"

"No," I said. "Have a good time. We've got a lot of work to do tomorrow, that's all."

I slapped a mosquito and tripped off into the dark. I hated myself for being so miserable, and now there was no pleasure in it at all.

The next day on the job Sunday was in fine spirits. I didn't ask him why. He didn't volunteer the answer. But everything he said on the phone ended with the word *po* – which was a Filipino term of respect, like "sir". If I asked him for a wrench, he said "Yes-po". When I asked him if he were tired, he said "No-po". We made three dives together and I didn't hear one gripe.

The day's work went well. On the first dive we laid about twenty-five sacks of sand, each weighing a hundred pounds, to shore up the next sections of pipe. The sandbags were lowered on the end of a hook-and-loop cable from a derrick on the barge. The eight-inch pipe came down the same way, one section at a time, and on the second dive we laid two sections.

The sections were joined by eight bolts which tightened down on a thick rubber gasket between the pipe flanges. We used ratchet wrenches to seat the bolts and a long-handled straight wrench to make the seal water-tight, and when the two of us got on the handle together, we were practically bumping heads. It was then that I could see him grinning inside his helmet. I didn't care, I told myself, so long as the job got done.

We were on our third dive, and I figured it would be the last of the day. A third section of pipe had been joined, and we were waiting for the fourth to come down. When that was joined, I planned to head topside, because we had piled up a final decompression time of almost three hours. The sky had been clear blue from one horizon to the other during our last rest period, so I wasn't worried about the weather.

Maybe I had been too sharp with Sunday the day before, I thought. Everything was going well.

And then, while we were waiting for the last section of pipe to start its 225-foot trip, we got a warning on the phones. It was trouble, and not the kind of trouble I had expected.

"Mr Shelnick. We have lost the pipe."

"What do you mean you lost it?"

"The pipe is loose," the engineer said. "It escaped from the cable."

"You mean it's in the water? It's coming down?"

"Yes, Monsieur."

"How do you like that?" Sunday said. "They dropped it in the drink."

"That's lovely," I said. "That thing is liable to come down anywhere."

The engineer's voice came on again – "You had better take cover, I think."

Sunday laughed. "*Sauve qui peut*, I think. Where the hell are we supposed to hide?"

"Sunday," I said "you'd better get over on this side of the pipe line. They've been dropping their stuff on your side."

"What difference does it make? I could be fifty yards from here and it still might land right on my skull."

"Play the odds," I said. "Come over on this side."

"I'll stand pat," he replied.

Suddenly there was an unnatural sound in his voice. He was scared, I realized. He had frozen where he was in some kind of superstitious hunch to stay put. And, for the first time, I understood Sunday. He was the kind of guy who handled danger, or his fear of it, by looking the other way.

I crouched up against the sandbags as close as I could, but there was no real cover. All I could do was wait.

"Shine your light up," I said. I aimed my light straight up, and then I saw his light slant upward. But we could see for only fifteen feet, and both of us knew that wouldn't be enough. Movement was slow down here. There would be little time to dodge.

We waited. Neither of us spoke. There was no sound from topside. I was remembering a crazy thing. A guy I knew back home, who worked in a power plant, always used to say – "The voltage doesn't worry me, but the warning signs make me nervous."

Several minutes passed. It's down, I thought. It's down somewhere. And then I saw Sunday's light swerve, and at the same instant I heard his voice. "Tom," he shouted. "Tom! Tommy!"

I got to him as fast as I could. He was down in the sand, writhing on his side, his light shooting in all directions. The pipe lay beside him. He was screaming – "No air! No air!"

I flashed my light on the top of his helmet. The air line was gone. It had been knocked off at the fitting. Quickly I closed the exhaust valve on his helmet. That should give him an air reserve of several minutes.

But he was still screaming, and his voice was shorting in and out on the phone. I turned my light on his face-plate. Water was cascading into his helmet. It was coming through the air-intake valve. The non-return button was unable to block the great pressure of the water. I clamped my left hand over the broken fitting, but I could feel the water still sucking into it.

I pulled him to a sitting position to let the water drain into his suit. His arms went around my legs in a tight grip. Oh, God, I thought – he'll drown unless I can block off that valve. Where's his line!

I dropped my light and started pulling down the radio cable with both hands. The air line was fastened to the cable at twenty-five-foot intervals, and if I could get my hands on it, I could pull in the broken end. But I knew there was no chance of repairing the broken fitting – no chance and no time. I would have to try something else.

"Slack," I shouted. "Slack!" There was slack, and when the marker came into my hands, I felt for the air line. I had it. I pulled in on the rubber air line and soon I saw a stream of bubbles swing into the lights. I grabbed the end of the hose.

Then I jerked out my knife, and, with the handle of it, I gave Sunday a sharp whack on the arm. His grip loosened and I pulled him to his feet. I grabbed a fold of his suit with my left hand, and with the right I sliced at the canvas just below the breastplate. Then I dropped the knife, ripped open the fabric, and started shoving in the end of the air hose with its broken fitting. I forced it up under the breast-plate.

Suddenly the screaming and gurgling in the phone stopped. I reached down, picked up one of the lights, and flashed it into the faceplate of Sunday's helmet. His eyes were wide. His cheek was a bloody gash. Against his cheek was the thing that had scraped it open – the broken fitting on the end of his air line. The water level was just below his chin.

"Turn up the air!" I shouted into the phone. "Engineer – turn up the air full blast."

I hoped that with the air on full force, the pressure would hold out the water. But there was still a dribble coming through the broken fitting. Once again I put my left hand over it. This time I felt no water sucking in, and the dribble stopped. Now all the air coming out of the end of the hose inside the helmet would escape down into the suit and out the rip I had made. The air pressure – thank God – was great enough to keep the water level below his chin.

All we have to do now, I thought, as I looked at his dazed eyes, his wet hair, and his dripping cheek – all we have to do is get through three hours of decompression time.

"Tom," he said weakly.

"You're all right, Sunday," I said.

"Tom," he said – "we'll never make it through decompression."

"Yes, we will," I said. "We'll make it."

I began giving the orders to get us out of there.

"Engineer."

"Yes, Mister Shelnick."

"That lousy pipe was right on target."

"I am sorry, Mister Shelnick. The wind came up."

"What's the sky look like?"

"Clear."

"Well, listen . . . this is going to take a long time. Now listen to this. Sunday's coming up with me. I've got one hand on his air valve, and one arm around his waist. I want you to bring us up like two kids in a cradle. You understand?"

"Yes, I understand."

"All right. This is what you will do. First, you will keep the compressor running full blast. Second, we are not going to use the guideline, and I can't hold a light, so you are going to keep track of the time, and the depth. Pull our lines together. Draw them in *together*. We must not be separated."

"I understand."

"All right. Take us up to sixty feet. Count off six markers and a little more. We'll stay there eighteen minutes."

"Slowly," he said.

"Right," I replied.

I felt the slack come out of our cables, and we began to rise foot by foot. The two lights on the floor grew dim. Then we were in total darkness. The phone was silent.

The time passed almost completely in silence. Sunday answered a few questions at first, and then for a long while he had nothing to say.

"Are you hurt?" I asked him. "Did you get hit below the helmet?"

"No."

"Did my blade catch you when I cut open your suit?"

"I don't think so."

"How do you feel? Does your cheek hurt?"

"I'm cold."

That was all. There was no use asking him what had happened. I knew what had happened. The black pipe had come out of the darkness and slammed him to the bottom. Only his hard hat had saved his life. Now, during our long climb to open air and light, we hung in a cramped grip upon one another and smarted from the glancing blow of near death. We were both afraid.

Only when he saw the glow of daylight, finally, in the next to last stage of decompression, did Sunday reveal what was going through his mind. His voice sounded raw. "When I was on Yerba Buena," he said, "I crossed the bridge every day back and forth."

"Yes," I said, "I remember."

"Sometimes the fog was heavy. I couldn't see the water, and I couldn't see the top of the bridge. It was strange – like hanging in a dream."

"Yes."

"I feel that way now."

I nodded to myself. "I know what you mean."

There was a pause, and then he said, "Tom, do you know I haven't been home in seven years?"

"I didn't know that, Sunday."

He was quiet while we were pulled up to the last decompression stage. Clearly visible now were the bottom of the tug and the large square bottom of the barge. Our cables swept up into the changing, mirrored ceiling.

During our last and longest wait, Sunday spoke only once. "Tommy," he said, "I can't believe it. I can't believe it."

And then we were out. Our helmets were off and the air was fresh. The sky was a white blaze. As we rode a motor launch to the island, I lay on my back and looked up into space, and I had a feeling I remembered from childhood – that at any moment I might fall headlong into open air. This time the feeling did not scare me.

After a few days of rest, Sunday left the Islands. I never saw him again. It took me three months to finish the job alone.

"We had rapture of the depths . . ."

RAPTURE

Jacques-Yves Cousteau

In 1946 Cousteau, the famed inventor of the aqualung, led an expedition to the mysterious cave of the Fountain of Vaucluse in southern France.

Our worst experience in five thousand dives befell us not in the sea but in an inland water-cave, the famous Fountain of Vaucluse near Avignon. The renowned spring is a quiet pool, a crater under a 600 foot limestone cliff above the river Sorgue. A trickle flows from it the year round, until March comes when the Fountain of Vaucluse erupts in a rage of water which swells the Sorgue to a flood. It pumps furiously for five weeks then subsides. The phenomenon has occurred every year in recorded history.

The fountain has evoked the fancy of poets since the Middle Ages. Petrarch wrote sonnets to Laura by the Fountain of Vaucluse in the 14th century. Frederic Mistral, a Provençal poet, was another admirer of the spring. Generations of hydrologists have leaned over the fountain, evolving dozens of theories. They have measured the rainfall on the plateau above, mapped the potholes in it, analysed the water, and determined that it is invariably 55° Fahrenheit all the year round. But no one knew what happened to discharge the amazing flood.

One principle of intermittent natural fountains is that of an underground syphon, which taps a pool of water lying higher inside the hill than the water level of the surface pool. Simple overflows of the inner pool by heavy rain seeping through the porous limestone did not explain Vaucluse, because it did not entirely respond to rainfall. There was either a huge inner reservoir or a series of inner caverns and a system of syphons. Scientific theories had no more validity than Mistral's explanation: "One day the fairy of the fountain changed herself into a beautiful maiden and took an old strolling minstrel by the hand and led him down through Vaucluse's waters to an underground prairie, where seven huge diamonds plugged seven holes. 'See these diamonds?' said the fairy. 'When I lift the seventh, the fountain rises to the roots of the fig tree that drinks only once a year.'" Mistral's theory, as a matter of fact, possessed one more piece of tangible evidence than the scientific guesses. There is a rachitic hundred-year-old fig tree hooked on the vertical wall at the waterline of the annual flood. Its roots are watered but once a year.

A retired Army officer, Commandant Brunet, who had settled in the nearby village of Apt, became an addict of the Fountain as had Petrarch six hundred years before. The Commandant suggested that the Undersea Research Group dive into the Fountain and learn the secret of the mechanism. In 1946 the Navy gave us permission to try. We journeyed to Vaucluse on 24 August, when the spring was quiescent. There seemed to be no point in entering a violent flood if its source might be discovered when the Fountain was quiet.

The arrival of uniformed naval officers and sailors in trucks loaded with diving equipment started a commotion in Vaucluse. We were overwhelmed by boys, vying for the privilege of carrying our air cylinders, portable decompression chamber, aqualungs, and diving dresses, up the wooded trail to the Fountain. Half the town, led by Mayor Garcin, stopped work and accompanied us. They told us about the formidable dive into the Fountain by Señor Negri in 1936. He seemed to have been a remarkably bold type, for we were informed that he had descended in a diving suit with a microphone inside the helmet through which he broadcast a running account of his incredible rigours as he plunged one hundred and twenty feet to the lower elbow of the siphon. Our friends of Vaucluse recalled with a thrill the dramatic moment when the voice from the depths announced that Señor Negri had found Ottonelli's zinc boat!

We already knew about Negri and Ottonelli, the two men who had preceded us into the Fountain, Ottonelli in 1878. We greatly admired Ottonelli's dive in the primitive equipment of his era. We were somewhat mystified by Señor Negri, a Marseille salvage contractor, who had avoided seeing us on several occasions when we sought first-hand information on the topography of the Fountain. We had read his diving report, but we felt deprived of the details he might have given us personally.

The helmet divers described certain features to be found in the Fountain. Ottonelli's report stated that he had alighted on the bottom of a basin forty-five feet down and reached a depth of ninety feet in a sloping tunnel under a huge triangular stone. During the dive his zinc boat had capsized in the pool and slid down through the shaft. Negri said he had gone to one hundred and twenty feet, to the elbow of a syphon leading uphill, and found the zinc boat. The corrosion-proof metal had, of course, survived sixty years immersion. Negri reported he could proceed no further because his air pipe was dragging against a great boulder, precariously balanced on a pivot. The slightest move might have toppled the rock and pinned him down to a gruesome death.

We had predicated our tactical planning on the physical features described by the pioneer divers. Dumas and I were to form the first *cordée* – we used the mountain climber's term because we were to be tied together by a thirty-foot cord attached to our belts. Negri's measurements determined the length of our guide rope – four hundred feet – and the weights we carried on our belts, which were unusually heavy to allow us to penetrate the tunnel he had described and to plant ourselves against currents inside the syphon.

What we could not know until we had gone inside the Fountain was that Negri was over-imaginative. The topography of the cavern was completely unlike his description. Señor Negri's dramatic broadcast was probably delivered just out of sight of the watchers, about fifty feet down. Dumas and I all but gave our lives to learn that Ottonelli's boat never existed. That misinformation was not the only burden we carried into the Fountain: the new air compressor with which we filled the breathing cylinders had prepared a fantastic fate for us.

We adjusted our eyes to the gloom of the crater. Monsieur Garcin had lent us a Canadian canoe, which was floated over the throat of the Fountain, to anchor the guide rope. There was a heavy pig-iron weight on the end of the rope, which we wanted lowered beforehand as far as it would go down. The underwater entry was partially blocked by a huge stone buttress, but we managed to lower the pig-iron fifty-five feet. Chief Petty Officer Jean Pinard volunteered to dive without a protective suit to attempt to roll the pig-iron down as far as it was possible. Pinard returned lobster-red with cold and reported he had shoved the weight down to ninety feet. He did not suspect that he had been down further than Negri.

I donned my constant-volume diving dress over long woollens under the eyes of an appreciative audience perched round the rocky lip of the crater. My wife was among them, not liking this venture at all. Dumas wore an Italian Navy frogman outfit. We were loaded like donkeys. Each wore a three-cylinder lung, rubber foot fins, a heavy dagger, and two large waterproof flashlights, one in hand and one on the belt. Over my left arm was coiled three hundred feet of line in three pieces. Dumas carried an emergency micro-aqualung on his belt, a depth gauge, and a *piolet*, the alpinist's ice axe. There were rock slopes to be negotiated: with our heavy ballast we might need the *piolet*.

The surface commander was the late Lieutenant Maurice Fargues, our resourceful equipment officer. He was to keep his hand on the guide line as we transported the pig-iron down with us. The guide rope was our only communication with the surface. We had memorized a signal code. One tug from below requested Fargues to tighten the rope to clear snags. Three tugs meant pay out more line. Six tugs was the emergency signal for Fargues to haul us up as quickly as possible.

When the *cordée* reached Negri's syphon, we planned to station the pig-iron, and attach to it one of the lengths of rope I carried over my arm. As we climbed on into the syphon, I would unreel this line behind me. We believed that our goal would be found past Negri's see-sawing rock, up a long sloping arm of the syphon, in an air cave, where in some manner unknown Vaucluse's annual eruption was launched.

Embarrassed by the wealth of gadgets we had hanging on to us, and needing our comrades' support, we waded into the pool. We looked around for the last time. I saw the reassuring silhouette of Fargues and the crowd round the amphitheatre. In their forefront was a young abbé, who had no doubt come to be of service in a certain eventuality.

As we submerged, the water liberated us from weight. We stayed motionless in the pool for a minute to test our ballast and communications system. Under my flexible helmet I had a special mouthpiece which allowed me to articulate under water. Dumas had no speaking facility, but could answer me with nods and gestures.

I turned face down and plunged through the dark door. I rapidly passed the buttress into the shaft, unworried about Dumas's keeping pace on the thirty-foot cord at my waist. He can outswim me any time. Our dive was a trial run: we were the first *cordée* of a series. We intended to waste no time on details of topography but to proceed directly to the pig-iron and take it on to the elbow of Negri's syphon, from which we would quickly take up a new thread into the secret of the Fountain. In retrospect, I also find that my subconscious mechanism was anxious to conclude the first dive as soon as possible.

I glanced back and saw Didi gliding easily through the door against a faint green haze. The sky was no longer our business. We belonged now to a world where no light had ever struck. I could not see my flashlight beam beneath me in the frightening dark – the water had no suspended motes to reflect light. A disc of light blinked on and off in the darkness when my flashlight

beam hit rock. I went head down with tigerish speed, sinking by
my overballast, unmindful of Dumas. Suddenly I was held by
the belt and stones rattled past me. Heavier borne than I,
Dumas was trying to brake his fall with his feet. His suit was
filling with water. Big limestone blocks came loose and rumbled
down round me. A stone bounced off my shoulder. I remotely
realized I should try to think. I could not think.

Ninety feet down I found the pig-iron standing on a ledge. It
did not appear in the torch beam as an object from the world
above, but as something germane to this place. Dimly I recalled
that I must do something about the pig-iron. I shoved it down
the slope. It roared down with Dumas's stones. During this
blurred effort I did not notice that I had lost the lines coiled on
my arm. I did not know that I had failed to give Fargues three
tugs on the line to pay out the weight. I had forgotten Fargues
and everything behind us. The tunnel broke into a sharper
decline. I circled my right hand continuously, playing the torch
in spirals on the clean and polished walls. I was travelling at two
knots. I was in the Paris subway. I met nobody. There was
nobody in the Metro, not a single rock bass. No fish at all.

At that time of year our ears are well trained to pressure after a
summer's diving. *Why did my ears ache so?* Something was
happening. The light no longer ran around the tunnel walls.
The beam spread on a flat bottom, covered with pebbles. It was
earth, not rock, the detritus of the chasm. I could find no walls. I
was on the floor of a vast drowned cave. I found the pig-iron,
but no zinc boat, no syphon, and no precariously balanced rock.
My head ached. I was drained of initiative.

I returned to our purpose, to learn the geography of the
immensity that had no visible roof or walls, but rolled away
down at a forty-five-degree incline. I could not surface without
searching the ceiling for the hole that led up to the inner cavern
of our theory.

I was attached to something, I remembered. The flashlight
picked out a rope which curled off to a strange form floating
supine above the pebbles. Dumas hung there in his cumbersome
equipment, holding his torch like a ridiculous glow-worm. Only

his arms were moving. He was sleepily trying to tie his *piolet* to the pig-iron line. His black frogman suit was filling with water. He struggled weakly to inflate it with compressed air. I swam to him and looked at his depth gauge. It read one hundred and fifty feet. The dial was flooded. We were deeper than that. We were at least two hundred feet down, four hundred feet away from the surface at the bottom of a crooked slanting tunnel.

We had rapture of the depths, but not the familiar drunkenness. We felt heavy and anxious, instead of exuberant. Dumas was stricken worse than I. I thought: *This is not how I should feel at this depth . . . I can't go back until I learn where we are. Why don't I feel a current? The pig-iron line is our only way home. What if we lose it? Where is the rope I had on my arm?* I was able in that instant to recall that I had lost the line somewhere above. I took Dumas's hand and closed it round the guide line. "Stay here," I shouted. "I'll find the shaft." Dumas understood me to mean I had no air and needed the safety aqualung. I sent the beam of the flashlight round in search of the roof of the cave. I found no ceiling.

Dumas was passing under heavy narcosis. He thought I was the one in danger. He fumbled to release the emergency lung. As he tugged hopelessly at his belt, he scudded across the drowned shingle and abandoned the guide line to the surface. The rope dissolved in the dark. I was swimming above, mulishly seeking for a wall or a ceiling, when I felt his weight tugging me back like a drifting anchor, restraining my search.

Above us somewhere were seventy fathoms of tunnel and crumbling rock. My weakened brain found the power to conjure up our fate. When our air ran out we would grope along the ceiling and suffocate in dulled agony. I shook off this thought and swam down to the ebbing glow of Dumas's flashlight.

He had almost lost consciousness. When I touched him, he grabbed my wrist with awful strength and hauled me towards him for a final experience of life, an embrace that would take me with him. I twisted out of his hold and backed away. I examined Dumas with the torch. I saw his protruding eyes rolling inside the mask.

The cave was quiet between my gasping breaths. I marshalled all my remaining brain power to consider the situation. Fortunately there was no current to carry Dumas away from the pig-iron. If there had been the least current, we would have been lost. *The pig-iron must be near.* I looked for that rusted metal block, more precious than gold. And suddenly there it was, stolid and reassuring. Its line flew away into the dark, towards the hope of life.

In his stupor, Didi lost control of his jaws and his mouthpiece slipped from his teeth. He swallowed water and took some in his lungs before he somehow got the grip back into his mouth. Now, with the guide line beckoning, I realized that I could not swim to the surface, carrying the inert Dumas, who weighed at least twenty-five pounds in his waterlogged suit. I was in a state of exhaustion from the mysterious effect of the cave. We had not exercised strenuously, yet Dumas was helpless and I was becoming idiotic.

I would climb the rope, dragging Dumas with me. I grasped the pig-iron rope and started up, hand-over-hand, with Dumas drifting below, along the smooth vertical rock.

My first three hand-holds on the line were interpreted correctly by Fargues as the signal to pay out more rope. He did so, with a will. With utter dismay I saw the rope slackening and made superhuman efforts to climb it. Fargues smartly fed me rope when he felt my traction. It took an eternal minute for me to work out the right tactics, namely that I should continue to haul down the rope, until the end of it came into Fargues' hand. He would never let go. I hauled the rope in dull glee.

Four hundred feet of rope passed through my hands and curled into the cave. And a knot came into my hands. Fargues was giving us more rope to penetrate the ultimate gallery of Vaucluse. He had efficiently tied on another length to encourage us to pass deeper.

I dropped the rope like an enemy. I would have to climb the tunnel slope like an alpinist. Foot by foot I climbed the finger-holds of rock, stopping when I lost my respiratory rhythm by exertion and was near to fainting. I drove myself on, and felt that I was making progress. I reached for a good hand-hold, standing on the tips of my fins. The crag eluded my fingers and I was dragged down by the weight of Dumas.

The shock turned my mind to the rope again and I suddenly recalled our signals: six tugs meant pull everything up. I grabbed the line and jerked it, confident that I could count to six. The line was slack and snagged on obstacles in the four hundred feet to Maurice Fargues. *Fargues, do you not understand my situation?* I was at the end of my strength. Dumas was hanging on me.

Why doesn't Dumas understand how bad he is for me? Dumas, you will die, anyway. Maybe you are already gone. Didi, I hate to do it, but you are dead and you will not let me live. Go away, Didi. I reached for my belt dagger and prepared to cut the cord to Dumas.

Even in my incompetence there was something that held the knife in its holster. *Before I cut you off, Didi, I will try again to reach Fargues.* I took the line and repeated the distress signal, again and again. *Didi, I am doing all a man can do. I am dying too.*

On shore, Fargues stood in perplexed concentration. The first *cordée* had not been down for the full period of the plan, but the strange pattern of our signals disturbed him. His hard but sensitive hand on the rope had felt no clear signals since the episode a few minutes back when suddenly we wanted lots of rope. He had given it to us, eagerly adding another length. *They must have found something tremendous down there,* thought Fargues. He was eager to penetrate the mystery himself on a later dive. Yet he was uneasy about the lifelessness of the rope in the last few minutes. He frowned and fingered the rope like a pulse, and waited.

Up from the lag of rope, four hundred feet across the friction of rocks, and through the surface, a faint vibration tickled Fargue's finger. He reacted by standing and grumbling, half to himself, half to the cave watchers, *"Qu'est-ce que je risque? De me faire engueuler?"* (What do I risk? Being sworn at?) With a set face he hauled the pig-iron in.

I felt the rope tighten. I jerked my hand off the dagger and hung on. Dumas's air cylinders rang on the rocks as we were borne swiftly up. A hundred feet above I saw a faint triangle of green light, where hope lay. In less than a minute Fargues pulled us out into the pool and leaped in the water after the senseless Dumas. Tailliez and Pinard waded in after me. I gathered what strength I had left to control my emotions, not to break down. I managed to walk out of the pool. Dumas lay on his stomach and vomited. Our friends stripped off our rubber suits. I warmed myself round a cauldron of flaming petrol. Fargues and the doctor worked over Dumas. In five minutes he was on his feet, standing by the fire. I handed him a bottle of brandy. He took a drink and said, "I'm going down again." I wondered where Simone was.

The Mayor said, "When your air bubbles stopped coming to the surface, your wife ran down the hill. She said she could not stand it." Poor Simone had raced to a café in Vaucluse and ordered the most powerful spirit in the house. A rumour-monger raced through the village, yelling that one of the divers was drowned. Simone cried, "Which one? What colour was his mask?"

"Red," said the harbinger.

Simone gasped with relief – my mask was blue. Then she thought of Didi in his red mask and her joy collapsed. She returned distractedly up the trail to the Fountain. There stood Didi, a miracle to her.

Dumas's recuperative powers soon brought his colour back and his mind cleared. He wanted to know why we had been drugged in the cavern. In the afternoon another *cordée*, Tailliez and Guy Morandiere, prepared to dive, without the junk we had carried. They wore only long underwear and light ballast, which made them slightly buoyant. They planned to go to the cavern and reconnoitre for the passage which led to the secret of Vaucluse. As soon as they found it, they would immediately return and sketch the layout for the third *cordée*, which would make the final plunge.

From the diving logs of Captain Tailliez and Morandiere, I am able to recount their experience, which was almost as appalling as ours. Certainly it took greater courage than ours to enter the Fountain from which we had been so luckily saved. In the few minutes they spent just under the surface of the pool, getting used to the water, Morandiere felt intense cold. They entered the tunnel abreast, roped together. Second *cordée* tactics were to swim down side by side along the ceiling.

When they encountered humps sticking down from the roof, they were to duck under them and then return to follow the ceiling closely. Each hump they met promised to level off beyond, but never did. They went down and down. Our only depth gauge had been ruined, but the veteran Tailliez had a sharp physiological sense of depth. At an estimated one hundred and twenty feet he halted the march so they might study their subjective sensations. Tailliez felt the first inviting throbs of rapture of the depths. He knew that to be impossible at a mere twenty fathoms. However, the symptoms were pronounced.

He called to Morandiere that they should turn back. Morandiere manoeuvred himself and the rope to facilitate Tailliez's turnabout. As he did so, he heard that Tailliez's respiratory rhythm was disorderly, and faced his partner so that Tailliez could see him give six pulls on the pig-iron rope. Unable to exchange words under water, the team had to depend on errant flashlight beams and understanding to accomplish the turn. Morandiere stationed himself below Tailliez to conduct the Captain to the surface. Tailliez construed these activities to mean that Morandiere was in trouble. Both men were slipping into the blank rapture that had almost finished the first *cordée*.

Tailliez carefully climbed the guide line. The rope behind drifted aimlessly in the water, and a loop hung round his shoulders. Tailliez felt he had to sever the rope before it entangled him. He whipped out his dagger and cut it away. Morandiere, swimming freely below him, was afraid his mate was passing out. The confused second *cordée* ascended to the green hall light of the Fountain. Morandiere closed in, took Tailliez's feet, and gave him a strong boost through the narrow door. The effort upset Morandiere's breathing cycle.

We saw Tailliez emerge in his white underwear, Morandiere

following through the underwater door. Tailliez broke the surface, found a footing, and walked out of the water, erect and wild-eyed. In his right hand he held his dagger, upside down. His fingers were cut to the bone by the blade and blood was flowing down his sodden woollens. He did not feel it.

We resolved to call it a day with a shallow plunge to map the entrance of the Fountain. We made sure that Didi, in his anger against the cave, could not slip down to the drowned cavern that had nearly been our tomb. Fargues lashed a 150-foot line to Dumas's waist and took Didi's dagger to prevent him cutting himself loose and going down further. The final reconnaissance of the entrance shaft passed without incident.

It was an emotional day. That evening in Vaucluse the first and second *cordées* made a subjective comparison of cognac narcosis and rapture of the Fountain. None of us could relax, thinking of the enigmatic stupor that had overtaken us. We knew the berserk intoxication of *l'ivresse des grandes profondeurs* at two hundred and fifty feet in the sea, but why did this clear, lifeless limestone water cheat a man's mind in a different way?

Simone, Didi and I drove back to Toulon that night, thinking hard, despite fatigue and headache. Long silences were spaced by occasional suggestions. Didi said, "Narcotic effects aren't the only cause of diving accidents. There are social and subjective fears, the air you breathe . . ." I jumped at the idea. "The air you breathe!" I said. "Let's run a lab test on the air left in the lungs."

The next morning we sampled the cylinders. The analysis showed 1/2000 of carbon monoxide. At a depth of one hundred and sixty feet the effect of carbon monoxide is sixfold. The amount we were breathing may kill a man in twenty minutes. We started our new diesel-powered free-piston air compressor. We saw the compressor sucking in its own exhaust fumes. We had all been breathing lethal doses of carbon monoxide.

THE TRIALS OF A BATHYSCAPHE

Pierre Willm

The 1950s were a Golden Age of French underwater exploration; quite aside from the "aqualung" expeditions led by Jacques-Yves Cousteau, the French Navy was developing the F.N.R.S 3, an independent submersible, or "bathyscaphe", intended to go down to hitherto unexplored depths. Engineer Pierre Willm, along with Captain George Houot and Leading Seaman Piovano, comprised the first crew of the F.R.N.S. 3:

On 4 June, immediately after breakfast, we started the trials. I clambered on to the bridge while Houot and Leading Seaman Piovano . . . shut themselves into the sphere.

"The hatch-cover is bolted down," came the message from below.

There was no question of putting the bathyscaphe into a dive yet; we had first to make sure that the air-lock worked properly. This vertical shaft, fitted with two portholes at its base, has two functions. It provides access to the sphere, but at the same time it serves to control the trim, and when it fills with water the bathyscaphe submerges. The system is very simple. The sea-water inlet at the base of the shaft is fitted with two valves. One of them is controlled from the deck of the bathyscaphe. In the event of the *F.N.R.S. 3* surfacing while its passengers were too faint to open the hatch themselves, it would be essential for the rescuers to be able quickly to empty the air-lock. A hydraulic pump inside the sphere operates a second valve on the pipe between the first valve and the sea-water inlet. An opening at the top of the air-lock provides an outlet for the air when the sea water enters from below. This vent is likewise fitted with dual control.

The object of the present trial was not to immerse the bathyscaphe, which had not yet received either her ballast or her petrol. An increase in weight of about one ton would lower the waterline only three or four centimetres.

I stood on the conning tower and turned on the sea-water inlet.

"The water is rising, but very slowly," announced Piovano.

"How far has it got?"

"It's reached the lower porthole in the air-lock."

A full ten minutes elapsed before Houot picked up the telephone in his turn.

"It's reached the upper porthole. That's as far as it can go," he said. The first part of the test was finished. My calculations had led me to expect that the compartment would be flooded much more rapidly than this.

I was still vaguely preoccupied by this problem as I replied:

"You can blow out the water."

Through the telephone I could hear the rhythmic sound of the hydraulic pump that closes the air-vent. A few seconds later a blast of compressed air was discharged into the air-lock, and horrible groans suddenly shook the metal plates of the *F.N.R.S. 3* and set her superstructures vibrating. The abrupt increase in pressure was buckling the plates. When our vessel was floating at her normal waterline, the external pressure on the hull exerted by the sea would prevent any vibration. After we had finished blowing-off, bubbles disturbed the surface of the dock at deck level, and the ripples rolled across the water and broke against the quay.

We now had to repeat the operation from the beginning, but this time expelling the water from outside. On the quayside, workmen arranged cylinders and unwound a coil of spiral copper hose-piping.

"Ready," called Houot, as calm as ever.

I was worried about the air-lock filling so slowly. When I blew out the water, the hull again started to rumble and vibrate.

"Oh, don't worry about that," said Houot emerging from the top hatch. "All things considered, the trial's conclusive. We'll go on to the next."

But that evening I was not completely satisfied. The water had not risen fast enough. Could my calculations be at fault? I hardly had time to do them over again. I was now busy with the electric circuits and tomorrow we were going to start testing the electromagnets that held the shot ballast in the silos. The bathyscaphe's manoeuvrability while diving would depend upon the sensitivity of these magnets. Each silo had its separate control, but a fifth button controlled the whole lot and enabled me to jettison 10 kilos per second. I could already imagine myself pressing this central button and checking the bathyscaphe's course, bringing her to a halt or making her surface.

I also had to make sure that an instrument I hoped we would never have to use worked properly. The sphere contains a leak detector. If the sea were to flood our steel ball this device – faithful to us after our deaths – would break the current in the ballast circuits and the F.N.R.S. 3 would rise to the surface. Investigators would at least be able to determine the causes of the catastrophe. But enough of this grim possibility.

On this hot afternoon of 5 June, the air was balmy, the sky cloudless. The natives, who prefer to retire from the sun, and the summer visitors who invade the beaches of this coast only to get sunburnt, would have been much astonished to see so many bathers on the edge of the Vauban dock. In fact the swimmers placed at our disposal by the Undersea Research Group were all wearing diving gear. One after another they clambered aboard the bathyscaphe with their compressed air cylinders on their backs and made the acquaintance of a machine which, as we well knew, would always need their services. When the bathyscaphe reached the site of her dive, their job would be to remove the safety clamps that are bolted over the electromagnets controlling the shot silos while the vessel is under tow. These safety devices enable one to cut off the current and keep the batteries at full strength.

I climbed down into the sphere in my turn, while Houot remained outside to direct the diving work. The divers from the U.R.G. were smiling, and seemed happy to be back with an officer who had long worked with them. I pulled down the switch and turned on the electromagnets. The current was normal. I was surprised to hear the sound of the divers' breathing as it re-echoed in the resonant sphere around me. From time to time a head, legs, or a body appeared outside the porthole. The safety clamp which the frogman was taking up to the surface gave a metallic flash as it passed.

It was reassuring to watch this marine ballet. The divers had at once adopted the *F.N.R.S. 3*, that peaceful sister of the warships on which they usually worked.

The telephone buzzed.

"What shall we start with?" inquired Houot.

"Ask the divers to take up their watching positions. I shall jettison the normal ballast, the safety ballast, and the guide chain in that order."

"Better start with the guide chain," he replied.

I pressed the button. Perhaps one day some emergency on the sea-bed might compel us to shed this 10-metre chain which dangles below the sphere when she goes down. As she approaches the bottom the weight of the links is taken by the ground, thus lightening our submersible and allowing her to hover in equilibrium. As I watched, the ammeter needle gave a jump, indicating a break in the current.

"Guide chain normal," came word from the bridge.

A few minutes later a dull rumble began the instant my finger pressed the button marked "Safety Ballast". The flaps of the two bunkers under the float had just swung open and two tons of lead shot was falling towards the bottom of the dock.

"Safety ballast normal," said Houot, to whom the divers had passed on their observations.

Then for five seconds, timed by the watch in my hand, I pressed down the "port bow" and a hissing noise told me that the steel shot was flowing out of the silo. I repeated the operation three times more; each time some eighty kilos of steel went down to join the two tons of lead at the bottom of the dock.

When I returned to the bridge, everyone was smiling. The week was drawing to a close and the bathyscaphe had well earned a weekend rest.

"Till Monday. Forget your baby for the next couple of days," Houot advised me.

But I could not forget her. The dockyard was closed on Saturday and at home I wandered restlessly from room to room. My children were noisy; they got on my nerves. No doubt my wife noticed it.

"Pierre, I've got some shopping to do in the town," she told me.

"All right, Jacqueline, I'll take the car out."

And there we were, almost on the road to the dockyard. My wife stopped me at one shop and then a second. Waiting at the wheel was exasperating. It would be so easy to leave Jacqueline to get on with her shopping – in no time at all I could drive to the dockyard. But there she was again, and I gloomily set off for home.

"You seem to be miles away," she remarked.

It was true. I could think of nothing but the bathyscaphe, and the least thing irritated me. It seemed then as if there might develop a rift in our family life. But fortunately the future proved the contrary and, little by little, in the course of the summer, we came to realize the strength of our mutual confidence. In fact we even profited from the experience – but I am anticipating . . .

For the rest of the weekend I was in a state of nervous tension. The family visits to the beach seemed interminable. I sat and scribbled sums in my notebook and impatiently worked out a fresh programme of tests for the coming week, but the sun seemed to remain fixed in the sky. I could not help gazing at the immense expanse of blue sea; it was a positive challenge. When I had said "Yes" to Gempp I had not believed in the call of adventure; but now it was no longer a question of plans and working drawings. I was caught in the snare; the game had to be played out to the end.

There was a full programme for the week just beginning. Workmen went in again on Monday morning. A gang finished installing the petrol and ballast level-gauges. The nerve centre, the sphere itself, was coming alive. When the *F.N.R.S. 3* disappeared below the waves, her pilot would need to be constantly informed of the state of the controls at his disposal. The cables and pipes that converge on the porthole are the vessel's spinal cord; they form the essential links between the inside and the outside.

We had first to try out all the devices controlled by these links. After that, Houot and I would turn our attention to the bathyscaphe's sensory organs. She had a single eye, with searchlights to light up the water in front of it; and, like the fish of the great deeps, she would also possess other senses for detecting distant objects. Besides a pressure-gauge which acted as a depth-recorder and gave us our distance from the surface, we should employ an echo-sounder to record the depth from the bottom and a similar obstacle-detector to probe for danger ahead when cruising at the bottom. An asdic set, with a microphone directed upwards, would enable us to communicate between the sphere and the convoy ship – provided that the ship were almost directly over the submersible. Wireless waves do not travel under water, so it would be impossible, while diving, to use the radio-telephone, with which the sphere is also equipped.

This work kept us so busy that Houot had to wait till the end of the week before carrying out a second air-regeneration test. On Saturday morning we shut him in, this time from the outside and while he philosophized with his companion Badre, a dispenser from the Centre des Études Pratiques des Sous-Marins, I made ready for the petrol to arrive. A great many safety precautions had to be taken.

When I arrived on the site at about seven in the morning on Monday 15 June, I was challenged by an armed sentry. He was guarding the only entry through the barbed wire entanglement. "No Entry", "No Smoking", proclaimed a multitude of notices. A few workmen were already on the job, but today their steps were soundless; they had exchanged their heavy boots for rubber-soled shoes. A single spark from the friction of a shoe-nail against the deck-plates might unleash disaster.

Houot was waiting for me at the edge of the quay. The sky was cloudless, it looked like being a fine day. A tanker drove through the dock gate. Since I was uncertain what weight the dock would bear, I had given orders that the vehicle's payload should be reduced to 10,000 litres. The tanker would therefore have to make eight trips. It came through the gate without hindrance, drove up to the embankment, and stopped level with the bathyscaphe. The workmen immediately connected the pipes. The first litres of petrol were flowing into our tanks.

"If you ask me," said Houot, "the bathyscaphe's only dangerous when she's on the surface."

I smiled, and hoped that the future would confirm his confidence in this paradox.

At 5.30 p.m., the float, having drunk 78,000 litres (17,160 gallons), at last settled down to a graceful waterline. We could not help admiring her from the height of the quay.

The next morning was spent in meticulously loading the safety bunkers with lead shot and filling the silos with steel shot.

As soon as the shot was loaded, Houot decided to go right ahead with the first dive. While he shut himself in, accompanied by Leading Seaman Piovano, the big crane came to a stop abeam of the conning tower. The spreader that had been used when the bathyscaphe was first lowered into the water was once more lowered from the crane and its ends shackled to the deck. In this way we could check her from diving too violently and bumping on the bottom of the dock. I stayed on board to see to the last ballasting, a sort of "weighing-in" which would prove or disprove my calculations. It was a moving moment. The machine was about to disappear beneath the waves for the first time.

"I'm opening the valve," Houot informed me over the telephone.

A little water ran into the air-lock and then stopped. Nothing happened. Everyone looked very disappointed. The air-lock had inexplicably failed to fill.

"I'm going to blow out the water."

The next moment the plates began to vibrate and creak. A quarter of an hour later, I entered the air-lock and joined my companion, who was climbing up from the sphere. He stopped in front of the lower porthole, round which beads of water were forming.

"The first leak," he announced.

In itself, the accident seemed harmless. At three metres below the waterline, the pressure was only 300 grammes per square centimetre. On the other hand, once the vessel was under water the pressures on the two sides of the wall would balance one another. A leak at one of the portholes in the air-lock was therefore only a surface incident.

Workmen immediately started to dismantle the sea-water inlet valve. The cause of all our worries was a large rag blocking the pipe. At last we knew why the water had risen so slowly into the air-lock at the previous test. Meanwhile, Houot put on an aqualung and went down to smear the seating of the porthole with sealing compound. The leak was stopped, at least-temporarily, and first thing the next afternoon – after twenty-four hours' delay – our craft was finally ready to dive.

There were more bystanders than on the day before. People had begun to talk about the bathyscaphe and someone had even been spreading a rumour about the rag which had blocked the sea-water inlet.

"Hoho! Supposing it had been a sardine," suggested a voice with a strong Southern accent.

The chief of the dockyard appeared at the edge of the quay. The interest he was now taking in the submersible was flattering.

Houot and his leading seaman had clamped the hatch of the
sphere behind them. The hawsers under the spreader were
dangling from their shackles. With my watch in my hand, I
checked the time the air-lock took to fill up: eight minutes. So
the original calculations had been correct. The foot of the
conning tower submerged.

"The water has stopped rising," complained Houot over the
telephone.

"That's because you've stopped going down. But Willm's
looking after it," replied Cabarrou, into the telephone on the
quay. He was chief medical officer of the Undersea Research
Group, and had turned up on the quay to prove that the medical
corps was taking an interest in the bathyscaphe.

As a matter of fact, it was the moment I had been waiting for
to top up the ballast. I had a boat ready, and on our first trip we
took 400 kilos of steel shot; the "weigh in" of 2 June was to
check her total weight, now we should find her exact displace-
ment while diving.

"One bag in each silo."

I gave the orders myself. By carefully dividing the ballast we
could keep her trim even. Four bags. I was a long way out. Four
times more I crossed the dock in the dinghy. I enjoyed these
short trips. The bathyscaphe was going to dive. She did it in her
own way – quietly. The spreader was lowered by crane and
followed our craft as she slowly disappeared.

"All's well. The water is filthy; we're on the bottom,"
proclaimed Houot, whose words were relayed by the powerful
voice of Dr Cabarrou.

At a sign, two divers threw up a spurt of water and then
disappeared. They were going to disconnect the shackles of the
spreader so that the crane could hoist it out of the water. But
that was not all. They also had to slip two large bins under the
float to catch the lead shot when Houot discharged it. The
divers met with some difficulties.

"Ready!" announced Cabarrou at last.

A few seconds later, the *F.N.R.S. 3* shed her safety ballast
and surfaced. She was on a perfectly even keel and her screws

churned the air as though her motors were running, although, in point of fact, they were not yet installed. The vertical movement through the water was alone responsible for this most effective little touch.

Twenty minutes later Houot emerged from the air-lock. Words were superfluous; the look we exchanged expressed our mutual confidence in the future. We both knew that in another two days we should have fresh evidence of our submersible's abilities.

A dive in the sea to twenty-eight metres was on the programme and on that day the bathyscaphe was going through the dock gates for the first time. The trial was intended to test the efficiency of the system for jettisoning the outside accumulators. These batteries are arranged in two groups, one on each side, and held in place by electromagnets. They supply the searchlights in front of the porthole, and their power also serves to turn the driving motors. Like the guide chain, these two batteries can be jettisoned and also act as additional safety ballast. Together they have an apparent weight (weight in water) of more than a ton. There must be no risk of the rollers that support them jamming on their skids. Hence the trial had to be carried out on full scale, and we had manufactured dummy accumulators for the occasion.

We were thrilled that at last we should be working outside the hospitable shelter of Vauban dock.

"I'm afraid this north-east wind may mean the mistral's blowing up. We'd better dive under Canier Point instead of off Cape Brun. The Vignettes Roadstead is completely exposed," said Houot to me.

We were both equally impatient. It was scarcely day-break. The tug *Fort* was waiting for us in the roads, and the Harbour Authority launches had entered the dock.

We had just carried out various checks and the commanding officer consulted his notebook for the last time.

"Soda lime, Willm?"

"Twelve baskets full."

"Oxygen?"

"Four cylinders at 125 atmospheres."

"Compressed air?"

"195 atmospheres in Group One, 190 atmospheres in Group Two."

We had topped up the charge in the various batteries the night before and personally supervised the men filling the shot bunkers.

Now, shoulder to shoulder in the cramped space of the conning tower, we watched the launches manoeuvring. The bathyscaphe cast off from her pontoon and glided towards the gate. Today, 19 June, she was at last going to show us what she could do. Like the worthy ship of the Marine Nationale that she was, she would obey the directions contained in a Ministerial order governing the smallest details of her departure from the dock. The *Élie Monnier* was not available, so the *Fort* was taking her place. Commander Tailliez had been detailed to direct operations. The divers from the Undersea Research Group were naturally in the happy party.

When we reached the middle of the roadstead, the launches stopped and the *Fort* passed a tow-rope. Our little spaniel was on her lead. We left her regretfully. It seemed to us that she was being watched from all the vessels around. We joined Commander Tailliez on board Launch 771.

When we arrived at the diving site, the various people concerned gathered in the wardroom for a conference. Dr Cabarrou was present. The skipper of the tug, who was overwhelmed by his responsibilities and who had no idea what a bathyscaphe might be, nodded his head and took little or no part in the discussion. This conference forged the first links between men destined to work together, on more than one occasion, in carrying out a great enterprise. It is no easy matter to coordinate operations on the surface and at the bottom.

Throughout this first dive in the sea, the bathyscaphe was to remain connected by telephone to a boat. Later on, of course, we should cut this umbilical cord. There could be no question of descending into the great deeps trailing a cable, however light.

The palaver went on for a long time and it was 12.30 before we went on board the *F.N.R.S. 3*. The water proved denser than I expected, which involved us in a further delay. A ballast-shot working-party was called for. The dinghy shuttled to and fro helping us to load the 50-kilo bags. Houot slipped and gave a cry of pain: he had twisted his back. Fortunately, the job was almost done, but it was already 1.30 by my watch when Houot joined me in the sphere, after checking the number of the safety clamps the divers had removed from the electromagnets.

Our overhead lamp spread a lovely yellow light and all our instruments were gleaming. The porthole was a patch of green. While Houot set about bolting down the hatch-cover, I picked up the telephone to talk to Tailliez, who was still in the conning tower; then I suddenly changed my mind, and insubordinately brushed the bathyscaphe's skipper aside.

"No, let me do it, I want to see how it's done."

So saying, I seized the ratchet spanner. It was the first time I had had the honour of shutting myself up between these narrow walls which I had festooned with every kind of instrument. I gave the spanner a last twist and turned round.

Houot was operating the oil pump that closes the first of the two valves that divide the filling pipe of the air-lock. I then telephoned through to Tailliez to open the second one from the deck. We were now free to choose our own moment of departure.

The seconds ticked by. Were they having trouble on deck?

"Open one half-turn," announced Tailliez.

"That's not enough," replied Houot. "Give it at least two turns."

"Wait a minute I'll start again," came the obedient reply, from our Commanding Officer.

For three full minutes the line remained silent. It seemed to us a long time, and I wondered if they realized on deck just how long it seemed. Does the surgeon worry about his patient's waiting agony while he is washing his hands? The dialogue began again.

Tailliez: "The valve won't open more than a half-turn."

Houot: "We must have two full turns. Get someone stronger – get Cabarrou!"

This was a good idea: our doctor's strength was legendary.

After a fresh silence the deck crew admitted its impotence. Action was imperative. I raised my arms and flung myself on the hexagonal heads of the screws and undid them one after the other. Pushing open the hatch, I scrambled up the air-lock ladder and flung back the hatch-cover. The light dazzled me. I must have looked like a Jack-in-the-box popping up. Two sharp blows on the valve control and it opened obediently.

"*Voilà! Au revoir!*" And with these three words I shot back into my hole.

Ten minutes later the hatch was closed again. We could dive at last. The valve was open. Through the porthole in the hatch, we watched the water rising in the air-lock. Suddenly it stopped. The bathyscaphe needed a further increase of ballast. The dinghy went into action again bringing 20-kilo pig-iron weights which were thrown loose into the conning tower by the deck party, who were in as much of a hurry to finish the business as we were. Two hundred kilos was enough.

"You're going under . . . You're under," announced the telephonist crouching in the dinghy.

We were entirely preoccupied with our instruments and scarcely gave a thought to the divers swimming away in the water above our heads. 9 metres, 10 metres, 11 metres. The needle of the shallow-depth pressure-gauge* turned regularly.

The porthole grew darker and darker. 16 metres, 17 metres, 18 metres. We were rapidly approaching the bottom, which, according to the sounder on the launch, was at only 30 metres. Perhaps we ought to slow down our descent. We thought of doing so, but it was already too late. The end of the guide chain

---

* This low-pressure gauge is graduated from 0 to 5 kilogrammes per square centimetre, that is to say down to 50 metres (165 feet). After that it is automatically shut off, and a high-pressure gauge comes into action.

must have touched bottom. 24 metres, 25 metres. A delightful meadow of green seaweed rose to meet us.

Although we were used to seeing such sights when aqualung diving we were both deeply moved, and for us these minutes were historic. 28 metres (92 feet) down, the bathyscaphe rested on a strip of sand bordered by fields of seaweed.

We had landed without a bump, but prudence demanded that, before bringing the machine finally to rest on the sea-bed, we should keep her a short distance off the ground. There was a slight risk of burying the sphere in the mud. Chronometer in hand I gave the word, "One, two, three, now!" And for thirty seconds Houot pressed the shot discharge button. Our toy answered our hopes. She went up with a bound and hovered obediently in equilibrium on the end of the guide chain. We could not feel the slightest oscillation.

Through the fifteen centimetres of perspex I could hardly make out the bottom, which had slipped away from my sight. But the dark green mass of marine vegetation stood out against the lighter-grey of the sand and it all looked like a garden.

"Look, Houot, there aren't many fish."

My companion moved over to the porthole and began to kneel down. I rose and backed away to make room for him. A bit too quickly perhaps . . . and I blessed the brainwave that had prompted me to put a detachable piece of perspex over the switches for the electromagnets. Had it not been for this protection, I should have backed into the switch-board and immediately jettisoned four tons of shot.

In my turn, I took over the telephone. The dinghy must have been drifting at the end of its 100 metres of cable and the watch sleeping peacefully in the sun.

It was past 4 o'clock and we had left the surface seventy minutes before. Where were the divers? No doubt they were waiting at a respectful distance, expecting us to jettison the dummy batteries at any moment. The dummies had buoys attached to them, to make them easier to recover. We had eaten nothing since seven that morning. The discussion and the series of delays had deceived our appetites for a while.

"Listen, Willm," suggested Houot, "let's bring a snack down with us next time."

"Good idea."

This time hunger prompted us to get the trial over quickly. The telephonist condescended to reply and our Commanding Officer informed us that we might proceed with the exercise as planned.

"The boats are moving off," said the man in the dinghy, "leaving you a clear field for surfacing."

Houot pressed a button; we heard a dull rumble.

15 metres, 10 metres. I read the figures on the pressure-gauge. Then, suddenly, the telephonist announced:

"Bathyscaphe on the surface!"

The dive had been too short for our liking, but it had gone off excellently. A touch of melancholy mingled with our joy. How soon could we pass on to the real trials? We still had no motors, searchlights, or outside batteries. The test of the machine's efficiency had certainly been conclusive, but all sorts of details still had to be checked. We were well aware that disagreeable surprises might await us.

"Perhaps we'd better get a breath of fresh air," remarked Houot.

Leaving the sphere involves a certain number of operations. Houot took up a position before the compressed-air control-board, I stood in front of that controlling the hydraulic-oil system. We did not waste time discussing the dive, but set about the jobs that would henceforth be ours.

"Ready?"

"Ready!"

I manipulated the three control cocks and started the oil pump. The pressure-gauge rose: 50, 70 atmospheres.

"Air-vent closed."

"I'm blowing out the water," replied Houot.

And a hissing, which surprised us for a moment, became audible. But everything was in order. The compressed-air gauge fell gently from 190 to 170 atmospheres. Through the porthole, we saw that the particles suspended in the water were going down and we also kept an eye on the U-shaped tube of the little differential pressure-gauge; it told us the level of water in the air-lock.

Ten minutes later we were on deck, where a task awaited us which proved far harder than we had expected. Even with eight of us on the job, we could not haul in the guide chain. It would be dangerous to leave it trailing behind while the bathyscaphe was being towed into port. On the narrow deck we fell over one another to no effect. In the end we attached a buoy to the troublesome object and sent it to the bottom. When the *Fort* had finished fishing up our dummy batteries she could deal with the chain.

As the sun went down our convoy set out for Toulon at a speed of three knots, and two hours later we were in the roads.

That dive of 19 June was a preliminary test. If she was properly trimmed, one could make the bathyscaphe disappear beneath the waves merely by flooding the air-lock; she went down slowly, maintained her equilibrium both on the bottom and at the end of her guide chain, and rose at the slightest discharge of shot; furthermore, she emerged on a perfectly even keel. Thus there was no risk of acid being spilt from the accumulators or of a disastrous loss of petrol at the moment she returned to the surface. I was entirely satisfied with these preliminary findings, and as I crossed the dockyard on my way to work on Monday 22 June, I looked forward to our next dives with confidence. There were several on our programme.

A fresh descent to a shallow depth would enable us to try out the searchlights. The bathyscaphe would then go down by herself to 1,500 metres. This would test the resistance of her joints to pressure. I was not much worried about the automatic surfacing release. I had confidence in the pressure-gauge which, at the proper depth, would cut off the current of the electro-magnets. Lighter by tons, the machine would set out on her return journey. Her inertia was still unknown; but by choosing a 2,000-metre deep for this trial we made certain that the descent would come to a stop before the bathyscaphe touched bottom.

The series of trials with passengers would start afterwards: 750, 1,500, 2,000 metres. Houot's aim was certainly to reach 4,000 metres, but the authorities in Paris did not propose to carry out the great descent until much later.

On the morning of Monday 22 June, I was concerned with less sensational problems. I was merely impatient to learn whether the bathyscaphe had spent a quiet weekend. The porthole in the air-lock might have played us up. The previous Friday, before leaving the vessel at about ten in the evening, we had taken the precaution of closing the hatch leading from the air-lock into the sphere, in case of a possible leak. A few gallons of water in the air-lock would not matter a scrap; on the other hand, if the sphere were flooded it would cause irreparable damage.

I spotted Houot on the edge of the quay. An earlier riser than I, he was already gazing at the dock and our baby. He turned at my approach, and gave me a wry smile. What had happened? One look at the *F.N.R.S. 3* was enough: she was not at her proper waterline, but ten or twenty centimetres too high.

"Have the magnets cut out?" I inquired.

"Yes, all your shot's gone down to the bottom."

Had some practical joker managed to get into the control-room? Had someone pressed the silo button? We had connected up a battery that was supposed to run for sixty hours. The accumulators couldn't have been properly charged. The voltage had fallen and this had released all the electromagnets.

There was a lesson to be learnt from this misadventure; we decided then and there to make safety clamps to lock the electromagnets of the silos. While the vessel was building I had thought of fitting the silos with some system of clamps like the one on the ballast bunkers, but the problem presented technical difficulties.

"We'll think up something," I said to Houot.

"We'll have to, but the week's started badly."

During the next few days, work gave me every satisfaction and made me forget Houot's pessimistic remark. The outside accumulators were in place. The searchlights ordered from private firms would not be ready until October so we had rigged up makeshift lights; there was nothing to prevent us going ahead with the series of trials. The next trip was therefore fixed for Friday, and the day drew rapidly nearer. The idea of going down to seventy metres filled me with such enthusiasm that I ceased to feel the weight of the hours. Everything was ready, or nearly ready.

On Thursday 25 June, with the help of a cohort of electricians, I checked the searchlight controls. The current ran from the quay and I had the pleasure of dictating my orders from the height of the conning tower down to the electrician in the sphere.

"Hallo, in the sphere, switch on the port searchlight."

"Searchlight on," replied the electrician.

"Now, switch off."

"Searchlight off."

At that moment a dull echo rang through the hull beneath our feet. In that single instant all the damned shot had once again gone to the bottom of the dock.

"Hallo, hallo . . ."

The telephone did not answer; it was dead. The workmen and the foreman looked at me. We were on a submersible with a relatively low reserve of buoyancy. For the bathyscaphe to sink, it only needed some one to open a valve accidentally. It is true that she would go down only very slowly.

I went down the ladder into the air-lock. The sphere was in darkness. A thick screen of smoke cut off the little light that might have filtered in through the porthole. An acrid smell of burning caught me by the throat. The electrician switched on his pocket torch.

"A short circuit," he explained. "Like this." He showed me what had happened. "My screwdriver touched the hull, which forms an earth, and this insulation. . . . It's no good at all!"

He was right, and the immediate consequences of his discovery was that tomorrow's exercise was cancelled. The insulation had got damp and must be changed. But that wasn't all.

There was a gremlin at work. We also had to rewire part of the searchlight circuit for at the end of the afternoon another workman discovered a fault in it. We also urgently needed a steel plate to fill in the lower porthole of the air-lock, which had inexplicably cracked. I had only just given the order for this job, on the following Monday afternoon, when another workman brought me more bad news.

"The level of pyralene oil in the electromagnet system is dropping alarmingly, sir. I was just filling it," he explained. "The more I poured in the emptier the pipe got. The leak must be under water."

He was not mistaken. I began to despair; the difficulties were multiplying too fast. At least I was lucky enough to share my disappointments with a friend. Houot had been called by telephone and arrived armed with an aqualung. I helped him to dress and fix the straps of the compressed-air cylinder. We had to hurry, for the shadow of the dock gate was already stretching across the water as the day declined.

I could follow Houot's course by the clump of little bubbles that rose to the surface. It seemed a long time. Then there was a swirl, a white patch, and there he was again, catching hold of the steps, straightening, climbing out of the water. He looked at me from behind his face-mask and spat out the mouthpiece of his breathing-pipe.

"The joint between the case of the quick-release gear and the silo chute on the starboard bow is leaking in big drops."

"Then we'll have to put her in dry-dock."

"I think so."

It was difficult to tell what Houot felt; I couldn't see his eyes. "What rotten luck," I said, but got no answer. Perhaps he was thinking, like me, of the implications of this discovery. The joints on the other chutes might be equally fragile. The whole fitting would have to be overhauled.

Before the bathyscaphe could be put into dry-dock 78,000 litres of petrol had to be drained off. We had never carried out this operation, but I did not think it would take more than forty-eight hours. On the third day, I had to admit to Houot that I had connected a hand pump, but that there were still 10,000 litres to be drained.

"Next time, you'll have to find a more efficient way of doing it," he said.

Nevertheless, by the evening of 3 July the bathyscaphe was resting on her cradle. I added up the days; she had spent a month in the water and we had dived only once.

On Monday 6 July, force of habit almost led me to the ladder down into the Vauban dock. But I had not forgotten our setbacks and the tasks awaiting me. On her cradle the bathyscaphe seemed to be back on the stocks again. The electricians had started changing the casings; the fact that the cables were already in place did not make their work any easier. Metalworkers were fitting the steel plate that was to block up the lower porthole in the air-lock. Other workmen were dismantling the chutes.

Houot joined me on board.

"She could do with a day or two in dry-dock, you'll see," he said to me.

He was referring to a general overhaul of the bathyscaphe's equipment. Naturally, after such a short stay in the water, the hull did not need scraping.

It took us all of ten days to change the fittings and modify the chutes. They were equipped with reinforced joints and the safety clamps were put in place.

One fine morning I was able to approach Houot:

"What do you say to fixing the seventeenth as the date for resuming our programme? It's about time we tested our searchlights under water."

"Fine," he replied. "Order the crane for 2 o'clock and dress ship. The newsreel people want to film the launching."

In the afternoon we all felt hopeful once more. A couple of blasts on the whistle and the bathyscaphe rose into the air. The French and Belgian colours fluttered gaily at her masthead. The cameramen went into action. Apart from a single detail, it was exactly like the ceremony of 3 June. Today the bathyscaphe was going to be lowered straight into the sea, for other craft were occupying the Vauban dock.

A few minutes later, we watched from the quay as the *F.N.R.S. 3* left. Launches towed her out towards an old disused dock that was to be her future berth.

Houot noticed my impatience. "What's the hurry?" he asked. But he was just as impatient himself.

A long hour passed before we were able to board the bathyscaphe and wriggle in turn into the sphere. All was darkness inside. I turned the switch, light blazed from the ceiling. As I had done six weeks before, I rushed to the porthole to check for leaks. The pipes were all perfectly dry, so were the aerial cable and the two ventilation ducts.

Then I examined the electric cables.

"No. 1, O.K. No. 2, O.K."

As my finger touched No. 3, I fell silent. Drops of water were oozing through and dripping into the bilge. When I raised the floorboards I found half a litre of water in the bilge. And the *F.N.R.S. 3* hadn't been in the water more than an hour. A leak at such low pressure plainly indicated an appalling fault in the gland. We exchanged a look of despair.

"Well, I suppose there's nothing for it . . ." began Houot.

". . . but to put her back in dock."

We had now compressed into a single sentence the same remarks that we had made two weeks ago at the edge of the Vauban dock. Today it was not a question of pyralene oil leaking into the sea, but of water leaking into the sphere itself – a far more serious problem.

"I don't understand, Willm. How do you seal the join between the cable and its casing?"

"With two centimetres of silver solder cast in a special cylindrical mould. It looks as though it's broken all the way through."

"It looks like it – but didn't you test this outlet in the high-pressure chamber?"

"Fittings of the same type have been tested at 1,000 kilos per square centimetre. A similar outlet has been in use in the pressure chamber for more than two years without breaking. Don't forget that we had to make these six casts *in situ*. To test them under pressure we should have had to build a pressure chamber big enough to take the whole sphere."

As we talked, we temporarily sealed the leak that cast fresh doubts on the joints of the cables and pipes that ran out from our new home. The muffled sound of the dockyard siren reached us. It meant that the bathyscaphe would have to wait till Monday to return to her stocks.

Three days later I breathed a sigh of relief. When we dismantled the gland we found a blow-hole. Never had I been so pleased to see an example of this well-known flaw in casting silver solder. The principle that had been adopted was no longer in doubt, and the very object of the unmanned dive to 1,500 metres was to disclose any faults of this kind which the *F.N.R.S. 3* might still have. For a long time I contemplated my discovery. Would water coming through such a small hole, one square millimetre in section, be fatal? I whipped out a pencil and a piece of paper. After various mathematical calculations I felt reassured. All the same, a sudden change in pressure might make the solder split into layers, and then . . .

"So what it amounts to," concluded Houot sardonically, after I had told him the result of my calculations, "is that the fault isn't serious. You think the repairs will be finished by Wednesday, the twenty-second? Will the twenty-fifth suit you for our shallow dive?"

Would it suit me? I felt my confidence returning, but when I saw the crane lifting the *F.N.R.S. 3* for the third time I found a new anxiety. There was a danger of the plates of the float working. This constant lifting and lowering had not been foreseen. But the bathyscaphe made her aerial journey without incident. If we wanted to have her ready by Friday we should have to hurry. We had forty-eight hours in which to fill up with petrol and shot.

The day before the trial, Commander Tailliez called a conference at the U.R.G. to settle the procedure for the next day's

exercise. Seated at the round table, we explained our programme. We should first test the echo-sounder, whose range
was supposed to be 200 metres (660 feet); it ought to give us the
distance from the bottom to the nearest metre. We should then
carry out combined tests, and keep in touch by using a code of
asdic signals. Tailliez agreed to the diving site that Houot had
chosen. This time there would be no telephone to the surface – a
great relief to both of us – and the bathyscaphe would go down
in a depth of 70 metres a few miles from the Cape Brun signal
station. This depth would have two advantages. It would allow
the divers to go down with us and at the same time would mark
an advance on our previous descent.

At 6 o'clock on the 25th, as the east grew bright with the
delicate colours of dawn, the *Élie Monnier* took our submersible in tow. Our hopes were very high. We were not the
only ones to admire the *F.N.R.S. 3* from the quarterdeck.
Draughtsmen, workmen, and technical staff had asked to be
taken aboard for the day. Each of them had contributed
something in building the machine and it was with pride that
they watched her tossing in the swell. I was touched by their
sympathy.

Around 8 o'clock, the cook discreetly brought me some pâté
sandwiches and a bottle of muscatel, which I slipped into my
briefcase among the plans. They might also come in handy – you
never can tell!

"I'll keep the bathyscaphe in tow until you are on board and
ready to dive," said Lieutenant Alinat, our friend the skipper of
the *Élie Monnier*.

We had now become quite used to carrying out the routine
operations before diving. Houot took charge of the guide chain
which had to be lowered into the water, and then made sure that
the petrol valves were open. I went down into the sphere and
checked the current in the various circuits. Outside, the divers
were removing the safety clamps, but I did not hear them. None
of them passed in front of the porthole.

"Your briefcase, Willm."

Houot handed it to me, then climbed up the ladder again and

closed the hatch of the air-lock himself. This precaution was not unimportant. The water can be expelled from the compartment only if it is completely shut.

At 10.40 we asked permission from those on the surface to cast off and dive.

A quarter of an hour later the loudspeaker brought us Alinat's serious voice.

"You're only half under. You've stopped going down."

"We're a bit light, could you add another 200 kilos of shot?" asked Houot.

The operation took another ten minutes.

At 11.14, Dr Cabarrou, who had stayed in the conning tower and was about to take a header into the water, told us we were diving.

"You're going under, you're un . . ." announced the loudspeaker as we did so. Then a breaker covered our aerial, which no longer picked up the wireless waves.

The shallow-depth pressure-gauge recorded our steady descent. 8, 10, 15, 30 metres. At the same time the echo-sounder showed us that the distance from the bottom was diminishing. To test our control of the bathyscaphe, Houot discharged shot for ten seconds. The usual pattering told us that everything was in order.

"But we're going up –"

As I knelt in front of the viewing port, I had just noticed that we were beginning to rise. The graph of the depth recorder ran level, then the stylus started to move towards the top of the chart. The shot level-gauge for the after starboard silo told us what had happened. The chute was empty. Lighter by at least 600 kilos, the *F.N.R.S. 3* was surfacing. The electromagnet had failed to close the chute when the current was turned on again after jettisoning the shot.

"Hallo *Élie Monnier*, bathyscaphe calling, can you hear me? Over."

They picked up our radio at once.

"Hallo bathyscaphe. *Élie Monnier* calling, what's happened?"

"Hallo *Élie Monnier*. Bathyscaphe calling. I'm going to dive by discharging petrol. Tell your swimmers to move off."

By discharging 1,800 litres of petrol into the sea, we should become a little more than 600 kilos heavier. With luck, this decrease in buoyancy would be enough; but the film of fuel might be a nuisance to the divers.

At 11.45 the *Élie Monnier* signalled that we were going under once more. The water, which was a beautiful deep blue, grew gradually darker. We impatiently switched on the searchlights. The result was disappointing. Not a glimmer was to be seen in the limpid water. We could not even tell whether the lamps were alight.

"We'll try lower down," decided Houot.

As she approached the bottom the *F.N.R.S. 3* slowed down of her own accord. We must have reached a colder and therefore denser layer of water. The inside thermometer confirmed this point: 15°C. (59°F.) instead of 18°c. (65°F.) on the surface. Our commonplace conversation hardly betrayed our wonder and excitement.

From time to time I inspected the cables and pipes round the porthole as well as the joint between the two hemispheres, without finding the slightest leak.

At 11.55 the descent reached its end. We were at 46 metres (151 feet). The weight of the guide chain was resting on the bottom and prevented us from bringing the bathyscaphe to rest on the ground, as we had done on the previous dive. We were too light and could jettison no more petrol from the dischargeable tank. Houot seemed disappointed. But I thought that today's experiment had been very interesting.

"Do you realize, Willm, that this sphere had made her first dive to fifty metres . . . with passengers?" he said.

"To forty-six, sir," I corrected him.

"All right, forty-six."

As we waited for the divers I suggested we should celebrate this achievement with our bottle of muscatel.

Houot hadn't extricated my briefcase from between the

compressed-air cylinders and the engine-control panel, before I cried:

"Here's Piovano!"

There he was indeed, diving head first towards the porthole. I switched on the searchlights and this time we could see the beam. It lit up the leading seaman's body as he rolled over and shot upwards again. We now had proof that the batteries worked perfectly under pressure. Although this was not essential, it was important. When we came to dive in the eternal night of the deep we should need a good light. The asdic signal trial was less successful. We received no reply to our transmissions. At last Houot got sick of playing with the Morse key; he sat on the step in front of the hatch and took our food out of the briefcase.

"Let's eat," he said. "Get to work with the corkscrew."

The cook's sandwiches were good. We drank the muscatel out of the bottle, and it was exquisite.

"Will it taste the same at two thousand metres?" I asked.

"Why not? We shall soon see," he answered.

Perhaps the thought of this next great stage to be passed may have given us a moment's apprehension. But we felt very safe in the sphere, and our confidence soon returned. In the great deeps the overhead lamp would shine as brightly and, apart from the figures on the pressure-gauge, the scene would remain unchanged. Through the porthole, it is true, we might perhaps see extraordinary, or at least unusual, creatures.

"We'll jettison 400 kilos," said Houot.

At 12.45 the bathyscaphe surfaced. We went out on deck to find a familiar world. The sun and the sea were sparkling; we blinked our eyes. It was good to see our friends again, to let them fire questions at us, to learn, for instance, that our asdic transmission had been received perfectly, and to tell them our adventures.

In the wardroom of the *Élie Monnier* lunch was served, and our shipmates began to tease us.

"I don't know what all the fuss is about," said Alinat. "You shut yourselves up in a ball to go down to forty-six metres. With a flip of my back I can dive to eighty. I hope we'll soon see you getting to work seriously."

"750, 1,500, 2,000 metres," said Houot. "We'll be making a date with you soon."

I thought it as well to remind him that we should first of all send the bathyscaphe down to 1,500 metres without passengers.

Following its successful sea-trials, the F.R.N.S. 3 made a record-breaking dive to minus 4,050 metres in January 1954.

THE LOSS OF *TEMPEST*

Charles Anscomb

The British submarine Tempest *was intercepted by an Italian torpedo-boat in the Gulf of Taranto in the early morning of 13 February 1942. Charles Anscomb was the* Tempest's *coxwain.*

She had seen us and was coming straight at us – to ram.

It was a crash-dive. It had to be. We went down steeply and heard the thumping of his engines. He was on us. My stomach went cold. Then I almost gasped with sudden intense relief as I heard the noise dying away again. He had missed us on the first pass.

Action always gave me an uneasy lurch in the pit of my stomach. I had it now all right. That destroyer was really going for us, no doubt about that. We were in for a very bad time.

It would be the first time for most of our green ship's company. Those kids must have had that sick feeling, that thumping heart I knew so well, but if they had they certainly did not show it as they went quietly and smoothly about their jobs like veterans. Of course, they didn't know what was coming. Being depth-charged is something which cannot be imagined. It is a terror which has to be experienced. Any minute now we were going to get it, and when we did it wouldn't be just the distant booming of a formal search. That Eyetie knew exactly where we were. There he is now – on top of us. My heart bumped as I watched the depth-gauge, sitting in my action station, at the after hydroplanes.

The captain gave an order.

"One hundred and fifty feet."

I turned the wheel. Rapidly we gained depth. I thought that first pattern will be keeping us company.

I had my eyes on the pointer. It was passing fifty feet. We'd never do it . . . The dial shook and the pointer danced before my eyes. There was a tremendous, gathering surge of clanging thunder . . . seat, wheel, hands, brain, dials, deck, bulkhead, deckhead, everything shook like an earthquake shock as if every atom in the ship's company were splitting. Then it was dark, nearly all the lights gave out. Instruments were shattered, wheels locked, glass tinkled over the deck.

We were still going down. I watched the pointer . . . 150 . . . 155 . . . 160 . . . 165 . . . We were out of control.

We fought her, second cox'n Burns and I. The pointer reached 350 feet. There, at last, we steadied her and managed to bring her back to 150 feet.

Swiftly the damage reports came in. Nearly all the instruments and lights throughout the boat had been put out of action. The fore hydroplanes and hydrophones were damaged beyond repair. Worst of all, one of the propeller shafts had shifted in its housing. That accounted for the loud continuous knocking sound we could hear. We had had trouble with this shaft before leaving England and it had been put right. Now the depth-charging had thrown it out of true again. The boat was trimmed at 150 feet and we maintained her level in the stop position with just the slightest movement of the motor or adjustment of the ballast. All ship's company not actually needed now were told to lie down at their station and to move as little as possible so as to conserve the limited oxygen supply in the boat and reduce telltale noise to try to cheat his hydrophones.

That was the only "evasive action" we could take now. Asdics and hydrophones were out of action, so we had no means of finding the bearing of our attacker. We didn't know where he was coming from next and we couldn't dodge what he was throwing at us. We just had to sit and take what was coming – until he finished us off for good and all. I began to get that this can't be happening to me feeling. So many times I had seen shipmates and chummy ships go out and never return – just, unbelievably, cease to exist, as if atomised into nothing. Failed to return from patrol. That was the official phrase. Wives and mothers sat at home and heard it over the BBC. Now our wives and mothers were going to hear it . . . "The Admiralty regret to announce that His Majesty's submarine *Tempest* has failed to return from patrol . . ." Now it was our turn.

But after the first pattern had done its worst my stomach settled down and we carried on as if all this were just a practice run. There were no more explosions for the moment. The moments lengthened and still we went free. After a little while the cook made some tea and cocoa, and this hot brew, with biscuits, was passed round the boat. It made us all feel a lot better, even though we could hear that destroyer's engines as he passed and re-passed above us, stalking us still, hour after hour.

But they dropped no more depth-charges. In fact by 7 a.m. we were beginning to have hopes that they had really lost us when we heard engines very close overhead once more and then another series of shattering crashes as a pattern went off right alongside us. After that they came again and again, dropping pattern on pattern and all of them so close you could smell them. Dazed and shaken and scared, we hung on and hoped against hope. You couldn't tell where he was coming from until you actually heard him.

The master gyroscope was smashed and we had to rely on our magnetic compass. One oil-fuel bulkhead connection in the control-room was damaged, and oil fuel poured into the boat. The chief stoker, George Spowart, and his men got to it quickly and soon stopped the flood. The electrical artificer, John Winrow, slaved to put the gyro right, but it was past all hope of repair and we had to give it up. The fore hydroplanes were out of action and the boat was being controlled for depth by the after planes.

We were at the mercy of that destroyer. At regular intervals we heard her rumble over us. We could hear the Asdic "pinging" us, the sound wave stinging our quivering steel flanks like an invisible whiplash, but never knew exactly where she was. Each time she turned and came back to try again. Each run did more damage than the last.

For a time the submarine was kept under perfect control. Then the ring main shorted on the pressure hull, blowing the main fuses. This put the ballast pumps out of action. This meant that the compensating tanks and auxiliary tanks had to be trimmed by using our compressed-air supply, when air was priceless to us. The boat was forced down willy-nilly to 500 feet, completely out of control. I was helpless on the planes. There wasn't a thing I could do to stop her.

The position was so desperate that we had to bring her to rest finally by trimming her on the main ballast tanks. To lighten the boat these main ballast tanks had to be trimmed either by venting the air into them, or blowing water out by means of compressed air. This was a far from satisfactory method of trimming and we were particularly reluctant to resort to it because it was very noisy at a time when silence was vital to give us any chance of surviving at all.

This started us on our way up again and to check the rate of rise we had quickly to flood the main ballast tanks again. All the time the sudden extra noise was playing right into the hands of our attacker. With deadly regularity she passed overhead, each time laying her eggs. They burst all round us as we sat and shook in the semi-darkness, with only the secondary lighting flickering palely like candles guttering in a dark tomb and the ship lurching and wallowing between 100 and 500 feet and things breaking loose and crashing about us. *Tempest* was a strong boat and she was withstanding a pounding that would have completely shattered a less well-found ship, but nevertheless the strain was beginning to show in the state of her machinery and on the faces and movements of her crew.

We went on steering blindly at any old depth between 100 and 500 feet. Bulkhead fixtures and spare parts were torn from their housing, and hurled across the narrow spaces. The boat was continually either bow up or bow down, and the angle was so acute at times that the bubble in the fore-and-aft spirit-level would disappear completely.

In the engine-room heavy spares like the big breech-ends from the diesels, each weighing half a ton, were sliding dangerously up and down the steel deck at each plunge and lurch. It was quite impossible to stop them, much less secure them again.

To make matters worse we were carrying a big load of extra spares for the submarines based at Alexandria – not to mention sack-loads of mail for the Fleet – and all these broke loose and started to smash about through the boat. All the time, as the relentless depth-charging went on, the always dim emergency lighting burned lower and lower until it was hardly more than a faint glow.

The position inside *Tempest* steadily worsened as more and more fittings were shaken loose. The earthings of the main electric cable against the hull increased the danger of fire and electrocution.

This hell went on until 10 a.m. Then, miraculously, unbelievably, there was a definite lull. We blinked, breathed again and looked around us to take stock of our position.

John Winrow, creeping through the submarine on the track of some electrical repair, accidentally kicked a bucket which clattered with a deafening noise along the deck.

"I'll have that man shot!" shouted the captain. It nearly made us jump out of our skins.

Then the attack began again. Again I thought this is not happening to me. I suppose many of us felt that. I know that no one, least of all the young submariners who had been civilians only a few months before, showed the slightest sign of panic or fear. They all behaved splendidly.

About 10.30 a.m. the battery securing boards showed signs of lifting. A closer inspection showed that salt-water had got into the battery compartment and several containers with sulphuric acid in them were broken.

When salt-water and sulphuric acid mix they give off chlorine gas. That is the ultimate horror of all submariners.

The boat started to fill with it. One whole battery was flooded now. We had reached the end. The boat was just a pitch-dark, gas-filled shambles, flooding at the after end, with no instrument working except "faithful Freddie" the magnetic compass. What use was a compass now? *Tempest* had nowhere to go any more, except to the bottom. At last, to save us from going with her, the captain decided to abandon ship.

Quietly the ship's company were told to put on Davis escape gear. Without any fuss everybody buckled the gear on. Then the order was passed for everyone except men at key positions needed to maintain the trim of the boat to muster in the control-room.

Then the captain gave the order "Abandon ship".

*"... the fireball would have used up all the precious oxygen
the crew had meticulously tried to preserve"*

KURSK: A TIME TO DIE

Robert Moore

*At exactly 11.28:27 on Saturday 12 August 2000 a shock wave
roared across the Barents Sea, causing the seismographs of the
Arctic Experimental Seismic Station (ARCESS) in Norway to
twitch a measurement of 1.5 on the Richter scale – the same as an
earth tremor. Two minutes later, the seismographs at ARCESS
registered another violent shock wave.*

*The reading at ARCESS on that morning in August were not,
however, caused by an earth tremor, or any other natural phenomena, but two explosions inside the Kursk, pride of Russian's
Northern Fleet and one of the largest attack submarines in the
world. The explosions, caused by the accidental detonation of a
torpedo in the torpedo room at the front of the ship, sent the Kursk
plummeting to the bottom of the Barents. The Russian navy began a
frantic effort to rescue the survivors, but was hampered by outdated
submarine rescue technology. Only after world opinion was roused
against Putin's government could the Russian establishment be
persuaded to drop their pride and paranoia and accept international aid.*

*Even so, it was not until 20 August that divers from Seaway
Eagle, a private diving support vessel run by Stolt Offshore, were
finally allowed to open the intact ninth compartment of the Kursk –
which they found to be flooded. Definitively, no-one was now left
alive in the Kursk. However, as the Russian navy's later forensic
investigation into the Kursk discovered, a number of Kursk crew
did survive the initial blasts but perished sometime before 20*

*August. A quicker, more efficient rescue effort may well have saved
these men.*

*This account of the recovery of bodies and forensic evidence from
the* Kursk *is from Robert Moore's study of the disaster,* A Time to
Die.

Admiral Gennady Verich was placed in charge of the recovery
operation. After the rescue débâcle in August there was no
hiding the need for foreign expertise, but divers would still not
be able to enter the submarine through the narrow ninth escape
tower. In their bulky suits, trailing umbilical cables and safety
gear, such a manoeuvre would be too perilous. The *Kursk*
would have to be cut open.

The underwater expertise of the offshore industry would
again provide the solution to the Russians' problems. This time
it would not be Stolt, but their rival, the US energy giant
Haliburton. Special equipment was needed, including high-
pressure water jets that used special diamond emulsion to cut
through the thick pressure hull, as well as a substantial support
operation above the divers.

But whatever technical assistance was accepted from the
West, it was politically unthinkable that foreign divers would
be allowed inside the *Kursk*. The task of scouring Russia for the
specialist divers willing to work inside a flooded, pitch-black
and corpse-filled submarine fell to Verich.

In the end, one diver was chosen from the Baltic Fleet,
another from the Black Sea Fleet, and the ten others were
selected from two secretive naval organizations that operate
near St Petersburg: the 328th Rescue Division and Institute
Number 40. Both serve the Ministry of Defence in the area of
underwater special operations, and in the absence of adequate
Russian diving ships neither had played a role in the original
rescue attempts.

Captain Vladimir Salutin was among the divers chosen. He
had served as a member of Russia's naval special forces, starting
his career clearing old Second World War mines from the Black

Sea. This was dangerous work that required stamina and steady nerves. At thirty-seven, he was already well used to seeing death at close quarters, having recovered bodies from a number of sunken fishing vessels as well as from helicopters and planes that had crashed into the sea.

The elite team was flown straight to the Northern Fleet Headquarters at Severomorsk where they were plunged into study of the *Kursk*, analysing diagrams and charts detailing the construction and layout of the submarine.

The divers moved from the classroom to the *Oryol*. The officers of this sister-submarine to the *Kursk* advised them where sailors might have taken refuge after explosions. They also practised alternative routes to the captain's personal safe, where codebooks and other secret documents were held. Then they blindfolded themselves and walked the passageways, negotiating their way by touch through hatches and down ladders.

From Severomorsk, the Russian divers flew back to St Petersburg and the Military Medical Academy. They toured the academy's huge morgues to study fatal injuries. They were shown men who had perished in fires, in car crashes and from drowning. They were asked to look closely at bodies in advanced states of decomposition.

The support operation comprised a mix of British and Norwegian divers based on the giant offshore platform Regalia, which was moved into the Barents Sea. The foreign specialists performed the underwater construction work, cutting openings in carefully selected positions through the *Kursk*'s double hulls, while the Russian divers prepared for their delicate mission. The scope for confusion, and entangled cables meant that only one diver at a time would be allowed to work inside the submarine. The second Russian would wait on the outer casing, while a Western diver remained inside the diving bell, ready to act as a rescuer at a moment's notice.

Warrant Officer Sergei Shmygin was the first man to enter the tomb of the submarine, manoeuvring his way cautiously down through one of the holes cut into the seventh compartment. His powerful halogen lamp barely penetrated water that was ink-black with oil and floating particles. To help his co-ordination inside the submarine Shmygin was wearing boots instead of fins. He also wore a plastic white covering over his normal diving gear, to be removed and discarded after he emerged from the submarine to ensure that no contaminants were taken into the diving bell. A long, wide hose was used to try to suck out some of the stale water from inside the submarine and to eliminate some of the floating waste from the decomposing bodies. It also helped to remove some of the chemicals and debris that obscured the view.

Floating past Shymgin was a blue-and-white-striped mattress. Like the bodies, many of the non-metal items inside the *Kursk* had gained neutral buoyancy and were drifting around the compartments. Shmygin was armed with a two-metre-long pole, with a small hook on the end, but he found no bodies during his first six-hour shift.

In fact, no corpses were found in compartments seven or eight. Over the next few days, the focus of the divers shifted to the crucial ninth compartment, where it was assumed the sailors would have gathered as they waited for a rescue that never came. The Russian divers immediately saw the evidence of an intense fire, with machinery and equipment heavily charred. The first body was found floating largely intact, its legs covered in thick green clothing, its torso naked. The divers attached a rope to the waist and, using the pole, eased the body through to the eighth compartment and up into the open sea. The *Kursk* had reluctantly given up the first of her sailors.

Soon afterwards, a second crew member was found, severely burnt. Outside the submarine, a large latticed steel container, painted a high-visibility yellow, was lowered from the Regalia. As each body was gingerly removed from the ninth compartment, it was placed inside and taken to the surface.

Directly underneath the hatch where Tony Scott had hammered, six bodies were recovered. One of them, Seaman Roman Kubikov, was lying just below the escape tower. Other corpses were visible further aft, down the narrow passageway, wedged so deeply that the divers failed to retrieve them, despite struggling for hours with their specially improvised pole. Eventually they were forced to give up. One body Vladimir Salutin touched simply disintegrated in his hands, limbs falling away in the water.

After they had explored the seventh, eighth and ninth compartments, the divers were then ordered to move down to the fourth. In this area, which included the private cabin of Captain Lyachin, in conditions of the greatest secrecy divers spent three hours unloading files and documents from a single locker.

They then moved forward towards the heart of the explosion, to compartment three, and attempted to approach the most sensitive area of the submarine, the radio room. But once the new hole had been cut through the double hull it was immediately apparent that what confronted the divers was an entirely new proposition. "It was something horrible," one of them reported. "We couldn't even swing our legs through the hole. It was full of broken parts, metal and plastic." The machinery and equipment was so chaotically entangled that the divers gave up.

At 1.15 a.m. on 26 October, the meshed-steel sleigh containing the first corpses emerged from the depths of the sea and was swung on to the vast open deck-space of the Regalia. The powerful floodlights gave the platform an eerie look amid the heavy swell and darkness of the Barents Sea. Winter was unmistakably arriving. The first two bodies were quickly carried the short distance to a large shipping container that had been converted into a temporary morgue. White drapes ensured the bodies were not glimpsed by any of the Regalia's curious Norwegian workers.

Standing expectantly inside the container, the size of a small room, were two naval pathologists and Colonel-Lieutenant Sergei Chernishov, who served in the office of the Prosecutor-General. There was also a staff member with a small video camera, recording the investigation for the military archives. The footage from this secret videotape provides an astonishing glimpse into the moment the investigation achieved its breakthrough.

The first body examined was partially burnt and heavily smeared with a mix of oil and soot. The hands had turned ivory-white after their long immersion in water. The examiners spent some time looking at the inner blue overall that had the sailor's barely decipherable naval number on it, which would help identify him.

The second corpse soon became the focus of the examiners' interest. The upper body was severely burnt and much of the flesh had peeled away in the area around the neck and head. But the footage captured the fact that there were still recognizable features and the lower body was in remarkably good shape. As the pathologists examined the body, they spoke aloud so that their moment-by-moment thoughts and impressions were captured on tape.

"There appears to be some kind of package on the body."

"Take a look," Chernishov encouraged.

The tight bundle, the size of a man's wallet, heavily covered in oil, was bound by waterproof wrapping that was stained almost black. The little packet was next to the corpse's upper body, squeezed into a breast pocket of the singed overalls.

"The front surface is solid. I am now removing it from the clothing. Everything is saturated, we're finding . . . I'm not opening it, I'm afraid to break it into pieces."

"Go ahead and open it," Chernishov authorized.

"It appears to be some writing, some letter." The excitement in the investigator's voice was impossible to disguise.

The pathologists knew that newsprint and paper survive surprisingly well under water. As many salvage divers have discovered, documents and labels on packaging are often legible after being submerged for decades, so long as they have been undisturbed. Even letters recovered from First and Second World War wrecks have been readable.

Wearing white surgical gloves, the investigators gingerly separated the note from the wrapping. It was written on a page from a logbook, printed lines running across the page in both a horizontal and vertical direction. The letter was folded into four, and the writing was obscured by moist oil marks, but it was still just legible. The note had survived immersion. The name at the end of it jumped out, visible even on the video footage.

Kolesnikov.

The body on the table was that of Captain-Lieutenant Dmitri Kolesnikov, commander of the *Kursk*'s seventh compartment.

On one side of the note was written the list of twenty-three survivors with the time 13.34 at the top. The pathologists gently turned the note over. At the top were five lines written to his wife:

Olichka, I love you.
Don't suffer too much. My regards to
GV and regards to mine.
Mitya.
12.08.2000. 1545.

GV were the initials for Galina Vasiliena, his mother-in-law; Mitya was his own nickname, the Russian diminutive for Dmitri.

Below these five lines, Kolesnikov had written his final note, in the darkness of the *Kursk*, estimating his chances of survival at between 10 and 20 percent and concluding with a phrase of astonishing stoicism:

Regards to everybody; no need to be desperate.
Kolesnikov.

For the first time here was incontrovertible proof that sailors had survived the initial explosions. Dozens of Russian specialists were called in to examine in minute detail every aspect of the bodies, clothing and notes. One laboratory revealed that the type of oil that was smeared over some of the corpses came from a lubricant only used in the stern glands leading from the propeller shafts. The water had leaked into the ninth compartment through the shaft seals and brought the oil with it. This was the confirmation that the submarine had been slowly flooding over several days, increasing the pressure within the compartment.

Everywhere the Russian investigators turned, there were now fresh clues to what had happened in the ninth compartment. They were able to piece together the terrifying final days of life in the aft of the destroyed submarine.

Most of the bodies were clothed not just in their normal dark-blue working overalls, but in a second layer of thick green insulation fabric. These were the emergency suits issued to submariners to ward off hypothermia.

Despite the strength of the twin blasts that rocked the *Kursk* at 11.28 and 11.30 on Saturday 12 August, the sailors in the after compartments had survived with surprising ease. None of the twenty-three crew members listed in Kolesnikov's first note had sustained serious impact injuries such as broken bones or severe bruising.

Following the explosions in the torpedo room, it appears that the survivors had dressed in their thermal suits and opened their emergency superoxide chemical cartridges to generate additional oxygen and fight the rising carbon dioxide. Video from inside the ninth compartment showed numerous used cartridges lying discarded on the upper deck.

Kolesnikov's final note highlights the terrible moment when the ninth compartment was plunged into darkness. Still, the men had known exactly what was happening around them. They could hear the slow flooding through the propeller shafts. They were also cogent enough to analyse its significance: realizing the risk was not only of drowning but of steadily increasing pressure that ended any hope of reaching the surface.

We know that the sailors confronted this devastating predicament squarely because of another note, this one found on the body of Captain-Lieutenant Rashid Ariapov, who wrote:

> We feel bad. Pressure is increasing in the compartment. If we head for the surface we won't survive the compression. We won't last more than a day.

This letter from Ariapov, who was commander of the sixth compartment, was hidden for many weeks by the Russian authorities, before the deputy prime minister, Ilya Klebanov, released it.

Prevented from escaping by the rising pressure, the only remaining hope for the sailors had been in a rescue submersible that could double up as a decompression chamber. Their best, perhaps their only, chance of getting out alive had been the retired Russian submersible commander Andrei Sholokhov, whose remarkable piloting skills almost overcame the defects of the Priz rescue vehicle. We will never know whether the *Kursk* sailors were still alive in the ninth compartment on Thursday, 17 August, when Sholokhov scraped over the escape hatch and came so tantalizingly close to docking.

Changing those chemical cartridges could not have been an easy task for men who were badly frightened, shivering violently from cold and short of practice in emergency drills. In the last glow of emergency light, finding and deploying the chemical kits was difficult; in total darkness it was a nightmare. What's more, the survivors were in an atmosphere that was rigged for a secondary disaster. The rising pressure meant a fire would ignite more easily and burn with greater ferocity, and the men were dealing with chemicals that react violently with water.

According to specialists in the Russian Navy's rescue department, at some stage one of the survivors ripped open the packaging around a chemical cartridge and appears to have fumbled and dropped it. As the cartridge fell into the water, highly flammable oil and lubricants floating on its surface, the chemical reaction was sufficiently violent to ignite a blaze. We know from the fire-line in the compartment that at this stage the water was nearly waist high.

In a sealed, high-pressure environment like the ninth compartment, a fire is not just a problem, not even a crisis, but a truly cataclysmic event. This was a flash-fire that would have rolled at high speed across the surface of the water. In just a second or two, the fireball would have used up all the precious oxygen the crew had meticulously tried to preserve.

Some of the sailors had fought to escape, ducking below the water. Their bodies were later discovered with a distinctive pattern of burns: backs badly charred, chests scarcely touched. Others, it seemed, had been grouped around the spot where the cartridge was dropped – they were found with thermal burns compatible with a violent chemical reaction. The lower limbs of all of the bodies recovered from the aft compartment were untouched by fire, confirming the view of Russian experts that the men had been standing deep in water when the fire erupted.

For those who had managed to duck under the water and emerge to breathe, they had faced an atmosphere utterly incapable of supporting life. One of the sailors had a mask seared to his face. The superheated gases would have burned their lungs, and they would have faced another killer. As the fire reacted with the paintwork and metals inside the ninth compartment, carbon monoxide was being generated in lethal quantities. Carbon monoxide is known as the silent killer. It comes with no taste or smell; it is not detectable by the human senses. Victims of CO poisoning feel no pain and rarely comprehend what is happening to them. For that reason, using the exhaust fumes of a car is one of the most common forms of suicide. The increase in carbon dioxide must have already left the survivors gasping for air, but when the monoxide hit them, they would have felt an incredible tiredness. Their muscles would have weakened, their vision greyed.

Their last vision of the ninth compartment would have been a rapidly narrowing tunnel surrounded by darkness.

The twenty-three men had certainly faced the hazards of carbon dioxide and drowning, but, as the Russian naval pathologists recorded on the death certificates, all of the *Kursk* sailors in the after compartments died of carbon monoxide poisoning. Their lower limbs, which had been underwater at the time of the fire, remained a bright pink, a healthy hue that is a tell-tale feature of death by CO. Several of the sailors who had avoided facial burn injuries while ducking underwater wore expressions that appeared so peaceful it looked as though they had just fallen asleep. After twelve of the twenty-three bodies were recovered and brought to the surface, with winter conditions fast approaching, the decision was made to seal the *Kursk* again. The recovery of the rest of the sailors and the retrieval of the missiles would have to wait for the salvage of the submarine, which would take many months of additional planning. The tomb of the nuclear submarine fell silent once again.

On the morning of 7 November 2000, all work stopped on the Regalia. The Russian divers, the Norwegian technicians and all the support staff stood on the deck, heads bowed. A gentle rain washed over them as a minute's silence was held in memory of the crew of the *Kursk*.

One week after the twelve corpses were recovered from the submarine, the coffins were taken through Courage Square in Severomorsk. The ranks of naval officers attending the ceremony dropped down onto one knee in the thin layer of snow as a mark of respect. The red coffins, draped in the blue and white Russian Navy flag, were carried atop armoured personnel carriers, as the High Command looked on. Marshal Sergeyev and Admiral Popov stood together, in their thick winter great-coats. Finally, Sergeyev stepped forward to the open-air lectern.

"Even the great Russian language fails to provide words for the bitterness of this loss and tragedy. Forgive us, and let the ground beneath you be as soft as down.'

A dozen warships riding at anchor in the bay sounded their fog-horns. The sirens resonated across the low hills and frozen landscape to the south.

Irina Lyachin, the widow of the *Kursk*'s commanding officer, stood poised and composed in the bitter cold. Not far away was Olga Kolesnikov, braving the weather without a hat or gloves. She watched the ceremony unfold in the gentle snow, with the battle-grey backdrop of Russian warships in the port. The first casket that passed contained the body of her husband. Dmitri had written her a poem before he had left on the exercise that now seemed strangely prophetic:

> When there is A Time to Die
> Although I try not to think about this,
> I would like time to say:
> My darling I Love You.

". . . the diver working up inside the rig was only attached to the bell by his umbilical. He was seconds from death"

DOWNTIME

Keith Jessop

Keith Jessop, a professional diver, made headlines in the 1980s when he salvaged the gold bullion cargo from the wrecked HMS Edinburgh *in the mid-Atlantic. Below he recalls an earlier period in his career, working as a diver on the oil rigs of the North Sea:*

I was now nearing forty – pensionable age for a diver – but I found that the younger divers valued my experience and I graduated to Diving Supervisor, controlling the dives and monitoring the safety of the younger men taking my place. I attempted to learn everything there was to know about deep-diving and a fair bit about crisis management, for the North Sea oilfields in those early days had a lot of the Wild West about them. The North Sea was a new environment even for the oil companies. A lot of learning was going on and lives were being lost. There was no government department then to deal with diver safety and the rules tended to be made up as you went along. Exploration rigs and construction barges cost tens of thousands of dollars a day to keep running and any suggestions that diving operations be suspended because conditions were too dangerous were apt to be treated with contempt. Divers' lives took a distant second place to the almighty dollar.

"When I holler for a diver," one Texan oilman told me, "the only answer I ever want to hear is 'Splash'."

I saw several examples of the dangerous consequences of this attitude while working as the supervisor on the dive ship *Northern Protector*. It was a DP – dynamic positioning – vessel, able to maintain its position precisely by the use of its propellers and bow thrusters, controlled by an on-board computer. When the ship was on station, a sonar beacon was lowered to the sea-bed. Its signal was picked up by four hydrophones. The computer continually compared the ship's actual and required positions relative to the beacon and made the necessary constant minute changes by the use of the ship's propellers and side thrusters to keep it precisely positioned.

We were doing non-destructive testing, checking the underwater condition of the giant Claymore oil-production platform. We stationed ourselves alongside the platform, which towered above us like a skyscraper. There was a constant barrage of noise from the giant generators on the platform, counterpointed by the din from our own engines as they strained to keep us on station, battling the heavy swell of the North Sea.

At night, everything was a blaze of light. Torrents of sparks cascaded from the torches of welders working on the structure, but they were mere pinpricks beside the flame belching from the giant flare stack as it burned off the excess gas. The heat from it would scorch your head, just walking out on deck. I was in charge of the night shift and worked from midnight until noon. It was a hard twelve hours and there were constant incidents caused by the oilmen's indifference to diver safety.

Many times we had to launch the diving bell even though the surge and swell of the sea were far above the safety limit. On one particularly wild night, I expected the captain of the ship to tell the dive superintendent that he wouldn't be able to hold his ship steady enough, but he said nothing. We looked at each other in the growing silence. Downtime was logged against the company who called it. Too much downtime against your name and you would be making a one-way trip back to Aberdeen. The captain of the ship, the diving superintendent and the diving supervisor all knew the safety limit for holding and launching the diving bell, but each wanted one of the others to make the decision. In the meantime, until somebody acted, the bell had to be launched.

On this occasion, I blew my top and told the superintendent exactly what I thought of him. He just stared back at me. "Why don't we let the divers decide?"

It was an apparently reasonable compromise, but every one of us knew that the divers' supposed free choice was really no choice at all. Anyone refusing to dive would have been shipped out immediately and blacklisted throughout the oil industry. Given the choice between diving in unsafe conditions or never working as a diver again, all the men made the inevitable decision.

The shrieking wind and salt spray were lashing at the rig as I made my way to the control van. I took up my usual position, monitoring the equipment and talking to the divers on the radio link as the diving bell was lowered 350 feet below the vessel. One diver stayed in the bell while the other worked seventy feet up inside the platform, photographing the welds around one of the joints. Suddenly the alarm bells in the control van began clanging and red lights flashed insistently. I knew immediately what had happened. The DP had failed and the ship was drifting off position fast. The diver inside the bell was safe because the stout steel cable for lifting and lowering it would not fail, but the diver working up inside the rig was only attached to the bell by his umbilical. He was seconds from death.

I had to pray that he hadn't tied himself off for stability. The wave action and the ocean currents pulled and pushed at you as you tried to work and though it was strictly forbidden on safety grounds, many divers tied themselves to the steel structure. If he had done so, or if his umbilical was wrapped around a couple of the horizontals or verticals of the structure, he would die. Once the weight of the drifting vessel took up the slack, the umbilical would snap like rotten thread and the diver couldn't swim to the surface because he'd die from the bends.

I had only those few seconds in which to save his life.

"Diver. Drop what you're doing and return to the diving bell." I kept my voice even and neutral. I couldn't allow any trace of the tension I was feeling to communicate itself, for panic underwater will kill you quicker than anything.

"What?" he replied. "Something wrong topside?"

This wasn't the time for an explanation. "No, just make your way back to the bell now."

"What about the camera?"

He was holding a £10,000 piece of equipment in his hands. "Just drop it."

"Surface? Should –"

I cut him off short. "Just get back to the bell now."

"Returning to bell."

There was nothing further I could do. The seconds dragged by as I watched the ship drifting steadily further from the rig. There was a sick feeling in the pit of my stomach as I waited, fearing that at any moment my headset would crackle and fall silent. It would be the only sign that a man's life had ended.

Finally the line did crackle, but instead of silence there was the diver's voice. "Clear of the structure. Shall I go back for the camera now?"

I almost cried with relief. "Not bloody likely."

On that occasion we were lucky, but there were other times – too many – when men died. One particularly bad accident happened aboard the *Drillmaster*. Two divers were on the bottom, one inside the diving bell, the other working outside it. The heavy drop-weight that took the bell down to the sea-bed was on a cable connected to a winch. There were two safety devices, a disc brake which was always locked on and a sprocket that was dogged firmly in place. The same safety system was used by the US Navy, but on this dive, both systems suddenly failed for some unknown reason.

Free of its brake and dog, the winch started to pay out and the bell began to rise, accelerating faster and faster as the gas escaping from inside acted like a propellant. The bell rocketed to the surface like a cork and both the divers died horrible deaths from embolisms and massive attacks of the bends. The bell drop-weight system was changed after that, but it was too late for the two divers.

On one job, working as a diver, we'd fallen well behind schedule on one pipe-laying job, but conditions were atrocious and my view was that we should have stopped diving. The dive superintendent, who I thought had been drinking, overruled the divers and the job continued in sea conditions so bad that I believe even a lifeboatman would have hesitated to launch his craft. When a diver became trapped at depth, another diver had to jump into that boiling sea to free him. It was almost a suicide mission, but more by luck than anything else, we managed to get them both safely back on board.

Another incident also affected me deeply, the more tragic because it was the result of such a simple and easily preventable error. Two divers were undergoing decompression in the chamber on board the rig when the dive supervisor in the control van noticed that the pressure was falling very fast in the chamber. He began pumping in gas to compensate for it, but the gauge continued to fall and he pumped in more and more in a desperate attempt to save the divers' lives.

A large leak had developed, but only in the small transfer chamber used to link the decompression chamber itself to the diving bell. The connecting door had closed and the pressure in the main chamber remained normal. The pressure gauges for each chamber had been interlinked, however, and all of them recorded the same rapid drop in pressure. By the time the error was realized the men were dead from hypothermia.

Once more modifications were made to prevent such an accident ever happening again, but once more it was too late for two divers.

Another tragedy, even more terrible because the men involved had much longer to contemplate their fate, killed a friend of mine. He was in the Far East doing saturation work in an oilfield construction barge. He was in the decompression chamber with the rest of his dive team when a hurricane developed and the barge began to founder. There are lifeboat chambers on barges and dive ships today, which can be launched over the side in such an emergency. The divers remain afloat in their chamber, controlling their own environment until a rescue comes. But there was no such system on that construction barge. The decompression chamber was fixed to the deck. There was no way of removing it and if the divers trapped inside had tried to leave it, they would have suffered an agonizing death from the bends.

Instead they were given time to write a last letter home, which they passed out through the hatch before the barge was abandoned. As the lifeboats moved away, the barge broke up and sank. The divers inside the decompression chamber went down with it to the bottom of the ocean.

Black humour was often the only response to such tragedies. We would just look at each other, shrug and say, "No problem. Just open another box of English divers."

SPYING ON A RUSSIAN'S BOTTOM

Don Camsell

Camsell joined the British Special Boat Service (SBS) in 1974, and saw action in Oman, the Falklands, and Northern Ireland. And, in a covert operation, on the British mainland itself:

Navy Intelligence wanted us to photograph the *Kirov*'s hull as she entered harbour. This rather depended on her arriving during the day. Then we'd do a hull recce at night. No specific timings could be planned on as no one person knew exactly what time she would arrive, and the Russians weren't about to tell us.

The photographic recce was a relatively simple task. Paul's idea was for the divers to be secured on the seabed while the cruiser steamed above. It would be loud and quite an experience, but seemed the best option. During our pre-diving training Paul and I had noticed a linked chain that ran from the South Mole to the Detached Mole along the seabed at a depth of about 55 feet. Our first idea was to attach Nikon cameras with flashlights on the seabed. As the cruiser manoeuvred into the harbour they could be switched on from ashore, and bingo – mission one complete. The powerful flashlights and the remote-controlled motor drives of the camera would do the rest. Great. However, how can we guarantee that the cameras would maintain a position? What if the remote control fails? What if the cameras run out of film?

It would give us better control if we did it manually, with

swimmers strapped to the line, cameras at the ready. An under-water version of the paparazzi to greet the Russian celebrity.

Lots of questions remained. What speed would the Russian cruiser enter port? There are speed restrictions within any harbour, but the cruiser would be very slow because it was entering a particularly tight area and would be required to make a sharp left-hand turn to the Detached Mole. Ocean-going tugs would help the giant cruiser into position, but they were not considered a problem as they would only help the cruiser if required or requested, once she was within the harbour. The *Kirov*'s likely approach speed would be about two knots. That's fast for a swimmer!

What was the ship's draught? Nobody knew. All we had to work on was an estimate of 32 feet. The next question could not be answered: what would be the tidal state on her arrival? The tidal range within Gibraltar harbour is about ten feet depending on the time of year. So it looked like we had a minimum clearance of ten feet, if the ship drew as much water as we thought and the tide was out. Ten feet is not a lot to play with when you have 25,000 tons of battle cruiser passing over your head.

To test out the plan, we resorted to our old friend HMS *Plymouth*. It went well. The noise was almost unbearable, like lying down on the railway tracks and letting an express train thunder over you. The wash from the ship's propellers was fearsome. The photos came out very clearly, but we all shared the same thought: a *Kirov* is five times the size of the *Plymouth* . . .

The night hull recce was a different story. The initial thought was to forget the basic method of a direct compass swim; there was too much room for error with the compass and possible chance of compromise. We were told that the cruiser was going be moored on the Detached Mole. Funny really, we often wondered why the Russian cruiser was being moored at this particular point. If this were to happen to a British ship there would have been a mutiny because you don't have direct access to the quayside. No chance of a run ashore from there. The reason was that the Russian navy had a big desertion problem, so when they visited foreign ports, they usually lay off shore rather than tying up in harbour and watching half their guys go AWOL. Russian sailors could go to the most exotic ports in the world, but only look, not touch. No wonder they wanted to desert.

We submitted our plan to No. 10. We intended to hit her twice. The first time would be the photographic run while she entered the South Mole entry/exit point. We'd be strapped on to the chain that lies across the bottom, between the two arms of the mole, attached with climbing harnesses lying on our backs, in broad daylight, cameras at the ready. A ship coming right over your head is a truly awesome sight – and it feels like the screws are going to suck you up and mince you to pieces.

As the *Kirov* goes over, we would fire the large motor-driven Nikon cameras taking a continuous sequence of shots as the hull thunders overhead. We would be after her sonar domes, towed array and any new subsurface electronic equipment.

For our nocturnal snoop around the *Kirov*, we planned to wait in position, ready for the tide to come in. Swimming across the harbour, we'd get directly under the ship and photograph the hull. We'd also go up and actually feel the hull surface, two men on each side, building up a mental picture of what it looked like, what was on it. Then, as soon as we got back to base, we'd sit down and draw the shape from memory. Then it would go up to the Int. guys to work out what the various lumps and bumps contained inside her hull.

One issue haunted us. What if the Soviets sent down a team of their own divers. We knew the Russian naval Spetsnaz (special forces) teams had a fearsome reputation. Underwater, with no witnesses, there was no telling what they might do to guard the *Kirov*'s secrets. It was impressed on us over and over again that our top priority was not to get caught. We were very competent and highly confident underwater. But our Russian counterparts are certainly a match for us: just as well-trained and just as fit. If it came down to kill or be killed, who would have the edge?

*   *   *

Whump, whump, whump . . . I could hear the slow beat of the *Kirov*'s screws as she lined up on the narrow entrance between the moles of Gibraltar harbour. Ivan was coming to pay us a nice little courtesy visit. And lying on my back, strapped to the wire by my climbing harness, I was going to spy on his bottom . . .

A gigantic shadow loomed over us. The noise went right through me. The hull was so broad, it blotted out the light. Had we got our sums correct or were we going to be squashed into the harbour mud? The *Kirov* travelled over us with agonising slowness, the thunder of her screws now getting unbearable. We squeezed the pressel switches in our hands. The flashes lit up the bottom of the hull. The ship was moving much less than 4 knots, the usual speed that ships enter Gib harbour. I think that even the tug captains were briefed to slow her down so that we could have a good look at her bottom. On and on it went. The turbulence was incredible even at this slow speed; it rocked us left and right as we tried to lie still, attempting to judge when to take the pictures and when to hold on to the pressel switches that controlled the lights.

It was just as well that it was daylight as the flashlights lit up the whole area, even 50 feet down. The difficult part was approaching; I kept on thinking that the props of a ship are usually tucked up along the keel. This particular ship was double propped and no one person was a hundred per cent sure how they were configured. We were about to find out. It seemed to get darker. I reached over and squeezed Paul on the arm; I received a reciprocal squeeze back; we were both still OK; now the most testing part: the stern.

The battle cruiser's giant screws were thrashing towards us, churning up the water as they came overhead. I was shaking with fear; the safety margin was going to be bloody slim. The cameras flashed in the hope we'd get something, but I had to put my free hand to my face mask to hold it on. The wake nearly yanked my mouthpiece out and I had to grip it hard in my teeth to keep it in.

At last the pressure started to ease. The water became less angry and I was able to peer up at the stern as it moved on to its mooring. I grabbed Paul's arm. He must have thought the same, as both our arms touched. We unclipped the harness, excited at what we had just achieved, just hoping that some good results had been gained. We swam to the start point which was located on the outside of the detached mole. There we would stay underwater until a signal was received that it was safe to surface. Eventually, we got the signal. The team dragged us out of the water, removed our set and ancillaries and we moved under cover. We watched the *Kirov* slowly being manoeuvred into position on the detached mole. Phase 1 complete, phase 2 next – 1–0 to us!

The following day was taken up with last-minute briefs, with time allowed for a bit of general relaxation. Trouble was, it was impossible to get any sleep. We kept double-checking our equipment.

The task was due to start about 0100 hours, dependent on traffic and movement around the *Kirov*. If there was too much activity or security around the cruiser, we planned to delay for 24 hours – and thereafter every night until she left. The crew were due to be in port for a total of seven days, so this gave us the "fudge factor" we required. We knew that the security around the *Kirov* would be tight so we more or less assumed that nights two and three would be cancelled.

H hour. All the moves from Coaling Island were done in covert vehicles to prearranged water entry points hidden from the public eye. Three pairs of swimmers would undertake the recce: one pair would take the stern, one pair the bows, while Paul and I studied her amidships – the area most likely to show any evidence of hydraulic doors from which the Russians might launch divers. The other teams would be looking for the prop configuration and any unusual sonar dome configuration.

The doors opened and we were out of the vehicle, down to the shoreline in the shadows. We prepared to enter the water, the surface calm and black. The final check on fins, mask, hood, gloves, set and body line. We went on to oxygen, completed our two minutes, cleared our counter lungs of any dirty air, and entered the water. We moved to about ten feet below the surface of the sea wall. We carried our compass board and constantly checked our direction just in case, so we didn't need to pop up to the surface to check our bearings, risking compromise by some sharp-eyed lookout. The total distance was approximately 1,800 yards. I swam on Paul's left, just above his left-hand shoulder. We kept at a depth of between 32 and 52 feet, going down to between 52 and 53 feet as we reached the *Kirov*. The phosphorescence from our bodies was very pretty, but alarmingly obvious, so we had to slow down.

It was a long swim. We had lots of time to think about the implications of being caught: Soviet interrogation procedures would make our experience on the *Plymouth* look like light entertainment. Never mind the political implications of letting our country down, we doubted we'd see our families again. (They might see us, I supposed, if they televized a show trial of the western spies.)

The noise of the great ship was all around us now. Under normal training circumstances the ship would be shut down, her props be locked in the water, intakes switched off along with anything else that might be hazardous to divers. This was different. The *Kirov* was a fully operational Russian battle cruiser with no reason to make things safe for us. Rather the opposite in fact. All her intakes would be working, her props could turn at any time – all standard anti-diver procedure in wartime.

The first leg went with no problems . . . second leg . . . third leg . . . and here we were. A quick check of the set: no leaks on the buddy line that we were about to depend on. The water cleared to reveal the silhouette of the *Kirov*. God, she was a massive beast!

We moved to the keel of the cruiser, starting our recce on the starboard side, nearest to the detached mole. Our plan was to move to the portside, complete the recce, then swim to safety. We swam deeper and deeper into the apparently bottomless harbour until we made our first physical touch with the *Kirov*. We immediately went into our routine. No time to hang about.

We ran our hands over every crack, hole or bump we could find. Using our 13-foot buddy line we measured everything, storing the information in our heads as we'd practised.

We moved all the way down the portside until the silhouettes of the long prop shafts could be clearly seen. It was at this point that we had the fright of our lives. A small boat had been patrolling the area around the cruiser. We heard the tell-tale splash of swimmers entering the water.

They were astern of us, how far it was difficult to tell. We pressed ourselves against the ship's hull so we wouldn't be silhouetted. We watched two Soviet divers swim along the prop shafts, but they did not come up as far as us. We dared not move. My hand clasped the knife strapped to my thigh.

We waited for what seemed like hours, but we later estimated at six minutes. It must have been a routine check of the *Kirov*'s propellers and propeller shafts. But why didn't they check along any further? In a roundabout way this suggested there was nothing of importance from amidships to the bows. On the other hand we did find a number of massive holes, over 13 feet square. Did this indicate anything peculiar about the cruiser? We could not answer that question as we were not about to commit ourselves into these black holes, especially with enemy divers in the water with us.

The Russian divers swam to the surface. After a final check we swam deep and away from the *Kirov*. The further we swam, the more elated we became. The swim was virtually over: we had completed a task against our biggest enemy. The phosphorescence flowed over our shoulders and around our bodies the faster we swam, but we didn't mind now. We got out of the water, tugged off our fins and masks and jumped into the van. Back to base.

We spent the next five hours drawing, describing and analysing the information. The report had to be on the plane to London the following day. Although there was no substantial proof of the ship conducting counter-espionage operations, the pictures and the results of the hull recce were a resounding success. The euphoria of it all made you want to shout from the rooftops and run up the submariners' traditional victory flag, the skull and crossbones. Two-nil to the SBS and above all Paul. For Paul's personal input in the success of the operation, Paul was awarded the British Empire Medal (BEM).

"I . . . floated through the opening,
wondering if this was the last thing my uncle saw"

THE GHOST OF SHIPWRECKS FUTURE

Patrick Symmes

Patrick Symmes is a New York-based travel writer. His books include Chasing Che.

It was an ugly ship, and still is. The steamer *Mohawk* was a 387-foot workhorse on the weekly run to Havana, carrying freight and discount passengers in both directions. When it sailed out of New York for the last time, on 24 January 1935, the *Mohawk* had neither fame nor beauty, and it has taken a damn serious beating since then.

The first blow was administered by the Norwegian freighter *Talisman*, which slammed into the ship a few hours from Manhattan, slicing a deep gash in the bow. It took 70 minutes for the *Mohawk* to sink, enough time for most of the lifeboats to get away with most of the 164 people aboard, though not all. Forty-five lives ended on that icy night off the coast of New Jersey, and the *Mohawk* plunged 80 feet and cracked open on the sea floor. For most of the world, the story ended then and there.

But the awkward little ship never had a final resting place, nor any peace. Sitting upright on the silty bottom, the wreck's tallest parts – the bridge and smokestack – were still hazards in the busy New Jersey shipping channels. Soon two tugboats were dispatched to wire-drag the wreck, forcing a heavy steel cable back and forth through the superstructure, snapping the deck plates apart, ripping the bridge from the hull, and scattering debris into the currents. A few years later, in World War II, the Coast Guard pummeled the *Mohawk* with depth charges; German U-boats had been hiding alongside wrecks in these waters, dodging sonar behind their bulky silhouettes.

With insult heaped on injury, the *Mohawk* was left to the mercy of the Atlantic. Decade by decade, the ocean shoved, pulled, twisted, flipped, and buried the ruins of the old boat and its rusting cargo of car parts and china. When scuba diving became a mass sport in the 1960s, a few visitors dropped onto the wreckage, but by the 1990s, as technology – advanced GPS, inexpensive side-scan sonar, and nitrox gas mixtures – made it easier to explore wrecks, a new wave of divers began to pick its bones. Hundreds of thousands of certified divers live along the Middle Atlantic seaboard, and nowadays a dozen or more of them can be found crawling over the vessel on any given summer Sunday.

Inevitably, those divers come back up with something: some trophy, some artifact, some souvenir. If they are lucky, or determined, they might find a porthole, bring it up, clean it, and slap it on the mantelpiece. Weekend by weekend, storm by storm, man and the elements are reducing the *Mohawk* to a memory. This would not concern me in the least, except that my uncle died on the S.S. *Mohawk*.

He was my father's eldest brother, William D. Symmes, a student at Williams College traveling with his geology professor and five classmates. They were scheduled to catch a plane from Havana to the Yucatán for an inspection of Mayan ruins. In the small world of families and acquaintances, 24 January 1935, was a black tragedy. A Massachusetts newspaper headlined a group photo of the six Williams passengers, taken right before they sailed: "JUST THREE RETURN ALIVE."

Time dissolves grief, just as rust undoes the strongest steel, and while the *Mohawk* slowly broke apart on the ocean floor, a few pieces of its history began to surface again. A chunk of that forgotten past fell into my hands last summer – and then dropped hard onto my big toe, before skittering across the floor and lodging under a sofa. The item in question was a modest ceramic tile, thick, hexagonal, sharp-edged, about the size of an Oreo, that fell unexpectedly from an envelope stuffed with documents about the *Mohawk*. I'd requested the paperwork from Steve Nagiewicz, executive director of the Explorers Club in New York, a group as famous for its annual dinner (where else can you dine on tarantula tempura with astronauts?) as for the grand scientific expeditions of its members. But Nagiewicz's interest in the *Mohawk* was personal, too – it lies just offshore from his New Jersey home. He runs a weekend dive-charter business, and like most Jersey divers, he knows the wreck well. Over the years he's brought up plates and a few tiles, and it was one of the latter that he slipped into the envelope. Recovering the cream-colored tablet from under the couch, I steeled myself for any number of reactions: sorrow at encountering this touch-stone from a tragedy, perhaps anger that this fragment had been rousted from a grave.

I wouldn't have been the first to be outraged at the desecra-tion of a lost ship. Ever since the early 1960s, when wildcat treasure hunters like the late Mel Fisher first pulled gold off Spanish galleons in the Florida Keys and marine archaeologists like George Bass of Texas A&M first sent frogmen down to Byzantine merchant ships in the Mediterranean, the rivalry between scholars and salvagers has deepened. Commercial salvagers, gold seekers, and souvenir hunters argue that they are rescuing value from the encroaching sea, that anything not removed will eventually be lost for good. Archaeologists counter that salvagers are disturbing vital cultural resources, like pot thieves defiling Anasazi ruins. Governments claim sunken war-ships as their patrimony. Insurance companies claim a share of lost treasure. Family members claim that wrecks should be left as undisturbed graves. The result has never been as simple as "finders-keepers," nor as absolute as the legal rulings of dry-footed legislators. But as wreck diving increases, the calls for regulation grow louder: California allows only permitted ar-chaeologists to remove objects from the 1,600 wrecks in its

waters, and Wisconsin arrested a diver in 1998 for taking a
porthole. In Britain, a group called Wreck Respect is agitating
to ban all souvenir diving, everywhere. Last July, Paris-based
UNESCO – the United Nations Educational, Scientific, and
Cultural Organization – promulgated a new international convention defining any shipwreck older than 100 years as a
"cultural deposit" and the "patrimony of mankind," subject
to restrictions including a total ban on amateur salvage. Lacking
any enforcement mechanism, the new policy is toothless. Most
wrecks lie in the shallow waters claimed by sovereign nations,
and most maritime powers, including the United States, have
refused to sign, claiming the convention contradicts existing
laws of the sea.

Emotions are another matter. Turning the tile over in my
fingers, I felt vaguely disappointed: It was cold, lifeless, a little
bit ugly. The humble reality was that it probably came from the
wall of a washroom or the floor of the galley. It wasn't the time
capsule I'd hoped for, and it carried no messages from the past.
Within days I had called Nagiewicz and arranged for a deeper
immersion.

"About nine twenty, as though from some unknown danger,
the room we were in fell into a deadly silence – no word was
uttered. Then came the crash." The final moments of the
Mohawk were chaotic, according to one of the surviving
Williams students. In a 28-page testimonial composed for
the college archives, Karl Osterhout described the departure
that blustery afternoon from Pier 13 in Manhattan and the
crash just hours later. The *Mohawk* sailed the day after what
the *New York Daily News* called the "worst storm since
1920"; 17 inches of snow had fallen on the city, and ice still
coated the ship's railings. As the vessel rounded Sandy Hook
and headed south, the college students had no inkling that the
steering system was freezing up. They ate dinner and then sat
in the lounge, playing cards. Osterhout had just dealt a hand to
my uncle when they heard a ship's whistle blow, and then
silence fell over the passengers. The *Mohawk* had veered out

of its sea lane; everyone seemed to sense some danger approaching. It was the *Talisman*, which surged out of the night and into the *Mohawk*'s port bow.

"It didn't seem like a big crash," Osterhout wrote, "but there was a sound like splintering wood. At the impact everyone stood up simultaneously. One woman screamed." The *Talisman* sheared off, drifting but intact, and after gawking at the disappearing freighter the *Mohawk*'s passengers rushed to their staterooms. Some sensibly put on warm clothing, but many paused to pursue bizarre urges. Osterhout encountered one of his friends sitting calmly in bed, scribbling a diary entry about "exactly how I felt when the crash came." One man stowed two teaspoons in his pockets, dejected that his shipment of antique silver was locked in the hold. Osterhout caught himself obsessively collecting his scattered playing cards. The *Mohawk* listed hard to port, then tilted to starboard. The pitching corridors were filled with families hauling steamer trunks, and old women in nightgowns. Falling pots and pans brained the cook. Few members of the 110-man crew were to be found: One officer, Osterhout noted, "tried to make the band play, but the men refused." Passengers stumbled up the gangways and skittered across the snowy decks. Some of the lifeboats could not be broken out of the ice; people filled others with their luggage, and handed their children out to strangers in departing boats. The lights failed, restarted, and failed again. In the darkness, the geology party became separated. Osterhout heard glass portholes shatter belowdecks, a sign that water was rising fast. He jumped into one of the last lifeboats, landing beside the waiter who had served him dinner.

Even those who made it into the lifeboats suffered severe frostbite during the two-hour wait for rescue, but my uncle didn't make it into a boat. If he did manage to escape the ship, the "suck" that followed the *Mohawk*'s dive would have pulled even a strong swimmer under, and as the downdraft subsided, the debris that rocketed back to the surface would have knocked even a strong man unconscious. More than a hundred people in lifeboats survived, but the lives of my uncle and 44 others ended quietly, a plunging body temperature leading quickly to exhaustion, then numbness, then blackness.

Two ships picked up the lifeboats and stayed on station until dawn as a formality; the *Talisman* did too, before being towed into port. When the *Mohawk* survivors docked in New York, they were thronged by photographers ("MORE SHIP DISASTER PICTURES PAGES 12, 18, 20 AND 21," crowed the *Daily News*) and the distraught families of passengers. Among them was my grandmother, still hopeful that her eldest son, initially reported to be safe, would come limping down a gangway. A few days later his body was recovered, and William D. Symmes was switched into the column of the dead. Most of the bodies were found, but not all, and the *Mohawk* began its long residence as a memorial to the lost.

I never knew my grandmother, but I find it hard to think of her on the dock that day, waiting. Things seemed to go wrong for my family after that. Within a few years my grandfather too died; my grandmother passed away shortly after that. My father's remaining brother died in the 1950s, and my father more than a decade ago. The youngest son of the youngest son, I was cut off from this lost generation. In the photos, Uncle Bill seems like a stranger – unfamiliar in the root meaning of that word.

There is an old photo of my father sledding in Central Park on a snowy day, and when I turned it over recently I was surprised to see, in my grandmother's neat writing, that it was taken on 24 January 1935, the day the *Mohawk* sailed. It was the last day of an old world, the day something broke between the past and present.

We cruised out to the *Mohawk* before dawn on a calm Sunday, leaving Point Pleasant Beach on Steve Nagiewicz's dive boat, the *Diversion II*. I sat on the aft deck with eight other divers, sipping coffee amid the odor of diesel fuel as the condos of the Jersey shore shrank away. My companions were members of a local dive club, veterans who teased one another as they squeezed into drysuits and strapped on knives, weights, guidelines, lights, and salvage bags. There wasn't much time to get ready, since the *Diversion* needed only 40 minutes to reach the *Mohawk*; the site is just eight miles out, close enough that you can sometimes smell the cheese fries of Asbury Park when you surface. As word spread that I had lost a relative on the *Mohawk*, the other divers offered to hold a moment of silence, but when I declined they went right back to ribbing each other and me about equipment ("You call that a knife?"). New Jersey is one of America's epicenters of wreck diving – the state has even created 14 artificial reefs out of sunken ships and scrap – and dive boats here are known for macho hazing. It's a normal defense mechanism as much as anything: Set amid tragedies of the past, wreck diving is also inherently dangerous. Author Bernie Chowdhury's book *The Last Dive* describes a fatal search for a U-boat in Jersey waters, and the *Mohawk* itself recently claimed a life, a diver who had a heart attack.

I climbed up to the flying bridge to watch Nagiewicz guide us toward the site. Finding a wreck used to require expert triangulation, factoring in travel time, land bearings, and currents, but now anyone can push a few buttons on a GPS and hit it on the first try. Stout and bearded, 48-year-old Nagiewicz lived up to his Explorers Club mystique – one of those hale-and-hearty specimens who can have fun at 6 a.m. Working the throttles, he grinned with contentment at the flat sea and clean air, and attempted to rouse me with a string of donuts, quizzing me about my uncle and railing against the UNESCO convention. ("They've gone overboard," he said.) His grin faded as we approached the site and found another large boat anchored over the wreck, with divers already plunging into the sea. Like our crowd, they all carried large mesh bags.

I let the club divers go first, and when their bubbles had vanished I waddled to the railing. Although there were three guides with us, the real authority on deck was Nagiewicz's four-year-old son, Travis, whose self-proclaimed duties included watching out for pirates and "assisting" divers into the water. He shoved me in with gusto, hurling oyster crackers at my bobbing head until I finally slipped under and followed the anchor line into a green void.

The water was thick with particles, limiting visibility to 25 feet – nearly perfect for this murky coast. It was obvious why souvenirs hold such a central place for Jersey divers: Without crystal waters, coral reefs, or exotic species, there isn't much to look at. But even in five feet of visibility, common here, you can feel your way along a wreck, hand over hand, picking up and examining things. The most successful souvenir hunters on the *Mohawk* were the diggers, who fanned away at the sandy bottom, groping through silt clouds for something solid. A couple of years ago someone found a pocket watch that way, and last year a crate of china.

As I dropped below 40 feet, the dark brine parted to reveal the *Mohawk* itself – it was less "cultural deposit" than junkyard, with steel plates and girders strewn randomly across the sea floor. Dropping onto midships, I landed between two massive winches, near what looked like a generator. I spotted a rusting Chevy grill, and a handful of tires. The sea surge tossed loose cables back and forth over the wreckage; fat blackfish flocked past islands of debris, and dark lobsters ducked under the scrap as I approached. The *Mohawk* is known as a great lobster dive, but after a few attempts to pry dinner out of a hidey-hole I gave up. Getting a meal here spooked me – like somehow skirting cannibalism.

I swam slowly across the wreck, steadily bumping into other divers; there were enough here to hold a cocktail party. Only near the end of my air supply did I see a ship shape loom out of the dark: an upright bulkhead, with a curving doorway attached. I purged a little air, dropped down, and floated through the opening, wondering if this was the last thing my uncle saw.

I threw up seven times during the surface interval, launching coffee and half-digested donuts over the *Diversion*'s port railing and onto this grave site of my clan. Diving squeezes the softer internal organs in unnatural ways, and I've found that even the best dive may be followed by a good puke.

"You're dunkin' those donuts, pal!" the Jersey boys heckled. Divers were crowding in and out of the water. A man staggered up the back ladder, holding a mesh bag. "Whadjaget?" someone asked. The bag disgorged an object, flat and brown, roughly triangular. We all gathered around and examined the trophy, which turned out to be a . . . stone.

"I thought it was a hinge," the embarrassed treasure hunter muttered, turning bright red. "He's got a rock!" one of his friends cackled. "Good job, a rock!" Over on the other boat, a diver popped up and scrambled on board. "Ooohhh," someone on our boat muttered. "He's got a big bag." We pressed against the rail to watch, but tradition demanded that we scorn the other crew, and no one called across to concede curiosity.

Watching the scene on the *Diversion*, I realized that whatever the legal or ethical protests, this sort of trophy diving was something larger than my own family's history. By traditions dating back thousands of years, wrecks are the property of whoever can first find and salvage them. "Salvage has been around since things have been lost," Robert Ballard, the discoverer of the *Titanic*, told me. "If they dropped a coin, they went down to pick it up." As far back as ancient Rhodes, the right to salvage wrecks was detailed in legal codes that rewarded divers for going deep. "The concept of preserving underwater cultural heritage is wonderful," Ballard continued, but the UNESCO convention could "throw out the baby with the bathwater" by severely curtailing serious exploration. "Porthole divers," as he derides them, can't reach deepwater sites – yet. But cheap robotic submersibles are already sold in dive magazines; it won't be long, Ballard warns, before "some asshole" clips off a piece of the *Titanic*. He still believes, however, that, with a few famous exceptions, only those wrecks over a thousand years old – not a hundred – should be protected for their rare archaeological heritage.

The *Mohawk*, of course, cannot qualify for legal caresses from anyone. Lying in the public domain, it isn't old enough to be covered by the UNESCO convention (although, within my lifetime, it will be). With every rivet detailed in existing blueprints, it holds no historic value. Resting within sight of the Jersey Shore, it has no meaning for ocean explorers. Filled with auto parts and luggage, it has no value for treasure hunters. It has no advocates, except for me, and even I wasn't sure how I felt.

George Bass, the 69-year-old father of marine archaeology himself, told me he'd long ago reconciled himself to the slightly gruesome mixture of souvenir diving and personal tragedy. Bass lost a distant relative on the S.S. *Atlantic*, which foundered in Long Island Sound in 1846, but he said it never bothered him that divers had picked the wreck over and brought up the ship's bell. "I always wanted to go see it," he admitted. So it was for me and the *Mohawk*.

Travis Nagiewicz pushed me into the water again, and I sank down toward the wreck to say a final farewell. This time I'd brought something along with me in the pocket of my dive vest, and it seemed to drag me down toward the ship like a magnet. The familiar scrap of girders and steel plates emerged from the gloom below me; a wall of steel stuck up from the mud, a section of the graceless hull. When I neared the turnaround point on my air supply, I floated quietly for a moment more, and in the darkness a last tall shape loomed: I thought I could make out a bit of the ship's bridge, 15 feet high, and beyond it a section of the bow still thrusting forward toward Havana. I pushed my fingers through the sand, thinking I might come across some of the old silver teaspoons that *Mohawk* passenger had left behind.

The water pushed back and forth, and I reached into my vest pocket and looked around for other divers – I didn't want to get ribbed about this later. Then I slipped the tile back into the silt, letting the currents cover it over for good.

*"I thought life on land was mean
until I saw what goes on under water"*

FISH DAYDREAMS

Michael G. Zinsley

Scuba instructor Michael Zinsley is the author of the diving-memoir The Rapture of the Deep, *1999.*

When asked where my favorite dive site is, I never hesitate to say New Dropoff. This underwater peninsula juts out like a thumb from Palau's barrier reef into the Philippine Sea. Living organisms are rooted into every square inch of it, covering the hard coral ridge with a soft colorful mantle. The exquisite natural architecture is fascinating, but the real entertainment is provided by the fish. When the tides change, strong currents wash fresh nourishment over the point, attracting tiny plankton feeders. These smaller fish draw larger predators that in turn attract the sharks. It doesn't take long for every link in the food chain to appear.

On the tip of the point, two wide vertical grooves add personality to the reef. The larger of these cuts drops to 120 feet, where a fantastic collection of wire corals and fans stick out from the wall. Sailfish, thresher sharks, oceanic whitetip sharks, and massive tuna cruise this neighborhood. Farther down, at the base of the smaller cut, the reef begins to overhang. At the base of this prominence is a small cave with an arch at its entrance. From there, the point looms above like the prow of a magnificent living ship, cutting the transparent water on an endless voyage. Below, a steep sandy incline drops 12,000 feet to the ocean floor.

When the current is strong, the vertical corridor of the smaller cut becomes a giant fire hose, funneling water straight up from the depths. A school of snapper loves to hover in the heart of the shaft when the torrent is rushing, and whenever a fresh gust barrels through, the hardy fish are tossed around like autumn leaves on a sidewalk. The blast continues 50 feet past the edge of the reef to the surface, where it "boils" hard enough to flatten waves – a helpful "landmark" when looking for the dive site.

Above the cuts, the reef flattens and stretches for hundreds of yards. Turtles wander this area, whitetip reef sharks lie in sand holes, and octopus slither from crevice to crevice. Alert divers occasionally notice manta rays passing overhead.

When the current kicks up over two knots at the tops of the cuts, the fish pack together to form a living fog-layer. A diver's objective is to get into that haze, hang on to the reef to maintain position, and spend the dive in sensory overload. Small fish dart back and forth among the coral heads, selecting their planktonic provisions. Schools of larger fish hover nearby in clouds. The largest fish hang out in twos or threes like schoolyard bullies, ready to dash in and gobble up any inattentive little guys. Dozens of gray reef sharks cruise past, arrogantly eyeing the buffet.

The most prominent predators are trevally, two-foot-long streamlined ocean swimmers whose silvery hides are tipped with yellow and blue fins. When a languid trevally spies a school of savory hors d'oeuvres and decides to *do lunch*, it snaps its tail hard, instantly accelerating into a carnivorous blur. I thought life on land was mean until I saw what goes on under water. Fish can't take coffee breaks. If they drop their guard for a second, they're snacks. Too bad Darwin wasn't a diver. He would have loved it.

When the current rips hard enough to suck divers' bubbles over the other side of the reef and down out of sight, the smaller fish swim hard or hide in the coral to keep from getting washed away. Only the hydrodynamic sharks soar effortlessly, similar to hawks on a windy day. They often glide up a few feet over the lip and hang in place. Once, in a moderate current, I carefully watched a shark doing this, and noticed that its angle of attack into the current was slightly downward. It was falling through the water, but motionless relative to the reef. I got an idea and tried it out. I exhaled hard and held my breath out to sink. I then straightened my body and angled downward. It worked! I could let go of the reef, breathe shallowly, and maintain my position with a minimal amount of fin twitching. By sloping my right shoulder down, I was able to glide slowly towards the shark until we were side-by-side, three feet apart. A few minutes later, another shark appeared, coming straight at me. When his mouth was two feet from my face, I realized that my head could easily fit inside it. I lost my nerve, gave up my spot, and swam over to join the other divers in relative safety.

This reef is also a great place to watch cleaning wrasse at work. These finger-sized colorfully striped fish run the cleaning stations in their neighborhoods. A cleaning station is the car wash of the reef. Larger fish pull up to the station, sometimes lining up behind each other to let the wrasse work over their skin, mouth, and teeth for parasites. They lift their heads and open their mouths, gills, and fins to let the smaller fish go to work. When they are finished, they wander off so the wrasse may attend to the next fish.

Surgeonfish add to the show by slowly changing the color of their bodies. Over the space of a minute, dark brown hides will flash three silver stripes across their skin, then fade to silvery light blue before returning to dark brown. Other surgeon species will go from dark brown with darker brown spots to brilliant blue with yellow gold near the head. Even their eyes change color!

When a shark pulls up, it doesn't wait in line. The others back off as the big fish holds open a yawn, allowing the wrasse to swim through its gill slits, clean its teeth from the inside, and exit through its mouth. Eating a cleaning wrasse is strictly taboo. In this symbiotic relationship, one gets fed, and the other gets cleaned. It is perfection in nature . . . almost – I once watched a large gray snapper seemingly daydream while it was being cleaned. It forgot there was a wrasse in its mouth and shut it. It seemed to gag a little, but nothing else happened. Several minutes later, I still hadn't seen the wrasse emerge.

I yelled through my regulator, "You're not supposed to do that!"

FREEDIVE

Colin Beavan

Freediving is any form of swimming underwater without breathing-
aids, but most celebratedly it is diving deep on a single breath of air.
"Competitive apnea" as the extreme sport of free diving is known
was immortalized in the cult movie The Big Blue, *1988.*
Divers compete to see who can go deepest on just one breath – and
who can survive the yet-more-perilous ascent to air.

One mile off the coast of Miami, Alejandro Ravelo, a small,
unshaven man, perches quietly at the edge of a floating white
platform, his neoprene-clad torso swaying without resistance to
the ocean's uneven rhythms. His submerged feet sport three-
foot-long fins. A heavy-duty clip clamps his nostrils closed.

Ravelo's breathing is slow and deep. His eyes are shut. By
calming his mind he will, he hopes, slow his body and quell its
thirst for oxygen as he attempts to reclaim his place as the
world's deepest breath-holding diver, unaided by breathing
equipment – a title that the Italian Umberto Pelizzari took in
1992. In his category of breath-hold, or "free", diving, called
constant-weight, Pelizzari descended 236 feet on a single breath
of air. Ravelo aims to descend ten feet farther, looking for a
"confirmation tag" attached to a blood-red guide rope that has
already been laid deep beneath the platform. If he grabs the tag,
the time he took to reach it – probably about a minute – will not
be the most impressive part of his oxygenless excursion: he set a

world record in 1993 by holding his breath for six minutes and forty-one seconds while lying motionless at the bottom of a hotel pool. The true feat is the tremendous exertion required to return to the surface. With his arms extended above him in a hydrodynamic Superman pose, Ravelo must kick against gravity the equivalent of nineteen stories back to air.

Around Ravelo's platform the faces of six scuba divers – white ovals emerging from dark wet suits – bob on the Atlantic's steely swells, waiting for Ravelo's move. Stationed at ten-meter intervals, the divers, who will later be joined by breath-hold divers, are ready to serve as links in Ravelo's underwater lifeline. If he passes out, no one of the safety divers can rush him to the surface: they will be anchored to their assigned depths by the perils of the bends, which threaten divers who breathe compressed air and ascend too rapidly. Instead they will pass his unconscious body back to the surface like a baton.

Spectator boats drift away; their engines must not taint the air. Momentarily lapsing from his trance, Ravelo signals to his manager, Rudi Castineyra, among the scuba divers. Castineyra extends his arm into the air and gives a thumbs-down sign – diver-speak not for "bad" but for "descend". Air hisses out of their buoyancy vests as the divers sink like paratroopers into the clouds. Ravelo's black form remains alone under the gray sky as he prepares his underwater *pas seul*.

In 1992, in Cuba, Ravelo set the world record for constant-weight free diving at 230 feet – the record Pelizzari broke only a few months later in Italy, where free divers are celebrated as fervently as bullfighters are in Spain. When Ravelo tried to regain his title in 1993, Cuban security officials refused him a boat, fearing that he would sail for America. Their refusal drove him to flee to Miami.

Ravelo's upper body grows larger and then smaller: his ribs are bowing outward from the pressure of his lungs as he breathes deeply, stretching their capacity for a gigantic last gasp. He makes the puh-puh-puh sounds of a bicycle pump as he swallows air into his digestive system, like a child wanting to burp. This may save Ravelo's life: on the way back up he will belch the gaseous discharge into his lungs. His twenty minutes of breathing techniques complete, a tingling in his fingertips tells him that his body is fully oxygenated. He blows off carbon dioxide with four hard exhales and gasps once. The water accepts him silently.

With a flutter of powerful fin kicks Ravelo propels himself downward. At fifty feet the increasing water pressure compresses the air-filled cavities in his body to a density sufficient for him to sink without effort. He stops kicking, and the force of gravity slices him through the water like an arrow surging toward its target.

Rino Gamba, of the Confederation Mondiale des Activites Subaquatiques (CMAS), has been verifying free-diving records, including Ravelo's, since 1967. "They aren't trying to beat nature," he says of the divers. "They have a deep love of the sea. You cannot understand the strength of their passion."

Gamba points out that human beings have long braved the sea unaided by gadgets. In 1913, thirty years before Jacques Yves Cousteau and Emil Gagnan perfected the self-contained underwater breathing apparatus (SCUBA), a Greek sponge diver, Stotti Geroghios, dove 200 feet without so much as fins and tied a line to the lost anchor of an Italian battleship. Archaeological digs have unearthed widespread evidence of breath-hold diving in seaside cultures. Mother of pearl, for example, harvested from the deep, adorns carved ornaments that date from 3200 B.C. in Thebes and 4500 B.C. in Mesopotamia. Today in Japan female divers known as amas scavenge the ocean floor for pearls and coral at depths of as much as 145 feet for up to three hours a day, returning to the surface as many as ninety times for air. Scuba divers at those depths for this duration would suffer decompression sickness. The ama practice of whistling before a plunge seemed only a custom until scientists discovered that whistling increases air pressure in the lungs, forcing blood out and leaving more volume for the next breath.

Rural peoples of the Mediterranean and the Caribbean buy the daily catch of local spearfishers who hold their breath as they dive. Ravelo himself, before becoming the youngest-ever member of the Cuban national spearfishing team, helped his father support the family by spearfishing. With his spear gun attached by rope to a buoy on the surface, he searched beneath underwater rocks and in caves for groupers, which can be as large as 140 pounds. Once the fish was speared, a buddy at the surface gathered in the line while Ravelo, fresh air in his lungs, returned to untangle the line from rocks or sometimes to fight his catch hand to fin. Today spearfishing has become a sport for thousands around the world. At international championships judges tally points for each fish caught and for their weights; the record for a bluefin tuna caught with a spear gun stands at 398 pounds.

Free diving is not without risk. In the European countries of the Mediterranean alone about fifty-five free divers die each year, many from "shallow-water blackout". With increasing depth, pressure compresses the chest, giving divers the false sensation that their lungs are full. But during ascent pressure drops rapidly and gas in the lungs expands, which can lead to a lack of blood-oxygen and loss of consciousness, often just before divers reach the surface. Pre-dive hyperventilation, as practiced by Ravelo and others, can also put divers at risk by lowering carbon dioxide levels so much that they do not feel the need to breathe soon enough. Mehgan Heaney-Grier, a nineteen-year-old model who established the US women's constant-weight free-diving record at 155 feet, and who accompanied her friend Ravelo to observe his most recent attempt to break a record, explains the danger all free divers face: "You override your brain's message telling you when to breathe. You're running on your reserve tank and there's no warning before you hit empty."

Most free divers neither hunt for fish nor seek to set records. They simply prefer to venture underwater unencumbered by pounds of scuba equipment. "Breath-holders often see things scuba divers don't," says Tec Clark, the assistant director of the YMCA's national scuba program (a U.S. federation of CMAS), based in Norcross, Georgia, which supported Ravelo's attempt as part of its plans to promote free diving more widely. "The aquatic environment accepts you more as a free diver. You get to see fish that might otherwise shy away from bubbles and the noise of scuba mechanisms." Heaney-Grier agrees. She tells stories of riding the backs of 25-foot whale sharks and giant sea turtles on a single breath of air.

The quest to make the world's deepest dive unaided by breathing equipment began in earnest about thirty years ago, when Enzo Maiorca, an Italian, and Jacques Mayol, a Frenchman born in Shanghai, separately developed methods using heavy weights to speed their descent. As they plummeted five feet per second, they grabbed their noses and blew like crazy, racing against time to equalize the mounting pressure that could otherwise burst an eardrum.

One method, which survives to this day, involves no swimming at all and is known as "no-limits" free diving. Divers hold on to a weighted, rope-guided sled. Delivered by this aquatic luge to the prescribed depth, they detach themselves from the sled and pull a pin that releases compressed air from a cylinder into a balloon, which they grab to buoy themselves back to the surface in a storm of bubbles. In an intermediate kind of free diving, "variable-weight" divers hasten their descent with a sinker of no more than a third of their body weight, which they shed before ascending unaided. In Ravelo's "constant-weight" type of free diving, he completes the round trip without assistance.

In the late sixties Mayol and Maiorca achieved depths approaching 240 feet. Physiologists, groups of whom curiously follow free divers, cautioned them against going deeper. The limit, they said, would be not breath-holding capacity but water pressure, which below 325 feet, they calculated, would collapse the chest like an empty soda can – an effect known as thoracic squeeze.

But Mayol was convinced otherwise. During his studies of the diving behavior and anatomy of dolphins at the Seaquarium, near Key Biscayne, Florida, he witnessed autopsies that revealed no obvious anatomical structure preventing thoracic squeeze. The lungs and thorax were essentially the same in a dolphin as in a human being, yet dolphins survived great depths. Mayol was sure that whatever protected them would also protect people. Testing himself in waters from the Mediterranean to the frigid lakes of the Andes, and helped by a group of scientists, Mayol sought to understand what happens to the human body underwater. In a typical experiment, Mayol descended to 150 feet and held his breath for nearly four minutes with a cardiac catheter inserted in his chest. When in 1976 he defied warnings and, helped by a sled, went to 328 feet, scientists confirmed the existence of "blood shift" in humans.

We share this mechanism to prevent crushing – a throwback to our evolutionary aquatic heritage – with dolphins, seals, and other diving mammals. In response to pressure, the body constricts the blood vessels on the periphery, forcing blood from the extremities into the chest cavity. The thoracic cavity becomes not like an empty soda can but like a full one, blood being incompressible.

Blood shift protected Francisco "Pipin" Ferreras, another native of Cuba who now lives in Florida, when in 1990 he broke Mayol's record for no-limits free diving by going to 367 feet. In 1991 Umberto Pelizzari, Ravelo's nemesis in constant-weight free diving, broke the no-limits record by going to 387 feet.

These records tempt divers to believe that there is no limit to the depths a diver can withstand, but scientists still say otherwise. They worry now not about the crushing of the chest but about cardiac arrhythmias, which they have observed during Ferreras's dives. Claes Lundgren, the director of the Center for Research and Education in Special Environments at the State University of New York at Buffalo medical school, has observed that blood shift causes the heart to swell. Lundgren is also concerned that mounting blood pressure will eventually burst the capillary walls inside the lungs. The potential looms for an unromantic death by cardiac arrest or by drowning in lungs full of blood. "No one seems concerned," he says. "But they will be when somebody finds out what the absolute limit is in a very unpleasant way."

Even without these dangers, the hazards of no-limits diving are drastic. Ferreras, in his most recent world-record attempt, off Cabo San Lucas, at the southern tip of Mexico's Baja Peninsula, successfully descended to and returned from 436 feet. But he had to abort a first attempt, because he drifted into shallow water. Effectively blind without a mask, he raced toward a rocky bottom. Safety divers had to get him off the sled to avoid a crash. Only a few weeks earlier one of Ferreras's safety scuba divers had been found floating dead on the surface. During a training dive he may have had convulsions and therefore returned too quickly to the surface; internal gases, expanding as water pressure decreased, caused the arteries in his organs to explode.

Because of the dangers, dive organizations refuse to sanction no-limits diving. In 1970 CMAS stopped ratifying records, saying that no-limits diving was not a sport but a brand of "applied experimentation", meaning experiments involving people. Many aficionados of free diving are unimpressed with Ferreras and his ilk. Constant-weight has much more finesse, they say. Jacques Mayol's son, Jean-Jacques, who now teaches free diving in Miami, says of no-limits diving, "It's turned into a circus. Anybody who can clear his ears and hold his breath for two minutes can set a no-limits record. It doesn't take a whole lot of skill to hang on to something. But constant-weight I truly admire. They train until every little cell knows how to hold its breath."

When Ravelo stops kicking at fifty feet, he orders his body to sleep for the rest of the ride. Down is the easy part. Everything is on his side. His body is saturated with fresh oxygen and depleted of carbon dioxide – it is an excess of the latter, not a shortage of the former, that causes the craving to breathe.

Somewhere in the primordial part of his mind the pressure and cold water trigger orders to conserve the oxygen supply in his bloodstream. His spleen shrinks substantially, raising the level of oxygen-enriched hemoglobin. Because blood shift takes blood from the limbs, the burning of oxygen is much reduced –

only the brain and vital organs are drawing it. Receptor cells around Ravelo's lips cue the slowing of his heart by as much as 50 percent – a phenomenon, known as diving bradycardia, that sometimes allows near-drowning victims to be revitalized forty minutes after sinking into icy water.

Certainly the human body has ways to survive this sort of maneuver – as free divers argue when they are criticized for going where they do not belong. If we are not meant to descend into deep water, they ask, why are our bodies adapted to it?

Yet Ravelo's maneuver remains risky. The blood shift has reduced oxygen circulating to Ravelo's legs, which must power his return to the surface. Muscular exertion without oxygen is common; the muscles of a champion running a hundred-yard dash operate anaerobically, taking chemical energy from stores within themselves. But Ravelo's anaerobic strength may run out before he hits the surface.

The stopwatch ticks off the hundred and twentieth second; the entire dive is expected to last no more than 135 seconds. Two breath-hold safety divers descend to monitor Ravelo during the last, most dangerous, forty feet to the surface. This is the nether region between conquest and death, where the success shimmering at the surface can yet be snatched away by shallow-water blackout. The two breath-hold divers, unencumbered by equipment or considerations of decompression, can rush Ravelo to the surface if his body goes limp.

They have been below for thirty seconds; the stopwatch has ticked fifteen times since Ravelo was due on the surface – an eternity in a realm where contingencies are planned to the second. Their finned forms shoot around like huge, nervous baitfish. They know that the current, blown up by recent windstorms, has caught Ravelo off guard. Only later, when the scuba divers return to the surface, will they learn the full extent of the drama. Ravelo achieved his depth but drifted sixty feet from the guide rope. Disoriented, struggling against the current, he grabbed at a video-camera light instead of the reflector to which his confirmation tag was fixed. "When he realized his mistake," his manager said afterward, "he tried to go deeper, thinking he had farther to go." Another twenty seconds was lost while he wrestled with the cameraman. "I thought he would take my spare air supply and breathe," his manager continued, "but he went for the tag and started his ascent."

By the time the divers spot Ravelo, his legs are powerless. Sinking, he desperately claws for the surface with his arms. Then he goes limp.

Two minutes and forty-three seconds. The safety divers burst to the surface with Ravelo's motionless form between them. "Breathe!" they shout. "Breathe!" With all their might they slap their friend's face. His limp floating body is as blue and dark as the ocean. The speedboat roars over and a medic has an oxygen mask over Ravelo's face before his fins are out of the water. No one cares that the record attempt has failed.

Bobbing in another swell, Mehgan Heaney-Grier looks at something in her hands. It is the confirmation tag, which she found floating on the surface.

A few days after he returns from the hospital, Ravelo sits comfortably in a friend's living room, planning the next attempt. He is not intimidated by the blackout he suffered: he "pinked up" right after the mask was put on his face; the blood he vomited was only seepage from burst capillaries in his sinuses. He's had that before. "What we've learned," he says through his manager, who interprets, "is that we have to be where the seas are calm. We may go to the Caribbean or the Mediterranean. A record of this nature can be attempted only in perfect conditions."

Nor is Ravelo discouraged. He claims that Mayol has aborted many of his dives in panic, and so has Ferreras. He must go forward. Now, he feels, he has an advantage: he reached the depth.

But has he not learned something about tempting fate? Is he not worried that he has gone too far?

Ravelo shrugs. "Even the fish were uncomfortable in the sea that day," he says. Then, more thoughtfully, in his rapid-fire

Spanish, he tells of the most painful time of his life. It was in 1994, when he was interred for a year at Guantanamo, the US military base on the island of Cuba, where refugees were processed before they could come to America. "Every day I could see the sea but I could not go to it." He craved the sensations of a deep dive. The ocean has become, after all, his second home.

*"On one of my dives I discovered
a coral castle of marvellous beauty"*

BENEATH TROPIC SEAS

William Beebe

*Beebe (see pages 10–15 and 75–100) was director of the New York
Zoological Society.*

Early on a Wednesday in March I prepared for an exploring
visit to Lamentin Reef, but as I went down the gangway I
found that I could see the bottom of the bay in our new
anchorage, sixty feet beneath the schooner. It was a faint
reflection and no clear details were visible. I decided to make
a record dive and improve on my descent of forty feet in the
Galápagos.

A rope, with a weight on the end, was lowered from the
gangway platform, and with two lengths of hose joined together
and a husky man at the pump, I was helmed and slid slowly
down the line. The great hull of the *Lieutenant* curving away
into dimness was all covered with a dense growth of seaweed
and various reef animals. A great school of Aurelia jellies
brushed slowly past, but as the hull faded to a dull shadow I
fixed my mind on the mass of water below. At my last upward
glance, part of the black shadow swerved outward toward me,
detaching itself and fashioning into a 25-foot shark. To be sure,
when I scrummaged into a ball on my slender rope and looked
carefully, the oncoming selacian dwindled to about a third of my
first estimate, and two young ones showed more curiosity about
me than she did. They soon melted again into the schooner

shadow and I was alone. Then my rope twisted slightly and I
found myself gazing at a huge bit of shark bait on a hook and line
dangling from the aft deck. In my present pose, crouched into a
ball on my own rope, there was altogether too much resemblance to the object in front of me, so I promptly unrolled and
slid down.

The shark bait proved to be my last touch with the upper
world. Slowly I slipped down and down, and, for all definite
feelings, I might have been just one additional translucent
aurelia floating in the turquoise ether. Now and then a tiny
but active jellylet brushed against the glass of my helmet, and
I involuntarily swept it away as one would a cobweb or a gnat
in the upper air. Then, without warning, I was aware of
having less adaptable organs of sense than the casual jellies,
and a needle-sharp pain shot through my right ear – my old
airplane ear. I scrambled up a yard or two and began to
swallow and wobble my neck about. Then I opened my
mouth, depressed my tongue and said *Ah-h-h-h-h* as I do
for a tonsil-interested doctor. Soon there came the reassuring
little squeak of equalizing air in the Eustachian tube or
somewhere in my head; the pain vanished and I went on. I
slid more slowly now and did not have to delay again, except
when my pet school of *Caranx latus* swept past – seven left of
the eleven which had first made our keel their happy hunting
ground. Three times they repassed, and circled once before
vanishing.

On and on I went, with only the slowly ascending hemp spiral
to make real the passage of space. I felt I was taking an
unconscionable amount of time, and had descended only a
few yards beneath the schooner, when my feet struck the
three-link weight which hung at the end of the rope. The thrill
which marks the unexpected arrival at a goal was mine, and did
something to my ears, so, like a monkey on a stick, I shot up
again. In a few seconds I was hanging from the last link, my feet
sinking in soft, age-old ooze. Even through my rubber sneakers
I could feel the silky, almost oily smoothness. The light was
surprisingly good, my ears were quite normal, and I sensed my

position vividly. I kneeled down and found I was in a chamber of visibility about ten feet square. In the surface of the slime were many small craters sheltering unknown occupants. At my feet and scattered here and there, appeared great maggots of holothurians, worthy tenants of this world of ooze. Each had a pattern and to prove my goal, I selected the most colorful and squeezing it into dumb-bell shape I caught it netsuke-fashion in my belt. Climbing slowly, and swallowing as I went, I made good time and at last lifted my seacucumber prize aloft above the water – an echinodermic Excaliber. My next goal will be one hundred feet.

When my sea-cucumber and I had rested from our unusual experience, I examined him more attentively. I got out a key to West Indian seacucumbers and from the fact that he was over a foot in length, lived in the mud, was olive-buff dotted thickly with clove-brown, and the happy possessor of twenty tentacles, and with hundreds of tube feet arranged in three series, I was able to call him by his correct scientific name, *Stichopus mœbii*. For an organism which, in the bloom of perfect health, resembles a giant maggot, the euphony of this binomial is not amiss.

A new lot of fish was calling for my attention, but I neglected them for a few minutes longer. I took a lens and surveyed more carefully my fellow tenant of ten fathoms down. His skin was knobby and thorny and olive and brown, and in a hundred places I saw tiny stems supporting circles of delicate tentacles. At first I thought of these as some minute structure of the holothurian itself. Then I took a pair of forceps and, almost at a touch, off came the hydra. More and more and more hydras were found – lowly cousins of sea anemones, living happily on this great creature, as gnats might perch upon an elephant. I placed four hydras under my microscope, and the very first one I looked at had a bulging parasite near the middle of a tentacle. "And so *ad infinitum*," I chanted, then turned the cucumber over to my preparateur, and began on my fish.

One windy day we took the motor boat and went a few

miles down shore. The water was choppy and, to an unaided
eye, quite opaque. The lighthouse passed astern and a big
bay opened out before us. Several natives were fishing and a
flock of pelicans watched and dived and rose again. We put a
water bucket overboard, threw up the blinds of the wave-
marred surface, and discovered Lamentin or Sea-cow Reef.
Unlike Sand Cay it was of a barrier or shore fringing type,
and lay parallel with the land, about four miles west of our
schooner. Also, unlike Sand Cay, its sea-fans and gorgonias
were subordinate to its corals – massive brain mounds as big
as automobiles, and elkhorn forests twelve and fifteen feet
high.

We found a beautifully graded transition from land to deep
water, and took elaborate notes for future technical papers. The
cocoanut palms gave place to a fringe of mangroves with their
toes wet by the high tides. Then came a sandy beach reaching
beyond low tide, next a zone of short, hair-like grass, and a wide
area of Thalassia or eel-grass. Rather abruptly this merged into
the reef. The inner side of the reef was level and shallow,
wadable at low water. Small heads of coral grew here – nubbin,
branched and millepores.

I found life in great abundance, and many forms that did not
occur farther out. Under every bit of coral swarmed starfish –
black, red, pied, grey, orange and purple. Sea-urchins vied with
them in numbers, – long, needle-spined chaps, short, stubby
club-spined ones, and others fashioned like chestnut burrs.
With these were hosts of hermit crabs, small worms, infant
fish and octopi.

Farther out, there came an abrupt drop to several fathoms,
the barrier wall being tall growths of elkhorn coral, down which,
with care, we could clamber to the general reef floor. It did not
do to attempt this in any but a calm sea, for every helpless toss
against the stone-thorned branches revealed the pitifully thin-
skinned defence of our bodies.

It always seemed that in the places most difficult of access
were to be found the greatest prizes. The *Isopora* or branched
corals, grew in a ghostly tangle of cylindrical, white thickets

fathoms down, quite impenetrable. As they neared the surface
the branches flattened into the moose-antlered type, and grew
less closely together. I ventured, more than once, to creep down
into these tangles of coral branches, testing each before I put my
weight on it, and striving to keep my hose free from being
jammed and perhaps torn in a crotch. In the open reef, no
matter what happened, one could always lift off the helmet and
swim up, but here there was a cruel, interlaced, cobweb of
sharp-edged ivory overhead, and escape was possible only by
slow deliberate choice of passage. As I painfully made my way
down nearer the level of the ground corals, I encountered
portierès of the stinging millepores. When I reached these I
unslung the hammer at my back and pounded off the outer
layers, and there, like jewels in a geode, were occasionally to be
found tiny trees, an inch or two in height, of the exquisite and
rare pink coral. I do not remember anything in my undersea
experience which gave me more sheer æsthetic joy than spying
out these beautiful bits of color-looking like the diminutive
wind-blown pines of Fujiyama.

Again and again on these reefs, although the general effects
are all on a big scale, as I sit on a bit of sand between great
animal forests, I see Japanese gardens. When I walk through
terrestrial gardens, whether old-fashioned or overlandscaped, it
is man's height masses of color which form the character of the
garden and the pride of the owner. Has no one, I wonder, ever
cared to have literally a squatter's garden, one which has to be
knelt to, in order to discern the tiny blossoms, or detect the
evanescent odors? My pink coral trees made such a thing real
and very desirable.

When clouds prevented photography, and a swell made
climbing too hazardous and bloodletting an enjoyment, I
would break off and send up great branches and heads of
half-dead coral from the debris of the reef floor. From where
I sat, where there was not sufficient nourishment or protection for the coral to grow luxuriantly, the aspect would be
characterized by sombreness – browns, dull purples, sage
greens.

But when we began to break open the coral debris sent up to the boat, Aladdin's caves were everywhere, and our eyes were flooded with imprisoned rainbows and spectrums. The flower worms, buried deep in the stony lime, glowed with hues from red to violet, their clustered gills revealing concentric rings of color like those of our grandmother's bouquets; the sea shells, dirty white outside, when opened glowed with sunset pink and opalescence; crabs were hiding in filched shells, which in turn were in coral chambers from which there was no escape, and the colors of their legs and eyes defied human names; mantis-shrimps imprisoned behind zenana-like windows of the sponge gratings, reflected, from antennae, tips to telson edge, all the subtle shades and hues which dodge in and out between the primary and secondary colors of the earth.

On Sea-cow Reef where the corals thin out, there appeared in force the more pliant ferns and nets, fans and plumes of gorgonias. Tall, slender clumps had exactly the manner of growth of candelabra cactus, but covered with a dense polyp fur of clove brown. Some of the fluffiest stung at a touch, and, at the same touch, withdrew every polyp, leaving bare the rich purple trunk and branches – an emotional autumn of fear which swept over the full-blown foliage swiftly as a shadow. Indeed, a shadow alone will work magic with supersensitive polyp tentacles, and the animal forests shaded by the hull of my boat floating overhead, were, judged by the foliage of terrestrial plants, a month behind their fellows in the sun. The fretwork gorgonia fans were frequently abraded, or showed great holes torn or worn in their substance. To my delight I found that these were used as scratching places by passing fish; the parrots especially enjoyed oozing slowly through these tears and rubbing back and forth against the broken ivory strands. I shall never forget looking up at a great sheet of purple grill stretching across my path, and seeing the head and pectoral fins of a blazing parrotfish projecting from a jagged hole. It watched me calmly from its perch, and backed out reluctantly only when I approached it too closely.

After the fish had left I continued to watch the gorgonia, pondering on its resemblance to vegetable growth. I was astonished to see the tips of some rather thick branches suddenly blossom into a field of white star-flowers. I now saw that these branches did not originate from the main stem, but began abruptly in mid-network, gaining strength and rotundity, and shooting out beyond the limits of the fan. As a jungle tree throws branches about some fatal parasite which is irrevocably covering it, so the gorgonia polyps had bravely grown their purple bark about the encircling tubes, but these pink and white worms thrived apace, shooting ahead in their tubes like slow motion sky-rockets, finally, high above their host, to burst into a blaze of snowy tentacles.

One of my favorite diving places on Sea-cow was along the outer edge, where the reef dipped into the breathless mystery of deep water. Here, in five to seven fathoms I would submerge until I was blue and shaking, then come up cursing my bodily limitations.

It was the most Galápagos-like place I had seen. But the walking was terrible, almost like clinkerglass lava, over sharp, up-ended coral, which would break off sufficiently to let one's bare legs slip down and be gashed on the razor edges. Here and there were small sand patches, deep hidden between staghorn branches, and the whitest of nubbin coral, which, like beds of sweet alyssum or candytuft, carpeted every vacant spot. Underneath was the fallen débris of years – rotting coral branches broken off high overhead by mighty storms, overgrown with lichen-algae, sponges and mock-moss. On the animal hillsides blossomed great variegated worm blooms, more delicate than any orchid, while lesser flowers – mauve, pink and scarlet-marked the trap-door worms, which far outdo the spiders of the earth, for these doors are part and parcel of the worms, and close automatically.

I climbed six feet up a coral mountain and crouched behind a chevaux-de-frise of fret-work panels, hewn out of sheer ivory, and as I well knew, not-to-be-touched, because of glass edges and stinging cells. I now looked down and down from the visible reef rim, down into the void of the sea – into that absolute blueness which leads the eye on forever, yet conceals everything. It was like night reversed, that sky darkness which seems impenetrable at arm's length, and yet suddenly reveals the moon and distant stars.

As I climbed I dislodged several coral boulders which fell slowly past me. An avalanche undersea could only be described in slow motion terms. Small fish, like vultures about a fallen chamois, gather at once, but unlike even the swiftest vulture, they are around and under and atop of the rolling coral heads long before the latter have come to rest.

For the next many minutes I used very little of the oxygen from the air faithful Serge was pumping down to me, for I sat quiet, barely breathing. Out of the blueness, blurred forms came, small and large. I was reminded of the time I was caught at early dusk in a salt plain in south Ceylon, and crouched, watching several foggy forms, hoping they were boars, fearful of their being wild buffalo. Only now I did not fear, I simply watched with the same absolute concentration and joy which every entrance into this no-man's-land filled me. Before long, I saw more clearly, and a mob of huge parrotfish came into full view, working slowly toward me, feeding and idly wandering about as they came. They drifted around a coral spur, but before the last straggler vanished, the vanguard appeared again out of the distant brilliance, and now their numbers were augmented. I counted up to one hundred and thirty-nine, and then realized that three hundred would be within reason. None were less than a foot, while most were more than two feet in length, and at least twenty measured a full yard. They were chiefly of one species – a *Pseudoscarus*, known at any distance by the great, green, parrot-beak teeth.

They reminded me of the surgeonfish of Galápagos, with apparently nothing to fear, and they sauntered, with absolute casualness, back and forth, working, however, steadily ahead. Twice they circled me and I was impressed with the strange details of this strange world. Never before had I realized the chameleon character of the parrotfishes' eyes. When several of the huge bodied creatures had passed me, and when there was presented only an extremely foreshortened rear view, I could see that they were still watching me. It was most uncanny and only in wooden dolls could such a thing be thought possible. The whole eyeball rotated so far back that only a portion of the pupil projected from the socket.

The strength which these fish exerted in wrenching off a head of coral was astonishing, and every time, a swirl of lime débris would ascend like a dust cloud. In and out among the fish dashed a school of wrasse, intent on securing the crumbs. But most amusing were the attacks made on even the largest whenever they stopped to feed, by tiny demoiselles who feared nothing that swam when it came to defending their homes. To see a three-inch black and yellow fury driving full force against the side of these blue enameled giants was to see courage at its height. And when the great fish had torn off its titbit, it good humoredly allowed itself to be butted aside, the general effect being of a single tiny tug striving to nose the *Île de France* into mid-stream. Although I have seen such fish as gar and barracuda thus attacked, I have never seen them turn upon their midget assailants and swallow them at a gulp as they could do so easily.

In the midst of one of these encounters, while several score of the green-beaked parrots were gathered about me, I saw the blue distance give up another great form, and a six-foot tarpon – the king of the reef – grew into solidity, swam toward me, passed unnoticed through the school of parrots, and almost immediately dissolved again.

More than ever before I was impressed with the difference between the world of fishes and my own. We both possess three dimensions, but in comparison with theirs, ours is a realm of but two and a quarter. The great enameled forms before me rose and fell, circled, approached and receded, all with equal ease. We likewise can run to and fro, but for the rest must leap and climb laboriously, or fall with danger to life and limb.

Within a few minutes of sighting the first of the school I was completely puzzled by a remarkable habit. A parrot would scull slowly up to a small head or branch of coral, deliberately take it in his mouth, and by some invisible muscular turbine movement break it off. Moving away a few feet, the great fish would then upend – head up, tail straight down in mid-water, and hang there. I watched carefully and saw no movement of the jaws although the mouth was open. For several minutes it would remain suspended and then move off to another coral titbit. Many times I have seen these fish push with the pectoral fins, leverlike, against adjacent coral to give them greater wrenching force in breaking it off. During the period of verticality, and internal mastication, if such it was, a school of little wrasse darted out and thoroughly cleaned cheeks, lips, teeth and scales of all particles of organic coral débris, the parrotfish remaining quite motionless all the while. It was an aquatic parallel of crocodile and plover, cattle and egret, rhino and tick-bird.

When we have watched and watched, when we have fished with every imaginable bait and hook, when we have netted and dredged, lured with light and shot with tiny harpoons, then, when finally we still see strange and beautiful fish quite unknown to us, we stoop to pothunter's methods – securing sticks of dynamite and detonating caps.

On one of my dives I discovered a coral castle of marvellous beauty. The simile was more than an empty phrase, for in outline, in castellated battlements, in turrets and an astonishing mimicry of a draw-bridge the comparison was irresistible. Even more exciting were the tenants, for in addition to the usual demoiselles, butterfly-fish and gobies, there was a school of most exquisite beings.

They were only two inches in length. Although resembling the demoiselles in general appearance, we found later that they were actually diminutive sea-basses belonging to the genus *Gramma*. The anterior two-thirds of the body was rhodamine purple, the head, jaws, scales and fins being equally deep colored. Abruptly, the remaining third changed to glowing cadmium yellow. But all this detailed description is forgotten, when we see the living fish, and we feel only an inarticulate appreciation of the fairy-like beauty, as we watch the school swimming in and out of their coral castle.

By guiding signs on shore, a coconut palm just below a notch in the second range of mountains, and one native hut lined up with another, I was able to return to this wonderful castle of coral and to study it throughout many dives. Again I went down and squatted and watched, and again I saw the paradise fish – evanescent, long-finned, with pigments so beautiful they will never desert the memory. Six of them floated slowly back and forth across the mouth of a great half-open cave beneath the castle's crags. At my feet was a wire trap baited with over-ripe bananas, soggy bread and succulent sea-urchins. Around it swarmed-on land we would say buzzed – a maze of wrasse, exquisitely colored, gracefully formed, all excited and pushing to get inside. But the fairy basses were not to be lured by such sordid bait.

In my palm I held a length of shoe thread, with the tiniest hook in the world on the end, and a nice, wine-colored worm wriggling on the hook. I held it close for fear of the parti-colored wrasse which swam about me and watched every movement. When near the coral dome I floated out the thread and let the worm descend slowly toward one of the new fish. The fairy bass cocked up its eye, a single fan of a fin drove it closer, then it deliberately turned its back and nibbled at nothing – as far as I could see – in the water. As I was watching the basslet, a garnet wrasse rushed my hook and swallowed it, and I had great trouble hauling in and freeing it – a fish which, in its turn, would have thrilled most fishermen and all artists with its unearthly beauty. I backed away and my eye wandered for a moment to a clump of beautiful worm flowers. At the same instant one of my purple and gold fishlets rushed across my field of vision, and like some horrid, ex-aggerated shadow a small barracuda dashed after. It cut the gold half clean off, then, with a twist, seized the entire fish and vanished. Not ten seconds later the same infant barracuda took

a small demoiselle near by. This settled any scruples I might
have had left. I went swiftly up my rope, and soon an innocent
looking white sausage of a dynamite stick was lowered close to
the great cavern of millepores. We rowed off a short distance,
then down went the plunger and the explosion jarred the boat
as if we had rammed a rock.

I descended at once and found an immense cone of impenetrable cloud where the coral had been.

I skirted it, now and then pushing in when I caught sight of a
silvery upturned belly. But these were all common parrotfish or
demoiselles and I knew that I must bore straight in. It was a
weird sensation to lose oneself completely in this submarine
smoke and, except for less than a foot away, vision was useless in
every direction. I felt and crept, peered and crawled, twice
stumbling so that the water flooded my face, and several times
reached far down and unmercifully scraped off skin on sharp
coral when I caught a glimpse of purple, only to find it was a bit
of sponge or seafan. I had scrambled along for some time and
began to look for clear water on the farther side of the explosion,
but the water seemed as opaque as ever. It then occurred to me
that the current might be carrying the cloud with me, so I
turned off at right angles. My air got rather bad, and the water
rose to my mouth, and I composed several pertinent sentences
to recite to my slacking pumper when I should get within
speaking distance. Then I forgot my bruised limbs and my
labored breathing, for there, dimly silhouetted through the
murk, balanced delicately as a feather in the crotches of two
broken coral twigs, rested my purple and gold little bass. I
grasped at it so quickly that it shot out from between my fingers
into the hopeless cloud. I feared that it had vanished forever, for
beneath me was a tangle of broken branches through which I
could never force my way. Sprawling quickly after it, I again
saw that glorious glint and this time cupped it in both hands.

It was too thick to try for more fish and I was gasping myself
like a fish on land, so I gave up and started back, suddenly to be
jerked almost off my feet by the unexpected tautening of the
hose. This might mean danger, so I climbed the highest crag in

sight and saw that I had become completely confused in the limey fog, and, headed straight out to the open sea, had abruptly reached the end of my tether.

An hour later I returned to the scene of desolation, and found shambles of coral, all covered thickly with gray dust. As I clambered over the wreckage, extracting a fish here and there, I suddenly realized an unexpected limitation of the explosive not a single worm was injured. Fish succumbed, but even close to the heart of the damage, great blooms of beauty raised their heads at all sorts of unexpected angles from the débris. They probably found good feeding in the coral dust. One great piece of coral weighing hundreds of pounds had been blown over on its side, and apparently from beneath the mass itself several feathery, mauve and white heads protruded. What poppies in Flanders took months to do, hundreds of these worm blossoms had accomplished in an hour.

In the course of our dynamiting, we obtained some very interesting results. On the fourth of May I let off two sticks at Sea-cow Reef and got seventy-one fish. The fallacy of generalization was well shown by an entry in my field note-book. Looking down at the lot of fish, I wrote, "The seventy odd taken today are exceedingly brilliant, most of them glowing with every color of the spectrum."

Later, I analyzed them, one by one, and found that the brilliant and the dull were about equal in numbers of individuals, thirty-seven to thirty-four. The species showed a less even result, sixteen being decidedly bright colored and seven dull. The details were as follows:

Brilliant	Dull
Red Amia	Black and white Eques
Holocentrus (3)	Scarus
	Scarus (9)
Blue Chromis (4)	Odontoscion (4)
	Atherina
Purple and Yellow Gramma	Brown Chromis (3)
	Eupomocentrus (15)

Red-spotted (4)
Yellow Apodus
Parti-colored Scarus (4)
Sparisoma
Hypoplectrus (4)
Thallasoma
Thallasoma (5)
Caranx (3)
Chloroscombrus
Lactophrys

After the first of these shots, I saw a large fish disturb the surface as it snapped at a floating victim. I went down with John Tee-Van to collect fish and to gather some pink coral I had located behind a veil of millepores. On our way, as we clambered over some bad going, I saw a dead Eques in a deep cavern, and to reach it I had to lie as flat as my helmet permitted. As I straightened up, I saw an enormous fish just ahead – a grouper. He showed no signs of fear, and in fact came still closer to examine us. He was of a monochrome elephant's-breath color, with darker fins, deep and heavy body almost as long as ourselves, and bulging yellow eyes. The great mouth was filled with irregular teeth, an inch or more of many being visible. From these and other characters we identified him as a large jewfish, *Garrupa*. He swam slowly and majestically out from the shelter of a coral crag, and, turning slowly and gently head down, almost at our feet, the great fish skilfully picked up and swallowed a dead parrot. As we watched, fascinated by the hulk of the big fellow, ready with my crowbar as I was uncertain of his mood, I saw a twelve-inch shark sucker, *Echeneis*, slipping over his body. It was hardly ever quiet, but kept slithering about like a skater on ice, over body, head, back almost to the tail and once even over the eyes. When the jewfish moved, the sucker took up a position on the nape and lay along the slope in front of the dorsal fin.

In the wake of the giant there followed a dozen blue-lined jacks, swimming slowly a few feet behind their great baron.

When he came to rest, they gathered in a huddled group, a little distance away, like whispering courtiers in an anteroom.

Not far from this part of the reef was a small projection of the shallow shore zone, and I found I could climb up the sides of a great globe of brain coral until my face was on a level with this upper floor – the attic of the reef, so to speak. One defect of the open helmet is that it cannot be tipped very far forward without flooding, so it is impossible to assume my favorite jungle attitude of observation – a worm's eye view. But here I found I could lean comfortably outstretched with my eyes on a level with the smaller coral, gorgonias, and a scattering of Thalassia or tropical eel-grass.

One of my first observations had to do with a common triggerfish, *Alutera*, of which I had taken many specimens, but had no clue to the cause of its shape and color. The solution came quickly as I watched, for one of these triggerfish swam toward me, and turned head downward when he reached a small clump of eel-grass.

He took hold of a bit of coral with his sucker mouth and immediately set both vertical fins in gentle, undulatory motion, the other fins, especially the long caudal, being furled, so that the general body shape was tapering, which, together with the mottled green color, transformed it into a sea-weed frond or eel-grass blade. Now and then the fish revolved on its base without letting go. The trigger spine, slightly elevated, conveyed the impression of a bit of shredded tissue. An additional aid in the deception was the considerable variation of color in these fish, shifting from plain dark cedar green to a mottled greyish or greenish white.

In an aquarium on the schooner I had at one time a baby seahorse, or seapony, in the same aquarium with an Alutera, and it was an amusing tribute to the success of the vegetative camouflage for the seahorse to anchor itself by curling its tail about the inverted triggerfish, much to the discomfort of the latter. The change from a healthy member of the class of fishes to a short, ragged, and somewhat mildewed bit of eel-grass was indeed rapid and convincing.

Carrying out my occupational classification of reef fishes which I began in the Galápagos,* I found new types on these reefs. My last census is as follows:

FREE NOMADS
Sharks
Eagle Rays
Carangids
Tarpon
Cornetfish
Mackerels
Groupers
Gars
Barracudas
Puffers
Dolphinfish

GRAZERS
Parrotfish
Triggers
Surgeons
Angelfish

PERCOLATERS
Snappers
Wrasse

SQUATTERS
Gobies
Blennies
Morays
Eques

VILLAGERS
Demoiselles
Butterflyfish
Gramma

BALLOONISTS
Young Bumpers

AERONAUTS
Sargasso-fish
Young Triggers
Pipefishes
Seahorses
Abudefdufs
Triple-tails

SURFACE MOBS
Anchovia
Silversides

FLYERS
Flying fish
Halfbeaks
Gurnards

SPONGE PEOPLE
Amias
Blue-lined blennies
Garmannia

SAND CRAWLERS
Skates
Flounders
Batfish

* *The Arcturus Adventure*, Chapter XII, page 297

This list hints of the fascinating future of research in this undersea field. Even after scores of descents, and the enduring of lacerations from coral, and the inevitable teeth-chattering chill which forces one up after a too-long submersion, one's observations are of the most superficial character. To the casual observer there seems nothing but terror for the small fish in schools, and, on the other hand, few or no dangers for medium or larger sized ones. These go about their business unconcernedly and with no appearance of being constantly on the lookout. The carnivorous wrasse dog one's footsteps and all but dash in between fingers when a head of coral is disturbed. The parrots paddle about, and solemnly browse, and as solemnly upend and let the food fall down their throats. Yet an examination of stomachs shows tragedies unnumbered, and tells of pursuits and captures, even fish within fish within fish, – the realities of which will come to our note-books only after months of watching.

One of my last days at Sea-cow Reef was rough and I made no attempt to select a favorable spot, but working the motor boat well to the eastward, I dropped anchor and slid over at a venture. It looked like a rather poor location and I was about to ascend, when I let the tide drift me some way along a narrow path of soft sand. In the distance I caught sight of an enormous wall of coral. I went back, picked up the anchor and shouldering it, towed the boat nearer. When I again went on I found a narrow gorge between two mighty coral masses, and passing through, I came to one of the most diversified and beautiful places I have ever been in under water.

The narrow gorge opened up into a large circular arena of sand, planted here and there with seaplumes, while the surrounding, lofty walls were covered with all imaginable shapes and shades of reef life, living tapestries which waved and nodded with every pulsation of the water. Large fish were abundant, a school of two-foot silver snappers appearing from some concealed cavern and milling with curiosity around and around me. Near the sand were purple surgeons and golden-lined hæmulons, both revealing their passing emotions by the ebb and flow of dark bands across the scales. I sat quietly at the entrance of a side valley and watched the scene shift and change. Two sharks looked in from opposite sides, and a third followed my trail from the boat.

With the first were three barracudas, passing quietly, with the supercilious expression which their projecting under lips always give. Finally a procession of two hundred and six blue surgeons made a circuit of the whole arena, examining the coral walls several feet up, and most vividly recalling to my mind the waters of Galápagos. One of the barracudas was wholly eclipsed by a dense mass of jellyfish which passed in front of his suspended form. As I made my way out, I saw my old friend the six-foot tarpon just turning past the anchor rope. He had two scales missing from beneath the mid-side, and this was the ninth time I had seen him. He was apparently the only one of his kind at this reef, and, as I have already said, time after time when I dived, he would swim over, and pass slowly within ten feet.

It was a worthy farewell to Lamentin Reef, and the last look I took around before I ascended fixed in my mind a seascape, most noble, most beautiful, and filled with unsolved problems of such compelling interest that my life overhead threatened in comparison to be drab and uneventful.

*". . . as the water came in each man would fill his lungs
with air and climb out as fast as he could"*

MORTAL BLOW

Edward Young

The "mortal blow" to the British submarine Umpire *recounted by
Edward Young occurred in July 1941. Later, Commander Young
DSO DSC became the first Royal Naval Volunteer Reserve
officer to command an operational submarine during World
War II.*

Umpire's dockyard trials had been successfully completed, including the usual static basin dive to prove that the hull was
water-tight. The last welding leads had been removed, the
bunks, cupboards and other wooden fittings were a bright
mahogany gleam, new curtains hung in the messes, and the
whole boat was resplendent with fresh-smelling paintwork,
white inside and battleship grey outside.

Mervyn Wingfield was plainly delighted with his new command, though he tried to conceal his pleasure behind a demea-
nour of severity and icy reserve. The First Lieutenant, Peter
Bannister, I had not met before; he was tall, energetic and
humorous, easy to get on with. Tony Godden, the navigator,
had been in the same training class with me at Fort Blockhouse;
I was delighted now to find we were in the same boat, for he was
a most amusing and endearing shipmate, and we had many good
evenings ashore together during our stay in Chatham.

Umpire moved out at last into the River Medway on a day
towards the end of July, spick and span, a brand-new white

ensign flying, bound north-about for the Clyde, where we were
to carry out sea trials and training with the Third Flotilla based
at Dunoon, before setting forth on a "working-up" operational
patrol in the North Sea. After that, the Mediterranean.

We stopped overnight at Sheerness to wait for a convoy of
merchant-ships leaving the Thames the next day. In the morning we got under way early and found the convoy congregating
off Southend under an escort of motor launches and Admiralty
trawlers. We took up our station astern, and by the time we
turned the corner at Shoeburyness the convoy had more or less
sorted itself out.

All day we moved up the East Coast, passing Burnham,
Clacton, Walton-on-the-Naze, Harwich, Felixstowe, Orford-
ness, and when we were somewhere off Aldeburgh a German
bomber came in low from seaward and began attacking the
leading ships of the convoy. I was officer-of-the-watch at the
time, and in accordance with our convoy instructions gave the
order to dive.

Now, we had never dived before at sea and under way.
Normally a brand-new submarine carries out numerous dives
in slow motion, with the crew already at diving stations, before
it is committed to a full-speed dive. We had to make our first
dive on the klaxon, and it is to the great credit of all concerned –
the Chatham men who built her; Wingfield, who as Captain had
thought ahead and trained his officers and men to his satisfaction; Bannister, who as Number One had organized the crew in
their duties and had also worked out the first trim; and the crew,
who went calmly to diving stations and performed their jobs
correctly – it is to the credit of all these that *Umpire*'s first dive
was a complete success. Within two minutes Bannister had
caught a trim and the Captain was able to concentrate on the
periscope. We did not want to stay down longer than we need,
because the convoy was drawing ahead of us. Five minutes later
the Heinkel seemed to have vanished, so we surfaced and
pressed on to regain our station in the convoy, which had
sustained no damage from the attack.

We felt very pleased with ourselves, and boyishly proud of

our boat that had behaved so well. Then, about nightfall, one of the diesels developed trouble and had to be stopped. At first this did not affect our speed, our propulsion being diesel-electric, and we continued to maintain our station. But as the evening wore on, the engine-room staff were unsuccessful in their attempts to get the defective engine going. The other one produced insufficient power by itself to balance the batteries' output when driving two propellers, and we were obliged at last to reduce our speed. The Captain flashed a signal to the Commodore of the convoy, reporting the situation. An M.L. was detailed to drop back and act as our escort, and we were to catch up as soon as possible.

We knew from the latest W/T situation report that, some twenty miles to the north of us, a southbound convoy was approaching down the same buoyed channel. The two convoys were due to meet somewhere about midnight.

The international rule at sea is that in a channel-way ships must keep to the starboard side. Ships meeting in a channel should therefore pass *port to port*. It was revealed afterwards that when the two convoys met, some miles ahead of us, they passed on the *wrong* side, starboard to starboard. So when Tony Godden, the officer-of-the-watch, presently sent down a message that the southbound convoy was approaching, Wingfield was surprised to find on reaching the bridge that the oncoming convoy was not on our port bow, as he expected, but right ahead, with part of it actually extending across our starboard bow. It was a calm night, very dark, but with reasonably good visibility; lights could have been seen at a fair distance. But the German E-boats were raiding the East Coast convoys nearly every night, and no one was showing any lights. Our escorting M.L. had lost touch with us some time earlier. We were quite alone and almost invisible to other ships even at close range.

The normal action would have been to alter course to starboard, but this would have taken us across the bows of the approaching merchant-ships and we might not have had room to get clear. Wingfield altered a few degrees to port, and the first six ships of the convoy passed safely down our starboard side about two hundred yards away. Although we did not know it, our own convoy, now several miles ahead, had taken the same action.

Suddenly a dark shape appeared ahead of us, detached from the nearest column of the convoy. Examining it through his binoculars, Wingfield saw that it was a trawler, presumably part of the convoy's escort, and that we were directly in its path. In the next second he realized that it was alarmingly near to us and apparently unaware of our presence. He had to decide quickly what to do. The trawler was fine on his starboard bow and seemed certain to pass dangerously close. By the rule of the road it was the trawler's right of way and our duty to keep clear. According to the rules Wingfield should have altered course to starboard, but only two hundred yards to starboard was the endless line of southbound merchant-ships forming an impenetrable barrier. With every ship fully darkened, this was a predicament not visualized by the authors of the Regulations for Preventing Collision at Sea. Wingfield ordered "Hard-a-port." But, even as we began to turn, the trawler seemed to see us, low and dark in the water, and turned instinctively to starboard. This made collision inevitable. Wingfield yelled his last order down the voice-pipe, "Full astern together!" – but before the order could be carried out, the bows of the trawler struck *Umpire* with a sickening metallic crash, some twenty or thirty feet abaft the starboard bow. The submarine lurched to port, and for a few seconds the two vessels stayed locked together, held by the impetus of the trawler's headway. During these seconds Wingfield clutched the trawler's side as it swung in towards him, and shouted furiously, "You bloody bastard, you've sunk a British submarine!" Then the trawler fell away, and Wingfield found his boat sinking under him by the head. In less than thirty seconds she plunged under, leaving Wingfield Godden and the two look-outs in the water. In the darkness there was shouting and confusion, but the four kept together at first. But presently one and then the other of the look-outs dropped out of the small circle. Tony Godden, who was wearing long fur-lined seaboots, gasped out that he could not kick them free and that he was sinking. For a while Wingfield helped to support him, but Tony finally let go and sank out of sight. It seemed a long time before the trawler's boat appeared, and Wingfield was unconscious when he was hauled on board. When he came to and realized that he, the Captain, was apparently the sole survivor, his feelings can be imagined.

When the Captain left the wardroom to go up on the bridge in response to Tony's message about the approaching convoy, Peter Bannister and I were sitting at the wardroom table, decoding a routine wireless signal that had been passed to us by the telegraphist on watch.

The wardroom was divided from the control-room only by a thin steel partition, and by curtains from the passage-way; at sea these curtains were drawn back, and Peter and I could hear the helmsman repeat the orders which came to him down the voice-pipe from the bridge.

When we heard him repeat the Captain's emergency order, "Hard-a-port," we pushed back our chairs and stood up, our eyes meeting in question and alarm. We stumbled out into the passage-way, and Peter at once gave the order to "Shut watertight doors!" Almost immediately we heard another urgent yell down the voice-pipe, but before this last order from the bridge could be repeated by the helmsman there was a violent crash for'ard in the torpedo-stowage compartment, followed by the blue-white flare and muffled thump of an electrical explosion. The boat rocked to port, stayed there a few seconds, and then slid drunkenly forward and over to starboard as she began her plunge to the bottom. If the water were deep here, its weight would crush us like an egg-shell. Most of the lights had gone out. Then men were running past us from the next compartment, Peter was yelling "Shut that door!" and I had my hand on it, letting the men run through, disobeying Peter because I hadn't the courage to deny any of them a chance so long as the water was not yet actually at their heels. Somehow the further door to the damaged compartment had shut, whether blown to by the explosion or deliberately shut from the inside by a last nameless act of self-sacrifice as the sea came flooding in, we shall never know. "Shut that bloody door!" repeated Peter in a fury, but by now all the men from the intervening compartment were through. With some difficulty, because of the angle of the boat, I pulled the door up towards me and clamped it shut.

I turned, and struggled up the tilting deck into the control-room. The boat was listing to starboard and sloping forward at an angle of about ten degrees. Water was pouring in from what seemed to be a hundred places. Peter was struggling with the outboard battery-ventilation-valve overhead, desperately seeking an explanation for this inrush of water, and acutely aware of the fatal danger of chlorine gas if the sea-water should find its way into the battery cells under the deck. I reached up to help him, glad in my numbed state of something positive to do. But the valve was already shut, as we knew it should have been, and we must look elsewhere for the breach in our defences. To my paralyzed brain it seemed that the shock of the collision had cracked the hull and started rivets along the whole length of the ship. Surprisingly enough, no water was coming down the conning-tower; presumably the upper hatch had fallen shut when the boat took on a list immediately before she went under.

Peter was now calling for more light, and one or two of the men searched about for the emergency hand-lamps. I remembered that I had a torch in my drawer in the wardroom, so I retraced my steps, moving with difficulty down the wet and sloping deck. In the passage-way the water was already knee-deep. I sloshed through it and pulled myself up into the ward-room. Streams of ice-green water were cascading from some-where overhead, drenching the beautiful new curtains and bunks in a universal deluge. If I had brought a conscious intelligence to bear on the source of this waterfall I should have hit on something that ought to have been obvious to all of us. But not until the whole thing was over did I realize that all this water must have been coming from the *ventilation shaft*, now open to sea pressure through the damaged torpedo-stowage compartment. By reaching up my hand over the Captain's bunk I could have shut the valve on the bulkhead quite easily, and the flow of water would have stopped. But my brain, as though stunned by the catastrophe, had become incapable of constructive thought.

I found the torch and splashed my way back to the control-room. As I did so, it occurred to me to wonder what depth we were at. I shone the torch on the depth-gauges and found, to my surprise, that they were both reading only a little over 60 feet. This meant we were in very shallow water, with the bow presumably resting on the bottom at something like 80 feet. I asked Peter whether it was possible to *blow* her up. It seemed unlikely, since we had been at full buoyancy at the time of the collision, and a vast quantity of water must have entered for'ard to have overcome that buoyancy so suddenly. It was obvious that a large gash had been torn at the top of the pressure hull in the torpedo-stowage compartment, and that the compartment had filled up in a matter of seconds. We should never get her up with all that weight of water in her. However, Peter thought it would do no harm to try, so one by one he opened up the valves of the high-pressure air-panel until all five ballast tanks and the two main internal tanks were blowing. But it was no use: the depth-gauges did not even flicker.

The sea continued to pour in on us, with a terrible and relentless noise, and the water in the compartment grew deeper every minute. As the level crept up the starboard side, live electrical contacts began spitting venomously, with little lightning flashes. Vaguely I wondered if we were all going to be electrocuted.

In the half-darkness the men had become anonymous groping figures, desperately coming and going. There was no panic, but most of us, I think, were suffering from a sort of mental concussion. I discovered one man trying to force open the water-tight door that I had shut earlier. "My pal's in there," he was moaning, "my pal's in there." "It's no good," I told him; "she's filled right up for'ard and there's no one left alive on the other side of that door." He turned away, sobbing a little.

For some reason we decided it would be useful if we could find more torches. I knew there must be one or two others somewhere in the wardroom, so I made yet another expedition down the slope, wading through the pool that was now waist-deep and already covering the lowest tiers of drawers under our bunks. I spent some time in the wardroom, shivering with fear and cold, ransacking every drawer and cupboard, pushing aside the forsaken paraphernalia of personal belongings – under-clothes, razors, pipes, photographs of wives and girlfriends. But I could find only one torch that was still dry and working. Holding it clear of the water, I returned to the control-room.

It was deserted.

The door into the engine-room was shut. Had I spent longer in the wardroom than I thought? Perhaps they had all escaped from the engine-room escape hatch, without realizing that I had been left behind. Even if they had not yet left the submarine, they might already have started flooding the compartment in preparation for an escape, and if the flooding had gone beyond a certain point it would be impossible to get that door open again. I listened, but could hear nothing beyond the monotonous, pitiless sound of pouring water. In this terrible moment I must have come very near to panic.

I could at least try hammering on the engine-room door. Looking round for a heavy instrument, I found a valve spanner and began moving aft towards the door. As I did so I heard a voice quite close to me say, "Christ, who's that?" I looked up and found I was standing under the conning-tower. In it, to my infinite relief, I saw Peter with an able seaman and one of the E.R.A.s. "Where the hell have you come from?" said Peter. "Where the hell's everybody gone?" I retorted. "Any room for me up there?" "We ought to be able to squeeze you in. The others are going to escape from the engine-room."

I climbed up through the lower hatch, grateful as never before for the company of my fellow-creatures. Four of us in the tiny space made a tight squeeze, Peter at the top of the ladder with his head jammed up against the upper hatch, the A.B. half-way up the ladder with his bottom wedged against the side of the tower, leaving just room for me and the E.R.A. standing at the foot of the tower, with our feet on the edge of the lower hatch-opening. The E.R.A. was in a bad way, vomiting continuously and hardly able to stand.

In the centre of the upper hatch was a small port, or round window, made of glass thick enough to withstand tremendous pressure. Number One said that he could see a glimmer of light through it, and supposed it to be caused by a searchlight from some vessel waiting overhead. This encouraged him to think we ought to be able to swim to the surface and be picked up without much difficulty. We knew the control-room depth-gauges were reading just over 60 feet; the upper hatch was something like 15 feet higher than the normal surface waterline (the point of reference for the depth-gauges) and was therefore probably only about 45 feet from the surface, say the height of eight men standing on top of each other. It ought to be easy.

"Shut the lower lid," said Peter, "and let's just think this out." I bent down, shut the hatch and pulled the clip over. We then discussed exactly what we were going to do. We agreed that to wear Davis escape gear would be an unnecessary complication in the confined space. One of the dangers was that on our way up we might crack our skulls on the cross-bar between the periscope standards, but we decided there was little chance of this owing to the starboard list. We hoped (vainly, as it turned out) that we might be assisted in our rise to the surface by the bubble of air which would be released from the conning-tower as the hatch opened. The drill was simple. Peter would open the hatch, and as the water came in each man would fill his lungs with air and climb out as fast as he could. Except for the poor E.R.A., who was sick beyond comfort or encouragement, we were by now quite calm, even cheerful.

How long we considered the situation I cannot remember; but at last Peter said, "Well, the next thing is to see if we can open this hatch against the sea pressure." Bracing himself against the side of the tower, he pushed upwards with all his strength. The hatch remained firmly shut. Somehow we must raise the pressure inside the tower.

It occurred to me that while we had been talking the pressure had still been building up in the control-room below us, owing to the continuing inrush of water. I eased off the clip of the hatch under my feet, and sure enough there came the sharp hiss of air forcing its way into the tower. I allowed the air to come in until, after a minute or two, I became aware of a peculiar, faint smell. Perhaps it was merely the odour of fear, but my first thought was that the sea-water had at last found its way into the batteries. "Hullo," I said; "I think I can smell chlorine gas." "All right," said Peter; "shut the lid again and I'll have another short at opening this one." This time he managed without much effort to lift the hatch slightly off its seat, allow-a trickle of water to come through.

"O.K.," said Peter. "Well, boys, take your time. There's no hurry. You say when you feel you're ready."

I said I was for having a go at once, before we weakened ourselves any further by breathing foul air, and the others agreed. We stripped down to vest, pants and socks.

"Ready?" asked Peter.

"Ready," we all replied, though I think the E.R.A. had reached the point in his sickness where he wanted to die more than anything else.

"Right. Stand by," said Peter cheerfully. "Here we go for fourteen days' survivor's leave. We're off!" – and he pushed up the lid with all his strength.

I took as deep a breath as I could, and then the sea crashed in on us. There was a roaring in my ears, a blackness everywhere, and there was nothing for it but to fight for life with all one's primitive instincts of survival. Hauling myself up by the rungs of the ladder, I found my head obstructed by the A.B.'s bottom. With the strength of a desperate man I pushed up at him, his heel struck me in the face, I pushed again, and then we were through the hatch and clear of the submarine. I swam upwards with quick, jerky breast-strokes. It seemed a terrible distance. Time stretched out of its normal span until I thought my lungs must surely crack before I reached the surface. And then suddenly I was there, coughing, spluttering, gasping in great draughts of the sweet night air and drinking in the blessed sight of the stars shining in the immensity of space.

The sea was fairly calm, with no more than a gentle popple. Seeing two heads in the water not far away, I called out and found they were Peter and the A.B., both in good heart. Of the E.R.A. there was no sign. We could make out the dark shapes of several ships around us, so we began shouting to attract attention. Some of them were throwing searchlights on the water, and one of these seemed to me nearer than the rest. "Come on," I said, "let's swim to that nearest one," and began swimming towards it with my rather feeble side-stroke. I pressed on for a few minutes, imagining the other two were following me, but after a while I turned and could see no sign of them, although I heard them shouting at intervals not far off. The vessel I was making for was farther away than I had thought. I am not a strong swimmer, so I turned over on to my back and relaxed into an easy backward leg-stroke, calling "Help!" at the top of my voice from time to time. Sometimes a wave lopped over my head and I swallowed a little more water. I seemed to be swimming for a long time. Whenever I looked round, the ship seemed to be as far away as ever. Surely, after all this, I was not going to drown in sight of safety? I began to feel rather exhausted. Suddenly I heard voices shouting, the churning of propellers going astern, and I turned to find a searchlight blazing in my eyes and below it the shape of an M.L. quite close, with a scrambling-net down over the side and men running along the deck. A heaving-line shot out, I grabbed it and was hauled in. A sailor clambered down the net and helped me on to the deck, where I fell into the arms of two R.N.V.R. officers. Exhausted and groaning for breath, with my lungs half full of sea-water, I must have appeared in a worse state than I was, but while they wrapped me in blankets and hustled me below I managed to tell them that there were some more of us out there in the water and many others still down in the submarine trying to escape from the engine-room.

In a cabin below they rubbed me down, gave me dry clothes, and put me into a bunk, where I lay shivering from delayed shock. About half an hour later they came and told me our men were starting to come up from the bottom. I couldn't bear to stay in my bunk while this was happening, so I wrapped myself in a blanket and tottered along to find out what the situation was. They were coming up at fairly frequent intervals, strange Martian creatures with their D.S.E.A.* goggles and oxygen bags, and rendered almost unrecognizable by black oil which had floated up from the bilges when they flooded the engine-room for the escape. But they were in extraordinarily good spirits, half intoxicated with their unexpected return to life. Every one of them was full of praise for the way in which the Chief E.R.A. and the Torpedo Gunner's Mate had organized the escaping party and carried out the escape drill. When finally these two reached the surface, the Chief E.R.A. last of all, they reported there was no one left in the engine-room. There had been enough D.S.E.A. sets for all but two of the party. Two men had volunteered to go up without them, each holding on to the legs of one of the others; one of these was never seen again. A final roll-call showed that the only other casualty of the engine-room party of twenty was a civilian technician from Chatham dockyard, who had joined *Umpire* as passenger for the trip north: the Chief E.R.A. and the T.G.M. had fitted him with a D.S.E.A. set and patiently explained its simple operation to him several times, but the man was so unnerved by the catastrophe that, although he succeeded in getting out through the hatch, he failed to reach the surface. But altogether the engine-room escape was a remarkable justification of the submarine escape drill.

It was only afterwards I discovered that, half-way through the escape, the Chief E.R.A. thought it would be advisable to make sure none of the escapers was getting caught up in any obstruction outside the hatch. He therefore clipped on the oxygen mouthpiece of his D.S.E.A. set, made his way up through the hatch, walked about on the outside casing of the submarine in the vicinity of the hatch, and then, although he could easily and without shame have made his ascent to safety, he climbed down through the hatch into the engine-room once

* Davis Submerged Escape Apparatus.

more and carried on with the business of supervising the escape of the remaining men. Not until every other man had left the compartment did he make his own get-away.

For his part in the escape Chief E.R.A. Killen was later awarded the British Empire Medal.

It was not until the M.L. landed us at Yarmouth that I heard Peter Bannister was missing. I had been told that another vessel had rescued some survivors from the water, and I had assumed these were Peter and the A.B. who had been with us. In fact only the A.B. had been picked up. When I saw him later at Yarmouth, he said that he and Peter had swum together for some time and that when they were rescued he had thought Peter was immediately behind. A long search failed to find him. I was staggered by this news, for Peter was a strong swimmer and had seemed in excellent fettle when we spoke together on the surface. To have got so far and be lost at the last moment was an appalling tragedy.

It was daylight when we reached Yarmouth and were met by Lieut.-Commander J. F. B. Brown, who had flown up from submarine headquarters in London to get the facts at first hand. During the day, in the intervals of answering questions, we enjoyed the generous hospitality of the Naval Base.

That evening I strolled alone after dinner in a small grassy courtyard. A gentle drizzle of rain was falling, and it was what one would call a miserable evening, but to me the sound of the soft rain falling like a benediction on the living grass seemed inexpressibly sad and sweet, and life itself so desirable that I could not imagine myself ever again being dissatisfied with it. For the first time I knew the delirious joy of not being dead.

At the same time I felt that in the emergency I had failed to act in the manner expected of a submarine officer. Running over again and again the sequence of events following the moment of collision, I was tortured by two nagging thoughts. First, why had I not had the sense to realize that all the water coming into the control-room had been pouring in through the ship's ventilation system? Secondly – and this has haunted me ever since – I knew that I should have been in the engine-room with the men.

There was also the problem of the future. At first I was sure I never wanted to see the inside of a submarine again. But the conviction grew in me that to ask to leave the submarine service would be such an admission of defeat that I should never recover my self-respect. For the purely egoistic reason of patching up my pride, I therefore decided to remain in sub-marines – if I was allowed to. On the principle of immediately remounting the horse that has thrown you, I resolved to ask to be sent on an operational patrol as soon as possible.

With thoughts like these crowding my brain, I was still awake when Wingfield walked into my cabin about midnight. He had just landed, having stayed on the scene of the collision until nightfall. He was looking ten years older, grey and haggard from worry and lack of sleep. He told me how Tony Godden had been drowned, and asked about Peter Bannister. I told him the story up to the point where we had separated after reaching the surface. He said the final casualty total was two officers and twenty men, almost half the ship's complement.

"It was an hour later when I came to . . ."

FROGMAN

Sydney Woollcott

Woollcott was one of the first British naval divers – "frogmen" – of World War II.

It was on a hot afternoon in July 1942 that opportunity knocked at my door. I was sitting on a pile of hammocks in the lost-baggage room in the R.N. Barracks, Portsmouth, engrossed in the task of furling a "tickler" for myself, and feeling pretty "chokka" with life altogether.

I had been resident in Pompey Barracks about three months then, patiently waiting to be sent away to take a course in copper work, in order to qualify as a coppersmith engine room artificer. Now, three months is a long time to wait doing nothing but check lost baggage, when you're wanting to do great things for your King and Country – so that's the reason I was so "chokka".

I was half-way through making the aforesaid "tickler", when the clarion call for action came over the barracks' tannoy system. It said "Volunteers are required for Special Service. Ratings wishing to volunteer should give their names in at the Police Office." That's all that was said. No mention was made of the nature of the "Special Service", but conjuring up in my mind all sorts of things I may have been required for, I finally plumped for a landing in France. "Just the thing," I thought, "to relieve this boredom a bit." So, after finishing making my cigarette, I wedged it under the crown of my cap, placed the hat on my head, and high-tailed it for the Police Office, where I had my name, rank and number entered on the list of "Volunteers for Special Service".

Well – nothing happened for a few days, until one afternoon, a few minutes after "First Dogwatchmen to Tea" had been piped over the tannoy, another call came over, to the effect that "All volunteers for Special Service should muster at the sick bay immediately." I did as I was commanded, and found outside the sick bay a crowd of about a hundred other volunteers, of all shapes, sizes, ranks and denominations, mustered under the critical eye of a red-faced, sarcastic-looking old sea-dog of a Gunner, R.N. By the way he looked at us, he didn't go much on the present-day jolly tar, or, in fact, on the whole business of Special Service at all. "Come on, you Commandos!" he bawled. "Fall in here!"

Then came the first stage of the process of elimination. First, all the non-swimmers were cast out, which depleted our ranks by about half. Then came a visual sizing up by the Gunner, and another officer, which meant another weeding out, cutting our number down to about thirty. I remember distinctly the Gunner looking at me with a particularly disapproving eye. I could tell by his expression what he was thinking:

"Here's a big, useless-looking specimen. Be all right to stand him up as a shield for the good blokes, and as he looks an obvious criminal type, I'll be doing Society a service if I pick him, and he never comes back." So I was picked.

That was that, until we were called to the sick bay again two days later for a stiff medical examination. As a result of this, our ranks dwindled again, this time to twenty. Another day's wait, and then we had to go across Pompey Harbour to H.M.S. *Dolphin*, the submarine base in Fort Blockhouse, for an interview with Lt.-Commander Shelford, who was to be in charge of our party, and from whom we finally found out the nature of the job for which we had been asked to volunteer. We were ushered one by one into his tiny office in the experimental diving tank building. This is a rough outline of my interview with him. After taking my name, he said:

"Now, I'm looking for volunteers to enable me to find out valuable information."

"Ah, espionage!" I thought. "Just up my street." Then he dashed all my hopes.

"Information," he went on, "about diving apparatus, and underwater working. How do you feel about diving and underwater work?"

Well, that suited me all right. I'm a pretty good swimmer, in a rugged, unpolished sort of way, usually spending most of my swimming time in diving under the surface of the water looking for objects on the bottom, and I told him so. He also asked me if I suffered from claustrophobia at all. I assured him that I didn't. In fact, I suffer from the opposite form of phobia if anything, and sometimes, instead of having a horror of being shut up in a confined space, I feel uncomfortable when walking across a large, open space or sitting at a table in the middle of a large restaurant. I always like to have my back to a wall. So the interview passed off all right. Our number was two less when we had all been interviewed, and we had another medical exam.

Then back to barracks, to wait a few more days till we were once more called out. This time, with our kitbags and hammocks packed, we were drafted to H.M.S. *Dolphin*, where for the first three days we received lectures on diving with oxygen breathing apparatus. As much knowledge was imparted to us as had already been discovered on the subject – which wasn't much in those days.

Most of our instructors were Chief or Petty Officers, who were submarine coxswains who had specialised in this work, and had carried out the initial and most dangerous experiments with the embryo of the diving dress which we were to wear. This was called the "Sladen Suit," after the man who had invented it, Commander Sladen, a former ace submarine commander.

We had our first dives at *Dolphin*. These were done in the 15-foot diving tank with the Davis submarine escape apparatus. After putting on the apparatus and receiving instructions by numbers in the correct way of loading the bottles, filling the bag with oxygen, emptying the bag of foul air, flushing our lungs with oxygen, and finally breathing from the bag, we were taken to the edge of the tank and shown how to use the apparatus in the water by one of the instructors. Then it was our turn. One by one, we climbed slowly down the ladder which went to the bottom of the tank, until only our heads were out of the water. Then, after a few last-minute instructions, we completely submerged ourselves, and waited with our heads just under the surface while the instructor had a good look for any tell-tale bubbles which would tell us if there were any leaks in our apparatus. Then the instructor patted us once on the head, and we broke surface again. He reported to us that everything was O.K., and patted us twice on the head. We then submerged again and climbed down the ladder to the bottom of the tank.

It was then that some stout hearts failed for a brief spell. One or two of the volunteers registered great horror at the last moment at having to go down to the bottom. However, after a few reassuring words from the instructors, and a few more desperate efforts, everyone finally made the plunge, and we all mustered at the bottom of the tank. Personally, the whole thing had the opposite effect on me. I was thrilled to think that I could go for a good swim underwater without having to break surface to take in air. But I could well understand some of the other fellows being a bit nervous at their first dive, not having spent the best part of their previous swimming time, as I had, crawling about in the mud at the bottom of a river, like an oversized newt.

We certainly looked a peculiar bunch at the bottom of that tank. A weird crowd of deathly white human bodies, each wearing only a tiny butcher's-apron-coloured pair of cotton slips and a D.S.E.A. set, and each with a pair of goggling eyes and hair that stood on end, as if the wearer were in a state of perpetual fright. I found it rather difficult to remain at the bottom when I first dived, and had a tendency to keep rising to the surface. I soon discovered the reason for my apparent lightness though. My breathing bag was blown up too hard with oxygen. I was able to remedy this by squeezing my bag and causing some of the oxygen to escape through the exhaust valve.

By experimenting with filling the bag a little and squeezing a little, I soon attained a perfect trim which gave me neutral buoyancy, and enabled me to stay perfectly still in any position I liked, on the bottom, near the surface, or half-way between the two. I found I could alter my position simply by gently flapping my hands, just as a fish uses its fins.

There wasn't much room for us to move about in that confined circular space, about twelve feet in diameter, but we had great fun all the same. The instructor had us turning head over heels and doing other queer acrobatic tricks, just to get us used to the gear and give us confidence in it. We also did a mock escape from a replica of a submarine escape chamber built next to and connected with the diving chamber. This is the drill that all recruits to the submarine service have to go through.

In one of the lectures we were given after this, it was explained why we had to breathe oxygen instead of plain air in the D.S.E.A. and the Sladen Suit. It would appear that each of us, as we stand here on earth at sea-level, are subject to an all-round air pressure of fifteen pounds per square inch on our bodies. If we enter the water, for every thirty-two feet we descend, we are subject to a further fifteen pounds per square inch. Therefore, this means that for every foot we descend, we are subject to an extra half-pound pressure per square inch. So it will be understood that, when a diver descends to a great depth, his body, being more or less hollow, would eventually cave in under the great pressure of water from outside, unless enough pressure is built up inside his body to equalize the pressure on both sides. This is done by pumping air down to him from above which he breathes, and so equalizes pressure inside and outside his chest.

Now, a person who is breathing air is just like a bottle of fizzy lemonade. While the stopper is screwed into the bottle tightly, the lemonade appears quite still, but if it is suddenly unscrewed, the liquid immediately becomes a mass of bubbles. This is exactly what happens to a person breathing air under pressure, when the pressure is suddenly released, just as it would be with a diver if he were drawn suddenly to the surface from a great depth.

The nitrogen gas, which comprises four-fifths of the air we breathe, and which is a dead gas – that is, containing no life-giving properties like oxygen – would immediately form into a mass of bubbles in the blood stream. They would then follow the stream around until reaching a joint in the limbs, and would lodge there, causing the muscles to contract and fix the limb in a bent and paralysed position. This is known as "diver's paralysis", "Caisson disease", or "the bends". The only way to obviate this is to let the pressure decrease slowly so that the nitrogen bubbles won't get a chance to form. This is done by bringing the diver to the surface very gradually. But when a man is escaping from a submarine with a D.S.E.A., or is on a job for which the Sladen Suit is intended (we had not yet been told what job this was), this slow process of decompression is entirely impracticable, as both have to go from a great depth to the surface in as short a time as possible. So they have to breathe pure oxygen, undiluted at all by nitrogen, thus making it impossible for them to get nitrogen bubbles into the blood-stream, and so keeping them free from "the bends".

Unfortunately, we are not yet out of the wood, because oxygen itself raises another obstacle in the path of the diver – the obstacle of "oxygen poisoning". Where a person is breathing pure oxygen under certain pressures, he is apt to be subject to blackouts which are caused by oxygen poisoning. It is for the purpose of finding out more about this that "Special Service" volunteers are required to be "guinea pigs" in experiments.

Well that, we at last found out, was the prime reason for which this particular bunch of volunteers had been raised.

We gained a little knowledge from our doughty instructors who had first donned the Sladen Suit, but we soon learned to our discomfiture, and often to our terror, that they themselves had not yet learned much. We were told that the first symptom of oxygen poisoning was a twitching of the lips ("lips", as we afterwards called it), but that this could be got rid of by wriggling the lips round and round the mouthpiece of the breathing set. We were also told that, once we'd got rid of the "lips", they would never occur again during that particular dive. Well – the "lips" part was dead right, as far as being the first symptom, but as for getting rid of them never to have them return – well, that was a polite fiction. As I later found out to my dismay. We were also told that oxygen poisoning only attacked a diver at a depth of fifty feet or more. That, too, we later found out to be wrong. We did find out that one thing we had been told was quite right, however, and that was that we could be put into a state of unconsciousness by oxygen poisoning. Yes – the flaking-out part hit us very strongly. Luckily, none of us reached the dying stage, because that is what we were told would happen to us if we could not be brought to the surface very quickly after flaking out. I expect that was true too – because it was a near thing for us on several occasions.

When our initial dives in the tank and our lectures were completed, we spent the next fortnight diving with the Sladen Suit. This was done in a long, rectangular artificial lake at Horsea Island at the far end of Pompey Harbour. We were taken there every morning and brought back every evening by launch. There we put on the first models of the Sladen Suit, and rather rough-looking models they were, too. Actually, they were a light diving dress made of thin silk and rubber, with a headpiece made from the facepiece of a service gasmask, and rubber. The breathing apparatus was an improvement on the D.S.E.A. We carried a larger breathing bag on our chests connected to the facepiece by a gas-mask breathing pipe, at the end of which was a rubber mouthpiece similar to that of the D.S.E.A. Instead of carrying one small oxygen cylinder under the bag, we carried two large cylinders strapped to our backs. It is perhaps interesting to note that these bottles were made in Germany, and were the oxygen bottles carried by German aircraft shot down over this country. They were marvellous jobs, and apparently our own experts had not yet made anything like them. They were made of some aluminium alloy, and were so light that when filled with oxygen they would float on the water. They were very strong too; we used to pump oxygen into them up to

2,400 lb. per square inch. When they came to us, they had not even been repainted, and still carried the German markings. We didn't wear frogman's flippers, but a pair of roughly made canvas diving boots, weighted with five pounds of lead each.

I could understand now why I had been asked if I had ever suffered from claustrophobia, because my first impression when wearing the suit was of being rather shut in, especially after the two circular eyepieces had been screwed in. This was the last operation in the dressing procedure, and I was then completely enclosed in the suit. My breathing, too, seemed constricted, but that was due to my own breath causing the Protosorb cannister to warm up. The Protosorb was soda lime crystals carried in a metal perforated canister inside the breathing bag, for absorbing the carbon-dioxide gases in the exhaled breath returned back into the bag. I remember on one occasion while diving with the D.S.E.A. in the tank, I had had to surface and change my breathing set because I had allowed some water to trickle down into my mouthpiece, into the Protosorb, and it felt as if I could not breathe and was taking strong acid.

When I entered the water in the Sladen Suit, however, I felt quite comfortable because the coldness of the lake soon cooled down my Protosorb canister. I no longer felt shut in – in fact, I felt in my natural element.

It is hard to describe the feeling I had when I got to the bottom of that lake. To look up and see the pale reflection of light from the sun faintly showing on the surface thirty feet above me, to see the grey-green water all around me, to see the clouds of mud rising at my every footstep, and to feel the great pressure of water on my legs and arms, gave me a great feeling of awe. I felt just a tiny speck in the centre of that lake, and this new world into which I had entered seemed enormous. And yet – there was also another feeling, a very pleasant feeling. I marvelled at the peace and quiet down here, and I felt that I was lord of all I surveyed. Here was I, completely cut off from the world of human beings except for a long, thin line attached to my shoulder harness, here in this big, new, peaceful world, where I can go where I like and do what I like. I am the

"Guv'nor" – nobody can tell me to do this and do that. I am protected by a friendly wall of water all around me.

At first, I found it rather hard to move around the bottom of the lake. I tried first to walk upright, but this was useless; as soon as I took one step, the resistance of the water in front of me caused me to rise a few feet off the bottom of the lake, and I came down again in exactly the same place. There was no future in that. I then tried leaning forward farther and farther, until I was almost lying flat. By doing this I presented a very small surface to the water, and so decreased the resistance. Then, by digging my toes in at each step and doing a sort of fin movement with my hands, I managed to get along pretty quickly.

After a very enjoyable time diving every day in Horsea Lake, all the volunteers finally became used to the gear and acquired perfect confidence in it. Our number had decreased to sixteen by now, two more having dropped out owing to sinus trouble, after making their first dip into thirty feet of water. The sixteen survivors were then sent to Messrs. Siebe Gorman's factory, where the experimental job for which they were recruited really started in earnest.

The sixteen of us who arrived at Siebe's that August afternoon were a motley crew. There was one Petty Officer Physical Training Instructor (known as "Clubs" in the Navy), one Leading-Seaman, three A.B.s, three Ordinary-Seamen (of whom I was one), three Leading-Stokers, two Stokers, and three Cooks. We were all under the charge of a Warrant Gunner named Mr Crouch, who was an old diver, and a very pleasant person to know.

That morning we were allowed to wander around the factory a bit, inspecting the diving tanks and compression chambers which were used by the firm for testing the diving apparatus which they made, and watching the factory workers assembling the D.S.E.A. sets and fire-fighting equipment. Naturally, Jolly Jack lived up to his reputation, and a couple of the lads soon fixed dates for themselves that night with a couple of the girls in the factory.

During our period at Siebe Gorman's, we were accommodated at a nearby R.A.F. camp, where our naval rig stuck out like a sore thumb among all the Air Force blue. However, the R.A.F. and the W.A.A.F. made us very welcome indeed – the beer in the canteen was very good, too.

The day after our arrival, we were taken to Siebe's in a three-ton lorry. The diving experiments there were carried out in a two-storied building containing a cylindrical tank, twelve feet deep and twelve feet in diameter, another tank, twenty-five feet deep and six feet in diameter, a twelve-foot tank about six feet in diameter, several dry compression chambers, and an infamous affair known to us as "The Pot."

The Pot was a diabolical contraption, as we found out very shortly. It was a pressure tank, about twelve feet in depth and six feet in diameter, with the edges rounded off – very much like one of Mr Churchill's famous hats. In the top, which protruded through a hole in the first floor, was an opening, oval in shape, about two feet six inches by two feet. The opening was sealed by a heavy, air-tight door, opening inwards, which was opened and shut by means of a twofold purchase. This door must have weighed about two hundred-weight. The tank contained about eight feet of water. Pressure was built up in the remaining four feet of the tank by connecting four large compressed-air cylinders to a pipe leading into the top. By this means, pressure could be built up inside the tank equal to that which is met at great depths. Any depth up to 150 feet could be produced in this manner. A pressure gauge on the outside of the tank told us the depth of water that had been equalled inside.

Our first dive was made in the twenty-five foot tank. We went down in pairs and stayed there for thirty minutes. We all completed this successfully, and by that time the first day's diving was over. The next day, we started diving in The Pot. This was where our troubles started. It was the intention of those in charge, who now included a Surgeon-Lieutenant, to send us down one by one to fifty feet for thirty minutes. The first diver to go into The Pot was Symington, a Leading-Seaman. In order to get into The Pot, the diver had a canvas harness put on him underneath his breathing apparatus. The harness was fitted with a big iron ring, into which was placed the hook of another twofold purchase, and in this manner the diver was hoisted into or out of the tank.

Symington went into The Pot, and everyone waited with apprehension. But the fellow who waited with the most apprehension was the next one due in. He sat on a chair at the other side of the room with his diving dress on, all except the head-piece. His apprehension increased considerably when, twenty-five minutes after Symington had entered The Pot, a sudden cry of "Up, Up!" was heard, and all hands went to panic stations. Two unclipped the door of The Pot, two more stood by the diver-lifting tackle, another grabbed the air-pressure release valve, and with a terrific rush of air, the pressure in The Pot was lowered to zero. The door was opened, tackle lowered, the two lifters weighed-off on the tackle, and Symington was lifted slowly out of The Pot. He was unconscious. As he was gently lowered to the deck and his diving dress was stripped off, we all gathered round, wondering. He had flaked out from oxygen poisoning, after spending twenty-five minutes at fifty feet. He soon came round again and, apart from a terrific headache, he was O.K.

The next chap down lasted only ten minutes, and he looked so bad when he surfaced that he was sent straight back to Portsmouth. His diving days were finished – and I guess he wasn't sorry either. After lunch, it was my turn. I began to wonder if I had been wise to eat such a heavy meal. I entered The Pot in the usual manner, and arrived safely at the bottom, without catching my chin on the edge of the opening, or the back of my head on the door. Above me, one of the instructors was seated on a wooden platform in that part of The Pot that was not filled with water. He wore a pair of waders up to his waist, as the space was so cramped that his legs had to dangle in the water. He held the other end of the life-line which was attached to my harness. He also wore a pair of headphones and carried a microphone. He was connected to another instructor who was similarly equipped outside The Pot. In this way, my actions could be reported to the doctor and others interested, and a log could be kept.

When I had signalled that I was O.K., the heavy steel door was slowly shut and clipped. This was a terrifying business in itself. When shut, the door was kept in position by two huge strongbacks weighing about half a hundredweight each, through which passed two bolts of about one and a quarter inches diameter, and screwed down with a couple of immense nuts. Now, that door leaked a little, and to get it shut really tight we used to put a hefty spanner on the nuts and whack it home with a seven-pound hammer. Well, you can imagine what it sounded like to the diver inside. Each stroke of the hammer seemed to shatter my eardrums. I was reminded of the sound some time later, when I experienced my first depth-charge attack in a submarine, and a couple of those "ashcans" dropped a bit too close for comfort.

When the banging stopped, it was a horrible feeling too. There was dead silence for a few seconds – the last stroke of the hammer sounded like the clang of a cell door shut behind me. Then there was a sudden terrific hiss as the compressed air came rushing into The Pot. My rubber mouthpiece began to press in on my face. I allowed some oxygen to trickle through the side of my mouth, which blew the rubber out again to the proper position. Then I found that my bag had been flattened by the increased pressure, and my breathing was getting weak through lack of oxygen. I blew it out again by giving myself a "guff" of oxygen, by opening the bypass valve on my bottles for a fraction of a second. Then my ears started to pain. I tried to clear them by swallowing. This didn't work, so I pressed my nose against the inside of my facepiece and blew down it. That did the trick. As the pressure became greater, I had to go through these actions again and again. Suddenly, the hissing stopped – I was at fifty feet. Dead silence reigned again. I went on a tour of inspection. Hanging by a string to the ladder was a small slate and a slate pencil. This was for the diver to write messages to the attendant. Walking around the perimeter, I found two small portholes about nine inches in diameter. These were divided into smaller holes filled with thick glass, and looked very much like a fly's eye. They were about seven feet up from the floor of The Pot, and by getting a precarious hold on the heads of a couple of bolts, I was able to lift myself high enough to look through one of them, and by placing my head in a certain position and nearly going cross-eyed, I was just able to see the time by the clock on the wall outside. Then, of course, the inevitable comedian (it's queer how every party has its comedian), had to come and smoke a cigarette outside, and with a horrible leer on his face, blow the smoke against the glass. A nice bloke – very funny!

Having got "chokka" with exploring (there wasn't much to explore, anyway), I turned a few somersaults; that made the attendant "chokka", because I was putting too many turns in the life-line. So I had to loaf around doing nothing. I did send a couple of messages up via the slate, but we didn't have much to talk about, so conversation fell a bit flat, and finally broke off altogether.

I had been down about twenty minutes when I felt the first twitching of the lips. I exercised my lips around the mouthpiece, and the twitching went off. Soon afterwards, the attendant told me the thirty minutes were up, and that I had completed the course. The pressure would be taken off the tank, and we would rise to ten feet. Here we had to remain for ten minutes, for it must be remembered that the attendant too was breathing under pressure, and as he was breathing ordinary air, he was liable to get "the bends" if our ascent was not delayed. With great thankfulness, I heard the hissing of the air and very welcome it was too, because this time it was on its way out.

Then it happened. I suppose the release valve had been open for about ten seconds, and the gauge outside registered about forty feet, when I suddenly felt a violent twitching of my lips. I tried to wriggle them around the mouthpiece again, my mouth was blown out like a balloon, and I was blurting out oxygen through my lips so much that it was hard even to keep the mouthpiece on my mouth. The twitching of my lips increased, and I felt a terrific tingling sensation at the side of my mouth, as if someone were touching it with a live wire. This increased, until it became a definite pain, and my lips became so distorted that it felt as if my mouth were stretched to somewhere near my right ear. I tried to climb the ladder, but by this time my whole body was convulsing, and I was only just able to get my head above water. I tried to shout to the attendant to grab me before I fell back. Although my lips formed the words, no sound came. It was a horrible feeling. I could feel myself falling back into the water, and the attendant's face seemed to dissolve into a black void. In his place, mounted on that black back-cloth, I could see my grandmother. Now this was a queer thing, because I have never seen my grandparents at all. They were dead before I was born. The only thing I knew of this particular lady was from a photograph hanging on the wall at home, and it was this likeness I could see. There was no mistaking that face, with its dark, glittering eyes, the high cheek-bones, the long, hooked nose, and the swarthy gypsy-like complexion. I sang out to her to grab me. But she too faded away – blackness closed in on me – I was out.

It was an hour later when I came to – in the factory sick bay, where I had been carried on a stretcher. So I must have been in a pretty rough state. I had a shocking headache, and felt as though I'd had a monumental night on the beer and was just waking up the morning after. It was quite a cheap hangover, but I think I'd rather have paid for it in the normal way. I was given a couple of aspirins by the factory nurse, a kindly old soul who treated me with a sort of kindly-sarcastic-scolding-proud-and-loving atti-tude of a mother whose son has hurt his knee by falling out of a tree while stealing apples.

After resting for about an hour, I went back to the camp, had some tea, got cleaned up, and went ashore to have a night on the beer, for which I had already had a hangover.

A flaking-out session, seen from the spectator's viewpoint, is much less uncomfortable than undergoing the experience as a diver. But even from the point of view of the onlooker it's a pretty grim experience. I've never seen a man hanged, but after seeing a diver hoisted out of The Pot, unconscious, at the end of that tackle, I've a good idea what one looks like. His head is slumped forward on his chest. From his mouthpiece come awful bubbling noises. His hands hang limply at his sides from sloping shoulders. His hands, all swollen and puffy, with water dripping from them, are a ghastly greyish-purple colour. When his feet are clear of the hole, he is gently lowered on to the deck, face uppermost. The water streams off his suit in little rivers down the folds, forming a pool all round him. His headpiece is removed, revealing a face of slate-grey colour, eyes closed and saliva drooling from his sagging, purple lips. At the doctor's discretion, he is either divested of his diving gear and removed to the sick bay, or left to lie where he is until he regains consciousness.

Well, this sort of thing went on for four months at Siebe Gorman's. One by one, the volunteers flaked out with oxygen poisoning. We did all kinds of experiments, many under Professor Haldane and Surgeon-Lieutenant K. Donald, R.N. Sometimes we would dive to seventy feet for twenty minutes, up to ten feet for five minutes, down to seventy again for twenty minutes, up to the surface again for five, then down to fifty for half an hour, then surface and finish. Exact notes were taken in the log of all divers' reactions.

All the time, the morale of the volunteers remained very high, and we were all very cheerful. We still treated The Pot with very great respect, though. Jokingly we used to say that there was a demon living in it who was apt to be very hostile to any hapless diver who wasn't very quick to heed the warning of "lips". One comedian even composed a poem, which he chalked on the blackboard. I've forgotten it now, except for the last two lines, which went like this:

> For down at the depth of seventy feet
> Lives a guy by the name of "Oxygen Pete".

We were paid five shillings a day extra for this work.

By this time our number had decreased by two more. Leading-Stoker Harman and Cruikshank the cook were suddenly sent away to some mysterious place called "Up North". We found later that they had been sent to fill a couple of vacancies in "the operational classes" (whatever that meant, at the time). Meanwhile, we carried on diving, performing many kinds of experiments. For instance, a couple of the chaps had to sit for four hours with their hands immersed in icy water. They came out with their hands swollen to the size of boxing-gloves. More medical examinations followed.

By this time we all had a pretty good idea what the gear we were experimenting with was to be used for. But we were told nothing definite. We'd heard rumours of an attack by Italian frogmen on the *Valiant* and *Queen Elizabeth* at Alexandria. And there was another rumour floating around of a similar attack by our own lads on German shipping – but still nothing definite. Strangely enough, round about this time, a certain friction started to spring up between some of our party. I suppose we were all keyed up and anxious to get cracking operationally. Then the rot set in. Cases of flaking out became more and more frequent, and as the good divers flaked out, so their nerve seemed to go. Many of them had had such a good run before undergoing that terrifying experience that they had no time to regain their nerve before the experiments finished. It was terrible to see the effect on some of these grand chaps. I remember one in particular, a well-built six-footer, trying to light a cigarette. The cigarette was dancing around on his lips, and his hands were shaking like those of a man with the palsy as he tried to get the match in contact with the box to strike it. I am sure that if, like me, he had passed out earlier, he would have had time to recover.

So time went on, until 15 December 1942, when the experiments at Siebe Gorman's came to an end, and after stowing our gear and saying our farewells to our friends at the factory and the camp, we returned to Blockhouse. Here, one by one, we had our last interview with Lt-Commander Shelford. I guess we must have looked different men from those carefree, eager, green volunteers whom he had last seen in that same little office four months before. But there was one happy man among them – and that one was me. I was told the glad news that I had been recommended to carry on diving, and that I would, if I wished it, be sent to join the next operational class in training for "Human Torpedoes". He didn't have to ask me twice – I said, "Yes." I learned that there were only ten survivors, and that I had been the only one picked to carry on. I was a very proud and happy man. Proud, when I thought of the hundred volunteers that day at Pompey Barracks, proud of the men I had worked with, and of the fact that I had been one of them. I have a medal now, but it does not belong only to me – it belongs to the other guinea pigs at Siebe Gorman's and the other chaps I met later in the operational class who didn't get the same chance that I did. I was happy that I had got what I went after. I felt that now, at last, I was really going places.

THE BULL OF SCAPA FLOW

Wolfgang Frank

The Second World War was barely six weeks old when, on 13 October 1939, the German submarine Unterseeboot-47 *penetrated the British naval base at Scapa Flow, sinking the battleship* Royal Oak. *It was an audacious blow, one made all the sweeter for the Kriegsmarine in that Scapa Flow had been the site of the scuttling of its High Seas Fleet in 1918. The crew of* U-47 *returned home to Wilhelmshaven national heroes.*

Günther Prien, the commander of U-47, *was a natural U-boat ace and had already claimed the first U-boat victory of the war, a cargo ship on 5 September. An ardent Nazi, Prien had been an unemployed merchant seaman before volunteering for the U-boat arm (all German submarine crew were volunteers) in 1938. He had been appointed commander of* U-47 *just before the outbreak of war.*

After the success of the Scapa Flow raid, U-47 *was sent to the North Atlantic where it wreaked havoc amongst Allied shipping. A type VIIIB submarine,* U-47 *was armed with an 8.8 cm deck gun, a 2 cm anti-aircraft gun and five torpedo tubes (one stern, four in the bows). Its crew was 44 strong. Most of its attacking was done at night, on the surface, with the deck gun, since torpedoes were expensive and the boat could only remain under- water for short periods.*

The following account of the illustrious career of U-47, *in- cluding the Scapa Flow raid, is by Wolfgang Frank, the press officer for the U-boat arm during the 1939–45 conflict. He both knew most of the U-boat aces personally and occasionally accompanied them on their voyages.*

It is worth pointing out that the most important consequence of the Scapa Flow raid was that it enabled the head of the U-boat arm, Captain Karl Dönitz, to persuade the Führer – hitherto uninterested in naval matters – to endorse a massive U-boat building programme. As Dönitz realized, single U-boat raids, though spectacular and morale-sapping for the enemy would not greatly influence the war effort: large numbers of U-boats, organized in flotillas, or "Wolf Packs", to strangle the sea-lanes to Britain could. By the war's end some 600 submarines of the same type as U-47 had been built.

In September 1939, one of the "canoes" operating east of the Orkneys found herself off the Pentland Firth, the passage between Scotland and the Orkneys. A strong westerly current caught the boat and swept her through the turbulent narrows. Finding that his engines were not powerful enough to pull him free, the captain, making a virtue out of necessity, carefully surveyed the movement of ships and the defences in the area. On his return he made a detailed report to Dönitz, who at once saw the possibilities of a special operation. After much deliberation he ordered one of his best young officers, Lieut. Günther Prien, to report on board the depot-ship *Weichsel* at Kiel.

As Prien entered the Commodore's cabin he found Dönitz in conference with his own flotilla-commander and Lieut. Wellner, the captain of the "canoe". Charts lay spread on the table before them and Prien's eye was immediately caught by the words "Scapa Flow". The Commodore addressed him.

"Do you think that a determined CO could take his boat into Scapa Flow and attack the ships there? Don't answer now, but let me have your reply by Tuesday. The decision rests entirely with you, and without prejudice to yourself." It was then Sunday. Prien saluted and withdrew, his heart beating fast. He went straight to his quarters and settled down to a thorough study of the problem. He worked away hour after hour, calculating, figuring, checking and re-checking. On the appointed day he stood once again before the Commodore.

"Yes or no?" – "Yes, Sir." A pause. "Have you thought it all out? Have you thought of Emsmann and Henning who tried the same thing in the First World War and never came back?" – "Yes, Sir." – "Then get your boat ready."

The crew could make no sense of the preparations for their next patrol. Why were they disembarking part of their food supplies and taking so little fuel and fresh water with them? Apart from giving essential orders, the captain was uncommunicative, and on the appointed day the U-boat slipped quietly through the Kiel Canal into the North Sea. The nights were dark, the seas running high. While on passage the crew watched their captain closely; although funnel-smoke was sighted several times he never attempted to attack. At last, early in the morning of 13 October, the Orkneys were in sight. Prien gave the order to dive and when the U-boat was resting easily on the sea-bed, he ordered all hands to muster forward. "Tomorrow we go into Scapa Flow," he began, and went on talking quietly, making sure that every man knew what he had to do. Then he ordered every available man off watch to turn in; they would need all their strength when the time came.

At four o'clock in the afternoon the boat came to life again and the cook served a specially good meal. Jokes were bandied about and Prien wrote in his log, "the morale of the ship's company is superb." At seven-fifteen all hands went to diving-stations, and the chief engineer began to lift the boat off the bottom; the ballast-pumps sang and the boat began to move as the motors stirred into life. Prien took a first cautious glimpse through the periscope. All clear. He gave the order to surface. The wind had dropped but the sky was covered with light clouds; although there was a new moon, the Northern Lights made the night almost as bright as day.

As they moved into the narrows a powerful rip-tide suddenly caught the boat, just as Prien had expected. He needed every ounce of concentration now and a good deal of luck. The rudder was swung from port to starboard and back again, with full use of diesel engines, to keep the bows steady against the stream. At one moment he had to go full astern to avoid colliding with a blockship. Then he suddenly bent down and shouted through the hatch, "We are inside Scapa Flow!*

At this point his log read, "I could see nothing to the south, so turned away along the coast to the north. There I sighted two battleships and beyond them some destroyers at anchor. No cruisers. I decided to attack the big ships." As the U-boat crept closer still, he could make out the details of the ships. The nearest to him was of the *Royal Oak* class. He went closer, until the bows of the second ship appeared beyond the first. She looked like the *Repulse*. He gave his orders, "Ready all tubes! Stand by to fire a salvo from Nos. 1 to 4!" Endrass, his first lieutenant, was taking aim; the forecastle of the *Repulse*† came into the cross-wires. "Fire!" He pressed the firing key.

The U-boat shuddered as the torpedoes leaped away. There was a moment's agonizing pause. Would they hit? Then a tall column of water reared against *Repulse*'s side. But *Royal Oak* lay motionless as before. A miss? Impossible. Defective torpedo? Unlikely. Minutes went by but the silence of the bay remained unbroken. Had the ships been abandoned? Was the whole of Scapa still asleep? Why no counter-attack from the destroyers? It is almost imposible to believe what happened next. Calmly deciding to make a second attack, the captain took his boat in a wide circle round the anchorage *on the surface*, while the spare torpedoes were being loaded into the tubes. For nearly twenty minutes he cruised round the main base of the British fleet while down below the sweating hands pushed torpedo after torpedo into place. As though the situation were not tense enough already, Prien suddenly noticed one of his

* The entry into Scapa Flow was made through Kirk Sound, which was inadequately blocked.

† Prien mistook the old seaplane-carrier *Pegasus* for *Repulse*, which was not in Scapa Flow. Only *Royal Oak* was hit in both attacks. For the next five months the Home Fleet had to use remote anchorages on the west coast of Scotland, until the defences of Scapa had been put in order.

junior officers, Sub-Lieutenant von Varendorff, calmly walking round the deck. "Are you crazy?" hissed the captain. "Come up here at once!" Once again Prien moved to the attack – this time at closer range – and once again the torpedoes raced towards their target.

Thunderous explosions shook the area. Huge columns of smoke and water towered into the air while the sky was filled with falling wreckage – whole gun-turrets and strips of armour-plating weighing tons apiece. The harbour sprang to life. Morse signals flashed from every corner, search-lights probed and swept, a car on the coast road stopped, turned and flashed its headlights on and off as though signalling, as it dashed back the way it had come.

"Emergency full ahead both!" ordered Prien. "Group up mo-tors. Give me everything you've got!" As the water bubbled and boiled beneath the U-boat's stern, he saw a destroyer coming swiftly towards him, sweeping the water with her searchlight. She began to signal with her Aldis lamp; Prien bit his lip as the bridge beneath him shuddered to the vibration of the screws. His wake showed up all too clearly yet he could not afford to reduce speed. Suddenly the miracle happened; the destroyer dropped astern, turned away and disappeared. A moment later he heard the crash of her depth-charges in the distance. The U-boat scraped past the end of a jetty and then – "We're through! Pass the word, we're through!" A roar of cheers answered him from below. Prien set course for the south-east – and home.

During the long hours of waiting before the attack, the crew had passed round a comic paper; one of the cartoons in it showed a bull with head down and nostrils smoking. "Harry Hotspur," someone had said; that was also their name for their captain. Now, on the way home, Endrass had an idea. Armed with paint-brushes and some white paint a small working party clambered on to the casing and painted on the side of the conning-tower the boat's new crest – the Bull of Scapa Flow.

While crossing the North Sea they listened to the wireless. "According to a British Admiralty report," said the announcer, "the battleship *Royal Oak* has been sunk, apparently by a U-boat. British reports say that the U-boat was also sunk." The men in *U-47* smiled. In the afternoon came an official announcement from the German Admiralty: "The U-boat which sank the British battleship *Royal Oak* is now known to have also hit the battleship *Repulse* and to have put her out of action. It can now be announced that this U-boat was commanded by Lieutenant Prien." For the first time the name of Prien was heard by the German people. Prien in Scapa Flow – where twenty years before, the German High Seas Fleet had gone to the bottom!

As the U-boat made fast to the jetty Dönitz could be seen standing next to Grand Admiral Raeder, the cornflower-blue lapels of his uniform clearly visible. The Grand Admiral came on board to congratulate the crew; offering his hand to each man he conferred upon every one of them the Iron Cross, Second Class, while the captain was awarded the First Class of the Order. "Lieutenant Prien," said Admiral Raeder, "you will have an opportunity of making a personal report to the Führer." Turning to Dönitz he then announced before them all that the Commodore had been promoted to Rear-Admiral. Henceforth he would be the Flag Officer Commanding U-boats. That same afternoon Prien and his crew were flown to Berlin. Hitler received them in the Reich Chancellery and conferred upon the captain the Knight's Cross of the Iron Cross.

In June, 1940, *U-47* was patrolling to the west of Scotland, still commanded by Lieut. Prien, the "Bull of Scapa Flow". The weather was calm and mild, the nights so light that one could read a book on the bridge at midnight.

Early one morning the haze lifted to reveal a ship – their first target for days. Just as *U-47* altered course to attack, the target turned too and came straight down at her. Prien lowered his periscope and dived as fast as he could to 180 feet, while the ship rumbled unwittingly overhead. Almost at once he surfaced again, ordering the gun's crew to their stations; but as they were closing up round the gun, an after look-out suddenly reported more smoke astern of the U-boat and Prien realised that a convoy was approaching. He abandoned his original plan and, after sending out a hasty sighting-report to head-quarters, he submerged again.

As soon as *U-47* was running smoothly at periscope-depth, he took a quick look through the lens as it broke surface for a few seconds. He could hardly believe his eyes. Forty-two ships were steaming majestically towards him in open order, seven columns of six ships of all shapes and sizes, escorted by two ancient-looking destroyers and three modern ones. For three hours, still submerged, Prien tried to close on the convoy, but his boat was too slow; steadily he lost bearing on the ships, until they were out of periscope sight. He started to surface but almost immediately a trawler hove in sight and he had to dive; at his next attempt a Sunderland zoomed out of the sun like a fat bumble-bee and forced him below again. Prien now realised that to catch up with that convoy he would have to chase it for at least ten hours, and by then it would be so close to the coast that he would never get near it for aircraft and surface-escorts. As he sat weighing up his chances and scanning the horizon, masts and smoke suddenly appeared to port and a straggler from the convoy came hurrying along, zigzagging violently. So he stayed below the surface, and everyone kept deathly still, as if the U-boat herself were holding her breath like a living thing. "All tubes ready!" Every man was standing tensely at his post. Suddenly the ship turned away; with a curse Prien called for the last ounce of power from his motors as he stood after his prey. "No. 5, stand by . . . fire!" Some seconds later there was a clanging crash. "We've hit her near the funnel!" called Prien triumphantly. "She's the *Balmoral Wood*★ – look and see how big she is, I'd put her at 5,000 or 6,000 tons." As the water closed over the sinking ship, all that could be seen on the surface were a few large crates, some of which had burst open to reveal aircraft wings and fuselages. "Well, *they* won't be dropping any bombs on Kiel, anyway," commented one of the crew.

All next day Prien carried out a searching sweep on various courses, but sighted nothing. "The Atlantic seems to have been

★ This ship was torpedoed and sunk on 14 June 1940.

swept clean," he wrote in his log. But his luck changed with the dawn of the following day, for a 5,000-tonner without lights came steaming past, barely 5,000 yards away. Despite the growing daylight, Prien tried to approach on the surface but he was soon forced under by a Sunderland; however, he was determined to get in an attack and once again he surfaced. This time his first hasty look round revealed warships ahead and merchant ships astern of him; quickly he sent out a sighting signal and dived again, realizing that he had chanced upon the meeting-place of a convoy with its escort. He moved in to attack but soon saw that the twenty ships in convoy were screened by at least four escorts of the *Auckland* and *Bittern* class, while a Sunderland flew above them. His original plan of attack would be of no avail against such a strong escort, so he waited awhile before surfacing and then made a wide sweep round, so as to try his luck from the other side. As night fell he closed in, once more at periscope-depth, and began to look for a likely target. The weather was favourable; white caps of foam on the waves would make it difficult for the enemy look-outs to spot his periscope, and although the sky was cloudy, visibility was good.

Despite all this, it looked as though the U-boat had in fact been sighted, for one of the escorts turned towards *U-47* and came down like a pointer sniffing into the wind for game. The range dropped quickly – 300 yards, 250, 200 . . . Prien was tempted to fire at the escort, but she suddenly turned away and disappeared on a course parallel to the U-boat. With a sigh of relief Prien ordered, "No. 1 ready . . . fire!" His target was a great tanker, deeply laden, which had caught his eye earlier in the day. He did not wait to see the torpedo hit, but turned immediately to his next victim, which was slightly nearer – a ship of about 7,000 tons. "No. 2 . . . fire!" While the U-boat was still heeling, Prien suddenly saw a column of water spouting up alongside a ship he had not aimed at. There had been a slight mishap in the torpedo compartment; the torpedo-artificer had been thrown off his balance by the movement of the boat and had saved himself from falling by catching hold of the firing-grip. As a result No. 3 tube had fired a fraction after No. 2 – but the torpedo had hit a second tanker.

Fifteen minutes later the U-boat surfaced and Prien sprang up to the bridge; it was not yet quite dark and the sea was getting up. Over on the port quarter lay the big tanker with a heavy list, her bows well below the surface, her decks awash. Prien sent for the silhouette-book and soon identified the battered wreck as that of the tanker *Cadillac*, 12,100 tons.† The other ship, of which nothing could now be seen, was presumably one of the *Gracia* class of 5,600 tons. The third had also disappeared. Now for the rest of them!

But it was not to be; a storm blew up and after two days' fruitless search Prien realised that he had lost the convoy. A day later, however, he sighted and sank the Dutch tanker *Leticia*,* 2,800 tons, bound for England from Curaçao with fuel-oil. Late that night, in a freshening sea, yet another tanker was sighted and Prien ordered the gun to be manned, having decided to stop the ship with a couple of well-placed rounds and then sink her at his leisure. "Only five rounds of ammunition left, Sir," warned the coxswain. – "Never mind, we'll use them just the same." Time passed but there was no sign of the captain of the gun. Prien called down the hatchway, "Control room! Where's Meier?" There was the sound of running feet below, then the voice of the control room petty officer. "Meier is lying in his bunk, Sir, and says there's absolutely no point in trying to aim a gun in this weather." Prien could hardly believe his ears; the bridge watch did their best to hide their amusement. "Give him a direct order from the captain to report immediately on the bridge!" When Meier at last appeared he did not trouble to hide his feelings. "In *this* sea, with only a couple of rounds?" – "They *must* hit, Meier!" – "Aye, aye, Sir." Indifferently he moved towards the gun and Prien gave the order to open fire. The tanker turned sharply away as the first shells screamed

* Probably the tanker *San Fernando*, torpedoed and sunk on 21 June 1940.
† Sunk on 27 June 1940.

towards her, but two of them hit her; Meier was excelling himself. "Hit her in the engine-room!" ordered Prien. Another hit – but the target was still moving away. The last of the five rounds went into the breech, and this time the shell-burst was followed by a cloud of grey smoke and a yellow flash. Soaked to the skin, Meier returned to the bridge; the tanker had stopped and the crew were hastily abandoning ship. Throwing a quick word of congratulation to his still impenitent gunner, Prien brought *U-47* into a good firing position and loosed off a torpedo. His log reads: "The torpedo hit and the ship began to sink. Despite the gunfire and the torpedo-hit, her radio operator continued to signal '*Empire Toucan* torpedoed in position 49°20″ North, 13°52″ West' and later 'Sinking rapidly by stern'. Finally he jumped overboard with a flare and was seen swimming away from the ship." Prien immediately steered towards the flare but when he reached the spot, there was nothing to be seen. A brave man had died. . . .

Weeks went by as Prien and his brother captains hunted and sank, watched and waited, shadowed the convoys and "homed" other boats on to them, in fair weather and in foul. When at length the U-boats returned to France for repairs and provisioning, their crews were sent to the new rest-centres at Carnac and Quiberon near Lorient, where they could relax on the beach, bathe, ride and do exactly as they pleased. Here they could let the world go by, as they took the pretty daughters of France by storm and quaffed the local wines; all too soon they would once more be at sea, the perpetual thunder of the diesels around them and the waves foaming and crashing on their decks.

Prien, too, was soon back at sea. One dark and rainy night, he and half a dozen other boats encountered a convoy, which they attacked from all sides at once. This was one of the earliest organized wolf-pack actions of the war, and will go down to history as the "Night of the Long Knives". Torpedo after torpedo raced from its tube to detonate against some ship's side. Ten thousand tons of petrol went up in a fiery ball of white-hot flame a thousand feet high; an ammunition ship exploded with a deafening roar and literally disintegrated; all around was nothing but the bright glow of flames. Some ships stood on end before finally disappearing, some listed heavily and turned turtle, others broke apart, to die a painful death. Everywhere, like a pack of wolves, the U-boats were at the convoy. With all his torpedoes gone, Prien reckoned up the tonnage he had sunk by identifying his victims from the "picture book". Then he took a signal-pad and wrote, "Have sunk eight ships in the convoy totalling 50,500 tons. All torpedoes fired."

The dawn came slowly, marking the end of the "Night of the Long Knives". The other commanders were also making their reckoning: Kretschmer, Schepke, Frauenheim, Endrass, Bleichrodt, Moehle and Liebe. In two days of operating together they had achieved the staggering figure of 325,000 tons sunk.* Within a few days *U-47* had returned to her base. Prien, as the first U-boat captain to top the 200,000-ton mark, now became the fifth officer in the armed forces to receive what was then the highest decoration – the Oak Leaves to the Knight's Cross.

AFTERWORD

The luck of U-47 ran out on 8 March 1941, when it was sunk by HMS Wolverine, *with the loss of all hands. During its career the boat had sunk 28 ships totalling 160,939 tons.*

* "Night of the Long Knives" – 18–19 October 1940.

*"The sunken fleet of Truk Lagoon
represents the . . . world's largest collection of artificial reefs"*

TRUK LAGOON

Sylvia A. Earle

*Dr Earle is acknowledged as the world's foremost woman marine
biologist. "Her Deepness" has dived solo to 1,000 metres and was
appointed explorer-in-residence at National Geographic in 1998.
Here she describes her 1976 exploration of Truk Lagoon (Chuuk),
north-east of Australia, where 60 Japanese ships were sent to their
grave during World War II.*

For one awesome moment we seemed to have chanced upon
a vast submarine cathedral. Framed against the surface, the
ship's mast and yard extended crosslike as if in benediction,
the coral-encrusted arms wreathed in halos of schooling
fish.

Turning to my diving partner, Al Giddings, I wrote on my
underwater slate, "Give nature time, and a sunken warship
resembles a place of worship."

Al gestured toward a heavily encrusted stern gun nearby, then
scribbled, "And guns have garlands."

The impression of a hallowed site was more than mere
illusion, for our sunken ship was both memorial and tomb
for scores of Japanese sailors killed during World War II.
On the morning of 17 February 1944, a United States Navy
air attack caught a fleet of Japanese merchant vessels and warships by surprise at Truk, in the Caroline Islands of the western
Pacific. After continued attacks, some sixty ships and thousands

of men lay at the bottom of the Pacific, to remain undisturbed for more than a quarter of a century.

For all its tragedy, that long-ago event presents marine scientists today with a unique opportunity. The sunken fleet of Truk Lagoon represents not only the world's largest collection of artificial reefs but also one whose age is precisely known. It offers invaluable clues to the growth rates and patterns of the abundant marine life that congregates around submerged reefs. It was this fact that had brought Al and me to Truk Lagoon.

Few undersea laboratories are more beautifully situated. The Truk Islands, now part of a United States trust territory, consist of 11 major islands and scores of islets within a 40-mile-wide lagoon surrounded by a protective coral reef. The water of Truk Lagoon is not only crystal clear but normally calm, an advantage both to me as a marine biologist and to Al as an underwater photographer. Sometimes called "a lake in the middle of the Pacific," Truk Lagoon is a quiet haven set in a broad expanse of open sea.

Arriving at the settlement on Moen Island last summer, Al and I chartered a 30-foot diving support boat for our research and signed on Kimiuo Aisek, a likeable 48-year-old Trukese scuba diver who had witnessed the 1944 air attack as a boy of 17. Kimiuo's memory of the event and his detailed knowledge of the lagoon floor saved us many days of searching for particular wrecks.

One of our early choices was the sunken "cathedral," an armed aircraft transport, *Fujikawa Maru*. Measuring 436 feet in length with a 59-foot beam, she had carried Zero fighter planes, drums of fuel, and assorted munitions that had failed to explode when she was attacked.

Such wrecks are controversial today, for Truk Lagoon has been designated a historical monument – a museum whose ships and artifacts are protected from removal by law. Recently there have been suggestions that those ships with explosives or high-octane fuel aboard be blown up to prevent accidents to the many divers who will be attracted to the site. Along with our other studies, Al and I hoped to assess the dangers these ships pose today to humans and to Truk's underwater environment.

My first dive on *Fujikawa Maru* emphasized the haunting dual image of human and natural history. Although the tips of both masts break the surface, the ship's deck lies in about 70 feet of water and the keel in 130. Descending along the aftermast, arms forward, Al and I landed softly on the stern deck. I looked back at the mast's crossbeam, silhouetted against a sunburst of light from the surface, then turned to view the submarine garden surrounding us. Over the course of 31 years the entire ship had been transformed from a bare metal monument to human tragedy into a richly productive reef of extraordinary beauty.

Fujikawa Maru's holds, once used to store tools of war, had now become homes for large groupers. Crew's quarters and passageways, essential features for long-ago human occupants, now offered aquatic residents an extensive system of tunnel and cave habitats. Hatchways were filled from sill to top with hundreds of small silver fish. Curtains of algae graced exposed portholes. A low jungle of marine growth carpeted every surface exposed to light.

Old Wounds Now More Than Healed

As I explored this lush submarine forest, my thoughts turned to the violent events from which it had grown. During our first surface inspection of Truk Lagoon, Kimiuo had described the scene on those February days in 1944.

"When the attack came," he said, "I hid in a cave on the side of Dublon Island. Several ships were hit and sank as I watched."

During the next 30 hours there was unremitting chaos – noise, smoke, uncertainty, and fear. "For more than two years afterward," Kimiuo recalled, "oil from ships and planes covered the beaches and reefs. But the sea is healed now."

More than just healed, I thought time and again, as I explored the array of plants and animals covering *Fujikawa Maru*. Any solid object placed in the sea is likely to become home for passing plankton, an effect known as the "substrate phenomenon."

Once, on an oceanographic expedition in the South Pacific, I scooped a drifting feather from the open sea more than 200 miles from any shore, and in so doing captured a host of unexpected travelers: three minute goose barnacles, attached to the base of the feather; a slender nudibranch; several young crabs; and a tiny jacklike fish that apparently had taken refuge under the frail umbrella.

Exploring Three Decades of Growth

Here in Truk Lagoon I was faced with this same phenomenon on a grand scale, in the form of *Fujikawa Maru* and some sixty other enormous artificial reefs.

No one had recorded the kinds of plants and animals that settled and grew on these ships during the first month, or the first year, or even the first quarter of a century after their sinking. It was now my goal to help document what had taken place during more than three decades.

Not all the large corals and giant mollusks on the sunken hulls could be 31 years old, but they positively could not be *more* than 31 years old. Studies by others elsewhere suggest that the rates of coral growth vary greatly, depending on the species and the ecological conditions in which the corals live. Individuals of the same species may develop at different rates, depending on their age and the amount of light, food, and space available.

I explained our task to Kimiuo: "I want to locate and tag the largest corals we can find. This will give us an idea of the maximum size reached since the ships sank. Dividing a coral's diameter by 31 – its maximum age in years – gives us the minimum average yearly growth rate. We'll also mark and measure small corals and return later to see how much they've grown. Once we've established a new starting point, measurements can be made at any time to see how fast – or how slowly – these corals grow."

As Al photographed, Kimiuo and I set about measuring and tagging. We encountered some unexpected giants among the corals. The largest, a species of *Stylophora*, grew like a chrysanthemum on the bow gun of *Fujikawa Maru*, supporting a thriving community of small fish, crabs, polychaete worms, and algae. More than five feet across, it had clearly increased its diameter at an average rate of no less than two inches a year.

An exceptionally large black-coral tree of the genus *Antipathes* grew in 60 feet of water on the starboard side of the ship. In my years of diving I have seen many examples of this commercially valuable coral, but most were in deep water and few exceeded a height of three or four feet. This specimen stood 15 feet high. Many of our measurements, in fact, exceeded those for the same kinds of corals elsewhere in the world.

To gain insight into short-term growth rates, I cleared a number of areas on several ships to bare metal, including a section of anchor chain, portions of rails and beams, several patches on decks, and a ring around the barrel of *Fujikawa Maru*'s stern gun. Within a few hours reddish-brown rust filled each of the cleared places. In time the living mantle that I removed will be replaced, and growth rates based on a new starting point can be established.

Live Shells Not the Only Dangers

Each day I became more fascinated as I worked with this beauty-and-the-beast paradox. Deadly weapons, tanks, and trucks were frosted with pink-and-white plants, sponges, sea squirts, and corals. A blue sponge indifferently covered the nose of an artillery shell 18 inches in diameter, one of several in a disorderly mound of ammunition in a hold of the freighter *Yamagiri Maru*. I admired the sponge but felt a ripple of apprehension as I touched the point upon which it grew, recalling that these shells had been intended for the giant guns of the Japanese battleships *Musashi* and *Yamato*. Each, when fired, had a range of more than 20 miles.

It remained for something with far less range – a mere two inches – to cause my most anxious and painful moments in Truk Lagoon. During several dives on *Fujikawa Maru* I observed a lionfish (*Pterois volitans*) that had taken up residence in the ship's stern gun. Lionfish are beautiful, but notorious for the painful, even deadly, stings they can inflict with their venomous spines.

I mentioned the lionfish to Al and he decided to photograph it, so we dived together to the gun, 70 feet down. The lionfish, however, refused to cooperate and remained half hidden inside a crevice. At length I decided to try and maneuver it out into the open, something I have done in the past, though with great caution.

Inching forward, I eased my hand along the fish's tail. It responded to my gentle motion and began moving into the open. Then it did something I had not anticipated: It made an abrupt tilt in my direction with its dorsal spines, a defensive motion. I waited a moment before moving again, but the fish was evidently alarmed, for it tilted again.

That was enough for me. I started to withdraw my hand, but the lionfish suddenly tilted once more, this time vigorously, and through my diving glove I felt a sharp jab below the nail of one finger. I'm sure I only imagined a look of self-righteousness on my attacker as it darted away. Removing the glove, I examined my finger and saw a trickle of green – blood, as it appears more than 50 feet below the surface.

An Hour Seems an Eternity

I was in trouble and I knew it. This was our second dive of the day, and we required an hour's decompression before surfacing in order to avoid the bends – the painful, and in some cases fatal, formation of nitrogen bubbles in the bloodstream.

Al escorted me to a point ten feet below the surface and

watched intently to see if my reaction to the lionfish's venom became serious. As pain began to spread through my hand, I tried to entertain myself by watching a graceful school of small damselfish flow around *Fujikawa Maru*'s stern mast. Never before had I tired of the sight of their electric-blue forms, but within ten minutes I closed my eyes and could think of nothing but the intense, stabbing agony that was building in my finger. Only twice before had I known such pain: briefly, in a dentist's chair, and during childbirth.

Tears came. I wanted to cry out, but with a regulator in my mouth and ten feet of water over my head, I could only remain silent.

After 45 minutes my finger had swelled to nearly double its normal size, and my arm and shoulder began to ache as well. But finally, as the hour ended, the sensation of fire began to diminish. Al helped me aboard and the worst of my ordeal was over. But the burning in my finger continued for two more hours, and tenderness and swelling were evident for several days.

From *Fujikawa Maru* we turned our attention to *San Francisco Maru*, an armed munitions transport that had been proposed for demolition. One morning Al and I asked Kimiuo to guide us to the wreck.

San Francisco Maru rests in 250 feet of water, substantially deeper than most divers would care to venture. The 30-minute excursion we planned required double tanks, and Al placed additional cylinders on the deck of the dive boat with regulators and long hoses attached for mid-water decompression.

The ship proved invisible from the surface. It was not until we approached the 100-foot level that its eerie outline appeared – perfectly oriented, upright and fully intact. Three small tanks and a truck were neatly in place on the foredeck, each beautifully embroidered with lacelike plants. Half a dozen more trucks, like metal skeletons in a catacomb, rested on platforms below.

We paused to look at the forward hold filled with hundreds of anti-landing-craft mines festooned with coralline algae, then glided aft and gazed upon row on row of torpedoes and other ammunition carefully stored there. All were secure, potentially explosive, but slowly eroding through the natural combined forces of sea chemistry and time. Ultimately each deadly object will be rendered harmless.

Few people will ever see *San Francisco Maru* and her ghostly cargo, for she rests in such deep water. Yet she, among the sunken ships, most eloquently symbolizes the tragic waste of war. She should remain undisturbed in her ironic final mission – as a laboratory for the study of new underseas life.

Ocean Jewelry Enlivens Long Waits

Long decompression was needed before we could return to the surface, a procedure that became routine but never dull. Occasionally reef whitetip sharks emerged from the green-blue water beneath us, made wide circles, then moved on. Large jacks often rose from the ships below and cruised nearby, apparently as curious about our presence as we were about theirs. Always, there was plankton to watch.

Women who long to be adorned with the world's fairest gems should come with me to Truk Lagoon. Diadems of translucent comb jellies with bands of iridescent cilia passed through my hair as I waited, and I touched chain after chain of fragile, sparkling salps with violet-blue spheres enclosed in a clear, jewel-like mantle. Sometimes, when I moved not at all, the salps became bracelets and necklaces and then drifted on, and more came in their place. Minute medusae, like crystalline beads, pulsed by or lingered when I touched them with my fingertips.

Most dazzling but most unpredictable in their comings and goings were the jellyfish. None of the several species that we encountered irritate human skin, although all are equipped with microscopic armament useful in procuring food. One day the water was so filled with transparent disks that the sea seemed more jelly than liquid. Most were a kind of *Aurelia*, a clear hemisphere laced with four lavender loops, but occasionally an unknown giant the color of lilacs and the consistency of firm aspic rhythmically undulated into view.

Several small jellyfish were accompanied by one or more minute fish that repeatedly thwarted Al's attempt to photograph the team, although he finally managed. "I think the fish watch," Al fumed. "When they know I'm ready to take a picture, they zip to the other side of the jellyfish!"

Sea Salad Gets a Mixed Response

Although often preoccupied with Truk's fascinating animals, I concentrated on the plants associated with the ships. As basic producers, plants set the pace for the number and kinds of animal settlers. If a habitat is suitable only for limited plant growth, then only limited food will be generated to support animals.

Some reef residents are wholly or partially dependent on various kinds of drifting plankton for food, and many corals flourish in combination with certain types of algae. Moreover, whole families of tropical reef fishes and numerous invertebrates graze directly on the local attached plants.

One day aboard the diving boat we were joined by Fumio Meres, a Trukese friend of Kimiuo's. Watching me retrieve my daily harvest of algae in plastic bags, Fumio looked puzzled. Grinning, Kimiuo explained, "She likes that stuff."

Since I am basically a botanist, I make no effort to hide my enthusiasm for plants. Rarely do I eat algae, but in this case I decided to turn the tables on the unsuspecting Kimiuo. I offered to share some freshly collected *Caulerpa racemosa* with him to see if he, too, might "like that stuff".

Kimiuo accepted my green, grapelike offering with some hesitancy. In Japan the alga is gathered for salads, and after a sample or two Kimiuo announced that a little oil and vinegar would improve the slightly salty flavor. But Steve Bowerman, Al's photographic assistant, was less enthusiastic. After a single mouthful he declared, "I'll take the oil and vinegar, and you can keep your *Caulerpa!*"

In the course of our diving I counted more than a hundred species of green, red, and brown algae, including 15 previously unknown in Micronesia. One minute red plant is a new genus of alga. Its closest relatives, independently discovered only last year in California, Australia, and the Comoro Islands in the Indian Ocean, have yet to be named – a small example of how much remains to be learned about the myriad plants and animals in the sea.

The most abundant and conspicuous plants on the sunken ships in Truk Lagoon were species of segmented green algae known as *Halimeda*. These plants hang on the ships' masts, sprout on the ladders, adorn the guns, lace the beams, and grow in extraordinary abundance on the decks. Adjacent to *Fujikawa Maru* the seafloor is literally paved with a thick sediment composed almost solely of dead *Halimeda* fragments, which we called chips.

Numerous small animals, characteristic of the lagoon floor, had taken up residence in the chips on *Fujikawa Maru*'s deck. They flourished like penthouse dwellers, 50 to 75 feet above their seafloor neighbors. Once, while digging among the chips near the stern, I displaced an elongated fish, a goby with spots and large eyes (below). I stopped digging and looked for others, and soon spotted 13 burrows close by. As I watched, I was amused to see a "bulldozer shrimp" scuttle from a burrow, pushing a load of chips.

Later, Al returned with Kimiuo to film the curious fish–crustacean association. Kimiuo was laughing when he came to the surface. "That fish!" he said. "He's the *boss*. The shrimp does all the work. The fish just sits there and supervises!"

The "boss" fish and shrimp were not the only chip dwellers. Occasionally I glimpse two or three ephemeral blue fish among the chips, each nearly five inches long; they seemed to dissolve as I approached. We found the same fish at a depth of a hundred feet, living in holes on the side of *Rio de Janeiro Maru*, a prewar passenger liner that had been converted to a troop transport.

One hole harbored 26 fish. They hovered several feet above the hole until a diver or large fish came near. Then, as if being poured down a funnel, all disappeared into the narrow opening. We sat quietly and watched, and within a few minutes heads reappeared, then a "morning glory" of fish blossomed from the ship's hull.

Intrigued about the identity of these fish and curious to know more about their habits close at hand, I used a small amount of quinaldine to anesthetize three specimens and eventually returned them alive to ichnyzological colleagues at the Steinhart Aquarium in San Francisco's Golden Gate Park. They were identified as *Ptereleotris heteropterus*, a fish that is rarely collected, dead or alive, and one that has never before been displayed in a public aquarium.

New Food Chain Starts With Plants

Plants, typically, are pioneers on sunlit surfaces newly introduced into the sea, whether warships, bottles, or old boots. Most of these plants grow rapidly, providing food and shelter for small animals, which in turn give sustenance to larger animals. When we arrived at Truk Lagoon 31 years after the ships settled to the seafloor, complex food chains were in evidence, originating with the plants. Hundreds of parrotfish, blennies, rudderfish, and certain damselfish species were conspicuously browsing on algae. In turn, these fish were food for larger resident predators, such as groupers, jacks, snappers, and barracudas. Above these were the roving, top-of-the-food-chain predators – giant oceanic tuna that occasionally cruised by, sleek and swift, or the slower but more ominous whitetip and gray reef sharks.

Among the most vigorous and persistent of the small predators were the red-speckled hawkfish that seemed to gather around the masts of *Fujikawa Maru* and a submerged munitions freighter, *Sankisan Maru*. Once I was drawn to vigorous hawkfish activity around a clear gray patch of eggs on one of the masts. At first I thought the hawkfish were doing their utmost to care for the eggs, but when I looked closely, I saw that the eggs belonged to a distraught damselfish and that the hawkfish were devouring them.

One patch of eggs laid on a truck tire and guarded by a pair of clownfish fared considerably better. I first noticed the eggs on 21 June in the form of a glossy black disk beneath a flap of the giant anemone in which the clownfish resided. Six days later I looked again at the egg patch, and was startled to see that it had changed from black to glistening silver. When I looked *very* closely, I could see two tiny silver-rimmed eyes in each transparent egg sac. The next day the cases were empty.

Cabins and Corridors Pose New Dangers

Moving from the outside of the sunken ships, Al and I began to explore their inner recesses to record cave-dwelling organisms that had taken up residence in the rooms once used by men. Such diving can be dangerous, for clouds of fine silt rise with the slightest movement, quickly reducing visibility to a few inches. Even with the help of a powerful light one's orientation becomes confused, and with a limited air supply at 90 feet there is little time to correct errors.

On one of our first such dives we explored the crew's quarters of *Shinkoku Maru,* an oil tanker with phenomenal numbers of corals thriving on her decks. In addition to Al's normal photographic gear we carried a thousand-watt light connected to a surface generator. While Al and I entered the crew compartment, Kimiuo stood by the light cable at the entrance to the passageway.

Inside we found that the ceiling had collapsed, exposing wires, pipes, and other fixtures. A layer of black oil inches above my head glistened and moved eerily as our air bubbles mixed with it. Several fragile, papery bivalves filled a high corner, and chalky white *Arca* shells lodged in the decaying walls. Red squirrelfish, normally confined to dark crevices by day, reacted only slightly to our presence. One peered out of a cabinet filled with teacups, plates, and bowls, all decorated with a rising sun and anchor insignia.

At the entrance of an adjoining compartment Al flashed his light inside and I noticed three unusual transparent shrimp with red markings on them. Collecting net in hand, I started through the hatch, when Al gently touched my arm and pointed to some human bones in the compartment, pathetic reminders of the 1944 holocaust.

Sobered, we slowly retraced our way back to the entrance, where Kimiuo, faint sunlight, and a garden of soft corals greeted us. At the surface once more, I recalled the blossomlike clusters of soft corals growing on the ship below and remarked to Al, "The sea tends her graves well."

Danger From Cargo and Leaking Fuel?

Our six weeks of work in Truk Lagoon gave us new insights into many aspects of reef ecology. A new genus and several new species of plants, records on coral growth, food chains, habits of fishes and invertebrates, and data reinforcing the significance of substrate – all were evidence of a rewarding and productive expedition. The most significant contribution may not be single discoveries, however, but rather the overall basic documentation that can be developed in years to come.

Numerous questions remain unanswered concerning the ecology of Truk Lagoon. One of immediate and urgent concern may affect the fate of the lagoon's underwater archipelago of ships: How significant is the impact of oil seepage and contamination by other cargo with respect to the lagoon environment?

One of our final dives resolved my doubts. It involved a 40-minute inspection of *Amagisan Maru*, a large freighter lying in 200 feet of water and still leaking small quantities of fuel. Even as we anchored above the ship, we noted two kinds of fuel rising to the surface. One type, apparently oil from the ship's own

bunkers, began as a rainbow-hued circle that spread until
dissipated by action of the surface waves. Another kind – most
likely volatile aviation fuel – spread with a shimmer of blue, red,
and gold, then contracted and disappeared in a few seconds.

Donning twin air tanks, Al and I went overboard and glided
down on *Amagisan Maru*'s bridge area. There we found the
ship's compass intact and a magnificent brass telescope, both
remarkably free of corrosion or encrustation.

I became engrossed in a kind of minute red alga, growing in a
barely illuminated crevice, and failed to notice that Al had
disappeared into a passageway. When I looked up, he was
emerging with an object that might have come from Poseidon's
personal art collection – a stark-white porcelain vase with an
outline of pine boughs and mountains raised in delicate relief.
For a moment I held it in my hand, turning it and enjoying the
combined beauty of what it was and where it was. Then I
returned it to Al, who put it back where he had found it.

Outside, on the flat surface of the ship's hull, we located the
vent from which golden globules of fuel were escaping. I moved
to the edge of the ten-inch pipe and peered in, just as a dozen
spheres of oil bubbled forth, floating upward till they disappeared from sight. Immediately surrounding the vent and lining
its sunlit upper end, we noted a profuse tangle of algae, corals,
and sponges, apparently unaffected by the emerging oil.

Ships' Future Still Uncertain

Later, as I clung to the decompression lines beneath our diving
boat, I contemplated the future of the giant ship below me.
Surely, the best course of action concerning her cargo is *no*
action. The gradual dispersion of fuel over the years should
have little or no damaging consequences, but releasing massive
amounts all at once would without question be detrimental to
the marine life.

That evening Al and I discussed the fate of the munitions ship
San Francisco Maru with Kimiuo, and we all concurred: Her

cargo is not dangerous if left untouched. The picric acid now locked in the unexploded mines will seep into the sea harmlessly through gradual corrosion, but detonation of those mines would have severe impact on the lagoon. Salvage techniques are dangerous, expensive – and in this case, unnecessary.

The destruction or modification of even one of the ships in Truk's underwater archipelago would mean lost opportunities for scientists, historians, and the many who in future years may benefit from that monument to the destruction of war.

What will become of the porcelain vase, the telescope, the peaceful undersea tombs, the living corals and plants? What of the ships themselves and the promising research now just begun? How can all this best be protected?

To us, the answer is clear: Nature is achieving the goals men seek. May we have the patience not to interfere.

". . . the utter silence in which the underwater wall
collapsed on me was intimidating"

THE HUNT FOR *MARY ROSE*

Alexander McKee

The Mary Rose, *flagship of King Henry VIII of England, was*
sunk off Portsmouth by French action on the balmy Sunday of 19
July 1545. More than six hundred English sailors went down with
her, "drowned like rattens". King Henry, who was watching the
engagement from shore, its said to have cried like a maid over his
"gallant men".

Almost immediately there was a salvage attempt, using ships as
pontoons, but this failed, leaving divers – presumably with diving
bells – to recover some miscellaneous ordnance. For 291 years the
wreck of the Mary Rose *lay undisturbed, but in 1836 she was*
sighted and explored by the famous salvage diver John Deane,
whose invention of the diving helmet, with its attached air hose, was
one of the great breakthroughs in underwater exploration. Deane
recovered numerous guns and artefacts, but interest in the Mary
Rose *wreck dwindled, and it was commonly believed that Deane*
had broken the wreck up. In the face of this assumption, the diver
and historian Alexander McKee set out to prove that a mound he
had discovered on the Solent floor was indeed the wreck of Henry
VIII's flagship:

Our amazing armada first sailed out to Spithead on 5 July 1969,
and took about two hours to get there, on top of an hour or so's
loading; and, of course, a couple of hours back, and an hour's
unloading. And when out there, it took time to anchor up so that

the boats rode above the point on the seabed where I wanted to dig. At least the boats cost nothing. They were frail pontoons about 18 feet long, propelled by low-powered outboard motors; one was loaned by Southsea BS-AC, the other by the College of Technology in Portsmouth, on a regular basis – once a week on a Saturday. As some Saturdays were spring tides, and others blew a gale, we managed about two days per month, with six hours of each working day perforce spent unproductively, coming and going at about three knots, loading and unloading. It didn't need a gale to stop us, for the Fire Brigade pump had to to be mounted precariously, high up on one of the frail pontoons, and often our hearts were in our mouths when a sudden breeze blew up. But as our total finances had now reached a peak of £4 – from the proceeds of a lecture and the contribution of one well-wisher – there was nothing to be done but get on with it.

I dived first that day, to mark up the mound, and then two 50-lb weights had to be lowered to the digging position in order to anchor the water jets, which otherwise would whip about the seabed like demented serpents, dragging the divers with them. Then, as team succeeded team, they reported progress to the surface by a telephone line which was combined with the airline of the leader's surface-demand set. They dug a six ft. by six ft. trench along the mound for 15 feet and, once they had dug themselves six feet into the seabed there was no visibility at all. I noted in my log:

> While trenching, Clark found an object six feet down which he gave to Parr to hold. It slipped out of Parr's grasp and fell into the trench and was lost. Parr said it was wood, and this was reported to us on the surface, so we had high hopes for a moment. On intercom, George said there were wonderful photographs to be obtained of the mud welling up; so I put on the tads and joined him.
>
> George appeared to be swimming forward with a heaving motion through the seabed, immersed to the shoulders in the trench, and towing intercom line (orange), surface-demand line (black) and the hose (white-grey canvas). No difficulty in

seeing these, because the bulk of the mud did not rise high at once, but welled from around his shoulders. It was like looking down from an aeroplane on a man walking jerkily through the clouds, with only his head and shoulders visible. A kind of off-grey, slow-swirling pattern of convoluted circles, evolving in slow motion from around George's head and shoulders as he dug the trench forward. He had a peculiar kind of bounding motion, half-swimming, half-walking, with this immense, intricately entwined mud pattern unrolling around him. It was extraordinarily beautiful, particularly when the silver bubbles burst up through the slow-motion patterns of the welling mud.

At the end of the day, Morrie Young noted that in the very deepest part of the trench a layer of stratification had been exposed, consisting of light shell and grit. This suggested an old seabed, possibly the Tudor one. In conjunction with the timber found at that depth, it looked as if we might have hit the disturbance area around the *Mary Rose*, for probing revealed no structure. But what sort of structure were we likely to find? There were two theoretical alternatives, based on depth of burial initially. Either it could have collapsed by stages as the upper parts were eaten and eroded away, leaving a partly flattened-out hull, or a deeply-buried hull might have been strong enough to retain its original shape, the unburied part only being eaten and eroded away to leave, in a steeply-heeled ship, a virtually one-sided wreck open on that side like a doll's house. Because his knowledge of ship structure and its weaknesses was so much greater than mine, Morrie undertook to work out a theoretical collapse sequence, while I explored the optimistic alternative of the "W" feature being a sonar reflection of the slanted decks and supports of a hull heeled at 45 degrees, cut off at a point I still had to determine. I also produced a site plan based on the many "pinger" runs along known transits, as a guide to deciding where it might be best to dig trial trenches. These would not be where the "W" came closest to the surface, at the south end of the site, because a shallow excavation would expose the remains to the destructive action of anchors, trawls and oyster dredges.

The summer of 1969 proved to be the best for ten years with underwater visibility up to 25 feet at Spithead, 40 feet at more favoured places off the Isle of Wight. In July we made three more sorties, having to turn back only once. George Clark and the other firemen began to instruct the rest of the team in the use of the water jets. A trained fireman using a branch and hose was one thing, but there had to be modifications for those lacking experience. One of those who took most readily to the method was Dick Millerchip, an aircraft engineer:

> I vividly recall one memorable dive. It was in the earliest days of the fire pump, which was lashed to the deck of our dive boat with twin hoses dangling over the side. I was down on the seabed, holding the nozzle, when the signal was given to switch on. I was immediately propelled to the surface by the force of the water, still clutching the nozzle. Never before or since, have I arrived at the surface from 50 feet in such a short time. It was hilariously unsatisfactory.
>
> The next step was to attach heavy weights to the nozzle by means of short lines, as a basic anchorage to prevent me losing control. My recollection is of one half-hundredweight sinker on about three feet of line. We then prepared for another trial! The signal was again given and the pump restarted. This time, although straining at its tether, it was crudely controllable.
>
> The results were quite dramatic. As the jet of water cut into the clay, visibility was immediately reduced to zero and one could only hang on and hopefully direct the jet at the clearance area. After ten or fifteen minutes the pump was stopped and the tide permitted to clear away the clouds of mud: one could then see the incredible results of this primitive but highly effective method of seabed excavation.
>
> This early dive was mainly experimental, to arrive at the most manageable weight and length of line required to effect a satisfactory anchorage.

Later, I introduced a weighted guide rail which both tethered the jet and indicated direction. The trenches tended to "smoke" for some time after digging had ceased and even after a week or more were very sensitive to water movement, belching up sediment if ships went overhead or a diver finned hard. They also tended to fill up with dense accumulations of the loose weed which circulates in masses at certain times of the year. After a short time they collected a permanent population of fish – the pretty, black-and-silver-striped whiting pout to begin with, then the big, green pollack as well – species which previously we saw only around wrecks and in rock areas. These were the most prominent colonizers of the trench, but there were many others.

I was ready to try anything once, but when first offered the use of a crane-grab dredger turned it down as probably too brutal for archaeology. But what we were doing was only the first stage – stripping off the overburden. At the second time of offering, I accepted, by then knowing much more of the composition and depth of the soil laid down since Tudor times. The dredger was 180 feet long and the depth of dig could be pre-set by the crane operator. By using a gravity-powered mud grab, a surprising amount of sensitivity could be obtained; so much so, that I feared this grab might not penetrate the consolidated layer of grit and shell which, we now knew, could be found some six feet down. The dig revealed an interesting, if expected, pattern. From the top layer came slipper limpets, indignant hermit crabs and un-speakable sponges. There were few artefacts in the first five feet, but under that was a distinct layer of anchorage 'gash', mainly modern, similar to that which lay unburied on the harder *Royal George* site: a strip of lead, a concreted staunch-ion, clay pipes, pottery, animal bones, and an enormous glass jug. In two days we removed 480 cubic yards of overburden and only once did I ask the crane driver to penetrate the shell and grit layer. The immediate result was a very old elm plank, holed by gribble, and found loose; exactly what one would expect to lie on and around the wreck of the *Mary Rose*.

A team of helmet divers from Portsmouth Dockyard, led by Mr S. J. Utley, offered their services; and I gladly accepted. With aqualungs we had to change over shifts of two men every twenty minutes, and in near zero visibility, whereas only one helmet diver was required on a jet, and he could stay one or two hours at a time, if necessary. He could also make himself heavy at will, was in telephone communication with the surface and would almost certainly survive a cave-in of a trench, whereas an aqualung diver almost certainly would not. Moreover, this team possessed a waterjet of their own which had been designed for the job and was automatically balanced by a reaction device.

Any connection with the organization of land archaeology was purely fortuitous. The helmet divers and their compressor were in one boat, which must be positioned exactly and could not drag its anchor without endangering the diver; while the pump for the water jet was in another boat which had to lie close by; the helmet men had to be guided directly from their boat to the particular part of the seabed where the guide rail was. The closest analogy would be to imagine oneself above a bank of cloud, trying to drop plumb lines on exact spots on the earth below from a couple of barrage balloons kiting about in a gusty wind, while attached to insecurely fixed winches. You cannot, alas, apply the brakes and park on a wave.

However, it all worked perfectly, and I saw Mr Utley's helmet disappear into the green water, the first helmet diver to visit the *Mary Rose* since John Deane in October 1840, almost 130 years before. A continuous stream of air boiled to the surface above him, supplied by the big dockyard compressor roaring away at my ear; in contrast to the bursts of bubbles which mark the breathing rhythm of an aqualung diver. The weather was perfect, with only a slight swell. Then there was a tremendous bang and I saw rubber rings fly out of the compressor before it died. And Utley was fifty feet down, without air. I was immensely relieved to see him rise slowly to the surface and be rapidly hauled in to the side of the boat by his safety line. The irony of the accident was that he had been careful to obtain a newly overhauled compressor instead of the old one his team normally used.

The aqualungers, many of them new recruits and inexperienced with jets, had to carry on the job alone; but briefed by George Clark, they succeeded. On my last dive of the day, at sunset, I found myself four feet below the seabed with the side of the excavation above me, like a moonscape without shadow, until the striped pout moved in so close-packed that I couldn't even see water, let alone seabed or trench. Outside my mask was simply a wall of living fish. We had all suffered from the insidious "clay psychosis", the deep conviction that nothing would shift enough of the seabed this side of Christmas. But now we had a continuous trench for the full 38 feet of the guide rail, five feet wide, three feet deep at one end, six feet deep at the other. We could probe for contacts along it.

As a further boost to our morale, the Royal Engineers Diving School at Marchwood, near Southampton, had offered to run their next advanced course for diving supervisors at Spithead, using a massive one-ton airlift with an eight-inch diameter tube powered by a gigantic compressor. Through no fault of theirs, or ours, this excellent plan became less promising. They had to alter their dates, and most of our divers who had arranged to take unpaid time off work could not alter at short notice. Instead of a low-profile "Z" craft mounting a mobile Coles crane to suspend the airlift and move it about, they had to use a high-sided RPL without a crane; with bow doors down, this 74 ft.-long landing craft made an excellent diving platform, but it caught the wind and kept veering about; and when we asked for moorings from another authority, we were refused. On the first day, fog delayed everything, followed by mechanical troubles. But the next day was 21 October, when Portsmouth celebrates Trafalgar Day: a good omen, we hoped.

For an hour or two the RPL held position. First, I tried a delimitation hole on the Isle of Wight side of the "W" feature; the airlift went in 17 feet in a few minutes, when the air was turned off to avoid a blockage – a firm negative. Then I had the

RPL dropped back towards Southsea so that it lay over the outskirts of the disturbance area. Sergeant Ferguson, the R.E. diver, dug a funnel-shaped cavity to eight feet and then came up to report trouble. Pete Powell, from Southampton BS-AC, guessed that the airlift had been stopped by something solid and went down with a manual corer made by Morrie Young. Lying head down in the cavity, he put the corer into the solid and brought up a sample of it – splinters of dark wood mixed with tiny shellfish. Lance-Corporal Flannigan was next; after digging a bit, he probed in a circle: "I got solid – solid – solid every time. Not a plank, but definitely solid timber." Then the RPL veered with the wind and tide and dragged the airlift out of the hole.

Next day, the RPL hung perfectly positioned for three hours during which the airlift broke down three times and was three times repaired. Only one useful cavity was dug, in which Percy Ackland of Southampton BS-AC used a hammer to drive home a probe into some soft solid, perhaps an iron concretion, he thought. The last two days of "R.E. Week" were ruined by high winds.

The last chance of the year was on 2 November, exhausting in further boat fees the last pennies of the £50 which had financed the season's work. I planned to use aqualungers *en masse* to probe for shallow contacts less than six feet down, and helmet divers with a waterjet to expose anything they found. I led off myself, followed by Ackland and Powell.

> The buoy was bucking and smashing and throwing up white water, the chain was shaking and jerking all the way down. Visibility on bottom a very clear 12 feet. Water warm for November.

South of our main trench I found a subsidiary excavation made by the dredger, some three or four feet deep – and in the bottom of it my hand spear went in full-length the first time, and stopped two or three feet down the second time. Exactly the easy depth required, which could be cleared during a short winter's day! Around it, Peter Powell got no contacts even eight feet down. This did not mean that it was not structure, because a wreck rarely presents a flat surface upwards. We then marked it up so that a water jet and weight could be lowered to it – an action I was bitterly to regret. I should have ordered an immediate hand-dig, less thorough but much simpler.

It was blowing Force 6 with high waves and white horses, but the two boats were riding easily together at their anchors – one boat carrying the helmet divers and their compressor, the other holding the aqualung divers and the fire pump. The contact was securely buoyed, the weight was down, and a Chichester fireman, Andy Gallagher, was swimming out the hose to the buoy. Perhaps the extra drag caused it, perhaps the veering breeze; or both together. With shocking suddenness, the pump boat went out of control, dragging her anchor to port. Tony Glover, our skipper, started his engine and put the wheel hard over, but there was no observable effect. It seemed that the pump boat must collide with the helmet divers' boat. That was the least of it, for Andy Gallagher was down on the seabed in what must now be a tangle of swinging, dragging lines; and the pump would probably be pulled bodily out of the boat on top of him.

Instantly, George Clark uncoupled the hose from the pump. With equal speed, some of the divers snatched the yellow line leading to the 56-lb weight beside the contact, and threw it out over the sea to the men in the helmet divers' pinnace, who caught it. We still had a line to the contact from a boat, plus a bottom line from a marker buoy. What we did not know was that the anchor of the pump boat had dragged across in a crazy tangle, with Andy Gallagher in the middle of it. By quick thinking, 45 feet down, he escaped and reached the white-capped sea. We roared out to him to swim down tide to a marker buoy and hold on to it. Then Dick Millerchip went racing by in his inflatable and with Leslie Lemin leaning right over the side they picked Andy out of the water, very flushed, excited and pleased with himself.

Mr Utley sent a helmet diver down at once and I jumped from the pump boat to the pinnace to listen to the crackling telephone as his diver reported: all lines carried away, my contact no longer marked. Back to square one. I put in Percy Ackland to make another search and against all odds, by following the drag marks through the mud, he found the contact; but he was out of air, so he gave the distance line to his companion to secure. But here the drawbacks to the aqualung showed: divers cannot talk to each other and they are blinkered like horses. His friend had not even seen the drag marks and did not understand that the contact crater had been relocated. So he just carried on swimming.

And that really was that, for 1969. But no one wanted to pack up yet, so I suggested a general survey of the excavated area to take note of any changes that might occur during the winter. For George Clark and myself, this meant the luxury of a dive instead of controlling events from the surface. George went first.

There was a great swell running, and although I had carried out one dive, I felt the last place for me was down on the seabed. However, by this stage of the project we had a fairly long trench several feet deep running in the direction which Mac felt would lie across the wreck. I was swimming along this trench, glad to be off the rolling boat, when I saw through the murky water what I thought was a large piece of newspaper lying against the trench. I slowly swam over to it and much to my surprise it was an enormous flatfish. I almost burst with excitement. I stopped breathing and was frightened to move for fear of spooking this fish. If I told my pals above about this monster of the deep, no doubt they would think it a fishy tale!

I slowly passed the tube of Morrie Young's auger through my hands, hoping I could impale the fish with it, only to find that I had the wrong end of the pipe. By sheer luck the fish remained motionless as I laboriously handled the pipe to get the other end. I aimed at the bit beneath the head and then placed it into the fish, screwing it into the mud. The creature went berserk and the slightly clouded water erupted into a big violent cloud of black ink. Visibility had completely gone and

I was plunged into darkness. I managed to get my hands on the fish which was now well and truly impaled and flapping about like a Vulcan bomber. Slowly I made my way to the surface where the boat was prancing up and down like a wild horse at a rodeo.

When they saw me wrestling with a 10-lb turbot, one of the divers managed to come down the boarding ladder and take the fish inboard.

I missed this spectacle, because I was already absorbed in my last inspection dive of the year. When I surfaced, Force 8 was almost upon us; we would never get back to Langstone Harbour by sea, so our boats fled for the shelter of Portsmouth Harbour. George Clark was good enough to write later that, "There was no doubt whatever that had it not been for Mac's enthusiasm and drive the whole project would have been dropped long ago; his perseverance has kept it alive." Actually it worked both ways: the team spirit and determination shown on days like this encouraged me to continue when, as happened now and then, everything seemed hopeless.

It seemed that 1970 might be such a year. We lost George Clark, the Fire Brigade chief, sent off on a three-months course; we lost Mr Utley, the leader of the helmet divers, drafted for three years to Gibraltar; we seemed likely to lose Lieutenant Bob Lusty, drafted to HMS *Reclaim* as diving officer to replace a casualty; and I learned in April that the person who was supposed to be making our application in March to Portsmouth City Council for a £100 grant, had failed to do so at all, let alone in time.

These setbacks only made us the more determined. A baker's dozen of us decided to band together as the Mary Rose Association, paying all costs out of our own pockets. We were able to do this because of an offer from Tony Glover for the use, one day a week at cost, of his boat *Julie-Anne*, which amounted to £7 10s. od. (compared to the £20–£25 a day such a boat would normally cost). As it was licensed for 12 people only, we all agreed to pay a minimum of 10/- per trip, the difference if any to be made up by myself. *Julie-Anne* was a converted *Queen Mary* lifeboat with plenty of open space at the back for mounting heavy machinery, stowing cylinders and kitting up, while the forward end gave semi-covered protection out of the wind for half-frozen, damp divers. Also, it was based at Flathouse Quay in Portsmouth Harbour, about four miles from the site, thus avoiding the long, slow haul round from Langstone Harbour which had in the past cost us so much precious working time. Tony, however, did not get quite what he expected.

> I saw an article in the Portsmouth *Evening News* by Alexander McKee about this old wreck, saying he could not get a boat to take them out; so I phoned him. He then told me they never had a lot of funds available. Anyway, I thought I would make lots of money with all the "pieces of eight" that might come up. I quickly realized what I was into: lifting compressors and water pumps onto my boat; other boats tied alongside; the compressor shaking my boat to pieces; and the biggest headache – anchors that would not hold in the soft mud. This was a problem every time; then I laid some moorings on site and this helped.

We still had no permission to lay buoys as surface moorings or mark the site in any way; it had to be laboriously rediscovered every time. As a temporary expedient, I now laid "drowned" moorings. Morrie Young made the concrete blocks, someone else supplied the wire hawsers to connect them in a line, another source supplied the manila which, when picked up, we would take to the surface for Tony to tie on. No more problems with anchors dragging, but the ropes had to be visually located by diver search; in visibilities often of only two or three feet, this also could be time-wasting. On 16 May the new moorings were laid and the trench inspected after the winter. It had filled in only slightly with soil. On 30 May I had the trench staked out with numbered rods at measured intervals, and further probing produced more contacts in it, which were marked up with lettered rods.

Andy Gallagher's contact was the shallowest, only two feet below the bottom of the trench which was five feet deep at that point. I sent down a succession of divers to expose it by hand-digging. Several took samples in case by some dreadful mischance – to which we had become accustomed – we lost it again. One diver reported: "We are not going to get any more off today – best to open up a bit more. It's a deck beam, I think. I should say it's part of the ship."

I dived at six in the evening. In the floor of the trench was a further excavation four feet deep, and dark in the dim light. As I sank down into the hole I did not expect to see much, so it was quite a feeling when for the first time my eyes focused on wood. Some five feet of timber about a foot wide was exposed there, both ends continuing in to the faces of the excavation, and part of it already lightly dusted over with sediment. The last diver had dug down beside the timber and then excavated underneath, so that I could see plainly that it was a plank, not a beam, a number of trenail holes showing where it had been pegged to a ship's frames. I wrote in my log:

> My impression was that this was not part of the ship's structure in situ, but a piece broken off or collected.

This turned out to be the case. Morrie Young thought the stagger of the fastenings indicated frames of approximately 12-inch siding; about right for the *Mary Rose*; and so it proved, in due course.

We spent three days carefully excavating around the plank before we lifted it, to determine its context; there was some evidence for a scourpit having existed at that point. To dig out the ends meant working into walls of clay and mud some eight feet high, mostly with our hands and a spade. Once, a partial collapse lightly buried my legs, but this was more alarming than dangerous; nevertheless, the utter silence in which the underwater wall collapsed on me was intimidating. There was no warning at all. After the plank had been raised I made a last inspection and found that the lads, assisted by my daughters, had played a joke on me. There, standing on the edge of the trench, was one of those well-known road signs depicting a man with a spade. A minute inspection of the bed where the plank had lain produced only a single artefact – a car key belonging to the diving officer of Southsea BS-AC. He was relieved to get it back.

The plank, which was badly eroded and showing marks of gribble and massive teredo attack, was drawn, photographed and expended scientifically. The better preserved end was to go to Margaret Rule's laboratory at Fishbourne for conservation tests with polyethylene glycol, the end most massively infested by teredo was to go to Patrick Board of the Central Electricity Research Laboratories who had developed extraordinarily fine techniques for X-raying teredo tunnels so that the habits of what is in fact a mollusc, not a worm, could be studied accurately. The sawing in two of the plank, which had the look and feel of soft, black, flaky cheese, produced the first surprise, for as the blade bit deep, there came an unexpectedly harsh noise – and sawdust! The second surprise was when the X-rays revealed not merely the species of mollusc – *Nototeredo norvavica* – but the remains of an actual specimen in one of the tunnels, probably the oldest teredo in existence. Lying underneath the plank we had found part of a ship's lantern dated to around 1700, suggesting that the scourpits were active even then. As teredo is very rare in the Solent area today, the evidence pointed to a change in the local underwater environment.

The next contact I decided to investigate was nearer to Southsea and the "W" feature in what was now a 100 ft. long trench overlapping it on both sides; this contact was also deeper, but as we had the Fire Brigade with us again, it seemed worth a try. We also had, for one day only, the loan of a miniature airlift for test purposes. This consisted of a 2½ -inch diameter plastic tube 10 feet long, powered by a small compressor which fed air down through a rubber hose to the bottom of the tube. The compressed air should rise up the tube, expanding it as it went, creating a suction effect at the bottom; and, with this size of tube, all our troubles would be little ones. While the jetting went on 50 feet down, I put the airlift over my shoulder like a rifle at the slope, and swam with it down the fire hose leading to the waterjet.

The first sign of the jet work was a white cloud of murk ("whiteout"), which meant trailing one finger along the seabed to try to feel when you came to the trench. Then there was a colour change of the murk from white to black ("blackout"). Occasionally, the whirling cloud broke up and one could look along a kind of tunnel some six feet below the seabed. I stopped for a test. I turned the tap on and compressed air gushed in and began to roar up the tube. I sucked at various distances from the seabed and found that, although the miniature machine could not clear the massive murk being stirred up ahead, it did improve my local visibility, in contrast to the jet, which made the worker blind. When we ceased to deal with mere overburden, the airlift was clearly the tool to use. At this size it was controllable and selective, capable of really delicate work. My logbook notes read:

> I spotted a small crab among the slipper limpets and moved the end of the tube over his back. ZING! BLAM! SWOOSH! and he had gone, taking a fast ride up the tube, and presumably being released in something of a state eight feet up and down tide. Then I started on the slipper limpets, and a stream of them followed the crab heavenwards. WHOOSH! ZING! BLAM! OOUCH!

The power was controllable in no less than two ways. Basically, by turning the tap a little or a lot, but also by varying the height of the tube above the seabed. One could use merely a touch of power, so that the effect on the sediments was minute. The trick was not to let the airlift dig itself into the ground, where it was liable to blockage, but to hold it always above the seabed at the appropriate sucking distance, so that it kept visibility clear while one dug manually. Easy at this size, we should have to learn how to perform the feat with a much larger and more powerful machine.

The contact being dug by the jets at this time was where the main trench was only about $3\frac{1}{2}$ feet deep. By 8 August the shaft being driven towards the contact was at least $3\frac{1}{2}$ feet deeper still, for a width of six feet – a classic cave-in situation. So my next order must be to widen, not deepen. While I was considering this,

> I inspected the walls for stratification. Near the top and some four feet from the original seabed level, there was a marked black discoloration. I took a sample, which felt fibrous to the touch. It proved to be the remains of an old weed bed, and consisted of: weed holdfasts only (no fronds) and some part of their attachments – small fragments of glass mixed with tiny pebbles and molluscs.
>
> This evidence of past organic activity and the presence of some major collection area was "locked in" under at least four feet of mud and clay.

On my second inspection dive, after further digging had taken place, I noticed little puffs of sediment bursting up through the clay, and actually managed to photograph one of these as it erupted. I thought this might be caused by the decaying organic matter building up gas which had been trapped by the clay layer above, until our jets removed most of it and the compressed gas was able to burst through. Suggesting how the weed got there in the first place was easy – all our trenches filled with weed in short order. And a scourpit is only a kind of trench dug by the tides. But wrecks also tend to fill up with this loose weed which drifts across the bottom or just off the seabed. Only a few days before I had been looking down an open hatch in the deck of a First World War German submarine, UB-21, and the boat seemed to be filled entirely by masses of dead weed.

It was entirely possible, I now thought, that the "W" feature shown by Professor Edgerton's pingers might not, strictly speaking, be the *Mary Rose*, but rather a layer of dense, dead weed which had collected in and around her. The ship itself would of course become an attachment surface not only for weed but for many other organisms, particularly oysters, so there would be a growth-and-death sequence lasting perhaps a century or more on the wreck itself.

A week later we had our first full-size airlift built for us by William Selwood Ltd, a plant-hire firm near Southampton. Of six-inch diameter, it was powered by a moderate-sized compressor which was capable of being manhandled into Tony Glover's *Julie-Anne*. The tube was light and semi-flexible and would require a weight to anchor it; it would not of its own weight sit on the seabed and damage artefacts or structure. The first time, it worked like a dream, swiftly cutting trenches with vertical faces. The second time, it seemed to have hardly any effect (being partially blocked); and by now we were down to our last few pounds and the good August weather was almost over. I decided to play last year's two major cards again – two days' work with the crane dredger followed by five days with the Royal Engineers.

Now, with more experience of the use of the mud-grab on the dredger and of the actual soil layers we would be excavating, I first cleared overburden on both sides of the trench, so that it could be widened easily; and then, with caution, began to enter the clay layer. Without damaging them, the grab raised two pieces of ship's timber from this level – part of a teredo-infested "fashion piece" and a large "staghorn", or cleat, which had not been attacked by teredo at all.

On the last of the two days, I decided to excavate deeply into the mound in the area where the concreted iron contact had been located eight feet down by the Royal Engineers the previous year. I had Morrie Young and Percy Ackland with me, to dive if necessary.

At 12.20 a very large concreted object appeared, so big that it was held between the jaws of the grab. Morrie commented later that I went into "a state of shock".

It was many years now since I had dreamed of finding clear, dramatic proof that the site held the wreck of the *Mary Rose* –

some single object, such as a built-up gun or a dead archer, which by itself, on top of the circumstantial evidence, would be conclusive. This object was like a long, thin sausage with knobs on it at intervals. I began to shout to the crane driver to be careful, I thought it was a built-up gun – and immediately found myself trying to explain the difference between "built-up" and "cast". We managed to get ropes round and so lowered it to the deck (instead of dumping it in the hold). There was a slight bump as it touched the deck and about three inches of the concretion broke off, exposing a triple ring of grey metal. The crew looked totally disbelieving: "You don't mean to tell us that's a gun!" they said. But by God it was!

They hosed down the concretion, which was studded with oyster valves, some stained yellow. This was exactly as John Deane had shown in his watercolours. But what did surprise me was the grey-blue, sharp-edged metal exposed where the concretion had broken off. This was exactly the colour of built-up guns shown in Tudor paintings, but from long study of such pieces recovered from the sea, I had come to think of them always in their rusted, degenerate state. What I was looking at now, for about ten minutes before it too rusted over, was the barrel of a built-up gun as it had appeared before the ship sank. However, within five minutes, we became aware of an insistent hissing noise coming from inside the concretion. The gun was not really in mint condition. It had gone through the classic process of deterioration and chemical change set up by immersion in salt water, had been buried and eventually become stable in an oxygen-free environment below the seabed; but now that I had lifted it back into its original environment, the gun was changing again and deteriorating further.

On shore at Southsea Castle, little more than a mile away, was a conservation laboratory used to dealing with guns. I got the dredger's master to radio a message for either Ken Barton or Bill Corney of Portsmouth City Museums:

Have what appears to be built-up iron gun from *Mary Rose*, same size as yours or larger. Collect today at RCY 5 p.m. Bubbling already.

After so many years of being denigrated behind my back as a mad chaser after wild geese, it was with great satisfaction that I saw that message go off.

THREE MILES DOWN

James Hamilton-Paterson

In 1994 James Hamilton-Paterson, a poet and writer, was invited to join a salvage expedition to the Atlantic coast of West Africa, the graveyard of the gold-carrying WWII Japanese submarine, the I-52. To try and locate the I-52 the expeditionaries hired the MIR submersibles of the Russian PP Shirsov Institute of Oceanography. Hamilton-Paterson joined one of the MIR's descents – to 4,828 metres down:

10.10: Inside *MIR I.* Our hatch man removes the conical polythene ring that protects the polished steel face of the rim. The hatch closes on a blue tropical sky and Viktor locks the lugs from within with the central wheel. All exterior sound ceases. Isolation begins. Viktor and Sergei are busy with the pre-dive checklist. It's very hot and cramped and sweaty.

10.15: We're swung out over the side. Even the crane's groaning hydraulics are inaudible. Departing faces: Quentin, Clive, Andrea in her blue jump-suit. She'll be diving in about half an hour. Blue water rushes up over the viewing ports, which are angled downwards. Swell, rocking. Colour and light values are those of a theme-park aquarium. Silvery bubbles, shafts of light as a window rolls partially clear. No fish.

10.30: I've missed the moment when Viktor took on ballast and we began to sink. So many switches being clicked, acoustical telephone crackle from the loudspeaker, general hummings and whooshings.

113 metres. The blue outside my little viewport is of a glowing dusk. It has lost the surface milkiness like rosemary in bloom and is now more the colour of delphiniums. This is about the maximum operational depth of a Second World War submarine: 377 feet and there's still light outside. I don't know why that's so affecting.

218 metres. Past twilight to late dusk. Surprised there's any light outside, but there is. Wish I'd been able to do this before writing *Seven-Tenths*, especially the "Reefs and Seeing" chapter. I also wish they'd turn the lights off inside. The sea's intense violet colour is strangely piercing and I think would steep even the MIR's interior. It's a quality of light I've never quite seen before. It doesn't exist on the earth's surface and perhaps can't even be produced artifically. It does something to the mind which feels like faint genetic meddling. The crew are fettling up Clive's computer, now programmed by demon nerd Nik Shashkov to help us navigate. The Anarchist is wearing his beret, which is the king of its species with a wick on top as thick as a slug of goose shit. From time to time he fluffs out and then preens down his magnificent beard, using the back of one paw like a cat. He catches my eye and smiles. Nothing bad can happen with the Anarchist aboard.

265 metres. I remember that an emperor penguin was once recorded at this depth on an eighteen-minute dive. A bird looking for fish at 870 feet.

10.37: *300 metres.* Midnight outside. In other words still not absolutely lightless. I really got that wrong but there's so little on record to go by. No sensation of falling, though there wouldn't be since we've long since reached our terminal velocity of 30m./minute. Silence. A tiny bead containing us, sinking into night. Like Quentin before me I think of the *I-52* beginning to break up at this depth. At nearly 1,000 feet its rivets would have begun popping and welds tearing. Watertight bulkheads imploding. Black water slamming into every secret recess and compartment, including wherever the gold was kept. Bodies in fragments; some open mouths. We cruise serenely on past, having scarcely begun.

364 metres. The first phosphorescent grains stream upwards beyond the viewport. It's like night diving in the archipelago, familiar and reassuring.

400 metres. It is no longer possible to distinguish the black overhang of syntactic foam (somewhere above us like the MIR's eyebrow) from the surrounding sea – i.e., to my eye all ambient light has gone. Possibly not to someone thirty years younger, though, and certainly not to squid and all the other biota of the Deep Scattering Layer which migrate up and down the water column daily. Viktor sucks toffees and exchanges jokes with Sergei who strokes his beard and plots our course.

10.55: *800 metres.* For me this represents some kind of grand climacteric, a psychic barrier, in that it's the point Beebe and Barton reached – half a mile or so – in 1934 off Bermuda. Beebe was my boyhood hero. He was then 57; I'm now 53. It has taken a long time. Luminous granules still drift upwards, sometimes eddying around the viewport's frame like the lone snowflakes that presage a long storm.

871 metres. Now a few green banners slide past; faint phlegm studded with stars. The crew are communicating with Control about the computer, joking. Their voices and laughter are beginning to echo as they bounce around the water column.

922 metres. Not banners, but sacs containing fiery points. Siphonophores?

11.04: *1 kilometre.* Condensation beginning to bead around the edge of the hatch overhead. Hope it *is* condensation. Quentin said that on his dive Nik Shashkov ran his finger around the connectors where they enter the sphere, then licked it to taste for salt. It's too late to worry. Anyway, water has been known to leak around the edges of *Pisces*'s windows at low pressure, though it stops as you go deeper. They, like the MIRs', are not conventionally sealed. This dry seating of tapered acrylic into steel is technically known as an "interference fit".

11.11: *1,210 metres.* More jellies sidle upwards, one like frozen smoke, another a snake outlined in green dots like a

Greek constellation. Hoffman's Anselmus again and Serpentina and tokens of nameless love. A slow, upward shower of fragments of light.

11.20: *1,461 metres.* The sphere is cooling rapidly. I've just put on another two pairs of socks.

1,517 metres. Oh, the far constellations that enwrap us all the same!

11.42: *2 kilometres.* Still a few sparks and jellies.

11.50: *2,240 metres.* The wandering granules seem to be sparser. As always, one wants to know what it is one *can't* see. Astronomers have their hypothesis of "dark matter" to account for interstellar stuff they can't observe and without which their sums won't come out right. Down here in this placeless place one wonders about the mass of creatures which don't operate at our wavelengths, that must rely on infra-red and pheromones and sounds, to whom this world is no "darker" than that of a bat. Placeless, because no matter how still and suspended the layers seem through which we're descending, each molecule of water making up this "place" is in motion and sooner or later does get its chance to see the sun. They say it takes 250 years for deep water to come to the surface and another 250 for it to sink back down. Everywhere these huge, slow, invisible wheels turning. Caught up in them, we ourselves are nowhere: just at a set of coordinates which not even Sergei could precisely define with Clive's computer on his lap.

12.10: *2,730 metres.* In the last 500 metres we've had lunch: a plastic box each of rolls, cheese, salami, a gherkin and a steak sandwich. Plus hot, sweet coffee in a stainless steel thermos. Apples, chocolate and peanuts to come. The language barrier has been partially solved. The Anarchist speaks German about as well as I do, Viktor marginally less so. All three of us know peanuts as *Erdnüe*, so communication is possible. I'm really sorry I can't understand their jokes with Control. "*Wörterspiel*," says Sergei regretfully. No decent pun could survive translation via two languages.

2,891 metres. The granules seem to have stopped but a faint ghost just passed us like a wisp of interstellar gas.

12.20: *3 kilometres*. There's now a long echo when Viktor talks to Control. Acknowledging their last reply, he always signs off with a double press of the "transmit" button on the microphone. We can hear the two pings clearly on the loudspeaker, like the soundtrack of one of those submarine warfare films. Three kilometres is a meaningless measurement; it could as easily be three thousand. Despite the communications, the glowing computer maps, the sonograms and all the bright switchgear, we're surely lost. Descending without the sensation of descent, beyond reach. Quentin said that passing 100 metres had made him sad for the submarine: that in some unfair way he was stealing a march on that doomed object of half a century ago, soon to be full of water and the collapsed bodies of nearly a hundred young men. That was 300 feet or so. Maybe as a significant figure 300 is to him what 47 is to me: my father's age at his death, the sense that each year by which I go beyond his span is a way of leaving him behind. How fascinated he would have been to sit in this tiny capsule now – he who barely lived to see Sputnik and maybe the dog Laika but not (by seven years) the first Moon landing. And his son – this half-recognisable man now his senior by six years – scribbles and jots and gazes at 3,480 metres, drifting down into nowhere and belonging to a time zone we could call Primordial Galactic, where years as humans recognise them thin out and vanish in a long oblivion.

13.05: *4 kilometres*. Extremest night for considerable stretches, but sporadic dim spores still straggle past. Something bursts against one of the camera brackets outside the viewport and for a frozen moment resembles the tenuous envelope of a supernova millions of light years distant. I suddenly find I can remember the name of the people from whom my parents bought the house I grew up in, in 1948, when I was seven. They were the Harbrows. A name from nowhere, to nowhere, and for no reason. Viktor's voice, enquiring about the Furuno sonar, bounces and fades away as through an endless gallery of metallic baffles, lost on the edge of no known universe.

13.15: *4,212 metres*. Viktor turns on the exterior lights to test them, making of the solid blackness a milky violet fog with a light upward snow of particles. These all appear to have red right-hand edges, a trick of the viewport looked through at an angle. I also remind myself that the optical properties of the tapered acrylic block change as it deforms under pressure (here about 7000 p.s.i.). Lights off again. The visual equivalent of sudden silence.

13.23: *4,400 metres.* Polythene bags of thermal clothing are pulled from various holes and compartments. Struggling into a one-piece padded suit without knocking one of the vital switches is like trying to get into a sleeping bag while lying in a crystal coffin.

13.28: *4,507 metres.* Still an occasional spark keeping us company. The Furuno gives 271 metres to the bottom. It's very cold.

13.55: Exterior lights on. For the first time Viktor kneels forward and leans at the controls beside me. We stare out through the milk. Faintly, faintly, a green lunar surface forms below. An asteroid is swimming upward to meet us.

13.58: *4,828 metres.* Touchdown. Level sediment. A tiny crab scuttles. Otherwise nothing stirs but the heart. Either tears or condensation on my window. I wipe vigorously. I'm looking out over a patch of planet never before seen. Since we're in a sphere, Viktor and Sergei are also looking out of their ports at a view which scarcely overlaps; three people in a single eyeball but with three distinct visions. Nor have the inhabitants of this planet ever seen such lights as the MIR sheds as it squats among the million wormcasts, blazing with energy at all sorts of wavelengths. Everywhere are the tracks of living creatures. A large white fish comes in slowly, head down, from the edge of our penumbra to investigate. It's probably 2–3 feet long with a heavy catfish fore-end and an eel-like tail. Close up, it somewhat resembles a large albino tadpole with scales. It has eyes with two dark markings in front of them which might be infra-red or other sensory organs. Is it attracted by our light? Sound? Smell (molecules of hydraulic oil)? Viktor moves a joystick and we glide off just above the surface at a brisk walking pace. Hardly any motor noise. More like ballooning. Large, blackish-red holothurian with fleshy plume on its back, *Pseudostichopus*. Beautiful red prawns, some the size of langoustines and with jewelled eyes whose retinas sparkle in our lights, beetle past in mid-air (so it seems) on feathered oars. A white/grey starfish. Again I think of night fishing on the sediment beyond the reefs, familiar and friendly.

14.30: There are a lot of floating particles in the water column. Quentin's wrong: it isn't just muck kicked up by the MIR's propellers (as he explained some of the "snow" on the video pictures of his own trip). Down here we're at the benthic boundary layer, where water column meets seabed. Much of the suspended matter drifting past our lights is resuspended partly as a result of the almost imperceptible current but mainly because of the activities of the various fish and animals. It's a slow, infinitely languid world. The particles are known as "nephels". (The word derives from the Greek *nephele*, meaning a cloud).

14.55: We're going round and round on the spot in a whirling ochre fog of our own making while Sergei tries to work out where we are. Occasionally we tack off in one direction or another into the clear, sometimes coming upon our own skid marks in the sediment like UFO tracks on some benighted American desert and giving a similar superstitious jolt that perhaps we aren't alone down here.

16.05: Our target turns out to be a dune. They're very steep, with sharp crests one imagines would have been slumped and flattened by currents and general erosion. Not so. A black, straight line appears ahead – looking amazingly like the edge of a submarine's hull if you happen to be keeping your eye open for one – and the sediment falls steeply away into an abyss. Once we're inside the valley we lose the signals of our navigation beacons which were laid in a pattern of three over this area before we came down.

How benign it feels here! I should like to come and live in a perspex igloo to watch just how the shrimp and fish and floating jellies and echiurid worms co-exist, minding their own business so successfully in this most un-barren place. Almost no scientist ever gets to see what my eyes are so greedily devouring. How, for instance, did Heezen and Hollister write their great descriptive textbook *The Face of the Deep* as early as 1971? So many species remain unidentified, so many behaviours unexplained. Everywhere in the sediment are spoke burrows: a central hole surrounded by a "clock face" of grooves made by the worm whose burrow it is when it flicks out a tentacle or proboscis and hauls in anything which happens to have settled on that patch. But how does it know where it has flicked before? The intervals of the spokes don't form a precisely regular dial, and some are shorter than others, but none ever seem to overlap. Why not? Come to that, there are many tracks in the sediment which are dead straight. How does an animal make a dead straight track in total darkness? No one knows.

16.17: I wonder what it smells of out there.

16.21: I like the silence. Ralph says he plays *The Ride of the Valkyries* at maximum volume on his dives, blasting it into the water column to "freak them out a little up there".

16.25: Viktor says, as if to set my mind at rest, "*Wir haben Pipi-Flasche.*"

16.30: Freezing, streaming metal surfaces. My toes, pressed up against the sphere, ache with cold despite three pairs of socks. The temperature out there is currently 2.31°C. There must be a pocket of particularly cold water; it's normally a pretty uniform 4°C.

17.00: *It isn't the sea.* "The sea" means nothing here. It is not where we are.

4,938 metres. Neither does it feel like an "abyss" or the bottom of anything; it feels like a planet taking place in the head. Nor does it feel contiguous with the nearest continent, unlike Madeira with Cornwall. You can't imagine this surface ever becoming fields or underlying the low, earthen towns of Africa.

18.00: Another matey snack. How does the time go so fast? Viktor drinks only UHT milk from the carton (Lancashire Dairies. Little did it think, the day it was packed in Clitheroe or somewhere, that it would be drunk at 4,791 metres beneath the Atlantic.) He explains that what he *really* likes is UHT milk and Pepsi, mixed 50/50. Is this bizarre admission designed to encourage further confidences? We have a brief conversation about Boris Yeltsin's future and gang warfare in Moscow, where both he and Sergei live.

19.05: No submarine anywhere. We encounter an obviously modern tonic water bottle. Otherwise nothing but the plains and dunes of this marvellous land. I can't believe we've been down for nine hours though it's true that, if asked, I wouldn't be able to guess how long had elapsed. More than twenty minutes and maybe less than twenty years. Not an instant's self-awareness, so not a moment's boredom. The sphere, despite having shrunk 6 millimetres overall seems to have expanded. It's now a large room, a gliding observatory, in which I spend long hours quite alone.

19.41: My birth-year, by chance. I've never encountered a landscape which has conveyed such a strong impression of happening *inside* the eye. Notions of some impartial, objective, "scientific" gaze have never seemed flimsier, less likely. The darkness, our wandering spark of light, the randomly unrolling view of a world happening without me and yet in me, the clear bursts of memory it triggers so that lying on the sand beside a holothurian I saw the name of a schoolfriend I'd loved when we were both about eleven – "one of those sterile but exquisite attachments of boyhood, when nothing is done, nothing even said; and everything taken for granted," as Norman Douglas puts it. A name I'd thought clean forgotten. Yet there it suddenly was, as though incised in the sediment. No wonder this land feels so benevolent: it's been here all along, and so have I. More and more I can't *not* believe in a form of genetic memory. Those millions and millions of years spent in this land before we were driven ashore by predators: surely they must have left their mark? Something that may not even show up as a collection of codons in our DNA but which the complete genome gives off like a whiff of brine?

19.57: This seafloor is really riddled with echiurid worms. I suddenly remember digging for lugworms at Swanage when

I was eight. I also remember a far more recent claim that all sorts of radioactive waste including plutonium gets locked safely into the sediment around the various outfalls of Sellafield. British Nuclear Fuels Ltd.? Nirex? Whoever made the claim didn't know – or hoped the public doesn't know – that echiurid worms like *maximillaria* simply kick it all out again.

20.20: Too much sweet coffee. Having a pee at 4,872 metres, the first in eleven hours, is fabulous. Sooner or later someone's going to say what a pity it was that I didn't happen to dive on a more photogenic site (no black smokers, not even the foothills of an underwater alp). The point about alps is that they are more impressive thought about than viewed by torchlight. You can't see things at any distance under water. Water so readily absorbs light that the sea's topmost 10 metres filter out roughly 90 percent of daylight. Down here maximum visibility with all our exterior lamps on is indeed about 10 metres. There are no panoramas on the seabed. The very nature of sea-water is to make one concentrate on detail: a patch of minerals, the tightly sinuous track of an enteropneust, a single spoke burrow, the light organ of a shrimp. To some extent the observer in his submersible *becomes* a microscope, peering through a thick acrylic lens set in a narrow tube of illumination, with the entire ocean's surrounding black rigidity forming the body of the instrument. It is said of the nineteenth-century poet Annette von Droste-Hülshoff that she had a peculiar optical condition which gave her extraordinary close-up vision. Her friend Levin Schücking described her "almost conical eyeball, such that when she closed her eyes one could see the pupils glitter through her delicate lids". She would wander the shores of Bodensee examining minute shells and grains of sand whose details were lost to any normally-sighted person. They were her worlds within worlds which enraptured her and afforded such a contrast with an outwardly uneventful, even grey, life. Maybe seabed studies should be approached in a similar manner, as being the more intense and focused for their apparent restrictedness, the more ravishing for their seeming drabness.

20.45: A sack lying draped over a worm hill. We back up,

hoping to see Japanese characters on it, for there is writing of sorts. Close up, I can see it's English. "*Kartoffeln*," I explain. They laugh. It's one of the sacks of spuds the *Keldysh* bought in Falmouth.

20.51: I'm not misled by the shadows things cast: the inch-long sperm (some creature's fry) swimming tremulously past one of our halogen lamps makes a boa writhe across the sediment. Fish hang in twos: the animal above, its shadow staggered below, both moving together and apart with the MIR's passage. I'm used to this after years of seabed spear-fishing by torchlight, knowing how shrimps can look like lobsters, how monsters duck behind rocks as you pass over them.

21.36: *4,978 metres.* We've been recalled by Control; our search is over. I feel sorry for Mike. I feel sorry for expectations. I feel sorry for those vanished men in their craft which might almost have dissolved completely away for all we've found of it. But what a land in which to leave your dispersing molecules! No coral, no pearls, but a sea-change all the same. The ballast pump sounds like old-fashioned windscreen wipers labouring. And now the place which doesn't exist begins to fall away, or we fall upward. Black milk floods back to fill the dwindling hole our light leaves. An appalling sense of loss as the features disappear according to their size. The privilege of having seen it is unaccountable. I doubt my luck ever to visit these regions again. Now everything's gone and the brief glare of our unnatural light withdraws, leaving the 50-million-year darkness as before. "*Auf Wiedersehen, submarine*," says Viktor.

21.55: "It took them five years to find the *Titanic* and she was 16 miles from where her coordinates said she was," Sergei says consolingly. Everybody is always quoting this, usually with varying figures. Neither he nor Viktor believes the submarine sank. They tell me so as the outside lights are clicked off and we embark on our three-hour rise to another world. Maybe she faked her sinking; maybe she was badly wounded and crept away after the Americans left her to die elsewhere; maybe she reached the African coast or even Japan . . . Maybe she did. I'm afraid I don't give a damn.

22.20: I am wondering why Beebe's description so differs from mine – at least in his finding that once all light had gone there was nothing but "chill and night and death". For the last twelve hours I've not thought at all about death in the sense that he means. For the first half-hour I considered in an academic sort of way the possibility of dying, but that was very different. Chill there certainly was: the MIR's steel hull conducts the ambient temperature most efficiently. But death? And then I think of how it must have been for Beebe, a true pioneer, the first man ever to go as deep as half a mile, way past the remains of light and with only interior lamps trained through the windows to reveal what was in the water column immediately outside. Although he wrote so well about light and the excitement of entering a strange place, he can never even have glimpsed that timeless land and its creatures far below him, nor felt its infinitely slow rhythms move in his blood. Nor did he have manœuvrability, but dangled helplessly on the end of a cable like a plummet on a string. If that cable had snapped, he would have gone. So it was different for us, with the comforts of a further sixty years' technology, eating our sandwiches on the bottom and touring effortlessly about with our headlights on. It was a different realm we saw. Death was there, all right, though not as an absence of the human, of light, of warmth.

23.05: Silence. Only the loudspeaker's hiss. We stare into space, dozing with our eyes open. My hand aches from writing and cold. The Anarchist has peed; I'm determined not to again.

23.27: But I wish we'd get a move on, all the same. This is the only part of the trip when I've become conscious of time. Watching the red LED display of the depth meter going steadily backwards, but not fast enough.

00.45: Exterior lights on.

00.49: Surface. Immediate rocking and tumbling in the swell. Does nothing for bladder. Or handwriting. The lights brighten and fade as they plunge in and out of the surf, reflecting off the bubbles but barely off deeper water. No sound from outside. A bright white foot waves at my viewport. Lonya's? Now *Koresh* is towing us: helical clouds of bubbles stream back from its screw.

We rest in a violent, tossing pool of *Keldysh*'s deck lights and suddenly the foam falls away from the windows and we are hanging over the sea.

01.28: *MIR I* secured. Outside I glimpse Viktor the engineer, Anatoly, Quentin and others. Cape Canaveral. The depth meter reads -29 metres. Had we been over the 5,000 metre mark? Who cares? The hatch is hard to crack: the air inside is still much cooler than out, so it has to be lifted against a slight vacuum. Ears pop. Stiffly I emerge, carrying my pee bottle in a plastic bag.

Before going to bed I write: It didn't feel like the bottom of the sea, the bottom of anything. The communications lag, the capsule, the navigation difficulties; everything suggested space travel. But I can now see why 17th century scholars like Thomas Burnet in *The Theory of the Earth* thought of the sea as godless, frighteningly ugly in the "unfinished", primordial sense of jagged reefs and cliffs and coastlines. With late twentieth-century eyes I turn all this into its unique virtue. Where I have just returned from is wonderful beyond anything I've seen before, and partly because it is so spectacularly ungodded, too remote to be anthropomorphised. This is why I can't assign a time to it but am tempted to borrow the naturalist Philip Gosse's term *Prochronic* for the "pre-time" that existed before the Creation story in Genesis. It was so alien and peaceful as to make one profoundly calm. Untouched, unfashionable. Here were no lovable cetaceans for people to have mystical blurts over. In its salutary insistence on the primordial nothingness which is the real groundswell beneath all our lives it was notably benign and reassuring. There was nothing to fear, nothing that would not return a level gaze: something nearly indistinguishable from affection.

04.07: It won't let me sleep, that land three miles beneath my bunk. It seems to fill every available space. So dark down there and yet so many eyes. What is it? A unified intelligence busy with tiny acts stretched over aeons? (When you get home, check that stanza towards the end of Stevens' *An Ordinary Evening in New Haven)*:

> It is not an empty clearness, a bottomless sight.
> It is a visibility of thought,
> in which hundreds of eyes, in one mind, see at once.

But what has it done to me? What were those names doing on the bottom? Why have I started remembering people from forty years ago in such detail? Slanted afternoons, the words of pacts, the nape of someone's neck. I have been moving through a bath of solvent which has thinned away crusts and membranes which had built up around certain memories. I don't understand why this should have happened.

"There is undoubtedly a morality . . . even more, an ethic of diving"

ENVOI: A LESSON FROM THE SEA

Jacques-Yves Cousteau

The following was written by Cousteau in September 1968, following an abortive search in the Caribbean for the wreck of the Spanish gold-carrying galleon, Nuestra Señora de la Concepción:

Alone in my cabin at night, I reflect on the frantic activity of the past weeks and on the unexpected denouement of our treasure hunt. I know that, in my heart, I am strongly relieved that we found no gold, no silver, no pearls, no emeralds. Only rusted iron, a few pieces of porcelain, and a medal of St Francis.

If things had turned out differently, if we had found the treasure that we sought, it would have been the first time in my life that I gained material wealth from the sea; and that fact would have changed something in my relationship with the sea. I think that, as a result, I would have been the loser rather than the winner – even though, in the opinion of many, money in the bank is the only measure of success.

I cannot speak for other men. For myself, however, for my wife, and for my friends aboard the *Calypso*, I can say now that our investment in the sea is too large to risk losing merely for the sake of a few dollars. That investment consists of what we have sacrificed to lead the life that we do: money, of course; but also time, family ties, and almost everything else that people generally regard as most precious in life. I do not mean to imply that we are martyrs, or ascetics. Certainly, our investment has already been repaid a thousandfold, in happiness, in satisfaction, in the joy of discovery, in the knowledge that we have been able to contribute something to man's understanding of his world and that we have succeeded in opening, however slightly, a door through which other men will follow. I cannot help feeling that this reward was that which came also to the men of the Renaissance, and to the seamen of the Age of Discovery whose ship we sought so diligently and so vainly. This tradition of non-material compensation on the sea is a very old one and is reflected both in history and in fiction. Captain Nemo, Jules Verne's protagonist, took gold from sunken ships – but only to turn it over to support causes that he considered just. There is undoubtedly a morality, an ethic, of the sea; and, even more, an ethic of diving. And, like every ethic, it implies sanctions. In my own case, I am certain that if we had found our sunken treasure, I would inevitably have lived to regret it; for it would have spoiled our Adventure.

These thoughts run through my mind as the *Calypso* cruises through rough gray water. The waves wash over the deck, returning to the sea the last of its coral that we took from it at the Silver Bank. And so it ends. Our work, the tons of limestone that we hauled aboard and broke open with our hammers and picks until our hands bled and our backs ached – all this is now no more than an episode in our lives, a chapter of marine treasure hunting in the story of the *Calypso*. It is good to be on the open sea again, to hear the sweet sound of our engines instead of the compressor's hateful roar. And, above all, it is good to be together, to have survived the gold fever that might have destroyed our team, and to be on our way to more rewarding adventures. I have before me a long list of future projects: an observation, at close quarters, of sea elephants, of walruses, of sea cows; an expedition to investigate the Blue Holes of the Bahamas; another to film the salmon and the otters of Alaska; another to dive on the Great Barrier Reef off the Australian coast; another to dive in New Caledonia and in the Sonde archipelago . . .

The men of the *Calypso* have returned to the open sea, to do the work for which they are best suited by temperament and training. But what are their thoughts? Are they bitter at the realization that their dreams of wealth have, once and for all, gone up in smoke? I know that they are not. At no time did our project on the Silver Bank, for all its psychological dangers, compromise the spirit of our team, its solidarity, or its good humor. I have the proof of this here, within reach of my hand: the interviews taped by Michel Deloire once it became certain that our sunken ship was not *Nuestra Señora de la Concepción*. Everyone aboard, from the galley hand to the captain, had made plans on how he was to spend his fortune; for everyone had believed in the treasure, in the same way that men believe they may win a lottery. Some had planned to buy houses and boats; some, fur coats for their wives; and others, stores or other businesses for their parents. Morgan, an inveterate bettor, planned to buy race horses. But not a single man expressed either regret or rancor at having worked so hard without material gain. Their reward is the adventure that they lived, and the sense of accomplishment that they have gained, a feeling not unlike that of a man who climbs a mountain.

I know that they are not merely concealing their disappointment for my sake, for I have exactly the same feelings as they; the same conviction that true wealth consists in living and in working. It consists of diving to a sunken ship – even if that ship turns out to be empty of treasure.

A sunken ship, for that matter, is never really empty. It contains history. It tells us about men who lived and suffered in a land that was, at that time, at the very edge of the world. While we were diving to what we thought was *Nuestra Señora de la Concepción*, we often would experience a feeling of sympathy and solidarity with the men of that ship; for they, like ourselves, had traveled over the world in search of adventure, even though their motives may have been somewhat different from our own. These were the men who had dared to be *first*, to venture into the unknown; just as we ourselves were the first to venture into the sea to the outer limits of human survival.

Some of the benefit drawn from our experience at the Silver Bank is of a practical nature. We carried out, for the first time, a systematic dig in a coral bank, and we have learned something very important: that we must not expect too much from archaeological research in tropical seas. Coral grows too rapidly, and buries too deeply the vestiges of man and human artifacts, from hulls of ships to cannon balls. Even so, our dig turned up several objects that are precious to me because of the difficulties involved in obtaining them. They are objects made familiar by daily use, by man's touch: pots, plates, belt buckles. Sometimes, they are things that a man carried around with him. I still smoke, with great pride, a clay pipe that we found, intact, near the mizzenmast.

Frédéric Dumas told me a story that illustrates the sense of human continuity that one gets from such objects. He was diving to a large 16th-century ship in the Mediterranean, probably a Genoese warship, a few years before our adventure on the Silver Bank. Dumas was able to establish the age of the ship by means of coins – 127 of them – that he found on the bottom. He did not find the coins, however, in a treasure chest, but at a distance from the wreck, in the sand. They were in a clump, all joined together by coral. And next to them was a rapier, covered with rust; and a skull and other bones. The soldier to whom the coins had belonged had been apparently drowned in the wreck. Three centuries after his death, he was discovered by a diver, to whom he gave his money, and the means of ascertaining the date of his ship. It was a face-to-face meeting, says Dumas, that was worth all the gold in the world.

We have much to learn from the experience of the conquistadors in the New World. And not the least lesson, by far, is this: that they were ruined by their determination to accumulate as much wealth as they possibly could. This lust for gold did not enrich them; it destroyed them and the economy of their country, and compromised, for several centuries, the quality of human life in Spain. "Here is the God of the Spaniards," the Indians used to say, holding up a piece of gold.

All activity on land and in the sea should have as its inspiration, and as its rule of conduct, respect for man and respect for all life forms.

Appendix

THE HISTORY OF DIVING

From the *US Navy Diving Manual*

1–1 Introduction

1–1.1 **Purpose.** This chapter provides a general history of the development of military diving operations.

1–1.2 **Scope.** This chapter outlines the hard work and dedication of a number of individuals who were pioneers in the development of diving technology. As with any endeavor, it is important to build on the discoveries of our predecessors and not repeat mistakes of the past.

1–1.3 **Role of the US Navy.** The US Navy is a leader in the development of modern diving and underwater operations. The general requirements of national defense and the specific requirements of underwater reconnaissance, demolition, ordnance disposal, construction, ship maintenance, search, rescue and salvage operations repeatedly give impetus to training and development. Navy diving is no longer limited to tactical combat operations, wartime salvage, and submarine sinkings. Fleet diving has become increasingly important and diversified since World War II. A major part of the diving mission is inspecting and repairing naval vessels to minimize downtime and the need for dry-docking. Other aspects of fleet diving include recovering practice and research torpedoes, installing and repairing underwater electronic arrays, underwater construction, and locating and recovering downed aircraft.

1–2 Surface-Supplied Air Diving

The origins of diving are firmly rooted in man's need and desire to engage in maritime commerce, to conduct salvage and military operations, and to expand the frontiers of knowledge through exploration, research, and development.

Diving, as a profession, can be traced back more than 5,000 years. Early divers confined their efforts to waters less than 100 feet deep, performing salvage work and harvesting food, sponges, coral, and mother-of-pearl. A Greek historian, Herodotus, recorded the story of a diver named Scyllis, who was employed by the Persian King Xerxes to recover sunken treasure in the fifth century B.C.

From the earliest times, divers were active in military operations. Their missions included cutting anchor cables to set enemy ships adrift, boring or punching holes in the bottoms of ships, and building harbor defenses at home while attempting to destroy those of the enemy abroad. Alexander the Great sent divers down to remove obstacles in the harbor of the city of Tyre, in what is now Lebanon, which he had taken under siege in 332 B.C.

Other early divers developed an active salvage industry centered around the major shipping ports of the eastern Mediterranean. By the first century B.C., operations in one area had become so well organized that a payment scale for salvage work was established by law, acknowledging the fact that effort and risk increased with depth. In 24 feet of water, the divers could claim a one-half share of all goods recovered. In 12 feet of water, they were allowed a one-third share, and in 3 feet, only a one-tenth share.

1–2.1 Breathing Tubes. The most obvious and crucial step to broadening a diver's capabilities was providing an air supply that would permit him to stay underwater. Hollow reeds or tubes extending to the surface allowed a diver to remain submerged for an extended period, but he could accomplish little in the way of useful work. Breathing tubes were employed in military operations, permitting an undetected approach to an enemy stronghold.

At first glance, it seemed logical that a longer breathing tube was the only requirement for extending a diver's range. In fact, a number of early designs used leather hoods with long flexible tubes supported at the surface by floats. There is no record, however, that any of these devices were actually constructed or tested. The result may well have been the drowning of the diver. At a depth of 3 feet, it is nearly impossible to breathe through a tube using only the body's natural respiratory ability, as the weight of the water exerts a total force of almost 200 pounds on the diver's chest. This force increases steadily with depth and is one of the most important factors in diving. Successful diving operations require that the pressure be overcome or eliminated. Throughout history, imaginative devices were designed to overcome this problem, many by some of the greatest minds of the time. At first, the problem of pressure underwater was not fully understood and the designs were impractical.

1–2.2 Breathing Bags. An entire series of designs was based on the idea of a breathing bag carried by the diver. An Assyrian frieze of the ninth century B.C. shows what appear to be divers using inflated animal skins as air tanks. However, these men were probably swimmers using skins for flotation. It would be impossible to submerge while holding such an accessory.

A workable diving system may have made a brief appearance in the later Middle Ages. In 1240, Roger Bacon made reference to "instruments whereby men can walk on sea or river beds without danger to themselves."

1-2.3 **Diving Bells.** Between 1500 and 1800 the diving bell was developed, enabling divers to remain underwater for hours rather than minutes. The diving bell is a bell-shaped apparatus with the bottom open to the sea.

The first diving bells were large, strong tubs weighted to sink in a vertical position, trapping enough air to permit a diver to breathe for several hours. Later diving bells were suspended by a cable from the surface. They had no significant underwater maneuverability beyond that provided by moving the support ship. The diver could remain in the bell if positioned directly over his work, or could venture outside for short periods of time by holding his breath.

The first reference to an actual practical diving bell was made in 1531. For several hundred years thereafter, rudimentary but effective bells were used with regularity. In the 1680s, a Massachusetts-born adventurer named William Phipps modified the diving bell technique by supplying his divers with air from a series of weighted, inverted buckets as they attempted to recover treasure valued at $200,000.

In 1690, the English astronomer Edmund Halley developed a diving bell in which the atmosphere was replenished by sending weighted barrels of air down from the surface. In an early demonstration of his system, he and four companions remained at 60 feet in the Thames River for almost 1½ hours. Nearly 26 years later, Halley spent more than 4 hours at 66 feet using an improved version of his bell.

1–2.4   Diving Dress Designs. With an increasing number of military and civilian wrecks littering the shores of Great Britain each year, there was strong incentive to develop a diving dress that would increase the efficiency of salvage operations.

1–2.4.1   Lethbridge's Diving Dress. In 1715, Englishman John Lethbridge developed a one-man, completely enclosed diving dress. The Lethbridge equipment was a reinforced, leather-covered barrel of air, equipped with a glass porthole for viewing and two arm holes with watertight sleeves. Wearing this gear, the occupant could accomplish useful work. This apparatus was lowered from a ship and maneuvered in the same manner as a diving bell.

Lethbridge was quite successful with his invention and participated in salvaging a number of European wrecks. In a letter to the editor of a popular magazine in 1749, the inventor noted that his normal operating depth was 10 fathoms (60 feet), with about 12 fathoms the maximum, and that he could remain underwater for 34 minutes.

Several designs similar to Lethbridge's were used in succeeding years. However, all had the same basic limitation as the diving bell – the diver had little freedom because there was no practical way to continually supply him with air. A true technological breakthrough occurred at the turn of the 19th century when a hand-operated pump capable of delivering air under pressure was developed.

1–2.4.2   Deane's Patented Diving Dress. Several men produced a successful apparatus at the same time.

In 1823, two salvage operators, John and Charles Deane, patented the basic design for a smoke apparatus that permitted firemen to move about in burning buildings. By 1828, the apparatus evolved into Deane's Patent Diving Dress, consisting of a heavy suit for protection from the cold, a helmet with viewing ports, and hose connections for delivering surface-supplied air. The helmet rested on the diver's shoulders, held in place by its own weight and straps to a waist belt. Exhausted or surplus air passed out from under the edge of the helmet and posed no problem as long as the diver was upright. If he fell, however, the helmet could quickly fill with water. In 1836, the Deanes issued a diver's manual, perhaps the first ever produced.

1–2.4.3 **Siebe's Improved Diving Dress.** Credit for developing the first practical diving dress has been given to Augustus Siebe. Siebe's initial contribution to diving was a modification of the Deane outfit. Siebe sealed the helmet to the dress at the collar by using a short, waist-length waterproof suit and added an exhaust valve to the system. Known as Siebe's Improved Diving Dress, this apparatus is the direct ancestor of the MK V standard deep-sea diving dress.

1–2.4.4 **Salvage of the HMS** *Royal George.* By 1840, several types of diving dress were being used in actual diving operations. At that time, a unit of the British Royal Engineers was engaged in removing the remains of the sunken warship, HMS *Royal George.* The warship was fouling a major fleet anchorage just outside Portsmouth, England. Colonel William Pasley, the officer in charge, decided that his operation was an ideal opportunity to formally test and evaluate the various types of apparatus. Wary of the Deane apparatus because of the possibility of helmet flooding, he formally recommended that the Siebe dress be adopted for future operations.

When Pasley's project was completed, an official government historian noted that "of the seasoned divers, not a man escaped the repeated attacks of rheumatism and cold." The divers had been working for 6 or 7 hours a day, much of it spent at depths of 60 to 70 feet. Pasley and his men did not realize the implications of the observation. What appeared to be rheumatism was instead a symptom of a far more serious physiological problem that, within a few years, was to become of great importance to the diving profession.

1–2.5 Caissons. At the same time that a practical diving dress was being perfected, inventors were working to improve the diving bell by increasing its size and adding high-capacity air pumps that could deliver enough pressure to keep water entirely out of the bell's interior. The improved pumps soon led to the construction of chambers large enough to permit several men to engage in dry work on the bottom. This was particularly advantageous for projects such as excavating bridge footings or constructing tunnel sections where long periods of work were required. These dry chambers were known as *caissons*, a French word meaning "big boxes". Caissons were designed to provide ready access from the surface. By using an air lock, the pressure inside could be maintained while men or materials could be passed in and out. The caisson was a major step in engineering technology and its use grew quickly.

1–2.6 Physiological Discoveries.

1–2.6.1 Caisson Disease (Decompression Sickness). With the increasing use of caissons, a new and unexplained malady began to affect the caisson workers. Upon returning to the surface at the end of a shift, the divers frequently would be struck by dizzy spells, breathing difficulties, or sharp pains in the joints or abdomen. The sufferer usually recovered, but might never be completely free of some of the symptoms. Caisson workers often noted that they felt better working on the job, but wrongly attributed this to being more rested at the beginning of a shift.

As caisson work extended to larger projects and to greater operating pressures, the physiological problems increased in number and severity. Fatalities occurred with alarming frequency. The malady was called, logically enough, caisson disease. However, workers on the Brooklyn Bridge project in New York gave the sickness a more descriptive name that has remained – the "bends."

Today the bends is the most well-known danger of diving. Although men had been diving for thousands of years, few men had spent much time working under great atmospheric pressure until the time of the caisson. Individuals such as Pasley, who had experienced some aspect of the disease, were simply not prepared to look for anything more involved than indigestion, rheumatism, or arthritis.

1–2.6.1.1   *Cause of Decompression Sickness.* The actual cause of caisson disease was first clinically described in 1878 by a French physiologist, Paul Bert. In studying the effect of pressure on human physiology, Bert determined that breathing air under pressure forced quantities of nitrogen into solution in the blood and tissues of the body. As long as the pressure remained, the gas was held in solution. When the pressure was quickly released, as it was when a worker left the caisson, the nitrogen returned to a gaseous state too rapidly to pass out of the body in a natural manner. Gas bubbles formed throughout the body, causing the wide range of symptoms associated with the disease. Paralysis or death could occur if the flow of blood to a vital organ was blocked by the bubbles.

1–2.6.1.2 *Prevention and Treatment of Decompression Sickness.* Bert recommended that caisson workers gradually decompress and divers return to the surface slowly. His studies led to an immediate improvement for the caisson workers when they discovered their pain could be relieved by returning to the pressure of the caisson as soon as the symptom appeared.

Within a few years, specially designed recompression chambers were being placed at job sites to provide a more controlled situation for handling the bends. The pressure in the chambers could be increased or decreased as needed for an individual worker. One of the first successful uses of a recompression chamber was in 1879 during the construction of a subway tunnel under the Hudson River between New York and New Jersey. The recompression chamber markedly reduced the number of serious cases and fatalities caused by the bends.

Bert's recommendation that divers ascend gradually and steadily was not a complete success, however; some divers continued to suffer from the bends. The general thought at the time was that divers had reached the practical limits of the art and that 120 feet was about as deep as anyone could work. This was because of the repeated incidence of the bends and diver inefficiency beyond that depth. Occasionally, divers would lose consciousness while working at 120 feet.

1–2.6.2 **Inadequate Ventilation.** J. S. Haldane, an English physiologist, conducted experiments with Royal Navy divers from 1905 to 1907. He determined that part of the problem was due to the divers not adequately ventilating their helmets, causing high levels of carbon dioxide to accumulate. To solve the problem, he established a standard supply rate of flow (1.5 cubic feet of air per minute, measured at the pressure of the diver). Pumps capable of maintaining the flow and ventilating the helmet on a continuous basis were used.

Haldane also composed a set of diving tables that established a method of decompression in stages. Though restudied and improved over the years, these tables remain the basis of the accepted method for bringing a diver to the surface.

As a result of Haldane's studies, the practical operating depth for air divers was extended to slightly more than 200 feet. The limit was not imposed by physiological factors, but by the capabilities of the hand-pumps available to provide the air supply.

1–2.6.3 **Nitrogen Narcosis.** Divers soon were moving into deeper water and another unexplained malady began to appear. The diver would appear intoxicated, sometimes feeling euphoric and frequently losing judgment to the point of forgetting the dive's purpose. In the 1930s this "rapture of the deep" was linked to nitrogen in the air breathed under higher pressures. Known as nitrogen narcosis, this condition occurred because nitrogen has anesthetic properties that become progressively more severe with increasing air pressure. To avoid the problem, special breathing mixtures such as helium-oxygen were developed for deep diving.

1–2.7 **Armored Diving Suits.** Numerous inventors, many with little or no underwater experience, worked to create an armored diving suit that would free the diver from pressure problems. In an armored suit, the diver could breathe air at normal atmospheric pressure and descend to great depths without any ill effects. The barrel diving suit, designed by John Lethbridge in 1715, had been an armored suit in essence, but one with a limited operating depth.

The utility of most armored suits was questionable. They were too clumsy for the diver to be able to accomplish much work and too complicated to provide protection from extreme pressure. The maximum anticipated depth of the various suits developed in the 1930s was 700 feet, but was never reached in actual diving. More recent pursuits in the area of armored suits, now called one-atmosphere diving suits, have demonstrated their capability for specialized underwater tasks to 2,000 feet of saltwater (fsw).

1–2.8 **MK V Deep-Sea Diving Dress.** By 1905, the Bureau of Construction and Repair had designed the MK V Diving Helmet which seemed to address many of the problems encountered in diving. This deep-sea outfit was designed for extensive, rugged diving work and provided the diver maximum physical protection and some maneuverability.

The 1905 MK V Diving Helmet had an elbow inlet with a safety valve that allowed air to enter the helmet, but not to escape back up the umbilical if the air supply were interrupted. Air was expelled from the helmet through an exhaust valve on the right side, below the port. The exhaust valve was vented toward the rear of the helmet to prevent escaping bubbles from interfering with the diver's field of vision.

By 1916, several improvements had been made to the helmet, including a rudimentary communications system via a telephone cable and a regulating valve operated by an interior push button. The regulating valve allowed some control of the atmospheric pressure. A supplementary relief valve, known as the spitcock, was added to the left side of the helmet. A safety catch was also incorporated to keep the helmet attached to the breast plate. The exhaust valve and the communications system were improved by 1927, and the weight of the helmet was decreased to be more comfortable for the diver.

After 1927, the MK V changed very little. It remained basically the same helmet used in salvage operations of the USS S-51 and USS S-4 in the mid-1920s. With its associated deep-sea dress and umbilical, the MK V was used for all submarine rescue and salvage work undertaken in peacetime and practically all salvage work undertaken during World War II. The MK V Diving Helmet was the standard U.S. Navy diving equipment until succeeded by the MK 12 Surface-Supplied Diving System (SSDS) in February 1980. The MK 12 was replaced by the MK 21 in December 1993.

1–3 Scuba Diving

The diving equipment developed by Charles and John Deane, Augustus Siebe, and other inventors gave man the ability to remain and work underwater for extended periods, but movement was greatly limited by the requirement for surface-supplied air. Inventors searched for methods to increase the diver's movement without increasing the hazards. The best solution was to provide the diver with a portable, self-contained air supply. For many years the self-contained underwater breathing apparatus (scuba) was only a theoretical possibility. Early attempts to supply self-contained compressed air to divers were not successful due to the limitations of air pumps and containers to compress and store air at sufficiently high pressure. Scuba development took place gradually, however, evolving into three basic types:

- Open-circuit scuba (where the exhaust is vented directly to the surrounding water),
- Closed-circuit scuba (where the oxygen is filtered and recirculated), and
- Semiclosed-circuit scuba (which combines features of the open- and closed-circuit types).

1–3.1 Open-Circuit Scuba. In the open-circuit apparatus, air is inhaled from a supply cylinder and the exhaust is vented directly to the surrounding water.

1–3.1.1 Rouquayrol's Demand Regulator. The first and highly necessary component of an open-circuit apparatus was a demand regulator. Designed early in 1866 and patented by Benoist Rouquayrol, the regulator adjusted the flow of air from the tank to meet the diver's breathing and pressure requirements. However, because cylinders strong enough to contain air at high pressure could not be built at the time, Rouquayrol adapted his regulator to surface-supplied diving equipment and the technology turned toward closed-circuit designs. The application of Rouquayrol's concept of a demand regulator to a successful open-circuit scuba was to wait more than 60 years.

1–3.1.2 LePrieur's Open-Circuit Scuba Design. The thread of open-circuit development was picked up in 1933. Commander LePrieur, a French naval officer, constructed an open-circuit scuba using a tank of compressed air. However, LePrieur did not include a demand regulator in his design and, the diver's main effort was diverted to the constant manual control of his air supply. The lack of a demand regulator, coupled with extremely short endurance, severely limited the practical use of LePrieur's apparatus.

1–3.1.3 Cousteau and Gagnan's Aqua-Lung. At the same time that actual combat operations were being carried out with closed-circuit apparatus, two

Frenchmen achieved a significant breakthrough in open-circuit scuba design. Working in a small Mediterranean village, under the difficult and restrictive conditions of German-occupied France, Jacques-Yves Cousteau and Emile Gagnan combined an improved demand regulator with high-pressure air tanks to create the first truly efficient and safe open-circuit scuba, known as the Aqua-Lung. Cousteau and his companions brought the Aqua-Lung to a high state of development as they explored and photographed wrecks, developing new diving techniques and testing their equipment.

The Aqua-Lung was the culmination of hundreds of years of progress, blending the work of Rouquayrol, LePrieur, and Fleuss, a pioneer in closed-circuit scuba development. Cousteau used his gear successfully to 180 fsw without significant difficulty and with the end of the war the Aqua-Lung quickly became a commercial success. Today the Aqua-Lung is the most widely used diving equipment, opening the underwater world to anyone with suitable training and the fundamental physical abilities.

1–3.1.4 **Impact of Scuba on Diving.** The underwater freedom brought about by the development of scuba led to a rapid growth of interest in diving. Sport diving has become very popular, but science and commerce have also benefited. Biologists, geologists and archaeologists have all gone underwater, seeking new clues to the origins and behavior of the earth, man and civilization as a whole. An entire industry has grown around commercial diving, with the major portion of activity in offshore petroleum production.

After World War II, the art and science of diving progressed rapidly, with emphasis placed on improving existing diving techniques, creating new methods, and developing the equipment required to serve these methods. A complete generation of new and sophisticated equipment took form, with substantial improvements being made in both open and closed-circuit apparatus. However, the most significant aspect of this technological expansion has been the closely linked development of saturation diving techniques and deep diving systems.

1–3.2   Closed-Circuit Scuba. The basic closed-circuit system, or oxygen rebreather, uses a cylinder of 100 percent oxygen that supplies a breathing bag. The oxygen used by the diver is recirculated in the apparatus, passing through a chemical filter that removes carbon dioxide. Oxygen is added from the tank to replace that consumed in breathing. For special warfare operations, the closed-circuit system has a major advantage over the open-circuit type: it does not produce a telltale trail of bubbles on the surface.

1–3.2.1   Fleuss' Closed-Circuit Scuba. Henry A. Fleuss developed the first commercially practical closed-circuit scuba between 1876 and 1878. The Fleuss device consisted of a watertight rubber face mask and a breathing bag connected to a copper tank of 100 percent oxygen charged to 450 psi. By using oxygen instead of compressed air as the breathing medium, Fleuss eliminated the need for high-strength tanks. In early models of this apparatus, the diver controlled the makeup feed of fresh oxygen with a hand valve.

Fleuss successfully tested his apparatus in 1879. In the first test, he remained in a tank of water for about an hour. In the second test, he walked along a creek bed at a depth of 18 feet. During the second test, Fleuss turned off his oxygen feed to see what would happen. He was soon unconscious, and suffered gas embolism as his tenders pulled him to the surface. A few weeks after his recovery, Fleuss made arrangements to put his recirculating design into commercial production.

In 1880, the Fleuss scuba figured prominently in a highly publicized achievement by an English diver, Alexander Lambert. A tunnel under the Severn River flooded and Lambert, wearing a Fleuss apparatus, walked 1,000 feet along the tunnel, in complete darkness, to close several crucial valves.

1–3.2.2 **Modern Closed-Circuit Systems.** As development of the closed-circuit design continued, the Fleuss equipment was improved by adding a demand regulator and tanks capable of holding oxygen at more than 2,000 psi. By World War I, the Fleuss scuba (with modifications) was the basis for submarine escape equipment used in the Royal Navy. In World War II, closed-circuit units were widely used for combat diving operations (see paragraph 1–3.5.2).

Some modern closed-circuit systems employ a mixed gas for breathing and electronically senses and controls oxygen concentration. This type of apparatus retains the bubble-free characteristics of 100 percent oxygen recirculators while significantly improving depth capability.

1–3.3 **Hazards of Using Oxygen in Scuba.** Fleuss had been unaware of the serious problem of oxygen toxicity caused by breathing 100 percent oxygen under pressure. Oxygen toxicity apparently was not encountered when he used his apparatus in early shallow water experiments. The danger of oxygen poisoning had actually been discovered prior to 1878 by Paul Bert, the physiologist who first proposed controlled decompression as a way to avoid the bends. In laboratory experiments with animals, Bert demonstrated that breathing oxygen under pressure could lead to convulsions and death (central nervous system oxygen toxicity).

In 1899, J. Lorrain Smith found that breathing oxygen over prolonged periods of time, even at pressures not sufficient to cause convulsions, could lead to pulmonary oxygen toxicity, a serious lung irritation. The results of these experiments, however, were not widely publicized. For many years, working divers were unaware of the dangers of oxygen poisoning.

The true seriousness of the problem was not apparent until large numbers of combat swimmers were being trained in the early years of World War II. After a number of oxygen toxicity accidents, the British established an operational depth limit of 33 fsw. Additional research on oxygen toxicity continued in the US Navy after the war and resulted in the setting of a normal working limit of 25 fsw for 75 minutes for the Emerson oxygen rebreather. A maximum emergency depth/time limit of 40 fsw for 10 minutes was also allowed.

These limits eventually proved operationally restrictive, and prompted the Navy Experimental Diving Unit to reexamine the entire problem of oxygen toxicity in the mid-1980s. As a result of this work, more liberal and flexible limits were adopted for US Navy use.

1–3.4   **Semiclosed-Circuit Scuba.** The semiclosed-circuit scuba combines features of the open and closed-circuit systems. Using a mixture of gases for breathing, the apparatus recycles the gas through a carbon dioxide removal canister and continually adds a small amount of oxygen-rich mixed gas to the system from a supply cylinder. The supply gas flow is preset to satisfy the body's oxygen demand; an equal amount of the recirculating mixed-gas stream is continually exhausted to the water. Because the quantity of makeup gas is constant regardless of depth, the semiclosed-circuit scuba provides significantly greater endurance than open-circuit systems in deep diving.

1–3.4.1 **Lambertsen's Mixed-Gas Rebreather.** In the late 1940s, Dr C. J. Lambertsen proposed that mixtures of nitrogen or helium with an elevated oxygen content be used in scuba to expand the depth range beyond that allowed by 100 percent oxygen rebreathers, while simultaneously minimizing the requirement for decompression.

In the early 1950s, Lambertsen introduced the FLATUS I, a semiclosed-circuit scuba that continually added a small volume of mixed gas, rather than pure oxygen, to a rebreathing circuit. The small volume of new gas provided the oxygen necessary for metabolic consumption while exhaled carbon dioxide was absorbed in an absorbent canister. Because inert gas, as well as oxygen, was added to the rig, and because the inert gas was not consumed by the diver, a small amount of gas mixture was continuously exhausted from the rig.

1–3.4.2 **MK 6 UBA.** In 1964, after significant development work, the Navy adopted a semiclosed-circuit, mixed-gas rebreather, the MK 6 UBA, for combat swimming and EOD operations. Decompression procedures for both nitrogen-oxygen and helium-oxygen mixtures were developed at the Navy Experimental Diving Unit. The apparatus had a maximum depth capability of 200 fsw and a maximum endurance of 3 hours depending on water temperature and diver activity. Because the apparatus was based on a constant mass flow of mixed gas, the endurance was independent of the diver's depth.

In the late 1960s, work began on a new type of mixed-gas rebreather technology, which was later used in the MK 15 and MK 16 UBAs. In this UBA, the oxygen partial pressure was controlled at a constant value by an oxygen sensing and addition system. As the diver consumed oxygen, an oxygen sensor detected the fall in oxygen partial pressure and signaled an oxygen valve to open, allowing a small amount of pure oxygen to be admitted to the breathing circuit from a cylinder. Oxygen addition was thus exactly matched to metabolic consumption. Exhaled carbon dioxide was absorbed in an absorption canister. The system had the endurance and completely closed-circuit characteristics of an oxygen rebreather without the concerns and limitations associated with oxygen toxicity.

Beginning in 1979, the MK 6 semiclosed-circuit underwater breathing apparatus (UBA) was phased out by the MK 15 closed-circuit, constant oxygen partial pressure UBA. The Navy Experimental Diving Unit developed decompression procedures for the MK 15 with nitrogen and helium in the early 1980s. In 1985, an improved low magnetic signature version of the MK 15, the MK 16, was approved for Explosive Ordnance Disposal (EOD) team use.

1–3.5 **Scuba Use During World War II.** Although closed-circuit equipment was restricted to shallow-water use and carried with it the potential danger of oxygen toxicity, its design had reached a suitably high level of efficiency by World War II. During the war, combat swimmer breathing units were widely used by navies on both sides of the conflict. The swimmers used various modes of underwater attack. Many notable successes were achieved including the sinking of several battleships, cruisers, and merchant ships.

1–3.5.1 **Diver-Guided Torpedoes.** Italian divers, using closed-circuit gear, rode chariot torpedoes fitted with seats and manual controls in repeated attacks against British ships. In 1936, the Italian Navy tested a chariot torpedo system in which the divers used a descendant of the Fleuss scuba. This was the Davis Lung. It was originally designed as a submarine escape device and was later manufactured in Italy under a license from the English patent holders.

British divers, carried to the scene of action in midget submarines, aided in placing explosive charges under the keel of the German battleship *Tirpitz*. The British began their chariot program in 1942 using the Davis Lung and exposure suits. Swimmers using the MK 1 chariot dress quickly discovered that the steel oxygen bottles adversely affected the compass of the chariot torpedo. Aluminum oxygen cylinders were not readily available in England, but German aircraft used aluminum oxygen cylinders that were almost the same size as the steel cylinders aboard the chariot torpedo. Enough aluminum cylinders were salvaged from downed enemy bombers to supply the British forces.

Changes introduced in the MK 2 and MK 3 diving dress involved improvements in valving, faceplate design, and arrangement of components. After the war, the MK 3 became the standard Royal Navy shallow water diving dress. The MK 4 dress was used near the end of the war. Unlike the MK 3, the MK 4 could be supplied with oxygen from a self-contained bottle or from a larger cylinder carried in the chariot. This gave the swimmer greater endurance, yet preserved freedom of movement independent of the chariot torpedo.

In the final stages of the war, the Japanese employed an underwater equivalent of their kamikaze aerial attack – the kaiten diver-guided torpedo.

1–3.5.2 **US Combat Swimming.** There were two groups of US combat swimmers during World War II: Naval beach reconnaissance swimmers and US operational swimmers. Naval beach reconnaissance units did not normally use any breathing devices, although several models existed.

US operational swimmers, however, under the Office of Strategic Services, developed and applied advanced methods for true self-contained diver-submersible operations. They employed the Lambertsen Amphibious Respiratory Unit (LARU), a rebreather invented by Dr C. J. Lambertsen. The LARU was a closed-circuit oxygen UBA used in special warfare operations where a complete absence of exhaust bubbles was required. Following World War II, the Emerson-Lambertsen Oxygen Rebreather replaced the LARU. The Emerson Unit was used extensively by Navy special warfare divers until 1982, when it was replaced by the Draeger Lung Automatic Regenerator (LAR) V. The LAR V is the standard unit now used by US Navy combat swimmers.

Today Navy combat swimmers are organized into two separate groups, each with specialized training and missions. The Explosive Ordnance Disposal (EOD) team handles, defuses, and disposes of munitions and other explosives. The Sea, Air and Land (SEAL) special warfare teams make up the second group of Navy combat swimmers. SEAL team members are trained to operate in all of these environments. They qualify as parachutists, learn to handle a range of weapons, receive intensive training in hand-to-hand combat, and are expert in scuba and other swimming and diving techniques. In Vietnam, SEALs were deployed in special counter-insurgency and guerrilla warfare operations. The SEALs also participated in the space program by securing flotation collars to returned space capsules and assisting astronauts during the helicopter pickup.

1–3.5.3 **Underwater Demolition.** The Navy's Underwater Demolition Teams (UDTs) were created when bomb disposal experts and Seabees (combat engineers) teamed together in 1943 to devise methods for removing obstacles that the Germans were placing off the beaches of France. The first UDT combat mission was a daylight reconnaissance and demolition project off the beaches of Saipan in June 1944. In March of 1945, preparing for the invasion of Okinawa, one underwater demolition team achieved the exceptional record of removing 1,200 underwater obstacles in 2 days, under heavy fire, without a single casualty.

Because suitable equipment was not readily available, diving apparatus was not extensively used by the UDT during the war. UDT experimented with a modified Momsen lung and other types of breathing apparatus, but not until 1947 did the Navy's acquisition of Aqua-Lung equipment give impetus to the diving aspect of UDT operations. The trail of bubbles from the open-circuit apparatus limited the type of mission in which it could be employed, but a special scuba platoon of UDT members was formed to test the equipment and determine appropriate uses for it.

Through the years since, the mission and importance of the UDT has grown. In the Korean Conflict, during the period of strategic withdrawal, the UDT destroyed an entire port complex to keep it from the enemy. The UDTs have since been incorporated into the Navy Seal Teams.

1–4 Mixed-gas Diving

Mixed-gas diving operations are conducted using a breathing medium other than air. This medium may consist of:

- Nitrogen and oxygen in proportions other than those found in the atmosphere
- A mixture of other inert gases, such as helium, with oxygen.

The breathing medium can also be 100 percent oxygen, which is not a mixed gas, but which requires training for safe use. Air may be used in some phases of a mixed-gas dive.

Mixed-gas diving is a complex undertaking. A mixed-gas diving operation requires extensive special training, detailed planning, specialized and advanced equipment and, in many applications, requires extensive surface-support personnel and facilities. Because mixed-gas operations are often conducted at great depth or for extended periods of time, hazards to personnel increase greatly. Divers studying mixed-gas diving must first be qualified in air diving operations.

In recent years, to match basic operational requirements and capabilities, the US Navy has divided mixed-gas diving into two categories:

- Nonsaturation diving without a pressurized bell to a maximum depth of 300 fsw, and
- Saturation diving for dives of 150 fsw and greater depth or for extended bottom time missions.

The 300-foot limit is based primarily on the increased risk of decompression sickness when nonsaturation diving techniques are used deeper than 300 fsw.

1–4.1   Nonsaturation Diving.

1–4.1.1   Helium-Oxygen (HeO$_2$) Diving. An inventor named Elihu Thomson theorized that helium might be an appropriate substitute for the nitrogen in a diver's breathing supply. He estimated that at least a 50 percent gain in working depth could be achieved by substituting helium for nitrogen. In 1919, he suggested that the US Bureau of Mines investigate this possibility. Thomson directed his suggestion to the Bureau of Mines rather than the Navy Department, since the Bureau of Mines held a virtual world monopoly on helium marketing and distribution.

1–4.1.1.1 *Experiments with Helium-Oxygen Mixtures.* In 1924, the Navy and the Bureau of Mines jointly sponsored a series of experiments using helium-oxygen mixtures. The preliminary work was conducted at the Bureau of Mines Experimental Station in Pittsburgh, Pennsylvania.

The first experiments showed no detrimental effects on test animals or humans from breathing a helium-oxygen mixture, and decompression time was shortened. The principal physiological effects noted by divers using helium-oxygen were:

- Increased sensation of cold caused by the high thermal conductivity of helium
- The high-pitched distortion or "Donald Duck" effect on human speech that resulted from the acoustic properties and reduced density of the gas

These experiments clearly showed that helium-oxygen mixtures offered great advantages over air for deep dives. They laid the foundation for developing the reliable decompression tables and specialized apparatus, which are the cornerstones of modern deep diving technology.

In 1937, at the Experimental Diving Unit research facility, a diver wearing a deep-sea diving dress with a helium-oxygen breathing supply was compressed in a chamber to a simulated depth of 500 feet. The diver was not told the depth and when asked to make an estimate of the depth, the diver reported that it felt as if he were at 100 feet. During decompression at the 300-foot mark, the breathing mixture was switched to air and the diver was troubled immediately by nitrogen narcosis.

The first practical test of helium-oxygen came in 1939, when the submarine USS *Squalus* was salvaged from a depth of 243 fsw. In that year, the Navy issued decompression tables for surface-supplied helium-oxygen diving.

1–4.1.1.2   *MK V MOD 1 Helmet*. Because helium was expensive and shipboard supplies were limited, the standard MK V MOD 0 open-circuit helmet was not economical for surface-supplied helium-oxygen diving. After experimenting with several different designs, the US Navy adopted the semiclosed-circuit MK V MOD 1.

The MK V MOD 1 helmet was equipped with a carbon dioxide absorption canister and venturi-powered recirculator assembly. Gas in the helmet was continuously recirculated through the carbon dioxide scrubber assembly by the venturi. By removing carbon dioxide by scrubbing rather than ventilating the helmet, the fresh gas flow into the helmet was reduced to the amount required to replenish oxygen. The gas consumption of the semiclosed-circuit MK V MOD 1 was approximately 10 percent of that of the open-circuit MK V MOD 0.

The MK V MOD 1, with breastplate and recirculating gas canister, weighed approximately 103 pounds compared to 56 pounds for the standard air helmet and breastplate. It was fitted with a lifting ring at the top of the helmet to aid in hatting the diver and to keep the weight off his shoulders until he was lowered into the water. The diver was lowered into and raised out of the water by a diving stage connected to an onboard boom.

1–4.1.1.3   *Civilian Designers*. US Navy divers were not alone in working with mixed gases or helium. In 1937, civilian engineer Max Gene Nohl reached 420 feet in Lake Michigan while breathing helium-oxygen and using a suit of his own design. In 1946, civilian diver

Jack Browne, designer of the lightweight diving mask that bears his name, made a simulated helium-oxygen dive of 550 feet. In 1948, a British Navy diver set an open-sea record of 540 fsw while using war-surplus helium provided by the U.S.

1–4.1.2 **Hydrogen-Oxygen Diving.** In countries where the availability of helium was more restricted, divers experimented with mixtures of other gases. The most notable example is that of the Swedish engineer Arne Zetterstrom, who worked with hydrogen-oxygen mixtures. The explosive nature of such mixtures was well known, but it was also known that hydrogen would not explode when used in a mixture of less than 4 percent oxygen. At the surface, this percentage of oxygen would not be sufficient to sustain life; at 100 feet, however, the oxygen partial pressure would be the equivalent of 16 percent oxygen at the surface.

Zetterstrom devised a simple method for making the transition from air to hydrogen-oxygen without exceeding the 4 percent oxygen limit. At the 100-foot level, he replaced his breathing air with a mixture of 96 percent nitrogen and 4 percent oxygen. He then replaced that mixture with hydrogen-oxygen in the same proportions. In 1945, after some successful test dives to 363 feet, Zetterstrom reached 528 feet. Unfortunately, as a result of a misunderstanding on the part of his topside support personnel, he was brought to the surface too rapidly. Zetterstrom did not have time to enrich his breathing mixture or to adequately decompress and died as a result of the effects of his ascent.

1–4.1.3 **Modern Surface-Supplied Mixed-Gas Diving.** The US Navy and the Royal Navy continued to develop procedures and equipment for surface-supplied helium-oxygen diving in the years following World War II. In 1946, the Admiralty Experimental

Diving Unit was established and, in 1956, during open-sea tests of helium-oxygen diving, a Royal Navy diver reached a depth of 600 fsw. Both navies conducted helium-oxygen decompression trials in an attempt to develop better procedures.

In the early 1960s, a young diving enthusiast from Switzerland, Hannes Keller, proposed techniques to attain great depths while minimizing decompression requirements. Using a series of gas mixtures containing varying concentrations of oxygen, helium, nitrogen, and argon, Keller demonstrated the value of elevated oxygen pressures and gas sequencing in a series of successful dives in mountain lakes. In 1962, with partial support from the US Navy, he reached an open-sea depth of more than 1,000 fsw off the California coast. Unfortunately, this dive was marred by tragedy. Through a mishap unrelated to the technique itself, Keller lost consciousness on the bottom and, in the subsequent emergency decompression, Keller's companion died of decompression sickness.

By the late 1960s, it was clear that surface-supplied diving deeper than 300 fsw was better carried out using a deep diving (bell) system where the gas sequencing techniques pioneered by Hannes Keller could be exploited to full advantage, while maintaining the diver in a state of comfort and security. The US Navy developed decompression procedures for bell diving systems in the late 1960s and early 1970s. For surface-supplied diving in the 0–300 fsw range, attention was turned to developing new equipment to replace the cumbersome MK V MOD 1 helmet.

1–4.1.4   **MK 1 MOD O Diving Outfit.** The new equipment development proceeded along two parallel paths, developing open-circuit demand breathing systems suitable for deep helium-oxygen diving, and developing an improved recirculating helmet to replace the MK V MOD 1. By the late 1960s, engineering improvements in demand regulators had reduced breathing resistance on deep dives to acceptable levels. Masks and helmets incorporating the new regulators became commercially available. In 1976, the U.S. Navy approved the MK 1 MOD O Lightweight, Mixed-Gas Diving Outfit for dives to 300 fsw on helium-oxygen. The MK 1 MOD 0 Diving Outfit incorporated a full face mask (bandmask) featuring a demand open-circuit breathing regulator and a backpack for an emergency gas supply. Surface contact was maintained through an umbilical that included the breathing gas hose, communications cable, lifeline strength member and pneumofathometer hose. The diver was dressed in a dry suit or hot water suit depending on water temperature. The equipment was issued as a light-weight diving outfit in a system with sufficient equipment to support a diving operation employing two working divers and a standby diver. The outfit was used in conjunction with an open diving bell that replaced the traditional diver's stage and added additional safety. In 1990, the MK 1 MOD 0 was replaced by the MK 21 MOD 1 (Superlite 17 B/NS) demand helmet. This is the lightweight rig in use today.

In 1985, after an extensive development period, the direct replacement for the MK V MOD 1 helmet was approved for Fleet use. The new MK 12 Mixed-Gas Surface-Supplied Diving System (SSDS) was similar to the MK 12 Air SSDS, with the addition of a backpack assembly to allow operation in a semiclosed-circuit mode. The MK 12 system was retired in 1992 after the introduction of the MK 21 MOD 1 demand helmet.

1–4.2 Diving Bells. Although open, pressure-balanced diving bells have been used for several centuries, it was not until 1928 that a bell appeared that was capable of maintaining internal pressure when raised to the surface. In that year, Sir Robert H. Davis, the British pioneer in diving equipment, designed the Submersible Decompression Chamber (SDC). The vessel was conceived to reduce the time a diver had to remain in the water during a lengthy decompression.

The Davis SDC was a steel cylinder capable of holding two men, with two inward-opening hatches, one on the top and one on the bottom. A surface-supplied diver was deployed over the side in the normal mode and the bell was lowered to a depth of 60 fsw with the lower hatch open and a tender inside. Surface-supplied air ventilated the bell and prevented flooding. The diver's deep decompression stops were taken in the water and he was assisted into the bell by the tender upon arrival at 60 fsw. The diver's gas supply hose and communications cable were removed from the helmet and passed out of the bell. The lower door was closed and the bell was lifted to the deck where the diver and tender were decompressed within the safety and comfort of the bell.

By 1931, the increased decompression times associated with deep diving and the need for diver comfort resulted in the design of an improved bell system. Davis designed a three-compartment deck decompression chamber (DDC) to which the SDC could be mechanically mated, permitting the transfer of the diver under pressure. The DDC provided additional space, a bunk, food and clothing for the diver's comfort during a lengthy decompression. This procedure also freed the SDC for use by another diving team for continuous diving operations.

The SDC-DDC concept was a major advance in diving safety, but was not applied to American diving technology until the advent of saturation diving. In 1962, E. A. Link employed a cylindrical, aluminum SDC in conducting his first open-sea saturation diving experiment. In his experiments, Link used the SDC to transport the diver to and from the sea floor and a DDC for improved diver comfort. American diving had entered the era of the Deep Diving System (DDS) and advances and applications of the concept grew at a phenomenal rate in both military and commercial diving.

1–4.3 **Saturation Diving**. As divers dove deeper and attempted more ambitious underwater tasks, a safe method to extend actual working time at depth became crucial. Examples of saturation missions include submarine rescue and salvage, sea bed implantments, construction, and scientific testing and observation. These types of operations are characterized by the need for extensive bottom time and, consequently, are more efficiently conducted using saturation techniques.

1–4.3.1 **Advantages of Saturation Diving**. In deep diving operations, decompression is the most time-consuming factor. For example, a diver working for an hour at 200 fsw would be required to spend an additional 3 hours and 20 minutes in the water undergoing the necessary decompression.

However, once a diver becomes saturated with the gases that make decompression necessary, the diver does not need additional decompression. When the blood and tissues have absorbed all the gas they can hold at that depth, the time required for decompression becomes constant. As long as the depth is not increased, additional time on the bottom is free of any additional decompression.

If a diver could remain under pressure for the entire period of the required task, the diver would face a lengthy decompression only when completing the project. For a 40-hour task at 200 fsw, a saturated diver would spend 5 days at bottom pressure and 2 days in decompression, as opposed to spending 40 days making 1-hour dives with long decompression periods using conventional methods.

The US Navy developed and proved saturation diving techniques in its Sealab series. Advanced saturation diving techniques are being developed in ongoing programs of research and development at the Navy Experimental Diving Unit (NEDU), Navy Submarine Medical Research Laboratory (NSMRL), and many institutional and commercial hyperbaric facilities. In addition, saturation diving using Deep Diving Systems (DDS) is now a proven capability.

1–4.3.2 **Bond's Saturation Theory**. True scientific impetus was first given to the saturation concept in 1957 when a Navy diving medical officer, Captain George F. Bond, theorized that the tissues of the body would eventually become saturated with inert gas if exposure time was long enough. Bond, then a commander and the director of the Submarine Medical Center at New London, Connecticut, met with Captain Jacques-Yves Cousteau and determined that the data required to prove the theory of saturation diving could be developed at the Medical Center.

1–4.3.3 **Genesis Project**. With the support of the US Navy, Bond initiated the Genesis Project to test the theory of saturation diving. A series of experiments, first with test animals and then with humans, proved that once a diver was saturated, further extension of bottom time would require no additional decompression time. Project Genesis proved that men could be sustained for long periods under pressure, and what was then needed was a means to put this concept to use on the ocean floor.

1–4.3.4 **Developmental Testing**. Several test dives were conducted in the early 1960s:

- The first practical open-sea demonstrations of saturation diving were undertaken in September 1962 by Edward A. Link and Captain Jacques-Yves Cousteau.
- Link's Man-in-the-Sea program had one man breathing helium-oxygen at 200 fsw for 24 hours in a specially designed diving system.
- Cousteau placed two men in a gas-filled, pressure-balanced underwater habitat at 33 fsw where they stayed for 169 hours, moving freely in and out of their deep-house.
- Cousteau's Conshelf One supported six men breathing nitrogen-oxygen at 35 fsw for 7 days.
- In 1964, Link and Lambertsen conducted a 2-day exposure of two men at 430 fsw.
- Cousteau's Conshelf Two experiment maintained a group of seven men for 30 days at 36 fsw and 90 fsw with excursion dives to 330 fsw.

1–4.3.5 **Sealab Program**. The best known US Navy experimental effort in saturation diving was the Sealab program.

1–4.3.5.1 *Sealabs I and II*. After completing the Genesis Project, the Office of Naval Research, the Navy Mine Defense Laboratory and Bond's small staff of volunteers gathered in Panama City, Florida, where construction and testing of the Sealab I habitat began in December 1963.

In 1964, Sealab I placed four men underwater for 10 days at an average depth of 192 fsw. The habitat was eventually raised to 81 fsw, where the divers were transferred to a decompression chamber that was hoisted aboard a four-legged offshore support structure.

In 1965, Sealab II put three teams of ten men each in a habitat at 205 fsw. Each team spent 15 days at depth and one man, Astronaut Scott Carpénter, remained for 30 days.

1–4.3.5.2 *Sealab III.* The follow-on seafloor experiment, Sea-lab III, was planned for 600 fsw. This huge under-taking required not only extensive development and testing of equipment but also assessment of human tolerance to high-pressure environments.

To prepare for Sealab III, 28 helium-oxygen saturation dives were performed at the Navy Ex-perimental Diving Unit to depths of 825 fsw be-tween 1965 and 1968. In 1968, a record-breaking excursion dive to 1,025 fsw from a saturation depth of 825 fsw was performed at the Navy Experimental Diving Unit (NEDU). The culmination of this series of dives was a 1,000 fsw, 3-day saturation dive conducted jointly by the U.S. Navy and Duke University in the hyperbaric chambers at Duke. This was the first time man had been saturated at 1,000 fsw. The Sealab III preparation experiments showed that men could readily perform useful work at pressures up to 31 atmospheres and could be returned to normal pressure without harm.

Reaching the depth intended for the Sealab III habitat required highly specialized support, includ-ing a diving bell to transfer divers under pressure from the habitat to a pressurized deck decompres-sion chamber. The experiment, however, was marred by tragedy. Shortly after being compressed to 600 fsw in February 1969, Aquanaut Berry Can-non convulsed and drowned. This unfortunate ac-cident ended the Navy's involvement with seafloor habitats.

1–4.3.5.3 *Continuing Research.* Research and development continues to extend the depth limit for saturation diving and to improve the diver's capability. The deepest dive attained by the U.S. Navy to date was in 1979 when divers from the NEDU completed a

37-day, 1,800 fsw dive in its Ocean Simulation Facility. The world record depth for experimental saturation, attained at Duke University in 1981, is 2,250 fsw, and non-Navy open sea dives have been completed to in excess of 2300 fsw. Experiments with mixtures of hydrogen, helium, and oxygen have begun and the success of this mixture was demonstrated in 1988 in an open-sea dive to 1,650 fsw.

Advanced saturation diving techniques are being developed in ongoing programs of research and development at NEDU, Navy Submarine Medical Research Laboratory (NSMRL), and many institutional and commercial hyperbaric facilities. In addition, saturation diving using Deep Diving Systems (DDS) is now a proven capability.

1–4.4 **Deep Diving Systems (DDS).** Experiments in saturation technique required substantial surface support as well as extensive underwater equipment. DDS are a substantial improvement over previous methods of accomplishing deep undersea work. The DDS is readily adaptable to saturation techniques and safely maintains the saturated diver under pressure in a dry environment. Whether employed for saturation or nonsaturation diving, the Deep Diving System totally eliminates long decompression periods in the water where the diver is subjected to extended environmental stress. The diver only remains in the sea for the time spent on a given task. Additional benefits derived from use of the DDS include eliminating the need for underwater habitats and increasing operational flexibility for the surface-support ship.

The Deep Diving System consists of a Deck Decompression Chamber (DDC) mounted on a surface-support ship. A Personnel Transfer Capsule (PTC) is mated to the DDC, and the combination is pressurized to a storage depth. Two or more divers enter the PTC, which is unmated and lowered to the working depth. The interior of the capsule is pressurized to equal the pressure at depth, a hatch is opened, and one or more divers swim out to accomplish their work. The divers can use a self-contained breathing apparatus with a safety tether to the capsule, or employ a mask and an umbilical that provides breathing gas and communications. Upon completing the task, the divers enters the capsule, close the hatch and return to the support ship with the interior of the PTC still at the working pressure. The capsule is hoisted aboard and mated to the pressurized DDC. The divers enter the larger, more comfortable DDC via an entry lock. They remain in the DDC until they must return to the undersea job site. Decompression is carried out comfortably and safely on the support ship.

The Navy developed four deep diving systems: ADS-IV, MK 1 MOD 0, MK 2 MOD 0, and MK 2 MOD 1.

1–4.4.1 **ADS-IV**. Several years prior to the Sealab I experiment, the Navy successfully deployed the Advanced Diving System IV (ADS-IV). The ADS-IV was a small deep diving system with a depth capability of 450 fsw. The ADS-IV was later called the SDS-450.

1–4.4.2 **MK 1 MOD 0**. The MK 1 MOD 0 DDS was a small system intended to be used on the new ATS-1 class salvage ships, and underwent operational evaluation in 1970. The DDS consisted of a Personnel Transfer Capsule (PTC), a life-support system, main control console and two deck decompression chambers to handle two teams of two divers each. This system was also used to operationally evaluate the MK 11 UBA, a semiclosed-circuit mixed-gas apparatus, for saturation diving. The MK 1 MOD 0 DDS conducted an open-sea dive to 1,148 fsw in 1975. The MK 1 DDS was not installed on the ATS ships as originally planned, but placed on a barge and assigned to Harbor Clearance Unit Two. The system went out of service in 1977.

1–4.4.3 **MK 2 MOD 0.** The Sealab III experiment required a much larger and more capable deep diving system than the MK 1 MOD 0. The MK 2 MOD 0 was constructed and installed on the support ship *Elk River* (IX–501). With this system, divers could be saturated in the deck chamber under close observation and then transported to the habitat for the stay at depth, or could cycle back and forth between the deck chamber and the seafloor while working on the exterior of the habitat.

The bell could also be used in a non-pressurized observation mode. The divers would be transported from the habitat to the deck decompression chamber, where final decompression could take place under close observation.

1–4.4.4 **MK 2 MOD 1.** Experience gained with the MK 2 MOD 0 DDS on board *Elk River* (IX–501) led to the development of the MK 2 MOD 1, a larger, more sophisticated DDS. The MK 2 MOD 1 DDS supported two four-man teams for long term saturation diving with a normal depth capability of 850 fsw. The diving complex consisted of two complete systems, one at starboard and one at port. Each system had a DDC with a life-support system, a PTC, a main control console, a strength-power-communications cable (SPCC) and ship support. The two systems shared a helium-recovery system. The MK 2 MOD 1 was installed on the ASR 21 Class submarine rescue vessels.

1-5 Submarine Salvage and Rescue

At the beginning of the 20th century, all major navies turned their attention toward developing a weapon of immense potential – the military submarine. The highly effective use of the submarine by the German Navy in World War I heightened this interest and an emphasis was placed on the submarine that continues today.

The US Navy had operated submarines on a limited basis for several years prior to 1900. As American technology expanded, the US submarine fleet grew rapidly. However, throughout the period of 1912 to 1939, the development of the Navy's F, H, and S class boats was marred by a series of accidents, collisions, and sinkings. Several of these submarine disasters resulted in a correspondingly rapid growth in the Navy diving capability.

Until 1912, US Navy divers rarely went below 60 fsw. In that year, Chief Gunner George D. Stillson set up a program to test Haldane's diving tables and methods of stage decompression. A companion goal of the program was to improve Navy diving equipment. Throughout a 3-year period, first diving in tanks ashore and then in open water in Long Island Sound from the USS *Walkie*, the Navy divers went progressively deeper, eventually reaching 274 fsw.

1-5.1 USS F-4. The experience gained in Stillson's program was put to dramatic use in 1915 when the submarine USS F-4 sank near Honolulu, Hawaii. Twenty-one men lost their lives in the accident and the Navy lost its first boat in 15 years of submarine operations. Navy divers salvaged the submarine and recovered the bodies of the crew. The salvage effort incorporated many new techniques, such as using lifting pontoons. What was most remarkable, however, was that the divers completed a major salvage effort working at the extreme depth of 304 fsw, using air as a breathing mixture. The decompression requirements limited bottom time for each dive to about 10 minutes. Even for such a limited time, nitrogen narcosis made it difficult for the divers to concentrate on their work.

The publication of the first US Navy Diving Manual and the establishment of a Navy Diving School at Newport, Rhode Island, were the direct outgrowth of experience gained in the test program and the USS F-4 salvage. When the US entered World War I, the staff and graduates of the school were sent to Europe, where they conducted various salvage operations along the coast of France.

The physiological problems encountered in the salvage of the USS F-4 clearly demonstrated the limitations of breathing air during deep dives. Continuing concern that submarine rescue and salvage would be required at great depth focused Navy attention on the need for a new diver breathing medium.

1–5.2 **USS S-51.** In September of 1925, the USS S-51 submarine was rammed by a passenger liner and sunk in 132 fsw off Block Island, Rhode Island. Public pressure to raise the submarine and recover the bodies of the crew was intense. Navy diving was put in sharp focus, realizing it had only 20 divers who were qualified to go deeper than 90 fsw. Diver training programs had been cut at the end of World War I and the school had not been reinstituted.

Salvage of the USS S-51 covered a 10-month span of difficult and hazardous diving, and a special diver training course was made part of the operation. The submarine was finally raised and towed to the Brooklyn Navy Yard in New York.

Interest in diving was high once again and the Naval School, Diving and Salvage, was reestablished at the Washington Navy Yard in 1927. At the same time, the Navy brought together its existing diving technology and experimental work by shifting the Experimental Diving Unit (EDU), which had been working with the Bureau of Mines in Pennsylvania, to the Navy Yard as well. In the following years, EDU developed the US Navy Air Decompression Tables, which have become the accepted world standard and continued developmental work in helium-oxygen breathing mixtures for deeper diving.

Losing the USS F-4 and USS S-51 provided the impetus for expanding the Navy's diving ability. However, the Navy's inability to rescue men trapped in a disabled submarine was not confronted until another major submarine disaster occurred.

1–5.3   **USS S-4.** In 1927, the Navy lost the submarine USS S-4 in a collision with the Coast Guard cutter USS *Paulding*. The first divers to reach the submarine in 102 fsw, 22 hours after the sinking, exchanged signals with the men trapped inside. The submarine had a hull fitting designed to take an air hose from the surface, but what had looked feasible in theory proved too difficult in reality. With stormy seas causing repeated delays, the divers could not make the hose connection until it was too late. All of the men aboard the USS S-4 had died. Even had the hose connection been made in time, rescuing the crew would have posed a significant problem.

The USS S-4 was salvaged after a major effort and the fate of the crew spurred several efforts toward preventing a similar disaster. Lt C.B. Momsen, a submarine officer, developed the escape lung that bears his name. It was given its first operational test in 1929 when 26 officers and men successfully surfaced from an intentionally bottomed submarine.

1–5.4 **USS** *Squalus*. The Navy pushed for development of a rescue chamber that was essentially a diving bell with special fittings for connection to a submarine deck hatch. The apparatus, called the McCann-Erickson Rescue Chamber, was proven in 1939 when the USS *Squalus*, carrying a crew of 50, sank in 243 fsw. The rescue chamber made four trips and safely brought 33 men to the surface. (The rest of the crew, trapped in the flooded after-section of the submarine, had perished in the sinking.)

The USS *Squalus* was raised by salvage divers. This salvage and rescue operation marked the first operational use of HeO_2 in salvage diving. One of the primary missions of salvage divers was to attach a down-haul cable for the Submarine Rescue Chamber (SRC). Following renovation, the submarine, renamed USS *Sailfish*, compiled a proud record in World War II.

1–5.5 **USS** *Thresher*. Just as the loss of the USS F-4, USS S-51, USS S-4 and the sinking of the USS *Squalus* caused an increased concern in Navy diving in the 1920s and 1930s, a submarine disaster of major proportions had a profound effect on the development of new diving equipment and techniques in the postwar period. This was the loss of the nuclear attack submarine USS *Thresher* and all her crew in April 1963. The submarine sank in 8,400 fsw, a depth beyond the survival limit of the hull and far beyond the capability of any existing rescue apparatus.

An extensive search was initiated to locate the submarine and determine the cause of the sinking. The first signs of the USS *Thresher* were located and photographed a month after the disaster. Collection of debris and photographic coverage of the wreck continued for about a year.

Two special study groups were formed as a result

of the sinking. The first was a Court of Inquiry, which attributed probable cause to a piping system failure. The second, the Deep Submergence Review Group (DSRG), was formed to assess the Navy's undersea capabilities. Four general areas were examined – search, rescue, recovery of small and large objects, and the Man-in-the-Sea concept. The basic recommendations of the DSRG called for a vast effort to improve the Navy's capabilities in these four areas.

1–5.6 Deep Submergence Systems Project. Direct action on the recommendations of the DSRG came with the formation of the Deep Submergence Systems Project (DSSP) in 1964 and an expanded interest regarding diving and undersea activity throughout the Navy.

Submarine rescue capabilities have been substantially improved with the development of the Deep Submergence Rescue Vehicle (DSRV) which became operational in 1972. This deep-diving craft is air-transportable, highly instrumented, and capable of diving to 5,000 fsw and rescues to 2,500 fsw.

Three additional significant areas of achievement for the Deep Submergence Systems Project have been that of Saturation Diving, the development of Deep Diving Systems, and progress in advanced diving equipment design.

1–6 Salvage Diving

1–6.1 World War II Era.

1–6.1.1 Pearl Harbor. Navy divers were plunged into the war with the Japanese raid on Pearl Harbor. The raid began at 0755 on 7 December 1941; by 0915 that same morning, the first salvage teams were cutting through the hull of the overturned battleship

USS *Oklahoma* to rescue trapped sailors. Teams of divers worked to recover ammunition from the magazines of sunken ships, to be ready in the event of a second attack.

The immense salvage effort that followed at Pearl Harbor was highly successful. Most of the 101 ships in the harbor at the time of the attack sustained damage. The battleships, one of the primary targets of the raid, were hardest hit. Six battleships were sunk and one was heavily damaged. Four were salvaged and returned to the fleet for combat duty; the former battleships USS *Arizona* and USS *Utah* could not be salvaged. The USS *Oklahoma* was righted and refloated but sank en route to a shipyard in the US.

Battleships were not the only ships salvaged. Throughout 1942 and part of 1943, Navy divers worked on destroyers, supply ships, and other badly needed vessels, often using makeshift shallow water apparatus inside water and gas-filled compartments. In the Pearl Harbor effort, Navy divers spent 16,000 hours underwater during 4,000 dives. Contract civilian divers contributed another 4,000 diving hours.

1–6.1.2   **USS** *Lafayette*. While divers in the Pacific were hard at work at Pearl Harbor, a major challenge was presented to the divers on the East Coast. The interned French passenger liner *Normandie* (rechristened as the USS *Lafayette*) caught fire alongside New York City's Pier 88. Losing stability from the tons of water poured on the fire, the ship capsized at her berth.

The ship had to be salvaged to clear the vitally needed pier. The Navy took advantage of this unique training opportunity by instituting a new diving and salvage school at the site. The Naval Training School (Salvage) was established in September 1942 and was transferred to Bayonne, New Jersey in 1946.

1–6.1.3 **Other Diving Missions.** Salvage operations were not the only missions assigned to Navy divers during the war. Many dives were made to inspect sunken enemy ships and to recover materials such as code books or other intelligence items. One Japanese cruiser yielded not only $500,000 in yen, but also provided valuable information concerning plans for the defense of Japan against the anticipated Allied invasion.

1–6.2 **Vietnam Era.** Harbor Clearance Unit One (HCU 1) was commissioned 1 February 1966 to provide mobile salvage capability in direct support of combat operations in Vietnam. Homeported at Naval Base Subic Bay, Philippines, HCU 1 was dedicated primarily to restoring seaports and rivers to navigable condition following their loss or diminished use through combat action.

Beginning as a small cadre of personnel, HCU 1 quickly grew in size to over 260 personnel, as combat operations in littoral environment intensified. At its peak, the unit consisted of five Harbor Clearance teams of 20 to 22 personnel each and a varied armada of specialized vessels within the Vietnam combat zone.

As their World War II predecessors before them, the salvors of HCU 1 left an impressive legacy of combat salvage accomplishments. HCU 1 salvaged hundreds of small craft, barges, and downed aircraft; refloated many stranded U.S. Military and merchant vessels; cleared obstructed piers, shipping channels, and bridges; and performed numerous underwater repairs to ships operating in the combat zone.

Throughout the colorful history of HCU 1 and her East Coast sister HCU 2, the vital role salvage forces play in littoral combat operations was clearly demonstrated. Mobile Diving and Salvage Unit One and Two, the modern-day descendants of the Vietnam era Harbor Clearance Units, have a proud and distinguished history of combat salvage operations.

1–7 Open-sea Deep Diving Records

Diving records have been set and broken with increasing regularity since the early 1900s:

- **1915.** The 300-fsw mark was exceeded. Three U.S. Navy divers, F. Crilley, W.F. Loughman, and F.C. Nielson, reached 304 fsw using the MK V dress.
- **1972.** The MK 2 MOD 0 DDS set the in-water record of 1,010 fsw.
- **1975.** Divers using the MK 1 Deep Dive System descended to 1,148 fsw.
- **1977.** A French dive team broke the open-sea record with 1,643 fsw.
- **1981.** The deepest salvage operation made with divers was 803 fsw when British divers retrieved 431 gold ingots from the wreck of HMS *Edinburgh*, sunk during World War II.
- **Present.** Commercial open water diving operations to over 1,000 fsw.

1–8 Summary

Throughout the evolution of diving, from the earliest breath-holding sponge diver to the modern saturation diver, the basic reasons for diving have not changed. National defense, commerce, and science continue to provide the underlying basis for the development of diving. What has changed and continues to change radically is diving technology.

Each person who prepares for a dive has the opportunity and obligation to take along the knowledge of his or her predecessors that was gained through difficult and dangerous experience. The modern diver must have a broad understanding of the physical properties of the undersea environment and a detailed knowledge of his or her own physiology and how it is affected by the environment. Divers must learn to adapt to environmental conditions to successfully carry out their missions.

Much of the diver's practical education will come from experience. However, before a diver can gain this experience, he or she must build a basic foundation from certain principles of physics, chemistry and physiology and must understand the application of these principles to the profession of diving.

SELECT BIBLIOGRAPHY

Ballard, Robert D., *Explorations*, New York, 1995

Beebe, William, *Beneath Tropic Seas: A Record of Diving Among the Coral Reefs of Haiti*, New York, 1928

– *Half-Mile Down*, New York, 1934

Bevan, John, *The Infernal Diver*, London, 1996

Benchley, Peter, *Jaws*, New York, 1974

Brown, Joseph., *The Golden Sea, Man's Underwater Adventures*, London, 1974

Carsen, Rachel, *The Sea Around Us*, New York, 1951

Cousteau, J-Y and Frederic Dumas, *The Silent World*, New York 1953

Cowan, Zelide, *Early Divers*, Great Yarmouth, 1977

De Latil, Pierre and Jean Rivoire, *Man and the Underwater World*, London, 1956

Diole, Philippe, *The Undersea Adventure*, London 1953

Dugan, James, *Man Explores the Sea*, London, 1956

Ecott, Tim, *Neutral Buoyancy*, London 2001

Gilpatric, Guy, *The Compleat Goggler*, New York 1957

Halley, Edmund, "The Art of Living Under Water: Or, A discourse concerning the means of furnishing Air at the bottom of the sea in ordinary Depths", *Royal Society of London Philosophical Transactions*, 29 July, 1716

Hancock, Graham, *Underworld*, London 2002

Hass, Hans, *Diving to Adventure*, London, 1952

– *Under the Red Sea*, London, 1953

– *Conquest of the Underwater World*, London, 1975

Kolar, Bohumil and Oldrich Unger, *Explorers of the Deep*, London, 1976

Kunzig, Robert, *Mapping the Deep*, London, 2000

MacCormick, Alex, *The Mammoth Book of Man-eaters*, London, 2003
– *Shark Attacks*, London, 2003

Madsen, Axel, *Cousteau: An Unauthorised Biography*. London, 1986

Marx, Robert F., *The History of Underwater Exploration*, New York, 1990

Pugh, Marshall, *Commander Crabb*, London, 1956

Talliez, Philippe, *To Hidden Depths*, London 1954

Waldron, T. J. and James Gleason, *The Frogmen*, London, 1954

Warren, C. E. T. and James Benson, *Above Us the Waves: The Story of Midget Submarines and Human Torpedoes*, London 1953

Winton, John, *The Submariners*, London, 1999

Young, Edward, *One of our Submarines*, Penguin, London, 1952

ACKNOWLEDGMENTS

The editor has made every effort to secure the necessary permissions to reproduce the copyrighted materials which appear in this volume. In the case of any inadvertent errors or ommissions the editor should be contacted c/o the publishers.

Anscomb, Charles, from *Submariner*, William Kimber, 1967. Copyright © 1967 Charles Anscomb

Ballard, Robert D. (with Malcolm McConnell), from *Explorations: An Autobiography*, Weidenfeld & Nicolson, 1995. Copyright © 1995 Robert D. Ballard

Beebe, William, "One Thousand and Four Hundred and Twenty Six Feet Below the Sea", from *Half Mile Down*, Harcourt Brace & Company, 1934. Copyright © 1934 William Beebe

– "Beneath Tropic Seas" and "Kingdom of the Helmet" from *Beneath Tropic Seas*, GP Putnam's Sons, 1928. Copyright © 1928 William Beebe

Beavan, Colin, from *The Atlantic Monthly*, vol 279, issue 5, May 1997. Copyright © 1997 The Atlantic Monthly Magazine/ 2004 Gale Group

Benchley, Peter, from *Shark!*, HarperCollins Publishers, 2002. Copyright © 2002 Peter Benchley

Borghese, Junio Valerio, from *The Sea Devils*, Melrose, 1952. English translation copyright © 1952 James Cleugh

Bright, Michael, from *Man-eaters*, Robson, 2000. Copyright © 2000 Michael Bright

Camsell, Don, from *Black Water*, Virgin Books, 2001. Copyright © 2001 Don Camsell

Capes, John H., from *Submarine Memories*, Gatwick Submarine Old Comrades' Archives, 1994. Quoted in *The Submariners*, ed. John Winton, Constable, 1999

Cousteau, Jacques-Yves, "Mentish" and "The Fountain of Vaucluse" from *The Silent World*, Hamish Hamilton Ltd., 1954

– (with Philippe Diolé), "A Lesson from the Sea)" from *Diving for Sunken Treasure*, Cassell, 1971, Copyright © Jacques-Yves Cousteau 1971

Diolé, Philippe, from *The Undersea Adventure*, Pan Books, 1955. Trans Alan Ross. Copyright © 1953 Julian Messner, Inc.

Earle, Sylvia A., (originally "Life Springs from Death in Truk Lagoon") from *National Geographic*, vol 149, no.5, May 1976. Copyright © 1976 National Geographic Society

Ecott, Tim, from *Neutral Buoyancy*, Michael Joseph, 2001. Copyright © 2001 Tim Ecott

Frank, Wolfgang, from *Sea Wolves*, Weidenfeld & Nicolson, 1951. Copyright © 1951 Wolfgang Frank

Gilpatric, Guy, from *The Compleat Goggler*, Dodd, Mead & Company, Inc, 1957. Copyright © 1938 Guy Gilpatric

Haberstroh, Joe, from *Fatal Depth*, The Lyons Press, 2003. Copyright © 2003 Joe Haberstroh

Hamilton-Paterson, James, from *Three Miles Down*, Jonathan Cape, 1998. Copyright © 1998 James Hamilton-Paterson

Hass, Hans, from *Diving to Adventure*, Jarrolds, 1952. Copyright © 1952 Hans Haas Houot, Georges and Pierre Willm, from *2000 Fathoms Down*, Hamish Hamilton and Rupert Hart-Davis, 1955.

Jessop, Keith from *Goldfinder*, Simon & Schuster, 1998. Copyright © 1998 Keith Jessop

McKee, Alexander, from *How We Found The* Mary Rose, Souvenir Press, 1982. Copyright © 1982 Alexander McKee

Masters, David, from *The Wonders of Salvage*, Eyre and Spottiswoode, 1944. Copyright © 1944 David Masters

Moore, Robert, from *A Time to Die*, Doubleday, 2002. Copyright © Robert Moore 2002

Schaeffer, Heinz, from *U-Boat 977*, Tandem, 1955.

Shelnick, Tom (with Ray Cristina), from *Above and Below*, Robert Hale, 1966. Copyright © Tom Shelnick and Ray Cristina 1965

Symmes, Patrick, from *Outside* magazine, April 2002. Copyright © Patrick Symmes 2002

Talliez, Philippe, from *To Hidden Depths*, William Kimber, 1954. Copyright © 1954 Phillipe Talliez

Todhunter, Andrew, from *The Atlantic Monthly*, vol 273, Issue 1, January 1994. Copyright © 2004 The Atlantic Monthly Magazine/The Gale group

T.J. Waldron & James Gleason, from *The Frogmen*, Elmfield Press, 1974. Copyright © 1950 T.J. Waldron and James Gleason 1950

Woollcott, Sydney, quoted in *The Frogmen*, Elmfield Press, 1974. Copyright © 1950 T.J. Waldron and James Gleason

Young, Edward, from *One of Our Submarines*, Rupert Hart-Davis, 1952. Copyright © 1952 Edward Young RNVR

Zinsley, Michael G., from *Rapture and Other Dive Stories You Probably Shouldn't Know*, 1st Books, Bloomington, Inc., 1999. Copyright © 1999 Michael G. Zinsley